W9-BLS-100

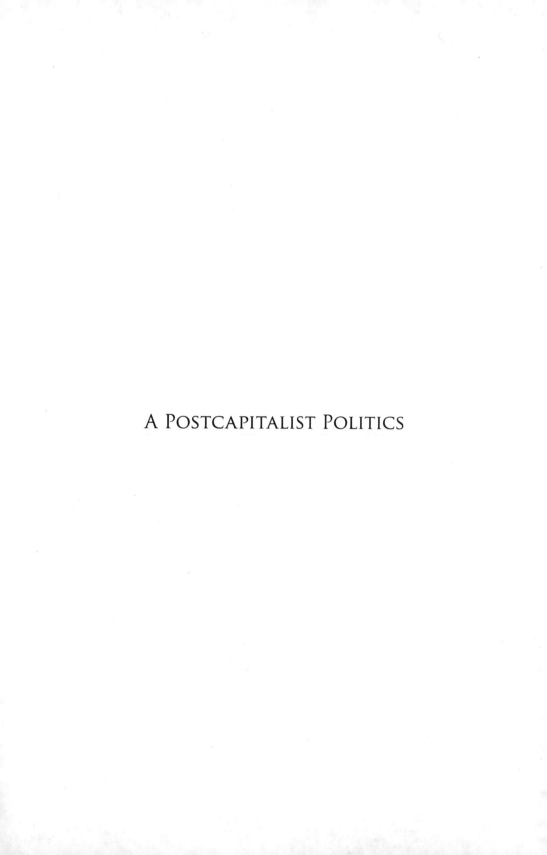

A Postcapitalist Politics

A Postcapitalist Politics

J. K. Gibson-Graham

University of Minnesota Press

Minneapolis · London

See pages 263–64 for copyright information on previously published material in this book.

Published by the University of Minnesota Press
111 Third Avenue South, Suite 290
Minneapolis, MN 55401-2520
http://www.upress.umn.edu

HD
87
G52
2006

Library of Congress Cataloging-in-Publication Data

Gibson-Graham, J. K.
    A postcapitalist politics / J.K. Gibson-Graham.
       p.   cm.
    Includes bibliographical references and index.
    ISBN 13: 978-0-8166-4803-0 (hc), 978-0-8166-4804-7 (pb)
    ISBN 10: 0-8166-4803-4 (hc : alk. paper) — ISBN 0-8166-4804-2 (pb : alk. paper)
    1. Economic policy.   2. Capitalism.   3. Political science.   I. Title.
    HD87.G52 2006
    338.9—dc22

                                                                2005032836

Printed in the United States of America on acid-free paper

The University of Minnesota is an equal-opportunity educator and employer.

12 11 10 09 08 07 06   10 9 8 7 6 5 4 3 2 1

For Bernice, Don, Elspeth, Eve, Helen, Jack, K, Megan, and Ramonda

CONTENTS

PREFACE AND ACKNOWLEDGMENTS

Hope is the difference between
probability and *possibility*.

—Isabelle Stengers,
"A 'Cosmo-Politics'—Risk, Hope, Change"

This is a hopeful book written at a time when hope is finally getting a hearing but also a battering. Between the completion of the manuscript and the writing of this preface, the seemingly intractable nature of the world's problems has impressed itself on us quite powerfully. A recently aired BBC documentary on "global dimming" showed how airborne industrial pollutants are blocking sunlight from reaching the earth; as these pollutants are reduced, global warming will presumably proceed at a much faster rate than is currently projected. According to the documentary, the Ethiopian famine that killed ten million people in the early 1980s was due to the failure over more than a decade of the yearly monsoon, as the water-laden tropical air mass was prevented from moving northward by the northern hemisphere's pollution haze—a shocking wake-up call about global responsibility. On top of all the environmental news, one of us has just discovered that she is not exempt from what feels like a breast cancer epidemic in women of the "developed" world. From the global scale to the place closest in, we have been presented with the enormity of "what pushes back at us" (to use the words of our inspirational activist friend Ethan Miller) when we attempt to imagine and inhabit a world of economic possibility.

Both of these "events" highlight in different ways the ethical imperatives and challenges of the interdependence that this book attempts to bring into focus. All too clearly we are being presented with the unintended effects of "development." All too starkly we can see that increased consumption, with its promise of heightened well-being, is bought at the expense of the destruction of the global atmospheric commons we have taken for granted over the past two centuries. It is not only African families who have borne the brunt of "our" development, but perhaps also women in wealthy countries and cancer sufferers in general, whose bodies are registering something counterintuitive—the downside of a "good life." We can only feel awed by and grateful for the complexes of committed and competent surgeons, oncologists, radiographers, and their instruments and institutions that interact with a state and privately supported knowledge commons to address breast cancer (something the feminist movement has made a priority). We can only feel ashamed that our respective nations (Australia and the United States) are the two industrialized countries that have refused to sign the Kyoto Protocol to limit greenhouse gas emissions and begin to arrest global warming. How is it that the wealth of nations readily flows into tackling one piece of this interdependent picture and is vigilantly restricted from addressing the other? In our bitter moments we are tempted to relate this asymmetry to the perceived workings of the economic growth machine in which low-cost coal and oil burning are seen to be central and women's post–childbearing bodies are basically irrelevant. Our respective governments are prepared to direct resources into breast cancer research and treatment, and will even foot the bill for much of the scientific research that has identified the interactions of global dimming and global warming, but agreeing to put in place the already existing technology and regulations that could halt destruction of our environmental commons is at present beyond them. For us, this is a matter for urgent discussion and a case where rethinking what constitutes an "economy"—if we are willing to countenance the continued existence of such a domain—may actually be crucial.

In this book, we broach global and local interdependence around economic issues of necessity, surplus, consumption, and commons. We bring these issues out of the realm of abstract theorizing and into everyday practices of living together and building alternative futures. Our own interdependence as the collective author J. K. Gibson-Graham gives us the fortitude (foolhardiness?) to address such monumental issues and the embodied insights into processes of self-cultivation that might equip us to become ethical subjects of a postcapitalist order. Emerging from the mutuality of our relationship and especially our interdependence with others, the book is the neatly bound tip of a ramshackle iceberg. We recognize that publishing and affixing our name to this volume consigns its contributing factors to subaqueous obscurity. "Authored, authorized, and authoritative," as Sadie Plant cautions, "a piece of writing is its own mainstream" (1997, 9). What is wondrous to contemplate is its emergence at the confluence of events, people, relationships, and things, and to watch it flow toward the pooling oceans of anonymity, to be dispersed and taken up once again in the hydrological cycle of de- and retextualization, and eventually transmuted into other streams and icebergs.

In less watery but no less embracing terms, we might simply acknowledge our understanding that "all and everything is naturally related and interconnected" (Plant 1997, 11; quoting Ada Lovelace) and leave it at that. But we will not get away so easily. Gratitude is not entailed in a moment of metatheoretical recognition; it is an orientation toward the world, indistinguishable from its embodiment in everyday practices. Here we wish to indulge in a practical exercise of gratitude by tracing a few of the interdependencies that made this book.

We'll start with the interdependence between *A Postcapitalist Politics* and its predecessor, *The End of Capitalism (As We Knew It): A Feminist Critique of Political Economy*, published in 1996. We are immensely appreciative of the offer of the University of Minnesota Press to reprint that book along with *A Postcapitalist Politics*, and we especially value Carrie Mullen's bracing enthusiasm for both projects. Separated by a decade of thinking, researching, and living, these two volumes are intricately interconnected and yet very different. In *The End of Capitalism*, J. K. Gibson-Graham was the quintessential "theory slut," happily and carelessly thinking around, playing with "serious" and consequential subjects like political economy, loving the theory she was with, offering ebullient arguments and heady claims about representations of capitalism and their politically constraining performativity. We spoke to our readers as somewhat wayward feminists who seemed to relish their positioning as mildly outrageous, quirkily funny, and ambiguously gendered. It might come as a shock, then, that *A Postcapitalist Politics* has a completely different feel; it reads like a wholesome, even earnest, treatise on how to do economy differently. The authorial stance is open, exposed, even vulnerable, entirely different from the shimmering armor of the earlier book (and much less fun, we fear). In writing that book we felt a perhaps unwarranted confidence, conferred by our lengthy training in political economy, that no one could say things about capitalism that we hadn't heard before and didn't have a response to. This book offers us no such safe havens.

What, apart from menopause and inevitable aging, has contributed to this shift in stance and affect? Perhaps it has been our awakening to the different kinds of politics that are possible, along with an enhanced ability to hear as well as speak. In our own relationship, which has spanned almost three decades as well as the Pacific Ocean, time differences of fourteen to sixteen hours (depending on daylight savings), and countless other spatiotemporal dis- and con-junctures, an opening up to listening to each other has had transformative micropolitical effects. As with the projects we review in this book, we have been confronted by the challenges of collaboration—the comforts and discomforts of collectivism, the bounds and liberties of (joint) identity, the struggle to make collaboration work not just for itself but for its participants. Our relationship has become a space for the exploration of techniques of self-cultivation that help us to observe ourselves more closely, listen to each other more openly, and constitute ourselves more proactively. From the theory sluts of 1996 to the self-help junkies of 2006, we have navigated a personal path that ever enriches as new challenges of relating and thinking/writing together arise.

This never-ending process of becoming has developed and extended our understanding of politics. It has affirmed the importance of the politics of the personal and the spaces closest in—the self-narratives that can plague and restrict or release and enable our experiments, the material and psychic interdependencies that we can celebrate and amplify or exploit and deplete. Both of us have been blessed with the gift of domestic communities that sustain and contribute to our collaboration. In the United States, the twelve or so members of the Cooleyville community have shared weekly Monday night dinners and interpersonal support with us for three decades, constituting a home and non-kin-based family that *is* a community economy. In Australia the small clan of David, Daniel, and Lillian Tait has provided a loving practice space for the best and worst performances of self and ethical decision-making by the mother of us, and a welcoming site for the enactment of our unusual (at least to suburban Canberra) collaboration.

Space and place have been crucial ingredients in our collaboration. In a relationship that spans the globe, neither can ever be taken for granted. Indeed, the materiality of distance has been an ever-present factor, and this is perhaps why we feel the need to acknowledge the places where we have met to work, for each has contributed its special quality to our thinking and feeling in this book: the large welcoming house on Town Farm Road in Shutesbury, Massachusetts; the end-of-the-road caravan at Merry Beach, New South Wales; Ann's Stepping Stones B & B in New Hampshire, with its astonishing two acres of flowers and shrubs; the family-sized swap house on College Hill in Eugene, Oregon; the little house graciously added on to 307 Antill Street in Canberra; tiny Tiri Crest on Waiheke Island and the comfortable big house in Moeraki, two New Zealand places with inspiring ocean views; the lovely garden cottage on Phillip Island, Victoria; the elegant sufficiency of the Maranese in Bellagio, Italy; and the Plymouth Harbor retirement community with its waterbirds and poetry readings in Sarasota, Florida.

In the attempt to enact a postcapitalist politics, the environment of academia has been a powerful and permissive factor in creating the world of possibility that enables "other worlds" to actually arise. Despite the encroaching commercialization, casualization, and rationalization of our institutions, academia in general and geography in particular have offered us a nurturing communal backwater in which to float our half-baked ideas and hare-brained projects. In our own and other departments and disciplines, we and our colleagues are free to attend each other's talks, offer and receive comments on each other's papers, teach and learn from each other's students, visit and speak in each other's lecture series, and draw on an intellectual commons that benefits from what Harvie calls "convivial competition" (2004, 4). None of these activities is free of dysfunction and some may be prone to it, but they nevertheless constitute a platform for "commons-based peer production" that values collaborative engagement, and respects and requires the sharing/gifting of output.

That the academic commons is hard won and not to be taken for granted is brought home to us daily by the evidence of what currently threatens it. Today, for example, we discovered that a colleague in political science has patented his solution to a game theory problem. The gift economy of academia (Harvie 2004) is neither a pleasant nor a productive place to be without an open affective disposition and a desire to relate to, rather than dismiss or colonize, the work and specializations of others. As an environment for creativity, the commons does not maintain itself, but requires a continual investment of effort and particular technologies to shape and replenish it. In the innovative philosophical workshops at Isabelle Stengers's institution, for example, the convenors promote a practice of slowing down, to allow for "people not just to express what they were thinking anyway but to feel their thought becoming part of the collective adventure" (2003, 252). By creating rules to preclude people "knowing what they think," the stewards of this environment allow for events in thought and feeling to emerge out of a "kind of collective stammering" (252).

Both at home and away we have been privileged to be in many such environments. One current instance is the seminar "The Rule of Markets" at New York University, chaired by Timothy Mitchell. Tim shares with us an interest in denaturalizing the "economy," pushes us to acknowledge the recent materialization of such an entity via the operation of a complex set of technologies and practices, and encourages us (as does Michel Callon, another participant) to pursue and develop our economic experiments. Another is the ongoing multiyear graduate seminar at the University of Massachusetts, including Ken Byrne, Kenan Erçel, Stephen Healy, Yahya Madra, Ceren Özselçuk, Joe Rebello, Maliha Safri, Chizu Sato, and Peter Tamas, in which the collective stammering occurs mainly at the intersection of psychoanalysis, poststructuralist Marxism, and the theory and practice of community economies. The Department of Human Geography in the Research School of Pacific and Asian Studies at the Australian National University provides yet another such environment, in which ongoing field and dissertation research and seminars produce events in thought that nourish, jolt, and transform the projects we are engaged in.

From friends and colleagues we have received what is necessary to our survival: new and old ideas, reactions, suggestions, criticisms, references, inclusion in other projects, intellectual support of all kinds, and the warmth and generosity of appreciation. So lavish have Jack Amariglio and George DeMartino been with their appreciation that our joint sense of possibility will never be the same. A central ingredient of our economic theorizing is the Marxian theory of class developed by our friends, colleagues, and coeditors Steve Resnick and Rick Wolff. Their anti-essentialist class language allowed us in *The End of Capitalism* to denaturalize capitalist dominance, opening the way to queering economic space and producing a language of economic diversity. In this book we foreground the class language more prominently in an alternative (counterhegemonic) discourse of economic difference and activate its core concern for an economics of surplus as a focus for the ethical dynamics of a community economy.

An economics of surplus is one of the major theoretical contributions of members of the Association for Economic and Social Analysis (AESA), an organization of economists and others that produces the journal *Rethinking Marxism* and has provided us with a great store of friendship and fun not usually associated with the dismal science. We would be unable to think and write as we do were it not for the insights of Jack Amariglio and Antonio Callari on (economic) subjectivity, among many other topics; Steve Cullenberg on diverse economies and class processes; George DeMartino and David Ruccio on imperialism, globalization, ethics, and politics; Kevin St. Martin on class and community; Yahya Madra on rethinking communism; Ceren Özselçuk on mourning and class politics; and many other AESA members whose work has added to and enriched the ideas presented in this book.

Arturo Escobar's ability to know what we are arguing before we do has had countless benefits for our work, for which we are truly grateful. One of the many catalysts for this book was the invitation to participate in the Women and the Politics of Place project, led by Arturo and Wendy Harcourt (editor of the journal *Development*) and involving more than twenty feminist activists and academics around the world. In the face of our reluctance to become involved in yet another project, Arturo twisted our arms ever so compassionately, bringing us into a conversation that eventually helped us to crystallize the feminist political imaginary we articulate in *A Postcapitalist Politics*.

In our perennial search for more freeing and complex understandings of affect, we revisited a familiar location, the writings of Eve Kosofsky Sedgwick, ever our muse. Her thoughts on queer theory guided us in *The End of Capitalism*, and her wonderful exploration of reparative and paranoid thinking in the book *Touching Feeling* enabled us to process the reception of our work in positive ways. That book draws to some extent on her earlier coauthored work on Silvan Tomkins, a psychologist who productively fails to distinguish the theory-affect interactions generated by individuals processing their own experiences from the interplay of intellect and emotions in what usually passes for "theory."

William Connolly and Jane Bennett have been inadvertent collaborators with us in writing *A Postcapitalist Politics*, their work having provided both philosophical and practical encouragement to take heed of micropolitical shifts in affect and to chart a politics of possibility in the face of incredulity and sometimes disdain.

Our long-standing project of rethinking economy has gained force, clarity, and insight from the work of many others who are similarly engaged. Economic anthropologist Stephen Gudeman's important book *The Anthropology of Economy* and his earlier writings with Alberto Rivera have influenced our thinking in profound ways, encouraging us to conceptualize a community in terms of its commons and stimulating us to pursue action research as a conversation with both the voices in the air and those on the ground. Steve Gudeman, Tim Mitchell, and J. K. Gibson-Graham have been drawn into a loose affiliation of academics and activists interested in challenging and rethinking "economic representations" instigated and shepherded over the past few years by David Ruccio and, more lately, Steve Cullenberg. We have gained insights and inspiration from the work of fellow scholars and friends Lau Kin Chi, Ruben George Oliven, Evan Watkins, Dwight Billings, Judith Mehta, David Ellerman, and Will Milberg, among others.

One of our greatest debts of gratitude is to the readers who spent valuable time and energy processing the unwieldy first draft of this manuscript and whose comments were extraordinarily helpful when we came to revise and clarify the argument of the book. Larry Grossberg offered enthusiasm and challenging judgments in just the right mix; Eric Sheppard likewise provoked and affirmed in equal measure; John Pickles and his graduate reading group at the University of North Carolina gave us targeted reactions and imaginative responses far beyond our expectations of a manuscript review. Ethan Miller's review became our oracle as we embarked on the rewriting process; he enabled us to recognize that the book had a structure and a tripartite political vision incorporating a language politics, a politics of the subject, and a politics of collective action. All readers were able to grasp what we were struggling to express, and their assistance in helping us bring what we wanted to say to the fore was a gift of collegiality in the best possible sense. To experience it as a gift nevertheless required a conscious exercise in gratitude on our parts and a daily undertaking to treat the sometimes painfully honest reviews as a positive resource and input to our work. That this practice had only beneficial results probably does not need saying; that it produced a new relation to ourselves, our reviewers, our work, and the review process in general probably does. It was a first shared instance of taking to heart the Buddhist injunction to practice gratitude for adversity, difficulty, and opposition (in this case criticism) as part of a path toward a more open and joyful way of being in the world.

During the past decade we have engaged in a number of action research projects with large research teams made up of colleagues, students, community members, nongovernmental organizations, and local government authorities. Each project has produced its own research community with a knowledge commons that we draw on in many of the chapters of this book. On the U.S. side, action research for "Rethinking Economy: Envisioning Alternative Regional Futures" in the Pioneer Valley of Massachusetts was supported by a grant from the National Science Foundation (Grant No. BCS-9819138) and conducted by members of the Community Economies Collective (co-researchers Brian Bannon, Carole Biewener, Jeff Boulet, Ken Byrne, Gabriela Delgadillo, Rebecca Forest, Stephen Healy, Greg Horvath, Beth Rennekamp, AnnaMarie Russo, Sarah Stookey, and Anasuya Weil). Seventeen community researchers were employed part-time by the project, and they and their interviewees are identified pseudonymously in the text. All of the team, but especially Becky, Ken, and Stephen, devoted themselves to the project with the unstinting energy that is known as "lifeblood," creating an extraordinary team process and product. The insights and analyses of the research team are inextricable from our own, and their presence is palpable in all we have written.

In Australia, action research in the Latrobe Valley was supported by grants from the Australian Housing and Urban Research Institute and the Australian Research Council (grant numbers A79703183 and C79927030), with further financial and in-kind support provided by the Latrobe City Council. The research was conducted with colleagues Jenny Cameron and Arthur Veno and employed community researchers Yvonne Joyce, Stephen Lister, Leanne Vella, Nicki Welsh, and Alan Riley. Institutional support for this project was skillfully offered by Julie Hocking and David Powell of the Latrobe City Council. Many community members formed enterprise groups and participated in the project; their voices are heard in the text, though their names have been changed.

Research in the Latrobe Valley would not have been possible without the incredible commitment, skill, and insight of Jenny Cameron, our colleague, dear friend, comrade, and Community Economies Collective member. Jenny "ran" the project day to day and night by night for its duration. She was the constant academic face of the project in the community, and we would like to acknowledge her huge contribution to what it achieved. Her reflections on the process of subject-becoming that the project initiated have provided inspiration for much of the analysis included here, and her own writings and our coauthored outputs about the project must be seen as companion pieces to chapter 6.

Our work with the Asian Migrant Centre in Hong Kong was initiated in collaboration with Lisa Law, who must be sincerely thanked for bringing J. K. Gibson-Graham's writings to the notice of this organization and especially to Rex Varona and Bien Molina. We have benefited enormously from Lisa's sensitive volunteer work with the AMC, which provided a secure and trusting base on which our own research collaboration has been built. May-an Villalba, Nimfa Lloren, and Rosario Cañete of Unlad Kabayan Migrant Services Incorporated have been enthusiastic supporters of our work and co-researchers and facilitators of the Philippines action research project that we report on here.

Action research in the Philippines has been funded by the Australian Research Council (Grant No. LP0347118) in partnership with the Australian Agency for International Development as part of the project "Negotiating Alternative Economic Strategies for Regional Development in Indonesia and the Philippines." We gratefully acknowledge the contribution of colleague Deirdre McKay specifically to the conceptualization and conduct of the Philippines aspect of the project located in Jagna, Bohol, and Linamon, Mindanao. In chapter 7 we draw on invaluable field research done by Joy Apag, Maureen Balaba, Amanda Cahill, Nimfa Lloren, and Deirdre McKay as part of the Jagna research team, and Kathylen Cocomas and Noel Salonga on the Linamon research team. All members of the wider research group, including Amanda Cahill, Deirdre McKay, Kathryn Robinson, Andrew McWilliam, Jayne Curnow, Ann Hill, and

Catharina Williams, have provided scholarly input into the clarification and application of ideas around the community economy.

A number of social researchers have helped us to understand and practice action research as a collaborative endeavor. We learned from Steve Gudeman to experience social research as a form of conversational interaction; from Ceren Özselçuk to steer a path between pressing one's own agenda and refusing out of fear or guilt to intervene in a community; from Michel Callon to think about practicing research *alongside* rather than *on* a group or organization, collaborating with what he calls "researchers in the wild," not by becoming an activist, but by maintaining the specificity of one's activities as a social scientist and making connections with other knowledge producers.

In all of our action research projects we encountered the wonderful generosity and interest of local residents who participated in the processes we initiated. For this input we are immensely grateful. Our experience of research as a series of orchestrated conversations in localities/sectors confirms our intuition that the power dynamics often represented as contaminating the academic/nonacademic relation are neither as simple to understand, nor as difficult to negotiate ethically, as some might think.

Our work on diverse economies has been extended and developed by participants in the "diverse economies conversation" within English-speaking geography, a loose association formed after a series of sessions organized with Andrew Leyshon at the annual meetings of the Association of American Geographers in 2003. This growing network of geographers includes old and new colleagues who are excited by the prospect of researching and performing diverse political and economic geographies. Recent conferences and conference sessions co-organized by Andrew Jonas, Roger Lee, and Colin Williams have stimulated the activities and interactions of this emerging research community.

Over the period of gestation of this book we have been generously supported by many institutions and their support staffs. Most consistently our homes in the Department of Human Geography in the Research School of Pacific and Asian Studies at the Australian National University and the Department of Geosciences at the University of Massachusetts Amherst have hosted our writing retreats, supported our research leaves and fieldwork visits, and offered congenial environments for our joint work. Sandra Davenport from the Australian National University has contributed her excellent copyediting, bibliographic, and indexing skills to our book and for this, as well as for her ever cheerful and encouraging aura, we are deeply grateful. With little more than strong European chocolate as an incentive, Peter Tamas of UMass spent hours clipping and tailoring the film stills for chapter 1 to our demanding specifications. Cartographer Kay Dancey from the Australian National University contributed her design expertise with enthusiasm and grace to the figures and maps that illustrate the book.

A collaborative writing residency at the Rockefeller Foundation's Bellagio Study and Conference Centre in 2005 provided a once-in-a-lifetime experience of validation and luxurious support that contributed in major part to the completion of this manuscript. A fellowship at the International Center for Advanced Study at New York University in 2004–2005 supported Julie during most of the period of the writing of the book. A visiting fellowship and a sabbatical fellowship at the Humanities Research Centre at the Australian National University afforded another wonderful institutional context for our joint writing process in 2003. Extended visits to The Johns Hopkins University at the invitation of Jonathan Goldberg and Michael Moon and to the University of North Carolina at the invitation of Arturo Escobar, Larry Grossberg, and John Pickles affirmed and cemented collaborative friendships across decades and disciplines.

Each chapter of *A Postcapitalist Politics* has its hidden collaborators, only some of whom we have space to mention. Steve Cullenberg and the other organizers of "Marxism 2000" at UMass Amherst and Phil O'Neill, Bob Fagan, and Pauline McGuirk, organizers of a session at the meeting of the Institute of Australian Geographers in Perth in 1998, got us working on the response to *The Full Monty* that ended up in chapter 1. Kay Anderson, Nicholas Brown, Jane Jacobs, and Tim Rowse drew our attention to key source materials, and Graeme Byrne offered reflections on growing up in Yallourn, all of which made their way into chapter 2. Michelle Billings transcribed sections of the focus group discussions reported in that chapter. David Ruccio and the above-mentioned members of the graduate seminar at UMass offered formative comments on chapters 3 and 4. Race Mathews and Fred Freundlich helped Katherine Gibson organize a visit to Mondragón in 1997, and the Australian Research Council provided financial assistance for the trip, contributing directly to early versions of chapter 5.

Friends not previously mentioned whose work and support have inspired and nourished us include Kathy Addelson, Marta Calas, Dipesh Chakrabarty, Ruth Fincher, Nancy Folbre, Michael Garjian, Gay Hawkins, Richie Howitt, Maria Hynes, Lesley Instone, Sharon Livesey, Linda Malam, Katharine McKinnon, Michal Osterweil, Mary Louise Pratt, Gerda Roelvink, Debbie Rose, Scott Sharpe, Linda Smirich, and Sophie Watson. Friends whom we cannot imagine life without (not all of these are living) can never be fully acknowledged for their contributions to our sustenance, but we offer our infinite gratitude to Affrica, Alfie and Megan, David and Lisa, Georgia and Greg, Helen, Helene, Jack and Christina, Jenny and Ramonda, Judy and Jack, Julie, Laurie, Michael and Jonathan, Peter and Lillian, Sharon and Neil, Sophie and Jeri, and Susan and Stephen.

Finally, we would like to acknowledge the members of the editorial and production staff at the University of Minnesota Press for their attentiveness, good humor, professionalism, imagination, and unfailing helpfulness. Many thanks to Carrie Mullen, Jason Weidemann, Linda Lincoln, and others at Minnesota for a wonderful experience.

INTRODUCTION
A POLITICS OF ECONOMIC POSSIBILITY

ORIGINS AND OVERTAKINGS

It seems that the making of a new political imaginary is under way, or at the very least a remapping of the political terrain. Coming into being over the past few decades and into visibility and self-awareness through the Internet, independent media, and most recently the World Social Forums, this emergent imaginary confounds the timeworn oppositions between global and local, revolution and reform, opposition and experiment, institutional and individual transformation.[1] It is not that these paired evaluative terms are no longer useful, but that they now refer to processes that inevitably overlap and intertwine. This conceptual interpenetration is radically altering the established spatiotemporal frame of progressive politics, reconfiguring the position and role of the subject, as well as shifting the grounds for assessing the efficacy of political movements and initiatives.

We glimpse the broad outlines of a new political imaginary in the performative self-designations of the "movement of movements"—*We Are Everywhere, Other Economies Are Possible, One No, Many Yeses,* "Life after Capitalism"[2]— and in the statements of movement activists like John Jordan:

> Our movements are trying to create a politics that challenges all the certainties of traditional leftist politics, not by replacing them with new ones, but by dissolving any notion that we have answers, plans or strategies that are watertight or universal. . . . We are trying to build a politics . . . that acts in the moment, not to create something in the future but to build in the present, it's the politics of the here and now.

> When we are asked how we are going to build a new world, our answer
> is, "We don't know, but let's build it together."[3]

Perhaps the most frequently acknowledged wellspring of this new imaginary is the Zapatista uprising in Mexico. Rejecting the old revolutionary order-
ing of means and ends and the "two-step strategy" of seizing state power as a
prelude to social transformation (Wallerstein 2002), the Zapatistas have moved
directly to institute what has been seen as a "postcapitalist" indigenous communalism (Neill 1997). Like the other movements for whom they have become both
ally and avatar of possibility, the Zapatistas' goal is not to wrest control, but to
create autonomous zones of counterpower (Klein 2002, 220):[4]

> By asserting and creating multiple other ways of being in the world,
> these movements rob capital [or the state] of its monopoly and sin-
> gular definitions of time, space and value, thereby destroying its he-
> gemony, while at the same time furnishing new tools to address the
> complex set of problematic power relations it confronts us with from
> particular and embedded locations. (Osterweil 2004, 8)

The Zapatistas' symbolically loaded performances of "local" action have
been instantly communicated via the Internet, and in countless other parallel
movements the ebullience and "event" of anarchic situationism have been given
new life. Some of these movements are short-lived, their antics embodying the
political value of interruption (as distinct from endurance), producing an affective shock wave that reverberates through the brittle architecture of established
forms. Describing the Reclaim the Streets (RTS) movement, for example, Rebecca
Solnit observes that

> humor, creativity, outrageousness, and exuberance were among the
> group's hallmarks. That RTS didn't outlive its moment was also a kind
> of victory, a recognition that time had moved on and the focus was
> elsewhere. Instead, RTS's incendiary carnival spirit, global Internet
> communications, and tactics of temporary victory became part
> of the vocabulary of what came next, the global justice movement.
> RTS decomposed itself into the soil from which new flowers sprang.
> (2004, 89)

Like the Zapatistas, these groups use playfulness and humor to toss us onto
the terrain of the possible (Bennett 2001).[5] Poetry and political action are united
in conscious attempts to disrupt and initiate.[6] In the words of Subcomandante
Marcos, Zapatismo is "an intuition" and a dream, and the Zapatistas are "the
voice that arms itself to be heard. The face that hides itself to be seen." Their "true
secret weapon" is language (Klein 2002, 212, 222–23). And also, perhaps, what
their language has enabled—a re-visioning of power and a retheorizing of revolution, from strategy and tactics to affect and energetics.

The Zapatistas, the World Social Forum, and movements like Reclaim the Streets are charting a globally emergent form of localized politics. This "place-based globalism" (Osterweil 2004) has a distinctive feel that Solnit lucidly captures:

> The embrace of local power doesn't have to mean parochialism, withdrawal, or intolerance, only a coherent foundation from which to navigate the larger world. From the wild coalitions of the global justice movement to the cowboys and environmentalists sitting down together there is an ease with difference that doesn't need to be eliminated, a sense that . . . you can have an identity embedded in local circumstances and a role in the global dialogue. And that this dialogue exists in service of the local. (2004, 113)

Place-based globalism constitutes a proliferative and expansive spatial imaginary for a politics that offers a compressed temporality—traversing the distance from "nowhere" to "now here."[7]

From our locations in academia at two ends of the world, we have a sense that events have overtaken us. Ten years ago, when we were writing *The End of Capitalism (As We Knew It): A Feminist Critique of Political Economy,* we imagined it as an invitation and perhaps a prelude to a new economic politics. Such a politics, we hoped, would venture along the obscure byways of noncapitalist construction, encouraging projects of economic experimentation, adding to the repertoire of what was considered legitimate political action. Feeling suffocated and disempowered by prevailing conceptions of what was possible, and when and how it was to be achievable, we located our dissatisfaction within the dead-end time-space of capitalism as it was usually theorized. Today we see ourselves as part of a movement that is actively retheorizing capitalism and reclaiming the economy here and now in myriad projects of alternative economic activism. Our project has been gathered up in the whirlwind of inventions and interventions, resonating with some, amplifying or amplified by others, and above all sharing sentiments and stances with respect to the tasks of transformation. The distinctive contribution we hope to make to this wider project stems from our starting point, as elaborated in *The End of Capitalism.*[8]

Wanting an economic politics that allowed us to think creatively and to start *now* and *here* to make new economies, we focused our attentions in *The End of Capitalism* on ways of thinking that distanced the economy from politics. These included the tendency to represent economy as a space of invariant logics and automatic unfolding that offered no field for intervention; the tendency to theorize economy as a stable and self-reproducing structure impervious to the proliferative and desultory wanderings of everyday politics; the tendency to constitute "the" economy as a singular capitalist system or space rather than as a zone of cohabitation and contestation among multiple economic forms; and the tendency to lodge faith in accurate representation that guaranteed and stabilized the prevailing substantive framings.[9] We noted that these tendencies contributed to an affect and attitude of entrenched opposition (on the left, at least), a habit of thinking and feeling that offered little emotional space for alternatives, and that instead focused the political imagination—somewhat blankly—on a millennial future revolution. If the "revolution" were to occur in a time-world discontinuous with this one, it would not be possible to talk about steps and strategies for getting there.

In the years since the appearance of *The End of Capitalism*, we have been gratified and encouraged by a profusion of alternative economic research that has challenged these representations, some of it inspired by our own deconstruction and queering of Capitalism, much of it welling up from the same productive dissatisfactions we had experienced with essentialist and abstracted thinking about economy. Here we acknowledge the proliferation of work in our own field of economic geography, and in cultural and political geography, as well as in the fields of economic sociology and anthropology, cultural studies, politics, feminism, Marxian political economy, and science studies.[10] If capitalism is still a dominant signifier in social analysis, it is, for many of us, less taken for granted in its character and configurations than ever before.[11]

The heady and hopeful message of *The End of Capitalism* was that our economy is what we (discursively and practically) make it.[12] The salutary and grounded message of *A Postcapitalist Politics* is that we must be ready with strategies for confronting what forcefully pushes back against the discursive imaginings and practical enactments we associate with building a different economy. What we feel is needed, and what we present here, is our own, admittedly idiosyncratic, practical guide to the politics of "taking back the economy."

Having completed our 1996 book with a desire for a new kind of economic politics, we pondered how to proceed. Situated as we are in academia, tied to teaching timetables and the administrative demands of our institutions, we devised action research projects that could be locally pursued. The need for proximity to our field sites meant that their siting was relatively arbitrary. They include the resource region of the Latrobe Valley in Victoria, Australia, the mixed agricultural-industrial-higher education-exhippy economy of the Connecticut River Valley in the northeastern United States, and most recently the agricultural community of Jagna Municipality in the southern Philippines island province of Bohol.[13] All these places have experienced economic dislocation wrought by processes including privatization, deindustrialization, sectoral restructuring, rapid growth, and stagnation. With the vision of a diverse economy in mind, we have spent much of the last decade participating in local-level conversations about the heterogeneous (capitalist and noncapitalist) economies of these places and engaging with people in a process of creating both the subjects and enterprises of "intentional community economies." Enlivened and supported by the emerging political imaginary we have outlined above, we have focused our energies on what we take to be the specific deficits and challenges (and thus pressing requirements) of economic politics: the need for a new language of economy to widen the field of economic possibility, the self-cultivation of subjects (including ourselves) who can desire and enact other economies, and the collaborative pursuit of economic experimentation.

THE MAKINGS OF AN IMAGINARY

From the earliest days of this political exploration, we recognized the special challenges of economic politics—the obduracy of the economic object as it had been discursively framed and practically constructed; the poverty of economic subjectivity, with its few identity positions and contracting (if also intensifying) desires; and the persistent conviction that large-scale, coordinated action was required for the task of economic transformation. In the search for successful political projects and practices to encourage and inspire us, we have turned primarily to second-wave feminism.[14]

We never fail to be amazed at how the feminist movement has transformed and continues to transform households, lives, and livelihoods around the world to different degrees and in different ways, rendering the life experiences of many women literally unrecognizable in the terms of a generation ago.[15] Here we are thinking of everything from the increased participation of women in public life, to the social recognition of and responsibility for domestic violence, to the proliferation of options of gendered embodiment. This is not to deny that these achievements are partial and embattled, but rather to affirm that they are recognizable and widespread.[16]

The crucial role of alternative discourses of "woman" and gender in this process of transformation cannot be overestimated. But second-wave feminism also offered new practices of the self and of intersubjective relation that enabled these new discourses to be inhabited in everyday life. The decentralized, uncoordinated, and place-based consciousness-raising groups that became the movement's signature intervention (at least in the English-speaking world) acted as the foundational site for a "politics of becoming" (Connolly 1999, 57), unleashing myriad practices and performances of "woman." The slogan "the personal is political" authorized women to speak of their intimate concerns in legitimate tones, enabling them to connect the private and public, the domestic and national, shattering forever the rigid boundaries of established political discourse. The practice of feminism as "organizational horizontalism" fostered alternative ways of being (powerful), including "direct and equitable participation, non-monopoly of the spoken word or of information, the rotation of occasional tasks and responsibilities, the non-specialization of functions, the non-delegation of power" (Alvarez, Dagnino, and Escobar 1998, 97).

Feminism linked feminists emotionally and semiotically rather than primarily through organizational ties. Without rejecting the familiar politics of organizing and networking within groups and across space, individual women and collectivities pursued local paths and strategies that were based on avowedly feminist visions and values, but were not otherwise connected. The "upscaling" or globalization of a feminist politics did not involve formal organization at the global scale to challenge global structures of patriarchal power.[17] It did not rely on (though it did not eschew) coordinated actions and alliances. The movement achieved global coverage without having to create global institutions, though some of these did indeed come into being. Ubiquity rather than unity was the ground of its globalization.

We are intrigued at the way the loosely interrelated struggles and happenings of the feminist movement were capable of mobilizing social transformation at such an unprecedented scale, without resort to a vanguard party or any of the other "necessities" we have come to associate with political organization. The complex intermixing of alternative discourses, shared language, embodied practices, self-cultivation, emplaced actions, and global transformation associated with second-wave feminism has nourished our thinking about a politics of economic possibility—impressing us with the strikingly simple ontological contours of a feminist imaginary: *if women are everywhere, a woman is always somewhere, and those places of women are transformed as women transform themselves.* The vision of feminist politics as grounded in persons yet (therefore) potentially ubiquitous has been extended in our thinking to include another ontological substrate: a vast set of disarticulated "places"—households, communities, ecosystems, workplaces, civic organizations, bodies, public arenas, urban spaces, diasporas, regions, government agencies, occupations—related analogically rather than organizationally and connected through webs of signification. A feminist spatiality embraces not only a politics of ubiquity (its global manifestation), but a politics of place (its localization in places created, strengthened, defended, augmented, and transformed by women). In this admittedly stylized rendering, feminism is not about the category "woman" or identity per se, but about subjects and places. It is a politics of becoming in place.[18]

The achievements of second-wave feminism provide, for us, the impetus for theorizing a new global form of economic politics. Its remapping of political space and possibility suggests the ever-present opportunity for local transformation that does not require (though it does not preclude and indeed promotes) transformation at larger scales. Its focus on the subject prompts us to think about ways of cultivating economic subjects with different desires and capacities and greater openness to change and uncertainty. Its practice of seeing and speaking differently encourages us to make visible the hidden and alternative economic activities that *everywhere* abound, and to connect them through a language of economic difference. If we can begin to see noncapitalist activities as prevalent and viable, we may be encouraged here and now to actively build on them to transform our local economies.

ENACTMENTS AND EMERGENCES

If the successes of second-wave feminism give us confidence that indeed "another world is possible" and offer the global outlines of a practical politics, specific projects of economic transformation suggest guidelines for how to proceed in an everyday sense. Locally based social movement interventions all over the world are already embodying many of the features of the political imaginary we have been tracing, building new economic futures within a clearly enunciated commitment to a politics of possibility. One such project is a slum dwellers' initiative, the Alliance, in Mumbai, India, where half of the 12 million citizens are slum and pavement dwellers; another is an overseas migrant worker initiative, the Migrant Savings for Alternative Investment (MSAI) program, which targets vulnerable Asian workers, especially those from the Philippines, where 7.5 million people (10 percent of the population) support their families by migrating overseas for employment.[19] Against the "tyranny of the emergency"—the poverty and privation that find people living on the street or working for years with no political rights in a foreign country—these initiatives practice a "politics of patience" and "utility" (Appadurai 2002, 30).

What distinguishes the two initiatives is the *constructive content* of their actions. The Alliance enrolls slum dwellers in saving for and constructing housing and in producing knowledge of their situation through self-surveying and enumeration. This contributes to a politics of visibility and self-affirmation, as well as giving them control of a large part of the housing policy process in Mumbai.[20] The MSAI program enrolls contract migrant domestic servants and seafarers in the practice of investing in community-based enterprises in their home countries. Migrant indentured laborers are trained in social entrepreneurship and in conducting alternative business feasibility studies, and helped to negotiate with officials from their home provinces to obtain business advice and assistance.

Savings groups are the consciousness-raising groups of the Alliance and the MSAI program. It is in these small groups that individuals embark on a project of *ethical self-transformation* in Foucault's (1997) terms, or a micropolitics of (re)subjectivation in Connolly's terms (1995, 1999). To join such a group is to engage in new practices of the self—setting aside savings from what is already too little to live on in the case of the women slum dwellers, or in the case of the migrant workers denying themselves or their families some portion of the enhanced consumption usually associated with migration.[21] In the process, new senses of self are instituted—through self-development as citizens, house designers, investors, or entrepreneurs, through self-recognition of their survival capacities as poor women and migrants, through daily recommitment to the cultivation of solidarity. The savings groups focused on individual self-transformation are the foundation on which alternative economic interventions are built.

In both instances, the transformation of the conditions of poverty is spearheaded by the poor themselves. Poverty and seeming powerlessness become the base from which daily action is sustained, rather than a grounds for its postponement. Possibilities for influencing change are identified in the face of a realistic understanding of the extent and limits of the forces that constrain them. Particulars of authority, domination, and coercion that might neutralize or negate their interventions are examined and *ways to exercise power* are found.[22] In an environment where domestic workers are legally denied freedom of movement or association for six days out of seven, domestic servants involved in the MSAI program meet in public spaces on their one day off to discuss investment and enterprise development plans. In a city where public demonstrations are viewed (and often suppressed) as an incitement to riot, the slum dwellers hold toilet festivals to inaugurate functioning public toilets with invitations offered to state officials, World Bank representatives, and the middle classes. Through this action, a daily public act of humiliation and major cause of disease is transformed into a scene of "technical innovation, collective celebration, and carnivalesque play" (Appadurai 2002, 39), as well as a site for policy promotion.

From the work of the Alliance and MSAI there is a lesson to be learned about the potential *global reach* of locally focused activities and organizations. The Alliance participates with similar federations in fourteen countries on four continents in the Shack/Slum Dwellers International. The federations make site visits to one another to learn from each other and to hasten the pace of innovation. Migrant savers and investors from all over the world who participate in the MSAI program also meet annually to share experiences and gain the knowledge and inspiration to further replicate the savings-investment-enterprise model.[23] The site visits and annual meetings facilitate supportive feedback and debate— questions and criticisms raised by a distant partner are often more fruitful than those of local allies, which may produce or exacerbate wounds and divisions. In general, international visits and gatherings are used to strengthen the organizations in place; the global scale of activities exists to facilitate success at the local level, rather than being the ultimate locus of transformative politics.

These interventions/organizations teach us about the *freedom to act* that is at the core of a politics of possibility. Each of them works with and accepts funding from governments, international agencies, foundations, or collaborating partners that may not share their values and goals. While recognizing the risk of co-optation that such relationships pose, they refuse to see co-optation as a necessary condition of consorting with power. Instead it is an ever-present danger that calls forth vigilant exercises of self-scrutiny and self-cultivation—ethical practices, one might say, of "not being co-opted." More generally, each group's *understanding of power* enlarges the field of their own effectivity. There is little if any representation of a global-scale apparatus of power that must be addressed and transformed before their activities can succeed or be extended. Indeed they could be seen as refusing to root their poverty and problems in any ultimate origin (such as capitalism) that might displace their antagonism from those problems themselves. As such, theirs is a political and ethical practice of theory, and an everyday practice of freedom.

In the theoretical practices and practical commitments of the Alliance and the MSAI, we can discern the lineaments of the *emerging political imaginary* that we have identified with a politics of possibility in the *here* and *now*:

- the centrality of subjects and ethical practices of self-cultivation;
- the role of place as a site of becoming, and as the ground of a global politics of local transformations;[24]
- the uneven spatiality and negotiability of power, which is always available to be skirted, marshaled, or redirected[25] through ethical practices of freedom; and
- the everyday temporality of change and the vision of transformation as a continual struggle to change subjects, places, and conditions of life under inherited circumstances of difficulty and uncertainty.

All these things are part of the ontology of a politics of possibility, and the theoretical commitment to such an ontology is an ethical act of enabling such a politics.

The (feminist) imaginary of possibility that underpins and motivates our politics did not arrive fully formed in our imaginations, but has been distilled from various experiences over the past decade and more. It has been crystallized in thought through our activities in the field and through interactions with ideas, projects, NGOs, and many people. In our various attempts to enact a noncapitalist economic politics, we have experienced the pushing back of dominant discourses and our own fears and feelings (see chapter 1 for an exploration of these). It is clear to us that a politics of possibility (and the theoretical choices that constitute it) cannot simply be put "out there" in the world with the hope that it will flourish. It needs to be sustained by the continual work of making and remaking a space for it to exist in the face of what threatens to undermine and destroy it. This work has involved addressing the materiality of other ways of thinking—other ontologies, competing political imaginaries, and sedimented affective and intellectual stances that claim superior status as approaches to theory.

Just as members of the Alliance and participants in MSAI have to work daily on cultivating themselves as subjects able to enact new futures—as thinkers of possibility, as strategic activists who confront all kinds of specific forms of domination, authority, manipulation, coercion, and seduction (Allen 2003) and who nevertheless continue to mobilize their local capacities for change—we must similarly cultivate ourselves as activists and subjects of noncapitalist economies. The self-education and formation of ourselves as thinkers of theorized possibility are crucial to this practice.

AN ETHICS OF THINKING

> Think the same, remain the same. (Octaviana Medrano, Mexican
> electronics worker, quoted in Peña 1997, 177)

> If you want to change yourself, change your environment. If you
> want to change the world, change yourself. (Varela 1992)[26]

Many years ago a favorite teacher said to one of us: "Your mind is a judging rather than a tasting mind." We took the comment as a reminder that the mind has the capacity for either or both. What was understood (though perhaps not intended) was that the capability for "tasting" was present in an undeveloped form and needed only to be cultivated, despite the categorical finality with which its absence was announced. Just as the Buddhist tradition understands the innate goodness of humanity as the capacity to be good under certain conditions of cultivation (Varela 1992), so we can recognize our "innate" capacity to linger with the object and process of thought in a ruminative space of not knowing. Extending this recognition, we might see that we possess the capability (and ever-present option) of opening to what is novel rather than familiar in situations, of cultivating the ability to produce more novelty, of providing an incubating environment for half-baked ideas, while at the same time working against impulses to squelch and limit. Acknowledging this option is the beginning of cultivating ourselves as theorists of possibility.

We were originally trained to see and represent a social object (the capitalist economy) structured by concentrations of power and qualified by deficiencies of morality and desirability. This vision gave way some time ago to a recognition of ourselves as theorizing, authorizing subjects of economy. Where once we believed that the economy was depoliticized largely through its representations, we have more recently come to understand that its repoliticization requires cultivating ourselves as subjects who can imagine and enact a new economic politics. Bolstered by the upwelling of various movements across the world, we see the need not only for a differently theorized economy, but for new ethical *practices of thinking* economy and becoming different kinds of economic beings.

The co-implicated processes of changing the self/thinking/world is what we identify as an ethical practice. If politics is a process of transformation instituted by taking decisions in an undecideable terrain,[27] ethics is the continual exercising, in the face of the need to decide, of a choice to be/act/think a certain way. Ethics involves the embodied practices that bring principles into action. Through self-awareness and transforming practices of the self that gradually become modes of subjectivation, the ethical subject is brought into being (Foucault 1985, 28).[28]

Writing, for Foucault, is an ethical practice, a way that the self relates to itself. It is an intellectual discipline that allows us to consider "the possibility of no longer being, doing or thinking what we are, do, or think . . . seeking to give new impetus, as far and as wide as possible, to the undefined work of freedom" (1997, xxxv). We would like to extend Foucault's vision of writing to the practice of thinking, recognizing as "technologies of the self" the cultivation of certain kinds and capacities of thought.[29]

The recognition that affect is crucial to ethical practice and interlayered with thought offers a clue to how one might cultivate oneself differently:

> An ethical sensibility . . . is composed through the cultural layering of affect into the materiality of thought. . . . To work on an established sensibility by tactical means, then, is to nudge the composition of some layers in relation to others. (Connolly 2002, 107)

It is difficult to imagine how to engage in such nudging, in part because it is difficult to apprehend what we are actually doing when we are thinking/writing. We are generally not conscious of our pervasive styles, that is, "how we deal with our selves and things in our everyday coping" (Spinosa, Flores, and Dreyfus 1997, 17), and certainly not of most of our ways of bringing feeling and thinking together to produce more thinking and feeling. Coming from a tradition in which the best thinking is held to be dispassionate, we recognize as a minority position the claim that all thinking is conditioned by feeling.[30] Yet it is possible that the most crucial aspect of our thinking is the emotional orientation we bring to it.

To make things even more difficult, our seldom-inspected common sense posits a separation—or even an opposition—between thought, understood as cerebral reflection, and action, understood as embodied engagement with the world. This makes it hard to see thinking itself as a kind of action—that we are *doing thinking,* in other words, touching the world and being touched by it and in the process things (and we) are changing.

The ethical self-cultivation we undertake to produce ourselves as beings who can act spontaneously in desired ways is therefore unlikely to be addressed by our thinking. In our functioning as casual or professional economic thinkers, for example, we do not often engage in reflective assessment—one of the tools of ethical self-cultivation—of the effects of our thinking practices on ourselves and the world. We are more likely to see ourselves engaging in a universally available, emotionally neutral process of enlarging understanding than as situated in a specific setting with particular social goals and affective entailments, localized products and standards of success, and urgent requirements of self-attention.

Yet the kinds of choices we continually make about *what to do* and *how to act* in particular situations are also required of us as thinkers. These include the *stances* we adopt, the affective dispositions that color our thinking and impinge on consciousness as feeling—practical curiosity and openness to possibility, for example, or moral certainty and the acceptance of constraint. They also include the *techniques* we employ to actualize those stances in particular thought undertakings. To cultivate new attitudes and practices of thinking is to cultivate a new relation to the world and its always hidden possibilities: "Thinking participates in that uncertain process by which new possibilities are ushered into being" (Connolly 2002, 1).

The spirit of our thinking is a matter for ethical decision, as is the choice of techniques and practices of thinking.[31] In this book we engage in three specific thinking techniques that both draw upon and prompt the affective orientations of openness/freedom, interest/curiosity, and joy/excitement. [32] Over the past decade, we have been living, experiencing, provoking, and promoting these techniques and the emotional stances that enable and accompany them. But it is only now, in the writing of this book, that our ways of *doing thinking,* as our core ethical practice, are starting to become clear. Cultivating ourselves as thinking subjects within a politics of (economic) possibility has involved us with techniques of ontological reframing (to produce the ground of possibility), rereading (to uncover or excavate the possible), and creativity (to generate actual possibilities where none formerly existed).

ONTOLOGICAL REFRAMING

The new political imaginary we have sketched presumes certain forms of being, enactments of power, modes of aggregation and connection, and pathways of change. Traversing the distance from a more familiar world (one perhaps structured by stable and inherently reproducible relations of domination) to this emergent one relies on *ontological reframing* as a technique of thinking. Reframing can create the fertile ontological ground for a politics of possibility, opening the field from which the unexpected can emerge, while increasing our space of decision and room to move as political subjects.

In *The End of Capitalism* we used one principal technique of ontological reframing, Althusser's (1972) concept of overdetermination,[33] which presumes that each site and process is constituted at the intersection of all others, and is thus fundamentally an emptiness, complexly constituted by what it is not, without an enduring core or essence. Adapted and extended by Resnick and Wolff (1987) to provide a provisional ontology for un-thinking economic determinism, overdetermination brings a rigorous anti-essentialism to the understanding of causation, working against the nearly ubiquitous impulse to reduce complex processes of eventuation to the operation of one or several determinants. Any attempt to assert centrality or simple causality in a complicated landscape confronts the practice of "thinking overdetermination" as an almost insurmountable obstacle.

This has made it invaluable to us in our positive project of rethinking economic identity and dynamics:

> Through the theoretical lens of overdetermination, a capitalist site is an irreducible specificity. We may no more assume that a capitalist firm is interested in maximizing profits or exploitation than we may assume that an individual woman wants to bear and raise children, or that an American is interested in making money. When we refer to an economy-wide imperative of capital accumulation, we stand on the same unsafe ground (in the context of the anti-essentialist presumption of overdetermination) that we tread on when we refer to a maternal instinct or a human drive to acquisition. (Gibson-Graham 1996, 16)

As we begin to conceptualize contingent relationships where invariant logics once reigned, the economy loses its character as an asocial body in lawful motion and instead becomes a space of recognition and negotiation. The economic certainties and generic stories of development discourse are effectively dislodged, as are the macronarratives of capitalist development (including most recently globalization) that loom in the vicinity of most social theorizing.

We have found that we need technologies for a more reticent yet also more ebullient practice of theorizing, one that tolerates "not knowing" and allows for contingent connection and the hiddenness of unfolding; one that at the same time foregrounds specificity, divergence, incoherence, surplus possibility, the requisite conditions of a less predictable and more productive politics. Here the underlaboring of contemporary social theorists and philosophers like Deleuze and Guattari has been particularly valuable. Many of these install difference and differentiation as a generative ontological centripetal force working against the pull of essence or identity.[34] Others attempt to theorize dynamics not as the simplicity of an unfolding logic that is "already within" an object, but as a very concrete process of eventuation, path-dependent and nonlinear, where a global system that explains its parts is not the privileged and predicted form of emergence (Law 2004).[35] What is bizarre about this theorizing (from the standpoint of common theoretical practice) is that it does not collapse what it aggregates into fewer categories, but spreads everything out to the limits of our tolerance for dimensionality and detail.

Lest ontological reframing be mistaken for a simplistic assertion that we can think ourselves out of the materiality of capitalism or repressive state practices, we should affirm that our orientation toward possibility does not deny the forces that militate against it—forces that may work to undermine, constrain, destroy, or sideline our attempts to reshape economic futures. The practice of thinking overdetermination as a mode of ontological reframing simply encourages us to deny these forces a fundamental, structural, or universal reality and to instead identify them as contingent outcomes of ethical decisions, political projects, and sedimented localized practices, continually pushed and pulled by other determinations.

TECHNIQUES OF REREADING

Thinking overdetermination can be seen not only as a technique of ontological reframing, but also as a technique of rereading—uncovering what is possible but obscured from view. Rather than attending to the regularities of discourse, overt or covert as these may be, an overdeterminist reading fractures and disperses the object of attention, dislocating it from essentialist structures of determination. Reading for contingency rather than necessity situates essentialized and universalized forms of being like "the market" or the "the self-interested subject" in specific geographical and historical locations, releasing them from an ontology of structure or essence.

Techniques of rereading adopt a stance of curiosity, rather than recognition, toward claims of truth. Rereading offers us something new to work with, especially useful if we are trying to produce raw materials for other (political) practices. Possibilities multiply along with uncertainties, and future possibilities become more viable by virtue of already being seen to exist, albeit only in the light of a differentiating imagination. The practice we call "reading for difference rather than dominance" has been our staple and most useful starting place. As part of deconstruction's subversive ontological project of "radical heterogeneity," it is also one of the preeminent tools of queer theory, one that we used throughout *The End of Capitalism* to "queer the economy" and to bring into visibility the great variety of noncapitalist practices that languish on the margins of economic representation.[36]

The practice of reading for absences is similar, though more agonistically recuperative. Briefly sketching a "sociology of absences" Santos (2004) confronts five key "monocultures" (or configurations of dominance) that produce everything else as "non-credible alternatives to what exists" (238). With the aim of transforming "impossible into possible objects," reading for absences excavates what has been actively suppressed or excluded, calling into question the marginalization and "non-credibility" of the nondominant.[37]

TECHNIQUES OF CREATIVITY

Creativity is usually seen to involve bringing things together from different domains to spawn something new—a practice that has been variously called "cross-structuring" (Smith 1973), "cross-appropriation" (Spinosa, Flores, and Dreyfus 1997), and "extension" (Varela 1992). Seldom are such techniques reflectively marshaled to the task of creating different economies, yet they constitute an important means of proliferating possibilities.

In *The End of Capitalism* we extended the thinking techniques of queer theory and feminist poststructuralism to our well-developed knowledge of political economy. Proceeding by analogy, we set to work on capitalism using the same analytical tools that feminists and queer theorists had been taking to patriarchy and heterosexuality, and from this cross-fertilization some of our most important insights emerged. While this was a theoretically generative technique, it was also a rhetorically powerful one, since we were applying ideas that were established and well-respected in their own domain and difficult to dismiss by virtue of their acknowledged effectivity and provenance.

Bringing practices "into contexts that could not generate them, but in which they are useful" is one of the tools of history making, in the view of Spinosa, Flores, and Dreyfus (1997, 4). And creating the context in which our "history-making" skills can be exercised is itself a skill of creativity. Here our action research projects have offered a potential environment in which to encounter/create the unexpected, while simultaneously posing the challenge of not thinking it away. As Connolly warns us, "thought embodies powerful pressures to assimilate new things to old habits of perception" (2002, 65). In the context of fieldwork, Sharpe (2002) sounds a similar warning and calls on us to discard the familiar vision of fieldwork as enlarging the known by domesticating and incorporating the unknown. This popular goal subordinates thinking to recognition and identity, rather than freeing it to participate in the always political process of creating the new. As an antidote, Sharpe offers a nonhumanist understanding of thinking that confers on matter (what is outside the symbolic order) a positive and creative agency, and sees the field as a site where matter and thought can come together to produce the "event in thought." When the field is understood in this way, "the act of thinking has a political dimension. Thinking creates differences" (258).

A POLITICS OF ECONOMIC POSSIBILITY

If politics is a process of transformation instituted by taking decisions on an ultimately undecideable terrain, a politics of possibility rests on an enlarged space of decision and a vision that the world is not governed by some abstract, commanding force or global form of sovereignty. This does not preclude recognizing sedimentations of practice that have an aura of durability and the look of "structures," or routinized rhythms that have an appearance of reliability and the feel of "reproductive dynamics." It is, rather, to question the claims of truth and universality that accompany any ontological rigidity and to render these claims projects for empirical investigation and theoretical re-visioning. Our practices of thinking widen the scope of possibility by opening up each observed relationship to examination for its contingencies and each theoretical analysis for its inherent vulnerability and act of commitment.[38]

As an ontological enterprise, our thinking practices are negatively grounded, starting in the space of nonbeing that is the wellspring of becoming. For us this is the space of politics, and its shadowy denizens are the "subject" and "place"—pregnant absences that have become core elements in our political imaginary.

The saliency of the subject derives from our reading of feminism as a project that explicitly affirmed women while implicitly affirming a new political being—the Lacanian "subject of lack," "the empty place of the structure" that is the opening for a politics of becoming.[39] To the extent that the figure of woman signals unfixed or incomplete identity, she is the subject to be constructed through politics. Her "failed" identity stands for the possibility of politics itself.

Place has been harder to locate negatively. We were stuck at first on its specificity, its dailyness and groundedness—what might be called the positivities of place. Over time, however, the negativity of place seeped into our awareness. Place became that which is not fully yoked into a system of meaning, not entirely subsumed to and defined within a (global) order; it became the aspect of every site that exists as potentiality. Place is the "event in space," operating as a "dislocation" with respect to familiar structures and narratives. It is the eruption of the Lacanian "real," a disruptive materiality. It is the unmapped and unmoored that allows for new moorings and mappings. Place, like the subject, is the site of becoming, the opening for politics.

Our thinking strives to render a world with an ever-replenishing sense of room to move, air to breathe, and space and time to act—a space of pregnant negativity. Our politics operates to create novel economic "positivities" on the negative ground of the "subject" and "place." Its practical engagements involve what we have come to see as three distinct (though intertwined) moments: a politics of language, a politics of the subject, and a politics of collective action.[40]

A POLITICS OF LANGUAGE

Any contemporary economic politics confronts an existing object: an economy produced, through particular modes of representation and calculation, as a bounded sphere "whose internal mechanisms and exchanges separate it from other social processes" (Mitchell, forthcoming). This economy is not simply an ideological concept susceptible to intellectual debunking, but a materialization that participates in organizing the practices and processes that surround it, while at the same time being formatted and maintained by them. A project of instituting a different economy must restore this obdurate positivity to its negative grounding. It must, in Laclau's terms (1990), produce a "dislocation," enabling a recognition that "other economies are possible." Something outside the given configuration of being must offer itself as an element or ingredient for a new political project of configuring. For us this dislocating element has been an economic language that cannot be subsumed to existing ways of thinking economy, and instead signals the ever-present possibility of remaking economy in alternative terms.

In *The End of Capitalism* we tried to open a space for thinking about "noncapitalism" and called for the development of a discourse of economic difference that was not *capitalocentric*. Through a process of deconstruction, we traced the contours of a radically heterogeneous economy in which noncapitalism lost its negativity, becoming a multitude of specific economic activities and relations, and capitalism simultaneously lost its abstract singularity. Liberating the "noncapitalist" occupied zone involved "widening the field of intelligibility to enlarge the scope of possibility,"[41] while at the same time dislocating the (discursive) dominance of capitalism. As what we have called our *language politics,* we produced the conceptual elements for projects of economic innovation and interpellation, and a discursive space in which they could be recognized as viable.

A language is fluid and mobile, not easily confined to a particular location or scale. Unlike a blueprint, it provides the contours and emphases of other worlds but cannot tell you what to say. It can share the space of power with other languages without having to "overthrow" them. We have imagined that a language of economic diversity might provide webs of meaning and intimations of possibility that could distinguish and invigorate a new economic politics. In *The End of Capitalism,* the development of this language was barely begun. In this book, we elaborate our economic language more fully in chapter 3 ("Constructing a Language of Economic Diversity"). In chapter 4 ("The Community Economy") we develop this language for a politics of (counter-) hegemony that aims to orient economic meaning around a noncapitalist point of identification.

A POLITICS OF THE SUBJECT

A language of economic difference has the potential to offer new subject positions and prompt novel identifications, multiplying economic energies and desires. But the realization of this potential is by no means automatic. Capitalism is not just an economic signifier that can be displaced through deconstruction and the proliferation of signs. Rather, it is where the libidinal investment is.

When unemployed workers in Argentina took over abandoned factories after the economic crisis of 2001, the obstacle they encountered was not the state or capital—which were, after all, in disarray—but their own subjectivities. They were workers, not managers or sales reps or entrepreneurs, and as one of them said, "If they had come to us with 50 pesos and told us to show up for work tomorrow, we would have done just that."[42] Instead, for lack of an option, they found themselves recreating Argentine manufacturing. Just as they had formerly constituted a capitalist economy through their identifications and daily practices as workers, so they are now constituting an economy and sociality of "solidarity" as members of the unemployed workers' movement (MTD). That this requires "a struggle against themselves" is one of their principal tenets and observances (Chatterton 2005, 26, quoting Colectivo Situaciones). For the MTD, combating capitalism means refusing a long-standing sense of self and mode of being in the world, while simultaneously cultivating new forms of sociability, visions of happiness, and economic capacities (Colectivo Situaciones 2004, 13). It is as though they had taken up the challenge of economic subjectivity that Foucault identified many years earlier, and made it the touchstone of their movement:

> The political, ethical, social, philosophical problem of our day is not to try to liberate the individual from the economy . . . but to liberate us both from the economy and from the type of individualization that is linked to the economy. We have to promote new forms of subjectivity through the refusal of this kind of individuality which has been imposed on us for several centuries. (1983, 216)

In this book, we circle around Foucault's challenge, confronting it from a number of directions. We turn our analytical lens inward in chapter 1 ("Affects and Emotions for a Postcapitalist Politics") to what in ourselves stands in the way of a contestable, transformable, politicized economy. We address the arts of revolutionary self-cultivation not only to those aspects of self that could be seen as accommodating and embodying capitalism, but to our oppositional and anticapitalist selves. What practices of thinking and feeling, what dispositions and attitudes, what capacities can we cultivate to displace the familiar mode of being of the anticapitalist subject, with its negative and stymied positioning?

Chapter 2 ("Reluctant Subjects: Subjection and Becoming") confronts the reluctant subjects, including in some ways ourselves, whom we stumbled on (and over) in the course of our action research projects. It poses the question, "How do we become not merely opponents of capitalism, but subjects who can desire and create 'noncapitalism?'" In the face of a new discourse of the diverse economy, participants in our projects could not easily identify with the alternative subject positions it availed. Most of them got up in the morning wanting a job—and if not wanting one, feeling they needed one—rather than an alternative economy. (Much as, on the left, we get up in the morning opposing capitalism, not imagining practical alternatives. In this sense, it is partly our own subjection—successful or failed, accommodating or oppositional—that constructs a "capitalist society.") In chapter 2 we address the question of how to understand the subject as both powerfully constituted and constrained by dominant discourses, yet also available to other possibilities of becoming.

Pursuing this subjective zone of possibility in chapter 6 ("Cultivating Subjects for a Community Economy") we recount our experiences of (re)creating ourselves and others as communal economic subjects collectively and individually. Here the *politics of the subject* involves the active and somewhat scary-sounding process of "resubjectivation"—the mobilization and transformation of desires, the cultivation of capacities, and the making of new identifications with something as vague and unspecified as a "community economy."

A POLITICS OF COLLECTIVE ACTION

In our fieldwork we have created spaces of collective endeavor and subjectivity, linking them to the project of constructing new economies. What we were doing, visible only in hindsight, was a form of "micropolitics" that recognized the world in the subject and worked to allow new subject-worlds to arise. At the same time, through introducing a new language of economy, we were producing novel foldings of "matter" and thought, experience and concept, participating in the creation of (economic) possibility. In collaboration with others we were propagating the seeds of the future.

We were also developing an interest in planting and tending them. And it seems to take a village, or a similar collection of kinds, to bring those seeds to fruition, to bring possibility into the next state of being, or even to keep it alive as possibility. For becoming to be supported and nurtured, some form and substance is required, some way of inhabiting three dimensions in space, extension through time, and a fifth dimension of intersubjectivity. Only through the bearing and harvesting of fruit can propagation continue.

A *politics of collective action* involves conscious and combined efforts to build a new kind of economic reality. It can be engaged in here and now, in any place or context. It requires an expansive vision of what is possible, a careful analysis of what can be drawn upon to begin the building process, the courage to make a realistic assessment of what might stand in the way of success, and the decision to go forward with a mixture of creative disrespect and protective caution.

In this book we document many cases of economic experimentation in which collective actions are taken to transform difficult or dire (or merely distasteful) situations by enhancing well-being, instituting different (class) relations of surplus appropriation and distribution, promoting community and environmental sustainability, recognizing and building on economic interdependence, and adopting an ethic of care of the other. We explore both long-standing and large-scale experiments like that of the Mondragón Cooperative Corporation (chapter 5, "Surplus Possibilities: The Intentional Economy of Mondragón"), as well as less well-known interventions including those stemming from our own action research projects that have resulted in the formation of small and in some cases short-lived community-based enterprises (chapter 7, "Building Community Economies"). Each of these interventions can be seen as enrolling a language of economic diversity and prompting new forms of identification and desire. Each is enacted in place, understood not only as the grounded specificities of locale, but also as the unmapped possibilities that are present in every situation—if only we are ready to encounter them.

1

AFFECTS AND EMOTIONS FOR A POSTCAPITALIST POLITICS

STANCES

Cultivating ourselves as thinkers of political and economic possibility has involved finding a stance that orients us, in a spirit of hopefulness, toward connections and openings. As academics schooled in thinking traditions that privilege critique, explanation, and caution, coming to feel comfortable in this stance has not been easy. Some of the reactions to our work have "impressed" upon us that our disposition toward the world sets us apart from and at odds with many contemporary social analysts.[1] As we have felt a way through the resistances to our projects, we have begun to tentatively identify structures of feeling that orient toward closure and brush with despair. It seems that what pushes back against our political imaginary and the techniques of thinking we employ are quite different stances toward theorizing and the world that, for many, stand in the way of a politics of postcapitalist possibility.

What we mean by "stance" is both an emotional and an affective positioning of the self in relation to thought and thus to apprehending the world.[2] Under the influence of rationalist traditions that have policed the mind/body, culture/nature divides, thinking has been seen to operate in a register above and separate from untamed bodily sensation. Yet we have all experienced the intense interconnection between thought and feeling. One has only to recall the inspirations that arise in the shower, the jubilant emotions that accompany discovery, or the pleasurable sensations that ripple through the body in the presence of a complex idea lucidly expressed. In conversations with Nietzsche, Spinoza, Deleuze, and others, contemporary theorists such as William Connolly and Brian Massumi draw our attention to the layered "inter- and intracorporeality" (Connolly 2002, 65) of thinking and the autonomy of affect "that pulls thinking beyond the steady control of intellectual governance" (76; Massumi 2002, chapter 1).[3] Their work suggests that paying heed to the body/brain processes that operate beyond representation and consciousness might give new impetus to political thought and action.[4] For us, this means paying attention not only to the intellectual arguments offered in response to our politics, but to the visceral intensities and emotive narratives that accompany their expression.

In this chapter we identify some of the stances that push back at our political imaginary. Committed to fostering a politics of becoming, we are compelled to explore their intersubjective nature. We consider what we can do to shift these organized "habits of feeling and judgment" (Connolly 2002, 76) that are lodged in our shared culture of inquiry and thus in ourselves as much as in our critics.

CAPITALISM IS NOT (ONLY) WHAT WE ARE UP AGAINST

Soon after completing *The End of Capitalism,* we became actively engaged in "rethinking economy," inventorying the many existing class processes and other economic practices that could be called noncapitalist or alternative, speaking and listening to other theorists and to local economic actors worldwide, and collaboratively and conversationally developing a less capitalocentric, more inclusive, more differentiated language of economy. Recognizing the inevitable performativity of language—its power to create the effects that it names (Butler 1993, 2)—we undertook action research projects with local officials and activists in Australia, the United States, and the Philippines, attempting to cultivate ourselves and others as novel economic subjects with new desires and visions of possibility.

What we found puzzling and unnerving (though certainly familiar) were the reactions to this project, and to our determination to represent capitalism as a set of economic practices scattered over a landscape, rather than a systemic concentration of power. With popular and academic audiences, in reviews and written rebuttals, in conversations with colleagues and friends, we confronted the same challenges over and over again. These resistances "spoke" to us not only at the level of intellectual argument: they also stirred uncomfortable feelings of dismay, recognition, and doubt in our usually relatively robust joint persona.

The assertions that capitalism *really is* the major force in contemporary life, that its dominance is not a discursive object but a reality that can't simply be "thought away," that it has no outside and thus any so-called alternatives are actually part of the neoliberal, patriarchal, corporate capitalist global order, were deeply familiar. This way of thinking was what we had been schooled in and were now militantly working against. It "impressed" itself on us as something we once were attached to, stirring up memories of the allure of a theoretical system that powerfully organized the world and appeared to promise guidelines for transformative action.[5]

More destabilizing was the criticism that politically we were barking up the wrong tree—that while we might help a few people in a few communities, our interventions could not make a dent in corporate globalization; that working at the local level would only foster fragmentation, not the unity and solidarity needed to build a global organization able to meet global power on its own terrain; that stepping in where the state had withdrawn and trying to make the best of it was only enabling the state's abdication, which should have been more directly opposed. These well-rehearsed views of the traditional left had authority over us, reluctant as we were to dismiss or denigrate past working-class victories with their specific strategies and tactics. Against these certainties we felt quite tentative about the potential efficacy of the new interventions we were advocating.

Last there was the judgment that looking for alternatives was escapist and irresponsible. We were not dealing with the emergencies of our time, with the "people who are starving out there." The projects we were involved in were risky and would attract the unwanted attention of the authorities, especially the IRS and the welfare bureaucracy. We were endangering the people we were trying to help. What is more, we were doing so in a way that furthered our own careers at the expense of the powerless. These implications tapped into feelings of guilt about the privilege and confidence that led us "out" into localities with a sense that we had something to offer.

While we had thought that our project was up against the discursive dominance of capitalism, we found that we were up against a culture of thinking (that had socialized us, as well as others) that made capitalism very difficult to sidestep or give up. Our familiar anticapitalist milieu was one in which we could not help but hear (even our own voices saying) that our projects of noncapitalist construction weren't going to work, that this kind of thing hadn't worked in the past, that it was naïve and utopian, already co-opted, off-target, too small and weak in the face of manifest challenges.[6] When we allowed these reactions to press heavily against us, we felt our political room to maneuver shrinking, almost as though a paralysis were setting in. In these moments of immobilization we recognized our own subjection, and that of the left more generally, within potent configurations of habit and desire that were incapable of supporting "experimentation with new possibilities of being and action" (Connolly 2002, 16). We puzzled over the emotional, theoretical, and historical conditions of this incapacity.

What was this all-knowingness about the world? Where did this disparaging sense of certainty come from, the view that anything new would not work? Why were experimental forays into building new economies, movements, and futures greeted with skepticism and suspicion? We found that we were not alone in our consternation and questioning. A growing number of contemporary thinkers have been drawing attention to the deep-seated negativity associated with an "epistemological practice" (Sedgwick 2003, 128), a "structure of desire" (W. Brown 1999, 20), "habits of feeling and judgment" (Connolly 2002, 76), the "reactive stance" (Newman 2000, 3) of critical, radical, left-oriented thinkers and activists. They identify what has come to be the accepted or correct "political" stance as one in which the emotional and affective dispositions of paranoia, melancholia, and moralism intermingle and self-reinforce.

Eve Sedgwick argues that the embracing reductiveness and confident finality associated with the practice of theorizing is a form of paranoia.[7] As a psychic disposition of the intellect, paranoia wants to know everything in advance to protect itself against surprises. It attempts to show intricately and at great length how everything adds up, how it all means the same thing. Paranoia extends the terrain of the predictable, casting its hypervigilant gaze over the entire world, marshaling every site and event into the same fearful order. Bruno Latour likens the thinking moves of contemporary theory to the beliefs of popular conspiracy theorists:

> In both cases, you have to learn to become suspicious of everything people say because of course we all know that they live in the thralls of a complete *illusio* of their real motives. Then, after disbelief has struck and an explanation is requested for what is really going on, in both cases again it is the same appeal to powerful agents hidden in the dark acting always consistently, continuously, relentlessly. Of course, we in the academy like to use more elevated causes—society, discourse, knowledge-slash-power, fields of forces, empires, capitalism—while conspiracists like to portray a miserable bunch of greedy people with dark intents, but I find something troublingly similar in the structure of explanation, in the first movement of disbelief and, then, in the wheeling of causal explanations coming out of the deep dark below. (2004, 229)

According to Sedgwick, the suspicious paranoid stance produces a particular kind of theory—"strong" theory with an embracing reach and a reduced, clarified field of meaning.[8] In contemporary left political analysis, the narrative of neoliberalism as global capitalism's consolidating regulative regime exemplifies strong theory at the cutting edge (Jessop 2003; Peck 2004). Most theories of neoliberal rationality assume a certainty and a sufficiency that blind us to the potential failures or faltering moments of this new governmental technology.[9] To the eye open to emergent practices that are emplacing neoliberalism, attempts to mobilize other economic rationalities that might foster noncapitalist practices are easily dismissed.

Strong theory definitively establishes what *is*, but pays no heed to what it *does*. While it affords the pleasures of recognition, of capture, of intellectually subduing that one last thing, it offers no relief or exit to a place beyond. If we want to cultivate new habits of thinking for a postcapitalist politics, it seems there is work to be done to loosen the structure of feeling that cannot live with uncertainty or move beyond hopelessness.

Another stance that undermines efforts toward imagining and enacting noncapitalist futures is what Walter Benjamin called left melancholia, in which attachment to a past political analysis or identity is stronger than the interest in present possibilities for mobilization, alliance, or transformation (Brown 1999, 20). Certainly the left has experienced monumental losses, and perhaps ultimately a loss of confidence—in the viability of state socialism, the resiliency of social democracy, the credibility of Marxism, the buoyancy and efficacy of solidary movements. Rather than grieving and letting go, the melancholic subject identifies with lost ideals, experiencing their absence as feelings of desolation and dejection (21). Whereas mourning frees the subject to move on, melancholia is stuck and isolated, looking backward rather than to the future, looking inward rather than seeking new alliances and connections.[10]

Nostalgia for old forms of political organization (like international movements of worker solidarity or unions that had teeth) and attachment to the political victories of yesteryear (such as the nationalization of industry or protection for key sectors) blinds us to the political opportunities at hand. "We come to love our left passions and reasons, our left analyses and convictions, more than we love the existing world that we presumably seek to alter" (W. Brown [1999, 21] paraphrasing Benjamin). Melancholia conserves and preserves, turning its hatred toward the new and blaming those—including poststructuralists and practitioners of identity politics (22)—who betray the old ideals.

It is from this stance that place-based activism of the kind we advocate is seen as accommodationist and divisive. As a departure from the politics of the past, place-based movements are suspect and likely to be seen as already incorporated into the capitalist world order. Here we have not only the melancholic attachment to the traditional paranoid style of theorizing, but the melancholic impulse to separate from and punish those who stray and innovate. Again there is work to be done to melt the "frozen heart of the putative leftist," where the "conservative, backward-looking attachment" to feelings, analyses, and relationships blocks any move toward present possibility and connection (W. Brown 1999, 22).

To be a leftist is historically to be identified with the radical potential of the exploited and oppressed working class. Excluded from power yet fixated on the powerful, the radical subject is caught in the familiar ressentiment of the slave against the master. Feelings of hatred and revenge toward the powerful sit side by side with the moral superiority of the lowly (and therefore good) over the high and mighty (and therefore bad) (Newman [2000, 2] paraphrasing Nietzsche). Moralism provides an emotional shoring up of the reactive stance of the weak, "who define themselves in opposition to the strong" (3).[11] With the dissolution in recent times of positive projects of socialist construction, left moralism has been energized by increasing investments in injury, failure, and victimhood (W. Brown 1995).

When power is identified with what is ruthless and dominating, it becomes something the left must distance itself from, lest it be co-opted or compromised

(Newman 2000). Fearing implication with those in power, we become attached to guarding and demonstrating our purity rather than mucking around in everyday politics. Those who engage in such work may find themselves accused of betraying their values, sleeping with the enemy, bargaining with the devil—all manner of transgressions and betrayals.

A moralistic stance fuels doubts about whether local economic experimentation can do anything but shore up a repressive state apparatus, or whether action research reproduces the power of the manipulative academic over the passive community. Focused on the glass half empty rather than half full, this angry and skeptical political sensibility is seldom if ever satisfied. Successful political innovation seems perpetually blocked or postponed because it requires an entirely new relation to power. It will need to escape power, go beyond it, obliterate it, transform it, making the radical shift from a controlling, dominating power to an enabling, liberating one (Newman 2000). But since distance from power is the marker of authentic radicalism and desire is bound up in the purity of powerlessness, the move to reinhabit power is deferred. If we are to make the shift from victimhood to potency, from judgment to enactment, from protest to positive projects, we also need to work on the moralistic stance that clings to a singular conception of power and blocks experimentation with power in its many forms.

Widely present if not fully manifest in any person or pronouncement, this culture of thinking and feeling creates a political sensibility that is paradoxically "depoliticized." The theoretical closure of paranoia, the backward-looking political certainty of melancholia and the moralistic skepticism toward power render the world effectively uncontestable. The accompanying affects of despair, separation, and resentment are negative and repudiating, inhospitable to adventure and innovation, at best cautious and lacking in temerity. From our perspective, these stances are what must be "worked against" if we are to pursue a new economic politics.

Thankfully those same theorists who have helped to identify the barely conscious contours of a habit of thinking that blocks possibility have also led us to potential strategies for loosening its hold over us. The practices of what Nietzsche called self-artistry or self-overcoming (Connolly 2002, 77; Newman 2000, 20) and Foucault called self-cultivation or care of the self are an important entry point for effecting changes in thinking and being in the world.[12]

If our goal as thinkers is the proliferation of different economies, what we most need is an open and hospitable orientation toward the objects of our thought. We need to foster a "love of the world," as Arendt says, rather than masterful knowing, or melancholy or moralistic detachment. To do this, perhaps we need to draw on the pleasures of friendliness, trust, conviviality, and companionable connection. Our repertoire of tactics might include seducing, cajoling, enrolling, enticing, inviting. There could be a greater role in our thinking for invention and playfulness, enchantment and exuberance. And we could start to develop an interest in unpredictability, contingency, experimentation, or even an attachment to the limits of understanding and the possibilities of escape.

SHIFTING STANCES

How do we disinvest in what we are, what we habitually feel and do, and turn ourselves to a project of becoming? How do we work against mastery, melancholia, and moralism and cultivate capacities that can energize and support the creation of "other economies"? If we want other worlds and other economies, how do we make ourselves a condition of possibility for their emergence?

Clearly there are powerful pressures that keep us thinking and feeling in the same old ways. But as Connolly points out, there are also

> countervailing pressures and possibilities . . . at work in the layered corporeality of cultural beings. Thinking bounces in magical bumps and charges across zones marked by differences of speed, capacity, and intensity. It is above all in the dicey relations between the zones that the seeds of creativity are planted. For thinking, again, is not harnessed by the tasks of representation and knowledge. Through its layered intra- and intercorporeality new ideas, theories, and identities are sometimes propelled into being. These new ideas, concepts, sensibilities, and identities later become objects of knowledge. Thinking is thus creative as well as representative, and its creativity is aided by the fact that the process of thinking is not entirely controlled by the agents of thought. (2002, 65–66)

There are, he suggests, experimental practices that we can employ to reeducate ourselves, to convince our bodies to adopt fundamentally different attitudes "that we intellectually entertain as a belief," thereby producing new affective relations with the world (78). We can work in the conscious realm to devise practices that produce the kind of embodied, affect-imbued pre-thoughts that we want to foster. And in the daily rehearsal of these practices we can hope that they will become part of our makeup, part of a cell memory that will increasingly assert itself without resort to conscious calling.[13]

PRACTICING WEAK THEORY, ADOPTING REPARATIVE MOTIVES, AND PRODUCING POSITIVE AFFECT

What if we believed, as Sedgwick suggests, that the goal of theory were not only to extend and deepen knowledge by confirming what we already know—that the world is full of cruelty, misery, and loss, a place of domination and systemic oppression? What if we asked theory to do something else—to help us see openings, to help us to find happiness, to provide a space of freedom and possibility? As a means of getting theory to yield something new, Sedgwick suggests reducing its reach, localizing its purview, practicing a "weak" form of theory that cannot encompass the present and shut down the future (2003, 134). Little more than description, weak theory couldn't know that social experiments are already co-opted and thus doomed to fail or to reinforce dominance; it couldn't tell us that the world economy will be transformed by an international revolutionary movement rather than through the disorganized proliferation of local projects.

Zen master Shunryu Suzuki reminds us that "[i]n the beginner's mind there are many possibilities, in the expert's mind there are few" (1970, 1). The practice of doing weak theory requires acting as a beginner, refusing to know too much, allowing success to inspire and failure to educate, refusing to extend diagnoses too widely or deeply.[14]

Weak theory can be undertaken with a reparative motive that welcomes surprise, entertains hope, makes connection, tolerates coexistence and offers care for the new. As the impulse to judge or discredit other theoretical agendas arises, one can practice making room for others, imagining a terrain on which the success of one project need not come at the expense of another. Producing such spaciousness is particularly useful for a project of rethinking economy, where the problem is the scarcity rather than the inconsistency of economic concepts.[15]

Reparative theorizing can be called on to open our assessments of repudiated movements and practices, fostering affinities and even affiliations. We can choose to cultivate appreciation, taking heart, for example, from the ways that identity politics has opened doors to class politics, or the ways in which a politics of recognition is already also a politics of redistribution.[16] We can practice relinquishing melancholic attachment to the past with its established narratives and entrenched blame. With a commitment to coexistence, we can work toward a way of thinking that might place us alongside our political others, mutually recognizable as oriented in the same direction even if pursuing different paths.[17]

Practicing weak theory allows us to deexoticize power, accepting it as our mundane, pervasive, uneven milieu. We can observe how we produce our own powerlessness with respect to the economy, for example, by theorizing unfolding logics and structural formations that close off the contestable arrangements we associate with politics. As we teach ourselves to come back with a beginner's mind to possibilities, we can begin to explore the multiple forms of power, their spatialities and temporalities, their modes of transmission, reach and (in)effectivity. A differentiated landscape of force, constraint, freedom, and opportunity emerges and we can open to the surge of positive energy that suddenly becomes available for mobilization.

In the last part of this chapter we present a reading of two films, showing how one, *The Full Monty,* portrays movements that sidestep the paranoia, melancholia, and moralism of traditional left thinking as exemplified in the other, *Brassed Off.*[18] Our aim is to illustrate the stance that we feel needs to be cultivated for the task of imagining and enacting a postcapitalist politics. What follows, then, is an experiment in reading that might nudge us toward a different affective relationship to the world and its possibilities.

ILLUSTRATING STANCES

Two British films that came out during the late 1990s, *Brassed Off* and *The Full Monty*, focus on the effects of deindustrialization on communities and masculine identities. As economic geographers who had been studying industrial restructuring since the mid-1970s, we were drawn to these films and found them to be equally emotively powerful. What we found fascinating and what clarified our subsequent interest in the issue of stances toward thinking and politics was the very different affects they produced. It was as though each offered a different extreme in the range of feelings that one could have about the world and its vicissitudes. *Brassed Off* presented the negative affect of despair and righteous anger associated with a strong theory of deindustrialization, while *The Full Monty* bubbled over with the positive affects of surprise and hopeful openings to possibility in line with a reparative reading of industrial change.[19]

The Full Monty hit us with the recognition of the kind of positive affect we wanted to cultivate in our politics. It provoked us to begin a weak reading of what wells up or erupts in the body to shape political possibilities and to think about how these emergences can be cultivated. It prompted us to clarify a potential relationship between class and community becoming. It both demonstrated how we could work on ourselves to become readers/theorists of possibility and was itself the thing demonstrated—a set of affect-driven movements that shift stances and open subjects to new becomings. In the varied responses to this film, however, and in the literature that quickly built up around it and *Brassed Off*, we saw the stark outline of the stance that our postcapitalist political imaginary was up against.

BRIEF SYNOPSIS

Both films are set in English working-class communities undergoing deindustrialization. *Brassed Off* takes place in a coal-mining town where the mine is slated to close. We see the losing battle to keep the pit open through the eyes of miners who are part of the Grimley Colliery Band—a brass band that becomes the symbolic voice of opposition in the film. After the mine has closed, they go on to win the national band competition in Albert Hall. This gives the terminally ill bandmaster a platform and an audience for the harrowing speech of protest and lament that closes the film. Although *Brassed Off* stretches a love story across the management-worker divide and coats itself with a thin layer of working-class humor, the principal affects evoked are pathos and rage. At the end we are left with powerful and painful feelings of loss.

Whereas *Brassed Off* has a documentary feel, *The Full Monty* is a utopian fantasy that starts sometime after the closing of the steelworks in Sheffield. The unemployed steelworkers spend their time at Job Club or pilfering scrap metal or hanging out on the street, feeling like "yesterday's news." But when a group of male strippers comes to town, some of the men who see the crowd of screaming women and the huge box office draw decide that they can do it, too. The film tells the story of six men who come together out of (mainly) financial desperation to become a collectivity of performers and friends. It ends in their striptease before a crowd of admiring, excited, and voluble women, where they take it all off and become reborn as "workers" and as "men." *The Full Monty* offers us surprise and hope while providing the joyful and forward-looking finale that is the hallmark of comedy.

Diverging Readings

What has attached us to these films are the diverging interpretations of what they have to say about economic politics. Many seem determined to read the films as realist texts sited upon the common ground of deindustrialization, with *Brassed Off* providing the awful truth of that process and *The Full Monty* trivializing (though unable ultimately to palliate) it. *The Full Monty* is variously seen as a film about the commodification of male bodies, a farce about the hopelessness of livelihood replacement for working-class males, or a testimony to the victories of capital and Thatcherism in the final years of the century (S. Pearce 2000; Kaplan 2004). For Slavoj Žižek, *The Full Monty* and *Brassed Off* are two ways of saying the same thing (1998). Both films are about coming to terms with catastrophic loss—of male identity, employment and livelihood, the grounds of community, the working-class tradition and modernist political project of social transformation, the struggle itself. *Brassed Off* shows us men gripped by melancholia who continue their colliery band despite the closure of the mine, affirming the empty symbolic form "as a sign of fidelity to the content," even as their ways of life and politics slip from their grasp. *The Full Monty* does it exactly the other way around: these men confront and indeed embrace the disintegration of their (no longer authorized) male dignity. Stripping before an audience of women, they heroically abandon their remnant pride in a sublime and spiritual rite of humiliation.

Žižek reads these films for what they say about left politics in the post-socialist era, arguably from a paranoid theoretical stance. Their despairing message, he concludes, is that there's no viable way forward, no politics confronting global capitalism with a program for its defeat or replacement. For Žižek, this absence suggests the impossibility of undermining "the global capitalist system" at the present time while the economy remains "depoliticized"—seen as a domain of neutral logics and requirements, and ostensibly removed from the sphere of responsibility and choice.[20]

We agree with Žižek that *The Full Monty* and *Brassed Off* are about the crisis of modernist class politics. But whereas Žižek sees the films as similarly configured around loss, we have always experienced *The Full Monty*—since our ecstatic first viewing in 1997—as an ebulliently hopeful film, and one that suggests a way forward (as well as an opening) for a postmodern politics of class.[21]

When we speak about class and politics here, we are not speaking of social groups in which individuals identify as working or ruling class; nor are we thinking about a modernist vision of politics involving two great classes struggling over the fate of the world or the economy. Rather, we are understanding class as a relation or a process—the process of performing, appropriating, and distributing surplus labor (see chapter 3 for more discussion of this conception). The class politics we are thinking of is focused on questions about who appropriates the wealth produced in a social labor process, how wealth is distributed and what kinds of societies it potentiates and sustains, and how noncapitalist class relations might be fostered.[22] It is oriented toward class becoming and transformation, rather than toward identities and struggles defined by capitalism and the traditional left.

Clearly any reading of these films is a political act that involves making ethical choices for one reading or another, for one reality or another, for one set of options or another world of possibility. Each reading is an ingredient, a condiment, a contribution to that feast of social possibilities that we all continue to produce and be nourished (or undernourished) by. In what follows, we offer our own idiosyncratic reading as an experimental demonstration of what a weak reading with reparative motives might look like. The reader can be the judge of whether this experiment works to generate positive affect.

Using stills and descriptions of clips from both films but primarily from *The Full Monty*, we aim to remove you momentarily from the world as we know it—where postcapitalism appears as an impossibility, where class politics is associated with nostalgia for the past and no present project of becoming, and where many of us experience a crisis of desire for communism, if we ever had one.[23] We begin at that negative point of departure with a clip from *Brassed Off*, which, like *The Full Monty*, ends with a performance—in this case the national band competition concert in Albert Hall, where the trophy has been won by the Grimley Colliery Band (see Figure 1).

Brassed Off is a film of and about closure—not only the closure of the pit, but closure around a particular masculine identity, the closing of the era of working-class politics, the closed and closed-off (hidden) nature of truth—whether it be the truth about the pit, or household finances, or health and death, or male emotions. *The Full Monty*, by contrast, is about openness and becoming—most visibly the becoming of new masculine selves who are physically aware and sexually diverse, in new gender roles and economic relations. It is about stripping away myths and falsehoods (including those that proclaim the fixity of antagonistic social distinctions) and the baring of the truth. These are radically different films, despite their similar settings and multiple points of connection.

Brassed Off angrily polices identity boundaries—between men and women, workers and management, us and them: "Why's your bird got a management logo on her key ring?" The film confronts us with the violence of belonging, pulling us toward ressentiment and righteous outrage—the signature emotions of modernist class politics (W. Brown 1995). *The Full Monty* gives us instead the relief and joy of recognition—of otherness as well as sameness, of self-value, of economic

The End

n. 1. closure (as in 140 pits since 1984)
2. termination (as in 250,000 jobs)
3. conclusion (as in draw your own...)

FIGURE 1. Bandmaster's speech in *Brassed Off* (1996). The bandmaster (Pete Postlethwaite), ashen and wheezing from terminal black lung, angrily refuses the award for winning the competition. He excoriates the government for its needless destruction of the coal mining industry and the press and populace for their heartless indifference to the desperate situation of mining communities. After he finishes the speech to a standing ovation, he leads his men off the stage for a night on the town (they grab the trophy on the way out). They are next seen on a double-decker tour bus with the band playing "Land of Hope and Glory" as they pass the houses of Parliament. The film ends with a freeze frame of definitions of "The End."

(and class) possibility as something that cannot be negated or denied. It is this buoyant emotional substrate, as much as the story line and characterization, that prompts us to read the film for lessons in a politics of becoming.

On one level, the crisis of modernist class politics is a crisis of desire, and where the two films diverge most is in the representation of that crisis. In *Brassed Off*, desire is stuck: on keeping the mines open; on being employed (and thus exploited by capital); on solidarity based on shared male experience, including that of capitalist exploitation; on keeping alive communities built on exploitation as well as life-destroying work. Desire is stalemated in a fixation on the demand of the capitalist Other—for labor and for an antagonistic political complement, the "working class."

The bandmaster recognizes the significance of labor's contribution to building and sustaining the larger national community and the communities around the mines. But he sees no alternative to the exploitative capitalist form of this constitutive relation. So as they celebrate labor's contribution, the miners are momentarily reliving the "satisfaction with dissatisfaction" that has been their principal relation to working life. With the closure of the pits, they have experienced a crisis of this compromised form of enjoyment, a crisis of *jouissance* (the complex French word for pleasure that is "tied up in knots" by others' demands and desires) (Fink 1999, 225–26).[24] Their response is to fix upon restoring their former modes and means of satisfaction. The prohibition of the worker identity has eroticized this identity in retrospective reflection, conjoining it with an image of quintessential manhood. Their fantasy is to reclaim this now prohibited state.

Anxiously fixated on a bygone capitalist order, *Brassed Off* acts out the fundamental fantasy of loss, staying with anger at the closure of the mines and within the experience of masculine crisis/castration.[25] What is so adventurous about *The Full Monty*, on the other hand, is that it *begins* with the hollowness of eroticized employment—Job Club has done a job on the job, it seems—and with the acceptance of masculine crisis: "A few years and men won't exist—we'll be extinct, obsolete, dinosaurs." It begins with castrated subjects and shows us a process of reeroticization, the forging of new desires, satisfactions, and masculinities freed from an anchor in a certain form of work.

The Full Monty liberates desire in two sorts of ways (and this liberation is probably what has made the film problematic for so many people, given its setting in devastating loss). Most obviously, with the closure of the steel mill the employed subjects experience a death, an interruption of subjection to capitalism, and thus the opportunity to be something else (though what that might be does not readily present itself). But their freedom is not just dependent on the withdrawal of capital and the symbolic death of the employed subject; it is also an internal potential of the subject, who is never fully subjected (Butler 1997). Liberation inheres in the failures of subjection—the potential of the subject to be other, the potential for unexpected changes of direction.

Jane Bennett sees this as the potential for enchantment, involving "the idea . . . of human *bodies* as an active, and potentially disruptive, force." Enchantment is

> a mood of lively and intense engagement with the world [that] . . . consists in a mixed bodily state of joy and disturbance, a transitory sensuous condition dense and intense enough to stop you in your tracks and toss you onto new terrain, to move you from the actual world to its virtual possibilities. (2001, 111)

Referring to "the spunk or swerve of bodies," (125) Bennett evokes a body with a mind of its own.[26]

The Full Monty presents quite a number of moments when bodies swerve away from familiar forms of subjection and toward alternative ways of being. In the following scenes (from which the stills in Figures 2a–d are taken) we see bodies swerving in immediate, almost unthinking response to humor, sexual desire, music, and encouragement.

In the scene where Gaz and Dave dash to the car, they swerve away from wage labor; in the next scene, Lomper and Guy swerve away from heterosexual masculinity and toward homosexual desire; and in the third and fourth scenes

FIGURE 2A. Dave's dash in *The Full Monty* (1997). Dave has finally succumbed to the pressure to get a job and is working as a security guard at the supermarket/department store. Gaz asks him to steal a coat to wear to Lomper's mother's funeral. "What color?" asks Dave. "Orange," says Gaz, deadpan, and after a hesitation, "Black, you bastard—it's for a funeral." Dave goes away, then comes back with two black coats and they both race out of the store, security bells clanging. It's as though Dave can't resist Gaz's humor; he has to throw respectability away and run off to be with his mates. And why should he stay in this pitiful job and not be there with the others at a funeral for a friend's mother? The unraveling of Dave's self-subjection to (capitalist) employment is palpable here.

FIGURE 2B. Lomper and Guy in *The Full Monty*. They have escaped the police raid on their rehearsal space and, wearing only red G-strings, are running through backyards and climbing over fences of the terrace houses. They reach Lomper's mother's house and clumsily climb through an upstairs window. Standing silhouetted against the window, they look at each other and swerve into what promises to be a kiss.

FIGURE 2C. Unemployment line dance in *The Full Monty*. In the unemployment office the men are in two different lines across the room from each other, waiting to collect their payments. On the radio in the background the deejay announces a 1970s disco hit, one of the tunes they have been practicing to. Their feet start tapping and hips start swinging, and as Gerald steps forward he can't resist doing a swivel turn. The music takes over their bodies and a collective dance presence takes over the room.

FIGURE 2D. Gerald's decision in *The Full Monty*. Gerald walks into the Job Club wearing a suit, and Gaz tells him that the show is on, with two hundred tickets sold. At first Gerald says he can't do it, but the other men urge him on and he changes his mind. After equivocating, he suddenly swerves into the possibility and excitement of it all.

there are swerves toward what might be called "embodied communality." These swerves prompted us to think about noncapitalist class relations and a postmodern politics of class.

As steelworkers, the men were subjected to capitalist exploitation. They were paid a wage (the monetary form of their necessary labor) and their surplus labor, over and above what was necessary for subsistence, was appropriated as surplus value by the capitalists, the board of directors of the steel-producing firm. This wealth belonged to the board to distribute as they saw fit—perhaps to shareholders as dividends, perhaps to managers as bonuses, perhaps to purchase firms in other industries and drain investment away from steel.

Despite their exploitation, understood and resentfully accepted, as wage earners the men had experienced an imaginary economic completeness, an apparent self-sufficiency and independence from society at large. But their situation has now been reversed. In the line at the unemployment office they are positioned as insufficient and dependent individuals, their subsistence needs being met by the state (albeit through redistributions of social surplus to which they have probably contributed). While their newly experienced incompleteness is a condition of community, it is one that has not yet taken (and may never take) a positive form.

But as the men's shoulders start to swivel and their hips begin to thrust in time with the music, we see a shared bodily pleasure in group play and performance that begins to overcome their individuation as bodies in crisis over masculinity and employment. And as the performance takes shape and takes hold in their minds, we see their growing recognition that by working together they have more earning capacity, as well as direct control over the economic resources generated by the group. (This is presented as fantasy rather than as a business plan, though not fantasy in the sense of illusion.) We see acceptance of a fluid hierarchy as leadership roles circulate around the group, from Gaz, whose original idea it was to become strippers and who raises the money to rent the club, to ex-foreman Gerald, who has the skill to teach dancing and who therefore "directs" the group, to Dave, who takes on the public role as announcer at the final performance. All this adds up to a willingness to become communal subjects, to accept their incompleteness, interdependence, and connection across differences of age, race, sexuality, body type, financial need, and social status. It also enables them to exploit their bodies in a jointly conceived "communist" class relation in which surplus will be communally produced and collectively distributed. What emerges is a videographic fantasy of a class relationship understood from the reparative perspective of potential and connection, rather than separateness, rip off, and alienation.

The bodily swerves are only momentary glimmers, however. How can such instances of enchantment lead to more sustained practices of communality and even to permanent escape from old forms of subjection? The film shows us the way. As Gerald equivocates, weighing his new job and social standing against the pleasure of the dance, the others gently encourage him: "Come on, Gerald. . . .

Yeah, you can do it, Gerald," they say. The next set of clips (see Figures 3a–b) illustrates the effectivity of what might be called the "constitutive outside"—the potentiating force, not in this case of the body with a mind of its own, but of a becoming community with desires that call forth resolve and energetic enactment from the neophyte performers.

The actual performance begins to take on reality from the energies of a community that forms around each of the participants to encourage him. It's almost as though the performance is a promise, an unreality to all of them until these moments of community are enacted. The women gathered around the men actively call forth new performances of masculinity, brazenly and tauntingly in the case of the women on the street, and with shy delight in the case of the rehearsal audience—Horse's mother, sisters, and niece Beryl. This reflection of pleasure gives the blokes a glimmer of the potential (including for their own enjoyment) of the performance.

The demand for a performance, the desire and anticipation of pleasure, the acceptance of the men physically, just as they are, by the potential audience, all enact a performativity of the constitutive outside. New masculinities are elicited

FIGURE 3A. Girls on the street in *The Full Monty*. Two women acquaintances taunt the men about what they have to offer compared to the Chippendales, and Gaz is goaded to promise the full monty ("this lot go all the way"). With lecherous but sincere enthusiasm the women promise to be there. As they walk away, the men are overcome with self-consciousness about their equipment (with the exception of Guy), but when Gaz asks, "Are you in, or are you out?" no one shies away.

FIGURE 3B. Relatives at the rehearsal in *The Full Monty*. Horse's female relatives watch a rehearsal and gradually get into it, smiling and shyly taking in the sexual message. As audience reaction develops, the men start to visibly enjoy themselves—before being interrupted by the police.

by the community, not simply by male agents of self-transformation. And masculinity is only one of the things being produced here—what's also being constituted (in our admittedly specialized and interested view) is a communal class relation, and one that would not have come into being without the community to encourage and foster it (see Figures 4a–d).

The Full Monty is, for us, about the potential for multiple productions—the making of masculinities released from the symbolic centrality of the erect phallus and manual labor; the creation of new forms of community energized by pleasure, fun, eroticism, and connection across all sorts of divides and differences; and experimentation with a communal class process in which interdependence and incompleteness are accepted as enabling aspects of individual subjectivity. These productions speak to us when we turn to thinking about how we might cultivate a politics of postcapitalist possibility.

The affects associated with this becoming community are not those traditionally linked to left politics—the outrage and anger that cluster around heroic

FIGURE 4A. Two brief encounters in *The Full Monty*. While Guy is running, teenage girls shout out their unabashed appreciation of his body. Horse is asked by the employee in the unemployment office whether he has done any work during the past week, paid or unpaid; he responds in the negative, and she gives him a knowing and complicitous look: "That's not what I've heard."

FIGURE 4B. Lomper's band practice in *The Full Monty*. Lomper's brass band has conspired to play a striptease tune without telling him. At first he thinks he has the wrong music, then recognizes the joke and sits with a sheepish and gradually beaming smile on his face. The warmth and approval in this enchanted moment bring the performance closer to reality.

FIGURE 4C. Gaz on the street in *The Full Monty*. After the front-page news story on the upcoming performance, guys start bumping and grinding and egging Gaz on with an ambivalent mix of scornfulness and encouragement.

FIGURE 4D. Jean and Dave in *The Full Monty*. Dave comes home to find Jean holding his red G-string, weeping and furious. As she stands up to confront and hit him, he grabs her hands and shouts that it's not what she thinks. He explains what he's been up to, but then admits he can't go through with it: "Jeannie," he says, showing us his large belly, "who wants to see this dance?" She responds without hesitation: "Me, Dave. I do." They head into a kiss.

struggles, or the cynicism and righteousness that operate in left political movements as a powerful emotional undertow. Affect in the film has an enticing quality of wonder as awareness of and delight in otherness take hold of the characters. In this utopian atmosphere, distrust, misrecognition, and judgment are temporarily suspended and a solidarity develops that is based not on sameness, but on a growing recognition that the other is what makes self possible—climaxing in the moment when audience and performers come together and make possible both the performance and each other's roles within it.

The audience is made up of men and women, wives and exes, relatives, neighbors, and police (providing security) who are brought together by eroticized male bodies (of a motley sort) and the sweet, hot promise of pleasure. Circulating during the performance is a mood of enchanted possibility—the possibility of an enduring relationship/connection between Gaz and his boy and even his ex-wife, between Dave and Jean, between Gerald (soon to be employed as a foreman again) and his former workmates, between the women of the audience, who are now mostly "employed," and the men, who are mostly not. It seems that a new politics of class and community might draw on this positive affect, recognizing the co-implication of material existences as well as social identities, where the acknowledged interdependence of self and other is the basis of solidarity.

To end this experiment in reading with an attitude of hope and an orientation to what is possible, we offer the "full monty" (Figure 5). We ask you to join us in recognizing the glimmers of a communal class subjectivity, and in the glances and flows of energy between performers and audience to see the enchanted solidarity of those who exist in recognition of their interdependency.

FIGURE 5. *The Full Monty* (1997). Gaz joins the performance late, after a failure of courage in the dressing room. We hear Tom Jones singing "You Can Leave Your Hat On" and we watch the striptease along with the ecstatic audience. In the final moment the camera takes the performers from behind as the men remove their last bits of covering (hats held over genitals) with a triumphant upward-sweeping gesture. The credits roll to "I Believe in Miracles"—and at that moment, everyone does.

2

RELUCTANT SUBJECTS:
SUBJECTION AND BECOMING

> How, then, is subjection to be thought and how can it become
> a site of alteration? A power *exerted on* a subject, subjection is
> nevertheless a power *assumed by* the subject, an assumption
> that constitutes the instrument of that subject's becoming.
>
> —Judith Butler, *The Psychic Life of Power: Theories in Subjection*

In this chapter we engage differently with what we are up against—not as we did in the Introduction and chapter 1, by posing challenges to thought and affect, calling forth strategies and energies for thinking and feeling in new ways. Here we are more interested in dwelling on what "pushes back" at us in our political projects. The energy in the chapter is (almost all) on the other side—in the institution, stabilization, and naturalization of a regional *economy,* the production of its economic *subjects,* and the obduracy of both in the face of change.

The hope of this chapter is not so different, however, from that of the preceding ones. Undoubtedly we are foregrounding the subjection produced in place through processes of economic and spatial government, attempting to render the embedded, energetic materiality of that subjection. But what ultimately motivates us is the by now perhaps familiar quest for openings and possibilities. While trying to convey the strengths and staying powers of a hegemonic formation, we are doing so in order to contemplate its destabilization. Our preeminent question is "How might the potentiality for becoming arise out of the experience of subjection?"

The concept of subjection allows us to see subjects as "made" and as "making themselves" in and through discourse and practices of governmentality.[1] As Foucault has argued, governmental power is productive and enabling, as well as oppressive and limiting. Subjection does not only entail what "unilaterally *acts on* a given individual as a form of domination, but also [what] *activates* or forms the subject" (Butler 1997, 84). Following Foucault, Butler notes in the epigraph to this chapter that power is "*assumed by* the subject, an assumption that constitutes the instrument of that subject's becoming" (1997, 11, emphasis added). Exactly how subjects "become," and more specifically how they may shift and create new identities for themselves despite the seemingly hegemonic power of dominant discourses and governmental practices, is what interests us here. And this is why Butler's work is so pertinent. She has been particularly concerned with how new gender identities have emerged out of a dominant heterosexual or heteronormative order (1990, 1993). For Butler, insights into the productive tension between being and becoming have arisen from a consideration of subjection as an active process that is always ongoing and never completely successful. In her engagement with Althusser, she shows how the exercise of power is temporalized, made up of a continuous repetition and reiteration of ritualized practices that necessarily involve interruptions and productive intervals of discontinuity (1997, chapter 4). It is during these moments in the constitution of being, she claims, that opportunities for new becomings emerge.

For William Connolly, there is something productive about "the profound ambiguity within Being" because it allows him to set up "a tension between being and becoming in the political domain" (1999, 196). He is reluctant to see the subject as residing simply in the symbolic realm (192) and develops the notion of different "registers of being" to think through "points of intersection between the symbolic and tactics or disciplines not entirely reducible to the symbolic" (193). He proposes a role for the "visceral register"—a pre-representational site where "thought-imbued intensities below the reach of feeling" (148) give rise to affective responses, gut reactions, and embodied actions that cannot help but influence other registers of being. For Connolly it seems that the visceral register might contribute "fugitive currents of energy [that] possibly exceed the fund of identities and differences through which [the individual subject] is organized" (143). In these fugitive energies, then, he recognizes a potential ground on which a politics of becoming might be practiced. So while Butler suggests continual pauses in the performativity of discourse and subjection that can offer openings for new becomings, Connolly offers a speculative glimpse of the way that new identities (and subjections) might arise to occupy these discursive aporia.

Connolly's intervention is interesting to us for its political content. He emphasizes the role of an active politics of becoming that works on fugitive energies to release subjects from "preset judgements that sanctify the universality or naturalness of what [they] already are," thus allowing them to participate in new and surprising movements (146). He argues that macropolitical proposals will not get far until "micropolitical receptivity to [them] has been nurtured across several registers and constituencies" (149). Connolly's work speaks to us as we reflect on the patent lack of desire we encountered, in the early days of our action research projects, for new economic identities that could energize different enactments of a regional economy. In this chapter we attempt to understand that lack of desire through a detailed examination of the ways that a specific economy and its subjects have been produced and normalized in place. At the same time, however, we attempt to glimpse potential openings for a process of *becoming*.

This exploration of subjection is undertaken in the context of one of our action research interventions,[2] the Community Partnering Project in the Latrobe Valley of southeastern Australia. The Latrobe Valley is an area with abundant brown coal resources some two hours east of Melbourne by car, where the bulk of the state of Victoria's electricity has been generated since the early 1920s (see Figure 6). As a result of massive retrenchments in the electricity and mining industries and the privatization of the State Electricity Commission of Victoria (SEC)[3] during the 1990s, the valley has undergone a prolonged period of high unemployment. In the face of this dislocating experience, the Community Partnering Project has attempted to develop new identities and enterprises based on an expanded conception of economy and an expanded range of economic subjectivities.

At the outset of the Community Partnering Project we encountered a widespread belief in the naturalness of "what the valley economy was" that seemed to stand in the way of any micropolitical receptivity to new becomings. The "natural" and the "real" seemed to offer both obstructions to movement and a continued subjection that was problematic, but nevertheless embraced. This prompted us to examine governmental practices and technologies that had constituted the Economy as the central anchor of identity in the region, naturalizing it as singular and definitely "non-diverse."[4] In what follows, we offer a detailed analysis of three "devices of 'meaning production'" that rendered the Economy thinkable and manipulable in the valley, constituting it as a reality that had naturally emerged (N. Rose 1996, 130).[5] Each device was enmeshed in complex debates about economic understandings and futures that belie any easy history of hegemonic thinking, reflecting the ways that the exercise of rule is always contested and highly contingent (O'Malley, Weir, and Shearing 1997, 505).

In many governmentality studies, the voice of the subject is absent and the opportunity is thereby lost to explore the ways that the project of governing and subjecting is never complete (O'Malley et al. 1997, 503). We are particularly interested in the experience of subjection as the very context in which becoming is engendered (Connolly 1999, chapter 2). Throughout this chapter, therefore, we intersperse discussion of techniques of governmentality with the voices of current valley residents who participated in our preliminary focus groups,[6] in an effort to listen to their experiences of subjection and to identify the energies and intensities that might be harnessed by a politics of becoming. We treat the advent of privatization and retrenchment as a moment of interruption in ritualized practices of regional economic subjection, and thus as a moment in which a micropolitics of cultivating receptivity might be activated and a politics of becoming embarked on to produce potentially lasting effects.

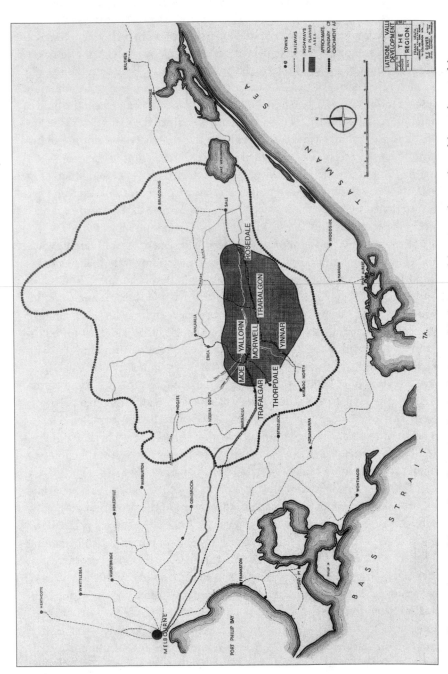

FIGURE 6. Map of the Latrobe Valley region showing the extent of the brown coal deposits and an outline of the catchment of the Latrobe River. From *Latrobe Valley Development: Interim Regional Survey and Report*, compiled by F. Heath and W. E. Gower, 1947.

SYSTEMS OF JUDGMENT: "THE NUMBERS"

Meet Harry, a contemporary resident of the Latrobe Valley—a migrant from a coalfield in the United Kingdom who was enlisted from halfway around the world to become an electricity worker in this region, which supplies most of the state of Victoria's electrical power:

> The problem with the valley, it's a place that's been artificially manufactured and that's the problem, that's how I see the problem. The valley was built by the government and the government wiped their hands of it when they had the responsibility to take it on to look after it. You'll never get over what happened because the valley is definitely an orchestrated built area. It was built to supply a need and the valley took on the people, and the governments encouraged the people to come here, but when the hard word went on, they wiped their hands of the place. And OK . . . we fought the hard fight in relation to it, but we knew the numbers were too much. There is no way that I could honestly sit here and say that for what was happening in the valley . . . the numbers is correct, but that's not the argument. The argument is the destruction that they left in the end when they finished. (June 1997)

Harry identifies his subjection in the region with government and with the numbers its economic accounting practices draw upon. A region is an area constituted by rule, as he points out.[7] But how this rule is enacted and why a subject like Harry accepts the ruling in such an unproblematic way are the issues that concern us.

Harry sets up a crucial distinction between the artificiality of the region, the governed entity ("manufactured" by government), and the reality of the "numbers," the accounting units representing the Economy whose forces gave birth to the region and ultimately devastated its community. Harry accepts the numbers as truths that could not be challenged because they were accurate indicators of an unmediated economic reality: "the numbers is correct," "we knew the numbers were too much." This attachment to the truthfulness of numbers and submission to the Economy's right to govern action (retrenchments) indicates an identification with rationality as an activating aspect of subjectivity.[8] From the nineteenth century onward, numbers have grown in importance to projects of governmentality, according to Theodore Porter (1995), who argues that their objectivity and "inoffensive impersonality" (51) imply the "rule of law, not of men," and "the subordination of personal interests and prejudices to public standards" (74). Taking a shorter historical view, we can perhaps trace Harry's acceptance that numbers are entitled to define his future to a form of regional economic subjection that originated in a series of tables and graphs devised in the early part of the twentieth century.

THE MERZ TABLES: ENROLLING POINTS/PLACES
IN RATIONAL ECONOMIC CALCULATION

> [S]uch tables became the fashion afterwards but up to then I do not
> think anything had ever been more completely or clearly stated and
> shown. (Charles Merz, quoted in Hughes 1983, 251)

In 1908, just seven years after federation of the six colonies into the Commonwealth of Australia, the premier of the state of Victoria commissioned Charles Merz, a consulting engineer based in London, to investigate "the power resources of Victoria and their possible development for the supply of Melbourne and District" (Merz 1908, 5). At this time, Melbourne's power supply was being provided by two small city-based power stations burning black coal imported from the New South Wales coalfields, and regional centers in Victoria all had their own power-generation facilities. Melbourne had developed as a key manufacturing and financial center in the aftermath of the gold rushes that had brought thousands of immigrants to the colony in the 1850s and 1860s and it was now the temporary host of the new federal government.

In commissioning Merz to write his report, the Victorian government entered into a complex web of international associations that were to connect British, German, and Australian engineering expertise and internationally accepted principles of economic calculation for many years to come. Charles Merz was the son of the founder and chairman of Britain's largest regional power utility, the Newcastle-upon-Tyne Electric Supply Company (NESCO) (Hughes 1983, 249). His firm, Merz and McLellan, pioneered the development of large-scale, regional, power-supply systems in Argentina, South Africa, India, and the United States, as well as in the United Kingdom and Australia. Hughes comments that he

> became an agent of technology transfer on a grand scale, taking with
> him the experience he gained in building the NESCO system on the
> northeast coast of England and bringing back state-of-the-art ideas
> from the rest of the world. . . . He was believed by many to be the most
> effective expert witness in the engineering world. In presenting his
> cases he used highly imaginative statistical tables, graphs, and charts
> prepared by his firm. (1983, 453)

A series of these statistical tables prepared by Merz for the Victorian state government first enlisted the Latrobe Valley, or at least a point within it, into an explicitly economic frame of reference and constituted it as a potential site of governmentality.

Merz's commitment to electricity as the most modern, adaptable, economical, clean, and safe form of power generation was strengthened by a belief in its role in economic development. In the introduction to his report, Merz placed the issues facing Victoria within the big picture of historical and contemporary industrial development on an international scale:

> Just as in former years the mills and factories of England were built by streams where water power was available and are to-day most thickly congregated near coal-fields, so the establishment of great centers of cheap electric power in various countries is beginning to exercise an increasingly important influence upon the distribution of factories. (Merz 1908, 6)

Merz was keen to link these progressive visions to the economics of least-cost calculation. He aimed to convince heavy industry to give up generating their own power in return for the lower costs of accessing power from a centralized system of mass-produced electricity.

The 1908 report to the state of Victoria relies on quantitative measurement, meticulous statistical detail, and the "explicitly mathematical reasoning" that was becoming normalized as a scientific tool of the new marginalist economics (Buck-Morss 1995, 462, quoting Mark Blaug). The report included a table drawn from the *Statistics of Manufactories, Works &c. (Metropolitan Area), for the Year 1906,* which showed the numbers and industrial sectors of factories operating in Melbourne, their degree of mechanization, type of power supply, employment, and value of plant and machinery. To add to his picture of the "existing conditions" Merz surveyed the size and type of plant currently supplying electric power and produced a ten-year forecast of the electrical requirements of Melbourne. This information, all marshaled and projected, along with the commitment to electricity as "good," set the stage for his "rational" recommendations about possible future courses of action.

The problem, as Merz saw it, was where best to locate a large new power station to service the growth in demand for electricity in Melbourne—in Melbourne itself or in situ on the vast brown coalfields of the Latrobe Valley. Merz produced a relative cost accounting to prove that, when demand was sufficiently high (as indicated by the "load factor," or the average demand for electricity as a percentage of peak demand), the cost of transporting coal to Melbourne would far exceed the cost of transmitting electricity by overhead wires from the Latrobe Valley to the city. His calculations (shown in Figure 7) showed that as the base demand for electricity grew, it would become more economical to undertake the long-term investment of building generating capacity in the Latrobe Valley. Merz argued that "it would pay best to run the Latrobe Valley Power Station and the transmission line at as high a load factor as possible" (1908, 19) and the resulting "efficiency" would create the imperative for more users, particularly industrial ones, to convert from steam to electricity.

This kind of table provided the conduit by which an emerging language of economic calculation was incorporated into the practice of governmentality.

TABLE V.

COST OF ELECTRICAL TRANSMISSION FROM LATROBE VALLEY COMPARED WITH THE COST OF FREIGHT ON BROWN COAL TO MELBOURNE.

LOAD FACTOR.	10 % Coal carried by rail to Melbourne.	10 % Electrical power transmitted by overhead wires.	20 % Coal carried by rail to Melbourne.	20 % Electrical power transmitted by overhead wires.	33 % Coal carried by rail to Melbourne.	33 % Electrical power transmitted by overhead wires.	40 % Coal carried by rail to Melbourne.	40 % Electrical power transmitted by overhead wires.	50 % Coal carried by rail to Melbourne.	50 % Electrical power transmitted by overhead wires.	75 % Coal carried by rail to Melbourne.	75 % Electrical power transmitted by overhead wires.	100 % Coal carried by rail to Melbourne.	100 % Electrical power transmitted by overhead wires.
Maximum H.P. delivered to 12,000 volt feeders over heaviest half hour	35,000	35,000	35,000	35,000	35,000	35,000	35,000	35,000	35,000	35,000	35,000	35,000	35,000	35,000
Maximum H.P. sent out of Generating Station	35,000	39,400	35,000	39,400	35,000	39,400	35,000	39,400	35,000	39,400	35,000	39,400	35,000	39,400
Capital cost of generating plant	£451,000	£514,000	£451,000	£514,000	£451,000	£514,000	£451,000	£514,000	£451,000	£514,000	£451,000	£514,000	£451,000	£514,000
Capital cost of transmission line and transforming substations	—	£286,000	—	£286,000	—	£286,000	—	£286,000	—	£286,000	—	£286,000	—	£286,000
Additional capital expenditure in the case of electrical transmission	—	£349,000	—	£349,000	—	£349,000	—	£349,000	—	£349,000	—	£349,000	—	£349,000
Fixed charges on additional capital, including interest, depreciation, maintenance, &c.	—	£38,390	—	£38,390	—	£38,390	—	£38,390	—	£38,390	—	£38,390	—	£38,390
Units per annum generated in millions	25·2	28·3	50·4	56·6	83·0	93·5	100·8	118·2	126	141·5	189	212·2	252	283
Tons of Black coal required per annum	31,000	—	62,000	—	102,100	—	124,000	—	155,000	—	232,500	—	310,000	—
Equivalent tons of brown coal required per annum	77,500	87,190	155,000	174,380	255,250	287,150	310,000	348,760	387,500	435,950	581,250	653,925	775,000	871,900
Cost of carriage per ton from mine to Generating Station taken at	4/-	8d.	4/-	8d.	4/-	8d.	4/-	8d.	4/-	8d.	4/-	8d.	4/-	8d.
Cost of carriage per annum	£15,500	£2,907	£81,000	£5,813	£51,050	£9,570	£62,000	£11,626	£77,500	£14,532	£116,250	£21,798	£155,000	£29,067
Cost of extra coal at 1s. 4d. per ton at mine	—	£646	—	£1,292	—	£2,130	—	£2,584	—	£3,230	—	£4,845	—	£6,460
Total variable charges	£15,500	£3,553	£31,000	£7,105	£51,050	£11,700	£62,000	£14,210	£77,500	£17,762	£116,250	£26,643	£155,000	£35,527
Total fixed and variable charges	£15,500	£41,943	£31,000	£45,495	£51,050	£50,090	£62,000	£52,600	£77,500	£56,152	£116,250	£65,033	£155,000	£73,917
Balance against electrical transmission	£26,443	—	£14,495	—	—	—	—	—	—	—	—	—	—	—
Balance in favour of electrical transmission	—	—	—	—	—	£960	—	£9,400	—	£21,348	—	£51,217	—	£81,083

FIGURE 7. Charles Merz's relative cost accounting in 1908: Table V in *Report upon the Production and Use of Electric Power*.

In least-cost economic calculations such as these, Buck-Morss notes, the social whole is dissolved, the Economy is set apart from society, and the broad concerns of political economy are rendered exogenous to the system (1995, 463). Merz's "comprehensive cost accounting" failed to include labor costs (or any of the costs of land resumption, housing, or providing for a labor force in the Latrobe Valley) and the costs of distributing power beyond one key point in Melbourne. This oversight appears to have been normal for exercises of this kind. As Hughes notes,

> Owners and managers of utilities, unlike the owners and managers of railroads, steel mills, automobile factories, and many other large-scale technological enterprises, were not diverted by harassing labor problems from a close analysis of, and emphasis on, capital costs. In the sources pertaining to the problems of the electric power systems, rarely was more than a passing reference to labor costs encountered. Instead, emphasis was on load factor. Load factor structured the decision-making environment. (1983, 463)

Merz's calculations contributed to the production of a "modern" economic reality in which order and predictive certainty were achieved by including a limited selection of production costs that were deemed to be the key determinants of efficiency (Ruccio and Amariglio 2003). The vision of economy that lurks in his report also constitutes centeredness as "natural" and necessary to survival—industrial growth is not only presumed but "demands" large-scale energy production and centralization of the ownership and management of power generation.[9]

The report's effect was to concentrate the focus of the state of Victoria on the Latrobe Valley as a "center of calculation." The human subject is, in this vision, an unaccounted and seemingly unimportant "labor cost" whose *being* in place is an outcome of "the numbers," and whose contribution to the *becoming* of a region is purely instrumental to the project of electricity generation. Brought into being as a site endowed with technical importance and economic meaning in relation to the metropolis of Melbourne and the demands of its industrial capitalists and residents, the Latrobe Valley is an economy and place (a point in relative economic space) that precedes the people.

These early representations of the Latrobe Valley—as an instrumental node in a network radiating out from a central metropolis, an invisible element of the economy of Melbourne/Victoria contained within its calculus but more or less dimensionless and certainly citizenless—still resonate today. Countless actors in Victoria and the valley have continued to valorize the least-cost representation authored by Charles Merz, thereby animating a form of subjection that arises from the subject's instrumental visibility only in the presence of numbers and economic accounts. When Jeff Kennett, then premier of Victoria, announced the decision to sell off the state-owned power stations in the early 1990s, he urged each station to rationalize and become "economical," so that it might survive in a privatized landscape. As Harry, a supervisor at the time, recalls:

> Just before we were being sold, we always demanded the figures of how efficient the plant was and how much profit was being made. . . . And so we were given this information for the first time and that information was the truth. When we were shown the truth we all got together and we started doing things that we would never do before. When it comes to having done things right . . . we have done things right to our own detriment. We've done the right thing and that's what the people in the valley have got to be proud of. (June 1997)

> Talk about the rest of it. . . . I've still got a job. My mate hasn't got a job, *some care should be taken of him.* [Break in which Harry is unable to proceed.] That's how I feel about the place. I was fundamental in the process of actually taking their jobs off them. [There] was nothing for them to be picked up [by] later and I felt really sorry for them. I've had a lot to do with those guys losing their jobs. But I knew it was the only way that the station I was in was going to survive in the long term. (June 1997, emphasis added)

These statements were uttered with increasing emotion and distress. A passionate and forceful voice trained in union oratory informed the first set of reflections. This was the voice that was able to accept the "truth," face the facts, and carry out the sackings demanded by the real and unchallengeable Economy to increase efficiency and maintain large-scale, least-cost operations. But in what followed, Harry's voice faltered, tears came to his eyes, and for a brief moment he was so overcome that he was unable to speak. His body seemed to temporarily escape the discipline of subjection to the numbers, refusing to "take it (or assume it) like a man." Following Connolly's lead, we could see Harry's tears as expressing a gut recognition that the "health" of the body economic—the paring down of the labor force, the closing of inefficient plants, the facing up to "economic truth," the selling off of public assets on the "free market"—does not equate with the health of the social body, and that his actions had produced injury to others. In this emotional moment, one could also feel a shift in the intersubjective relations of the focus group. The long embodied antagonisms between Harry as a worker and union man and the likes of the businessman who sat next to him drained away, as an empathetic atmosphere of care was established and past ideological enemies found themselves respecting each other in their honesty.

Drawing on Connolly's and Butler's work, we would like to see this instant in which Harry's intense and emotional response disrupts his speech as a potential interruption in the ritualized practice or assumption of subjection, a momentary opening for the expression of a different economic subjectivity based on an ethic of care for the other. It is from the embodied subject position of a "mate" (that potentially includes not only his union comrades, but also the business-people and bureaucrats in the focus group) that the numbers and their apparent rationality seem less legitimate, less "natural," and less able to dominate. This kind of opening was what we hoped to find, and to cultivate and develop in our action research.

VOCABULARIES: "CHILD," "CONSUMER," AND "CITIZEN"

Meet Mike, another contemporary resident of the Latrobe Valley—an artist who recently entered local politics in a newly amalgamated and democratically elected shire council that, for the first time, spans the entire valley:[10]

> The valley has always been perceived as a petulant child. It's a petu-lant child that you can't ignore, that you don't really want. It's the safest Labor seat in the state of Victoria and it's a seat of consequence that's spent most of its life in opposition. . . . Every now and then you have to attend to it because it screams so hard. But it's only when the ALP [Australian Labor Party] are the incumbent government that this region gets attended to. . . . It's always referred to as the industrial heartland. (June 1997)

> The SEC stood for slow, easy, and comfortable, but for all its shortcom-ings in that respect it's what kept this community going. It's what made the family, it's what made the stores flourish. It kept the economy going and the money went round and it stayed here. And, moreover, those people that had a job at the SEC, and were seen to be SEC bludgers by some on the outside, had a sense of worth and a sense of value; they had a job to go to. It might have been making lead sinkers for the SEC social club when there was no work out of recycled lead, but they had a job to go to and they felt worthwhile. (June 1997)

Perhaps you can hear the complex amalgam of emotions and identities introduced by these comments: the passionate attachment to the SEC (father/master); the complicity with its employment policies, which "valued" whoever was employed; the identification with "labor"; and the perversely proud attachment to an oppositional mode of us/them engagement where "we" are not only privileged and pampered compared to other workers, but also marginal and dependent. Mike's statements serve to remind us that subjection can be experienced as affirming, valuable, and desired as well as dominating, oppressive, and resisted. It is, after all, what constitutes the subject and, as Butler points out, recognition of one's subordination does not preclude its denial or its reenactment (1997, 9). The economic subjection expressed here involves a form of self-negation evidenced by the readiness of adults, as well as the valley as a place, to be interpellated as children—beings who are demanding, petulant, needy of care, and ultimately ignored.[11]

Discussing the desire for survival that drives us to "turn our back on our-selves," Butler questions the conditions under which we are required to exist as a "self-negating being in order to attain and preserve a status as 'being' at all" (1997, 130). "Being," in the Latrobe Valley, had been inextricably linked to the statutory authority of the SEC, which offered succor—stable employment, hous-ing, community services—as well as a robust masculine identity for the region as the "powerhouse" of Victoria. The SEC placed people in the valley and recruited them within an Economy that was growth-oriented, state-owned, and highly centralized, and to which they seemed to "belong" as valuable contributors. We can trace a dual address to the subject as both child and citizen/consumer within the vocabulary of cooperation and state development that was skillfully employed in the early days of the electricity authority by its authoritative head, Sir John Monash.

THE MONASH AUTHORITY: EMPLACING AND INTERPELLATING PEOPLE

> A plentiful supply of cheap power and of cheap fuel is the foundation
> of a nation's prosperity; upon that foundation rests also the well-being
> of its people as a whole, reducing, in all directions, physical toil and
> increasing the comfort and ease of every individual of every class of
> society. (Monash 1921, foreword)

The state of Victoria's Advisory Committee on Brown Coal acted on the rec-ommendations of the 1908 Merz report in 1917 as the Great War dragged on and Australian forces under the command of Lieutenant-General Sir John Monash continued to be slaughtered on the fields of France and Belgium. While Australia's experience of patriotic bloodletting forged a kind of political "coming to adulthood," it also heightened awareness of the economic dependence of the former colonies on their imperial parent. The 1917 report is imbued with a reac-tive isolationism and concern for economic independence, pointing to the "still ample scope for the development of industries to make Australia self-contained" (Victoria, State of, 1917, 9). It is also driven by a strongly competitive state devel-opmental agenda that belies a commitment to "national" prosperity (N. Brown 1995, 90). Despite federation and the sense of nationhood gained through par-ticipation in a "World War," the economic rivalry between the states appears at this time to be heightened rather than diminished.

One of the more immediate prompts for the Victorian government to act to develop its own brown coal resources was the frequent shortages of black coal imported from Newcastle, New South Wales (NSW), where disgruntled miners were causing industrial disruption (particularly during 1916 and 1917) (Gibson 1984; E. Ross 1970). The uncertainty of supply, as well as the rising costs of freight and coal, were strong incentives to become self-sufficient. The advisory com-mittee's report recommended that the more energy-efficient black coal imports from New South Wales be totally replaced by the local product from the state's brown coalfields (in the Latrobe Valley) and that a new power station located at Morwell be used to generate electricity. It also recommended that "the State should control and direct the co-ordination of all State and statutory generating and distributing schemes in Victoria" (Victoria, State of, 1917, 8–9). The outcome of this government report was the Electricity Commissioners Act of 1918 and the formation of the SEC in 1919.

Informing these recommendations was a conception of an Economy composed of both private capitalist and state capitalist enterprise in symbiotic relation.[12] In this vision, it was legitimate that problems caused by an inefficient capitalist black coal industry in New South Wales could be addressed by the formation of a state-run industry in Victoria, and that Melbourne capitalists could be assisted to access cheap and efficient power by means of a state-owned monopoly capitalist authority. A large-scale state enterprise was naturally seen as the only institution capable of translating the Latrobe Valley's least-cost location into something that could generate the lifeblood of state prosperity.[13]

Shadowing the efficiency of the proposed monopoly state authority was the inefficiency of labor—those people who fought for higher wages and better conditions and withdrew their labor power, as on the coalfields of Newcastle. A language of class had dominated debates over conscription during the war and the International Workers of the World had won many supporters during industrial conflicts in the mines and ports of Australia, both during the war and in its aftermath. In the very moment of the SEC's formation, this potential chink in the discourse of economic efficiency is identified and there is an appeal to the worker as a responsible citizen and participant in a project of communal (classless) progress. In his capacity as a military commander, Sir John Monash, who became the first appointed general manager and chairman of the commissioners of the SEC, was experienced in the rhetoric of social inclusion. He writes the following in his foreword to the public information booklet, *Power for Victorian Industries* (see Figures 8 and 9):

> The community can help greatly in this magnificent enterprise . . . by developing a healthy public opinion which will act in restraint of industrial unrest and in favor of honest labour, and all the good that flows from whole-hearted endeavour. (Monash 1921, 4)

In contrast to the language employed by Merz to "sell" a regional power supply scheme, in the documents and reports of the SEC the economics of technical efficiency are overshadowed by the economics of state boosterism and individual consumerism (A. Pratt 1921). The projections associated with this power scheme are not posed in terms of the growth of demand or the efficient management of load factors, but in terms of a population of economic individuals:

> [W]hen the scheme is completed its effect will be to reduce the cost of living, to facilitate the payment of high wages to improve working

Published by
The Industrial Australian and Mining Standard, 17th March, 1921

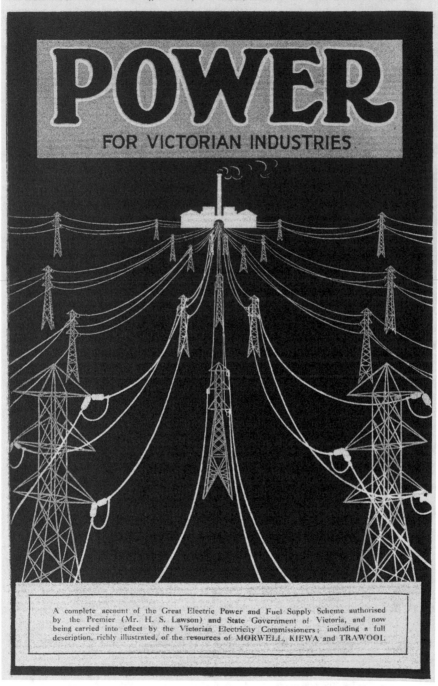

FIGURE 8. Cover of the public information pamphlet *Power for Victorian Industries*, edited by Ambrose Pratt in 1921, which outlined the Great Electric Power and Fuel Supply Scheme.

Lieut.-General Sir John Monash,
G.C.M.G., V.D., C.E.

who controls the work of the

Victorian Electricity Commission

Foreword

By Lieut.-General Sir John Monash
G.C.M.G., V.D., C.E.

Many of the men of Australia who answered the call upon them to devote, during the period of the Great War, the best years of their lives to the service of their country, have found themselves, at its conclusion, animated by the strong ambition to continue that service in the development of their country's prosperity which the peace, won by them in the field, has rendered possible. The realisation of such an ambition has, however, not come to many of them; and that is why I esteem myself fortunate that an opportunity to do so lies ready to my hand. The foresight and patriotism of the Victorian Government have launched a project whose possibilities are quite without limitation, and whose benefits to the community of this State no man can over-estimate. A plentiful supply of cheap power and of cheap fuel is the foundation of a nation's prosperity; upon that foundation rests also the well-being of its people as a whole, reducing, in all directions, physical toil and increasing the comfort and ease of every individual of every class of society.

While, however, the ultimate realisation of this great scheme is assured beyond all doubt, it is equally certain that because of the disorganisation of the world's industry, as the result of the war, the time which will be occupied in bringing it to fruition will be longer than in normal times. The community can help greatly in this magnificent enterprise, firstly by patience, so as to avoid, by a clamour for speedy fulfilment, the permanent burden of present highly inflated capital costs; and, secondly, by developing a healthy public opinion which will act in restraint of industrial unrest and in favour of honest labour, and all the good that flows from whole-hearted endeavour. The work to be done deserves such honest effort; for when it is completed, it will become a monument to every man, however humble, who has shared in its creation.

FIGURE 9. Sir John Monash's foreword to *Power for Victorian Industries* (1921).

> and living conditions, to plant a much larger population on the soil, to
> increase the purchasing power of the individual, to mitigate industrial
> troubles and to add vastly and progressively to the prosperity and hap-
> piness of the State. These are ideals worth striving for, worthy indeed
> of great sacrifices. They are all capable of achievement by means of the
> scheme. The power scheme has the intrinsic power to realise them all.
> (A. Pratt 1921, 5)

On the surface, this rhetoric hails the citizens of Victoria as consumers and as
potential employees of the SEC. Through an appeal to individual desires for a
higher standard of living, support is harnessed for a project of competitive state
development that will subsidize private capitalist activities. But alongside this address to adult workers and consumers, subjects are effectively interpellated into a
paternalist discourse, positioned as liable to be unruly, impatient, unreasonable,
and unfair if (reading between the lines) they engage in class-based behavior:

> [E]very individual citizen is under an obligation to "get behind" the
> Government and the Commission for the prosecution of this under-
> taking to success . . . to be patient while the scheme is being carried
> out, and to refrain from jeopardising its success by unfair or mischie-
> vous criticism of the methods of those responsible for its enforcement
> and effectuation. (A. Pratt 1921, 5)

Central to the promotion of industrial harmony was the provision of
housing for SEC workers (Freestone 1989, 124). The existing townships were
no more than small railway settlements servicing the surrounding farming and
logging communities. In keeping with the latest developments in urban planning at the time, and in the spirit of paternalism engendered by the SEC, it was
decided to build Yallourn,[14] a garden village "laid out on approved modern lines,
providing residential and factory areas, ample recreation grounds, and garden
space, together with the necessary school and public building accommodation"
(SECV 1921, 8).

To reside in Yallourn was to become the model economic citizen hailed by
Monash. The new town was owned and managed by the SEC and subjection to its
"authority" was almost total. One was housed, provisioned, schooled, employed,
entertained, policed, and watched by the SEC in one form or another.[15] One was
protected and pampered as well as infantilized and controlled. The classic tale
told by former Yallourn residents is that "if a tap or a light-globe went they would
ring up the SEC and somebody would come and change it for them" (community
member, Latrobe Valley, June 1997).

Permeating the quasi-socialist central planning that informed Monash's
project was a vision of the Economy as something that could be "tinkered with in
order to effect social outcomes at the macroeconomic level" (Buck-Morss 1995,
465). Monash's SEC animated the forces that had pointed toward centralization

of power—both electrical and economic—a decade before, producing the institutional order capable of creating and controlling industrial efficiency. With the building of Yallourn, a part of the Latrobe Valley became a physical site of governmentality, where bodies labored, the environment was radically altered, and subjects were constituted by economic and political discourses of Victorian state development. Attached by electrical transmission lines, as well as other circuits of finance and power, into the center of calculation that was Melbourne—itself representing the entirety of the state of Victoria—the valley was not accorded an independent regional economic identity. Though non-SEC workers were being attracted to the valley, the comprehensive governmental gaze included only the inhabitants of Yallourn—well-cared-for people who were positioned primarily as citizens of Victoria and consumers in a strengthening state economy.

As growth continued, Monash's earlier appeal for restraint was ignored—workers embraced expanding consumption and exercised their monopoly control by agitating for wage increases. The valley became known through the identity of the SEC workers; it was increasingly seen as a labor enclave, separated by economic privilege and industrial muscle from the rest of the state. This militant identity relied on the maintenance of a very public us/them boundary, and the private knowledge that power and privilege were attained through dependence on and compliance with state authority. The perception of valley workers as better off and more powerful than other members of the Victorian working class was mirrored at the local level as SEC workers and families became far more prosperous than other residents of the Latrobe Valley.

Infantilizing and paradoxical though it was, this discourse of identity sustained many through the decades of SEC growth. And it has been the loss of this strong personal and collective identity and the sense of inclusion in a project that has been most devastating in recent times:

> The changes and the subsequent decline in the power industry has . . . changed prosperity into misery. . . . Does the responsibility lie with the power industry for bringing up a vast culture and a way of life in this community? People were employed, grandfathers and fathers and kids got jobs at the SEC and I think the SEC established the social conditions in which people lived for a long, long time. . . . There were people I spoke to who were really quite traumatized that their culture or their way of life had just disappeared or at least was beginning to disappear. I think that was the beginning of what I saw to be a slow and miserable decline of many families and individuals. (Community-based financial counselor, June 1997)
>
> There are people out there who are doing it very, very hard. There is a lot of pain in the community and to a certain extent people do feel powerless, they do feel disenfranchised and they do feel hopeless. (Manager, government agency, June 1997)

One of the consequences of cooperating with the centralized power project of Victorian state development was that Merz's promised regional multiplier effects—the attraction of manufacturing industries and the development of a more diversified industrial region—were never realized to the extent predicted. With the exception of a major pulp and paper processing plant, the valley largely remained a single industry region with no alternative employment generators of any importance.[16] Now that the loyalty demanded by the SEC is no longer required, the actual costs of dependence on the state authority are being calculated. Residents in the valley are angry that they were forced to subsidize private capitalist industrial interests in metropolitan Melbourne, paying the same price as users throughout the state for the energy they produced and could have accessed more cheaply. The subsidy they granted others in the form of cheap power was never matched by standardized state gasoline pricing or telephone rates:

> We weren't allowed to compete on an economic basis. If we'd have been able to compete on an economic basis for the price of power, the real price of power in the Latrobe Valley compared to Melbourne . . . we would have been in a very good position to compete for a lot of industrial business. (Local planner, June 1997)

What is particularly disturbing is that the cooperation many readily offered has now been shunned. Echoing the entitlement of the obedient child, one person who grew up in the valley said,

> I can remember growing up in a very secure environment. There was a real sense of security and a great sense of belonging and I have seen that gradually eroded. . . . We were good, we did the right thing, we went along with all the changes, but what did we get? . . . Nothing. (Businesswoman, June 1997)

These statements were made with passion and a certain amount of anger and they evince a sense of injustice about the way the valley and its residents have been treated. It would be easy to see this anger as an expression of the ressentiment that accompanies subjection and victimization. But we are interested in a more nuanced reading and the suggestion that anger is also a productive expression of outrage in the face of unfair and irrational economic practices. Now that the social contract offering SEC workers escalating compensation in return for their "cooperation" has been broken, there is a willingness to face up to what lay behind this contract—the insecurity and unsustainability of a single-industry region run along state capitalist lines. While the heroic project of state development was paying out personal financial rewards, the community was blind to the regional underdevelopment to which they were a party. But when the rewards ceased, it was possible (and even perhaps inevitable) that people would see what had been created as deeply problematic and feel a mobilizing anger.

We sensed that the anger, overtly aimed at the SEC, was also directed at themselves. Animating their righteous blaming of the SEC was a certain self-hatred, some shame at their dependency, their going along, being bought off, slumbering through their economic lives, some uncomfortable sense that they had purchased their own well-being at the expense of the community. In such a moment of interruption in the way things are and should be, and in the angry feelings toward the world and self that the interruption provokes, demands may be forged to recreate what is lost, but a turning is also possible—one potentially based on economic diversity and more autonomous regional development, if such possibilities were to become imaginable.

GRIDS OF VISUALIZATION: THE "AREA AS A WHOLE"

Meet Tracy, a young businesswoman in the Latrobe Valley who grew up during the "good times" and remains committed to staying and contributing to a re-visioning of the region:

> There is an absence of security, there is no sense of permanency, it's evidenced by the architecture, by everything that we do. Everything's a quick fix or a band-aid approach to whatever it is that it might be. There's a greater sense of competition now, there's less trust, even between individuals, and on a greater scale between people in business. They don't want to work together anymore. Between the towns there's no longer this real sense that we can do anything *for the area as a whole*. Each person is out there wheeling their own barrow and protecting themselves. They're quite vulnerable to every aspect of competition or whatever it may be heading toward them. (June 1997, emphasis added)

Tracy's statement introduces the vision of the "area as a whole," an area in which towns and inhabitants once appeared to act in unity with a sense of purpose and that is now crumbling into fragments under current pressures. Her comments refer to a somewhat mythical image of cohesion that belies the class divisions, public/private sector cleavages, gender politics, and ethnic, racial, and town identities that have always internally differentiated the area. But they also point to the slapdash, unplanned nature of the built environment in the valley, and the heightened sense of competition between people, towns, and businesses across the region. In the face of what she sees as a rising competitive individualism, Tracy's mourning for the loss of trust and absence of community is at the same time an appeal for their re-creation and a call to a different kind of being.

We could see the competitive individualism that Tracy recognizes as a form of subjection in the valley as having roots in the reluctance to extend comprehensive social planning beyond the early experiments with Yallourn, and the failure to enact new techniques of governmentality during the period of unregulated growth that took place in the valley in the post–World War II period. Her appeal to the possibility of some kind of community resonates with the idealistic visions of the planners who first attempted to constitute the Latrobe Valley as a visible, governable, and naturalized "region."

THE HEATH AND GOWER SURVEY: MAPPING THE REGIONAL "PROBLEM"

> This work is offered as a contribution to the moulding of our corner of a molten world. (Barnett, Burt, and Heath 1944, 3)

> A plan that is soundly based and comprehensively inter-related to all services does not need to be assessed financially—it is essentially *an economy*. (Victorian Town and Country Planning Board 1949, foreword, emphasis added)

In 1947 the private architect and town planner Frank Heath, in collaboration with W. E. Gower, the chief architect for the SEC, presented the first regional survey and report on the Latrobe Valley. Commissioned by the SEC to review the "regional" impact of further development of the brown coal and briquette industry and to come up with a regional plan, this document brought the entirety of the Latrobe Valley region into formal policy focus. Until this time, the policies of development of the SEC had highlighted one point/place, Yallourn, and had ignored the preexisting dispersed spatiality of the area. Now the "region" appeared to have arrived, somewhat deformed and full of growth problems.

The maps of the Heath and Gower report for the first time showed people in situ in the towns of Moe, Newborough, Yallourn, Morwell, and Traralgon as part of the Latrobe Valley. Prior to this report, there appears to have been little or no use made of this visual technology, but from the late 1940s, countless maps and panoramic drawings brought the region into focus as an object of surveillance (see Figure 10). No longer could the valley be represented as a people-free point in a calculative frame centered on Melbourne, or as the extractive arm of a state authority manned by cooperative citizens focused on potentiating power (electrical and political) and generating Victorian state development. Now the valley was a thing in its own right, peopled with a range of subjects under the gaze of government.

The timing of this interest in the valley as a region in need of "planning" comes as no surprise, as it was during the immediate post–World War II period that "regions," as spatial entities that could be or needed to be managed, had become an object of direct policy interest. After the Japanese bombing of Darwin, Australia had become acutely aware of its "vulnerability" to attack; in the postwar years, the issue of decentralization was placed firmly on the agenda by the federal Labor government, which had successfully overseen the mobilization of national resources, industry, and manpower during the war effort. Many public figures were concerned with the detrimental effects of population concentra-

FIGURE 10. Panoramic view of the Latrobe Valley showing Morwell and Yallourn. From *Latrobe Valley Development: Interim Regional Survey and Report,* compiled by F. Heath and W. E. Gower, 1947.

tion, resource agglomeration, and political centralization in a few capital cities, and the need for spatial and social planning was hotly debated (see, for example, Santamaria [1945] and Harris et al. [1948]). Writing at this time, the academic economist H. L. Harris notes:

> Decentralization and regionalism offer us a vision of a rationally ordered nation in which natural regions balanced amongst themselves maintain internal balance and variety. . . . [D]ecentralization is not Planning under another name if by planning is meant the centralized direction of a total economy or complete submission to a blueprint. It stands for a principle to be applied co-operatively, continuously and flexibly, that the search must be made for a rational organization of our social life. (1948, 19–22)

Harris recognizes that the unchecked "invisible hand" has created one sort of order—now named a regional "problem"—but he is wary of being seen to advocate anything that could be construed as "socialist planning" ("submission to a blueprint"). His ambivalence toward the Keynesian vision of the economy as a machine to be tinkered with, as something that "might get 'sick,' 'derailed,' or need 'repairs'" (Buck-Morss 1995, 465), is countered by a reluctance to relinquish all agency in relation to economic growth and a desire to promote a more "rational organization of our social life."

The emphasis at this time on mapping and surveying indicates the importance placed on these key technologies as a means of communicating both the need for and the possibility of a logical and rational approach to spatial and economic planning (Mumford 1922). It was in this context of political debate about decentralization that Frank Heath and W. E. Gower produced their comprehensive survey of the Latrobe Valley and a plan for its future regional development (Heath and Gower 1947).[17] In it they discuss the importance of diversifying the industrial base of the valley by attracting ancillary industries and others that will employ young female labor, the need to allocate land in separate industrial districts for that purpose, and the importance that should be placed on the viability of the neighborhood, the basic cell of human society. They outline the conflicts between urban settlement and coal winning that have already become embedded in the landscape and strongly recommend careful zoning of land use, specifically proposing the relocation of Morwell to a new site east of the planned mining developments and major reroutings of the railway line and highway to the north of the valley, away from prime coal resources and in a more amenable relation to the existing townships (see Figure 11).[18]

Two years after the SEC's commissioning of the independent Heath and Gower report, the Victorian government's newly constituted Town and Country Planning Board gazetted a subregional plan entitled "Future Development of the Latrobe Valley Sub-Region: A Report and Planning Scheme." This plan bore strikingly little resemblance to the one drawn up by Heath and Gower. Its much more limited gaze and purchase belies the tensions associated with a change in the vision of Economy that had begun to inform policy. With the national ascendance of the Liberal Party and their more laissez-faire approach to economic matters (a precursor to the late twentieth-century neoliberal agenda), Heath's attempts to render the region thinkable and improvable met with strong opposition and his will to translate managed spatial and economic development into a practice of comprehensive regional planning was decisively shunned. The voices of sectional interests, already well established in many valley townships, appear to have been heard and the traditionally extensive influence of the SEC was curbed. All reference to the proposed removal and relocation of Morwell was dropped, as was any mention of plans to rationalize transport routes through the valley. Indeed, the major townships (Moe, Morwell, and Traralgon) are excluded from the subregional planning area and allowed to go it alone under the guidance of their respective councils (see Figure 12).

Only a weak note of repressed anxiety about economic matters infiltrates the otherwise "hands off" ethos of the 1949 Latrobe Valley subregional plan. In the preamble to the planning scheme, the fears of an unchecked economy are laid out and named:

> This sub-regional plan has been prepared and adopted by the Board as
> an insurance against an *uneconomic, haphazard and inefficient* series

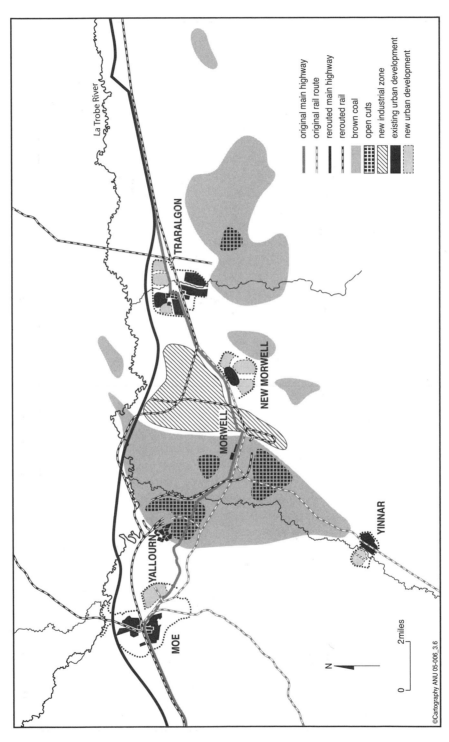

Figure 11. Key elements of the plan for Latrobe Valley development put forward by F. Heath and W. E. Gower in *Latrobe Valley Development: Interim Regional Survey and Report* (1947).

La Trobe River

TRARALGON

NEW MORWELL

MORWELL

YALLOURN

MOE

YINNAR

original main highway
original rail route
rerouted main highway
rerouted rail
brown coal
open cuts
new industrial zone
existing urban development
new urban development

N

0   2 miles

©Cartography ANU 05-006_3.6

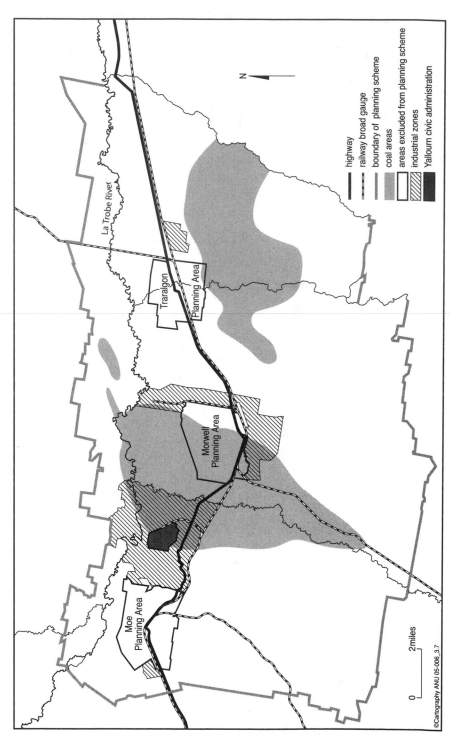

FIGURE 12. Key elements of the Latrobe Valley Sub-Region Plan as it was gazetted in 1949 by the Victorian Town and Country Planning Board.

highway
railway broad gauge
boundary of planning scheme
coal areas
areas excluded from planning scheme
industrial zones
Yallourn civic administration

La Trobe River

Traralgon
Planning Area

Morwell
Planning Area

Moe
Planning Area

N

0   2miles

of unrelated changes. Fast development of the region is already evident, and signs are not lacking of the enthusiasm of the land trader. . . .

The vital difference between having a practical plan to guide development of the area and having no plan is that the district grows harmoniously, smoothly and cheaply instead of *awkwardly, badly and wastefully*. It must cost less to adhere to a plan than to have no plan at all! (Victorian Town and Country Planning Board 1949, foreword, emphasis added)

Ultimately, however, the plan made no strong suggestions for control or management of business, land speculation, or service provision. Outside the gates of Yallourn, the SEC's model village where such control was maintained, topsy-turvy growth flourished virtually unchecked.

In casting a spatial frame across the different settlements, activities, and landscapes that constituted "the valley," maps and panoramic drawings served to situate points and places within a "unifying vision." The first regional plan continued to reinforce a centering of the regional economy on brown coal resource extraction and electricity generation, and the subjection of a singular economic identity was once again reinscribed. Despite attempts by Heath and Gower to de-center and denaturalize the Economy by inserting the human values of community, neighborhood, economic diversity, and social justice into the development calculus, the eventual plan betrayed a deep reluctance to constrain market forces and to fetter the drive for growth in energy-generating capacity. Subjection to a singular economic identity was readily embraced. If the Economy was real, it was "real good" from the perspective of the expanding male workforce—more power stations were built in the 1950s, 1960s, and 1970s, wage packages rose, and the growth potential of the single-sector resource economy seemed unbounded.

As with many struggles to create unity, disunity was the result—the plan had the effect of unleashing the sectional individualist interests it had identified, initiating the parochial competition for resources between the existing townships of "the valley" that has continued to the present. Each locality's hostile commitment to individual survival has produced an extremely inefficient duplication of facilities, a deep-seated suspicion of council amalgamation, and town loyalties and antagonisms that are manifest in everything from sporting rivalries to town stereotyping, most recently surfacing in the battle over the siting of the amalgamated shire's council chambers in Morwell. The failure of technologies of governmentality to effectively create a regional commons that could be "ruled" as a single community allowed a discourse of individualism to reign. When major rationalization and then privatization of the electricity generation and mining industries took place in the early 1990s, they were met by an individualistic response, despite the high union membership in the valley:

I was talking to a union leader about two years ago and he suggested that one of the mistakes the unions made was to individualize the problem. That is, the focus was on the size of the packages and ensuring access of their members to the best deal possible for those people individually. Looking back, his feeling was perhaps we should have looked at the wider community, perhaps we should have been looking at the social rather than the individual, and perhaps in the future the region needs to *socialize issues* or look at issues from a *social community* perspective rather than look at how it will affect individuals. And I think that's one of the problems. . . . issues seem to be defined individually, how they will affect me, how they affect you. And I think that contributes in turn to a sense of disempowerment. You are not part of a group and nobody else really understands. (Councillor, Latrobe Shire, June 1997, emphasis added)

In contrast to its collective form of address to the valley workforce during its establishment and growth, the SEC in dissolution interpellated subjects individually. The union movement, organized around slogans like "united we stand, divided we fall," was unable to mobilize a collective community response to rationalization, widespread retrenchment, and privatization.[19] As Tracy notes:

I think [the valley] was seen, and is seen now, as being a huge experiment, both socially and economically. The valley's been a bit of a hot potato—no one really wants to touch it. It's been thrown from one spot to the next and this whole "what's in it for us." . . . You know we've been good, we've gone the way, we've put up with the changes, now what are we going to get? What is the trade-off? And there really is nothing forthcoming, there is no compensation and there is no effort to try and mend the things that have torn things apart here. I suppose there is no real accountability. (June 1997)

The clarity of these visions of "what went wrong" indicates a psychic readjustment to the withdrawal of the paternalistic SEC. Abandonment and disempowerment here become the preconditions for a more "realistic" understanding of the deficits of valley life, potentially opening the way for a renegotiation of social and spatial collectivity beyond the individualism, town competition, us/them-ism and restrictive, solidary masculinist culture of "the valley." Later in the focus group Tracy reframed her earlier reference to diminished trust and community, evoking their positive presence in the valley and the group:

I think one of the best contributions that we have all made, probably as individuals, is that we've stayed. We've taken it all on board. We've taken all the ugliness and everything with it and said, "We are going to see this through." There are even individuals here today who have actually said that it's been painful, it's been hard, let's help someone else, let's make the blow a little less painful for them. This is a strong

community, it comes forward today, everyone's here prepared to work
together, but we need to sell that to a wider group. (June 1997)

Tracy can be heard expressing a desire for being "elsewhere or otherwise" (Deleuze 1986, 104; Butler 1997, 130) in the valley, despite its pain and ugliness. We see her both recognizing her subjection and putting forward the potentiality for a different kind of subjectivity based on the experience of *still being here* together. Her identification of an ethic of care among the focus group participants and her call to perform community in a different way was echoed by other community spokespeople. In an exhortative mode Mike added:

> The potential is still here. One wonders why some people haven't bothered to move, why we haven't all left, why we are all still here, why do we still call this home? Because the potential is still here. And the points that Bill raised about the spiritual life of people in the Latrobe Valley and the points I have raised about the cultural life in the Latrobe Valley . . . considerations that have never really been worked on through all of this, and they are still here. (June 1997)

The comments of Tracy and Mike suggest that we can indeed "reread 'being' as precisely the potentiality that remains unexhausted by any particular interpellation" (Butler 1997, 131). In these moments Tracy and Mike are open to and indeed they are performing other possible subjectivities. They and the others are ready to inhabit the sense of unavoidable collectivity, of just being together in place, that arose in the focus group, extending its life beyond this point in time and to a wider community.

A Politics of Becoming

We have explored the enactment of governmental power through an examination of its localizing effects—the emplacement of an economy and economic subjects in the Latrobe Valley of southeastern Australia. One of the avowed strengths of a spatial genealogical method is its ability to reveal the constitutive contingencies of history and geography, dispelling any sense of necessary unfolding.[20] We can see easily that "it could have been otherwise," that other economies could have been installed, that economic development is not a lawful natural process but one in which (in this case) economic "laws" were invoked politically—to justify, for example, the project of undermining the working-class communists in the older coal-producing region of Australia by establishing the brown coalfields, or to discredit an aggressive approach to social and economic planning and thereby dissociate from the long shadow of international communism. Complexly overdetermined rather than simply determined, the course of economic eventuation in the Latrobe Valley was unpredictable and full of (foreclosed because not taken up) possibility.

But while possibility exists, it is shadowy and negative, whereas the foreclosures enacted have shape and stability. What a genealogy conveys, in addition to possibility, is the performativity of discourse, the materiality of subjection, the sedimenting practices that leave relatively indelible marks on the landscape and its inhabitants, and resist change even if they cannot avoid it.[21] Through a genealogical tracing of the uneven application of three governmental technologies, we have provided one way of understanding the enduring subjection of contemporary residents in the Latrobe Valley; we have also revealed the ways that these contingent technologies brought into being a naturalized and abstracted Economy. Merz's numbers contributed to the successful performance in the valley of a calculable and lawful Economy singularly based on resource extraction and energy production, and dominated by large-scale enterprise. A lasting effect of Merz's initial enrollment of a particular space into the governmental calculus was the creation of subjects who could be manipulated by "the Economy" as a matter of rational course. Monash's rhetoric, in contrast, produced a more historically limited naturalization of the Economy as a sphere that could be managed and directed toward developmentalist goals, in which private and state capitalist enterprises could productively coexist. The creation of cooperative and dependent subjects whose collective masculinist identification with Victorian industrial growth and resource development in the valley was assured has been one effect that lives on, despite the disappearance of the institution through which this form of governmentality was largely practiced. Heath and Gower once again encountered the self-regulating vision of Economy, reinvigorated in post–World War II Australia, that had partially informed Merz's much earlier work; this had the effect of undermining the power of their maps and plans to naturalize a notion of the "Region" as an interdependent entity where nature, community, and alternative rationalities could tame and socialize economic forces. One possible legacy of this "failure" of governmentality to constitute a regional community is the amplified sense of competitive individualism that characterizes the valley today.

What we are describing here could be seen as a hegemonic formation of subjects, relationships, institutions, practices, and meanings that endures over time. And certainly the Latrobe Valley has its obdurate side. But a hegemonic entity such as a regional economy can be seen as continually performed in and through technical, material, and discursive devices. What if there is a break in the relations and practices constituting this performance, as undoubtedly occurred in the valley with the withdrawal of the SEC? What might this mean for the durability of economic subjection and the potential for new becomings?

Many of the technologies and practices of performing a regional economy based on mining and energy production have now been abandoned. Coal is still extracted and kilowatts generated, that is true, but most of the networks that once linked inanimate and animate materiality in the production system are now redundant. A discourse of economic rationalism that draws heavily on the self-evident logic of certain forms of numerical calculation and accounting remains dominant in Australian society (Hindess 1998), and in the valley "the numbers" blatantly show that the Economy no longer requires people like Harry and his workmates. Their initial invisibility in Merz's tables is now a reality—the labor factor of production in coal winning and electricity generation is minimal. The view that the regional economy is defined purely or primarily by its energy resources prevails, but it is *exclusion* from this instrumental vision that is today's subjection. What might this mean for the subject now deprived of economic citizenship?[22] Might this interruption caused by exclusion from a dominant economic calculus liberate new subjectivities and alternative forms of economic being?

Perhaps the only lasting connection between the performance of the resource-based economy and the majority of the population in the valley is the air people are forced to breathe, still laden with ash and chemical emissions from the power stations. But the break in the performance of established regional economic relations has not destroyed the legacy of a collective experience and the constitutive desire for a new kind of regional "being."[23] By listening for expressions of "fugitive energies" and emotions that exceed the fund of subjectivities institutionally provided and "assumed" in the valley, we have identified care for the other, concerns for justice and equity in and for the region, and calls for new practices of community as potentialities that have arisen out of subjection.[24]

Connolly warns us that without an active politics of becoming, such potentialities can easily become reintegrated into old discourses and "old piles of argument," rather than directed toward new ways of being (1999, 146). Momentary eruptions that break familiar patterns of feeling and behavior offer glimmers of possibility; but before we can actively cultivate these glimmers, we require a new discursive framing. At the very least we need a discourse of economy to supplant the one that has still has purchase in the valley, yet excludes its subjects from active economic citizenship.

In this chapter we have begun the task of denaturalizing the Economy and its capitalist forms of subjection; this provides a breathing space for fugitive energies of caring, social concern, and collectivity to be directed toward new performances of economy. But the very possibility of other economies has been suppressed both here in the Latrobe Valley and arguably elsewhere. A political project of economic becoming will require an imaginary in which economic possibility is plural and diverse. By speaking a language of economic diversity, we may be able to provide a context in which fleeting energies can be organized and amplified within alternative enactments of economy. It is to the task of language development that we turn in the next chapter.

3

CONSTRUCTING A LANGUAGE
OF ECONOMIC DIVERSITY

Why has Economy become an everyday term that denotes a force to be reckoned with existing outside of politics and society—a force that constitutes the ultimate arbiter of possibility? How is it that waged labor, the commodity market, and capitalist enterprise have come to be seen as the only "normal" forms of work, exchange, and business organization? When was it that capitalism assumed discursive dominance, becoming the only present form of economy and all that could be imagined as existing in the proximate future? And why do we have little to say these days about an expansive and generative politics of noncapitalist construction?[1]

We are convinced that the answers to these questions are connected to the almost total naturalization of "the economy" that has taken place in public discourse over recent decades, coinciding with the demise of socialism as an actually existing "alternative" and growing alarm that, with globalization, the autonomy of national economies, and therefore their manageability, is being undermined. This shift from an understanding of the economy as something that can be transformed, or at least managed (by people, the state, the IMF), to something that governs society has involved a hegemonic move by which representations of economy have slipped from their locations in discourse and landed "on the ground," in the "real," not just separate from but outside of society. In these postmodern times, the economy is denied the discursive mandate given to other social spheres and the consequences for the viability of any political project of economic innovation are dire.

If we are to enact new economies, we need to imagine "the economy" differently—as something that is created in specific geographical contexts and in historically path-dependent ways, but this is not an easy or straightforward project. As Timothy Mitchell argues, we are up against an already existing economic object materialized in socio-technical networks of calculation that have, since the 1930s, produced the economy as a "singular and self-evident totality" (forthcoming).[2] The economic landscape has been molded according to the imaginary functionings of a "self-contained and dynamic mechanism" known as "the economy," and this representation is difficult to dislodge. The advent of globalization and the failure of socialist economies have further compounded the identification of capitalism with this obdurate object.

This chapter outlines a strategy for taking back the economy, for re-presenting it in a way that dislodges the discursive dominance of capitalist economic activity and reclaims it as a contested space of representation. We propose to repoliticize the economy by challenging the representation of capitalism as the necessarily and naturally dominant form (or identity) of economy.[3] Others, such as Ernesto Laclau and Chantal Mouffe (1985), have de-economized the political by detaching it from its traditional identification with class struggles over the mode of production, opening revolutionary politics up to a wider array of social and cultural issues. We take up Callari's (1991) challenge to turn the tables and to repoliticize the economy by opening it up to potential interventions that are both class and nonclass focused.

In this chapter we construct a language of the *diverse economy* in which the economic landscape is represented as populated by a myriad of contingent forms and interactions. The thinking practice employed here is the technique of reading for difference rather than dominance (see the Introduction).[4] To read a landscape we have always read as capitalist as a landscape of economic difference, populated by various capitalist and noncapitalist institutions and practices, is a difficult task, for we must contend not only with our colonized imaginations, but with our beliefs about politics, understandings of power, naturalized conceptions of economy, and structures of desire (as we have argued in the Introduction and chapter 1). We are attempting to promote "collective disidentification" with capitalism, much as Judith Butler and other queer theorists have tried to do with heterosexuality and the binary gender categories that are its support (1993, 4). To do this we call on the theory of politics that Laclau and Mouffe (1985) have developed to help understand and dislodge forms of hegemony. Seen from their political perspective, our reading experiment is a counterhegemonic project.

A LANGUAGE POLITICS

Poststructuralist thinking offers insight into the ultimate undecidability of meaning and the constitutive power of discourse, calling into question received ideas and dominant practices, heightening an appreciation of the political effectivity of theory and research, and demonstrating how openings for alternative forms of practice and power can emerge (Gibson-Graham 2000). Laclau and Mouffe (1985) have developed a poststructuralist theory of politics that situates discourse (and therefore language) at the center of any political project. In their view, discourse is a relational totality in which the meanings of elements and identities are constituted in signifying sequences that are ultimately unfixed. Politics involves the continual struggle to fix meaning, to close the totality and stem the infinite processes of signification within language. Hegemony entails the persuasive expansion of a discourse into widely shared values, norms, and perceptions such that meaning *appears* to be fixed, even naturalized (Torfing 1999, 89, 302).[5]

The fixings attempted by hegemonic politics include techniques of negotiating equivalence and difference appropriate to the task of strong theorizing.[6] *Condensation* is a kind of conflation that fuses "a variety of significations and meanings into a single unity," thereby concentrating meaning by eliminating difference (Torfing 1999, 98). *Displacement* extends and transfers "the signification of meaning of one particular moment to another moment," producing contiguity and equivalence between what had been quite different meanings (98). Ultimately the partial fixings of meaning achieved through condensation and displacement establish nodal points, or dense knots of definite meaning that sustain the hegemonic discourse and the subjects it interpellates (303).

This theory of politics helps us to see the way in which a certain discourse of the economy (as real, as capitalist) has become hegemonic, and how alternative and different understandings of economy have been enrolled into the hegemonic project or outlawed as a threat to the hegemonic discourse. The representation of the capitalist economy as extradiscursive, as the ultimate real and natural form of economy, has gained additional ideological force since the demise of capitalism's "other." This is not to say that with the "disappearance" of communism and socialism social antagonisms that constitute the unity of neoliberal global capitalist discourse (and thus its hegemony) have been eliminated. The locus of antagonism has simply shifted and is now made up of multiple threats to the "free market," such as remnant public sector involvement in the economy, "democratic welfare statism" (Torfing 1999, 299), and the insistent "failures" of development—spaces where abject poverty and social disintegration have increased during the "age of development" and now harbor "terrorist threats" to wealthy nations.

In its current hegemonic articulation as neoliberal global capitalism, capitalocentric discourse has now colonized the entire economic landscape and its universalizing claims seem to have been realized. A distinctive social imaginary—a heady mix of freedom, individual wealth, unfettered consumption, and well-being trickled down to all—convenes a series of myths that constitute the (illusory) fullness and positivity of "capitalist" society, masking the social antagonisms on which this presence is posited. We have come to accept that "the economy" establishes the bottom line for action and "it" makes us perform in certain ways. This ideological fantasy has become safe and even enjoyable, directing and limiting politics to certain channels, blinding us without realizing it to the possibility of other options.[7]

The theory of politics advanced by Laclau and Mouffe suggests ways in which a counterhegemonic political project could be pursued through destabilization and dislocation of the seeming unity of the hegemonic discursive formation. We can, for example, uncover the condensations and displacements that have contributed to the understanding of the economy as extradiscursive and dominantly capitalist. We can begin to "unfix" economic identity by deconstructing the dominant capitalocentric discourse of economy in which capitalist economic activity is taken as the model for all economic activity. We can dislocate the unity and hegemony of neoliberal global capitalist economic discourse through a proliferative queering of the economic landscape and construction of a new language of economic diversity. This dislocation is a crucial prerequisite to the project of cultivating different subjects of economy.

UNFIXING ECONOMIC IDENTITY: CHALLENGING EQUIVALENCE

Capitalocentrism is a dominant economic discourse that distributes positive value to those activities associated with capitalist economic activity however defined, and assigns lesser value to all other processes of producing and distributing goods and services by identifying them *in relation* to capitalism as the same as, the opposite of, a complement to, or contained within.[8] A capitalocentric discourse condenses economic difference, fusing the variety of noncapitalist economic activities into a unity in which meaning is anchored to capitalist identity. Our language politics is aimed at fostering conditions under which images and enactments of economic diversity (including noncapitalism) might stop circulating around capitalism, stop being evaluated with respect to capitalism, and stop being seen as deviant or exotic or eccentric—departures from the norm.[9]

The expansive nature of hegemony is sustained as difference is harnessed and eliminated, meaning is condensed, and equivalence established. The specific economic meaning of, for example, nonmarket transactions, unpaid labor, and communal or independent modes of generating and distributing surplus are lost in the hegemonic move to represent capitalism as the only *viable* form of economy. A good description of the workings of capitalocentrism as a hegemonic discourse is given by Polanyi (2001) in his use of the term *economistic fallacy* to refer to

> the practice of analyzing all economic systems through the theoretical gaze that presumes that the horizons of the economy are fully comprehended by a map that includes only market exchange and the calculative behavior couplet. (Adaman and Madra 2002, 1046)[10]

Here the diversity of market exchanges (for example, in local farmers' markets, international commodity markets, niche markets) is condensed into a single unity of "market exchange" that is in turn conflated with capitalist economy. At the same time, the diversity of economic behaviors (for example, of solidarity, beneficence, stewardship, obligation) is interpreted through the lens of individual calculative rationality, displacing the significance and meaning of these behaviors by making them contiguous with a singular logic of self-interest or competition.[11] Our economic language becomes impoverished (yet paradoxically more powerful) through the processes of condensation and displacement.

A language politics is predicated on the understanding that a hegemonic discourse will always be riven by forces that work against the suturing practices that attempt to produce fixity. This gives us the confidence to begin the process of dislocation—identifying the alternative economic activities, events, and experiences that have been "domesticated, symbolized or integrated" (Torfing 1999, 301) within a dominant capitalocentric discourse of economy and giving them space to fully "exist."

DISLOCATING ECONOMY: LIBERATING ECONOMIC DIFFERENCE

Alongside the hegemonic discourse of the economy as capitalist many counter-discourses of economy have arisen from alternative strands of economic thinking— classical political economy, economic anthropology, sociology and geography, public sector economics, feminist economics—and from working-class, third-world, and community activism—the socialist, cooperative, and local sustainability movements, for example. Diverse languages of economy already exist but are rendered ineffectual by the hegemony of capitalocentrism. They have become, in Santos's terms, "non-credible alternatives to what exists" (2004, 238), subsisting in the shadows of mainstream economic thinking. To produce a potential dislocation of the hegemony of capitalocentric discourse, we need to identify and begin to liberate these alternative languages from their discursive subordination. In what follows, we briefly review three such languages arising from feminism, informal sector analysis, and Marxism.

The most controversial exposé of the discursive violences of dominant economic thinking has been spearheaded by feminist activists and economists.[12] Recognition of the exclusion of women's unpaid activities, like housework and child rearing, from understandings of the economy has led to multiple strategies to redress the situation—new metaphors to represent the "whole" economy and techniques of enumeration to measure the previously uncounted economic contributions of unpaid housework, voluntary work, and other non-market-oriented activities that sustain households and communities (Cameron and Gibson-Graham 2003). Empirical work on this subject has established that, in both rich and poor countries, 30 to 50 percent of economic activity is accounted for by unpaid household labor (Ironmonger 1996; Luxton 1997). There is now a call for the system of national accounts in many countries to be revised so that the total measure of economic performance, the gross economic product, includes both gross market product *and* gross household product (Ironmonger

1996, 38–39). But while feminist interventions have successfully expanded conceptions of the economy to include both paid and unpaid labor and market and nonmarket transactions, within the hegemonic framing of capitalocentrism this vast sea of economic activity is still situated in the "sphere of reproduction" that supports the real economy and is dependent on the determining dynamics of capitalist growth.[13] The intricate *inter*dependencies of household, community, and market-based economic activities are rarely explored, and the idea of *independent* economic dynamics within household economies, the voluntary sector, or neighborhood economies is rendered virtually unthinkable by the hegemony of capitalocentrism.[14]

Another significant challenge to the hegemony of neoliberal capitalism is presented by the vast literature on the informal economies of both "less" and "more" developed nations. The pressure to recognize that livelihoods are sustained by a plethora of economic activities that do not take the form of wage labor, commodity production for a market, or capitalist enterprise has largely come from the global "south" (Lipton 1982, Portes et al. 1989), though there is increasing evidence of the variety and magnitude of noncapitalist transactions and nontransacted subsistence practices pursued in the developed economies of the "north."[15] In the context of the so-called "developing" world, informal and subsistence economies are intricately bound up with what are often seen as "remnant" indigenous practices built around traditional rights of access to natural resources, indigenous laws governing the prohibition or practice of certain economic transactions, and relations of production, exchange, and redistribution governed by kin and community networks and rituals (Gudeman 2001). Increasing recognition of the persistence and magnitude of livelihood sustenance provided by informal markets and indigenous or traditional transactions (and the failures of growth-oriented capitalist models to increase well-being) has prompted development practitioners to take more notice of these different economic practices and begin to work with them (Benediktssen 2002). In support of the effort to redirect their interventions, a new language of "social capital" has emerged as promoted, for example, by the World Bank (Woolcock 1998; Fine 2001). The detailed concepts developed over many years by economic anthropologists to describe the performance and meanings of diverse transactions have been displaced, their specific significations decontextualized and reinterpreted as elements of the bonding, binding, and linking relationships that constitute "social capital." Dumped into this grab bag category, they are represented as bland relational ingredients of social cohesion or lack thereof, and indicators of the potential fertility of aid interventions and economic incentives. The choice of nomenclature, in which the term "capital" is liberally attached to certain social relations (as well as to the other four dimensions of the sustainable livelihoods framework—natural, physical, human, and financial), cannot be seen as innocent. The capitalocentric assumption is that the social relations addressed by these concepts are "investments" that can eventually be monetized, exchanged, and used to generate profitable returns.[16]

Historically, the most powerful contestation of the economic dominance and consolidation of capitalism has come from the Marxist and socialist tradition. In *Capital*, Marx developed a language of economic difference that focused on the relations between producers and nonproducers of surplus labor. His specification of the exploitative nature of capitalist production relations was theorized against the background of different kinds of exploitation that existed within feudal, slave, despotic, and ancient (independent) production relations, as well as the nonexploitative relations he identified with "primitive" and modern communism. In Marx's economic theory, capitalism was a specific historical form of economy centered on the exploitation of wage labor, animated by competition and the imperative of capital accumulation. It had emerged from feudalism and could be transformed through political action. Marx's and Engels's advocacy of a communist revolution was taken up by working-class and peasant movements around the world and their theories have inspired many local and national attempts at economic experimentation. Despite Marx's critical theory of capitalism and his inspirational role as an anticapitalist political agitator, however, his distinctive theoretical legacy has not been immune to the hegemonic displacements and condensations of capitalocentrism. His language of economic difference based on modes of production and exploitation has been (mis)interpreted by many as a historical stage theory of economic evolution in which capitalism is situated at the pinnacle of development and all other forms of economy are represented as precapitalist or as forms of primitive capitalism.[17] For the remnant true believers, communism, capitalism's other, is posed as a future utopia, yet to be realized in any concreteness, while capitalism remains the present, fully developed form of economy.

We have touched on just three languages of economic difference that are resources for our alternative project of reading the economy for difference rather than dominance and have shown how they remain caught within a hegemonic capitalocentric discourse that denies them credibility. To unleash the potential dislocative powers of these languages, we must resituate them on a different terrain. We need to de-domesticate the household, unpaid labor, and caring practices; to dis-integrate traditional economic practices and nonmarket transactions; and to de-historicize feudal, slave, and communist relations of production. That is, we need to step outside of the condensing and displacing powers of capitalocentrism and give the full diversity of economic relations and practices the space to exist in all their specificity and independence.

THE DIVERSE ECONOMY

It is clear from the preceding discussion that there already exists a substantial understanding of the extent and nature of economic difference. What has yet to emerge is a way of convening this knowledge that destabilizes capitalist dominance and unleashes new creative forces and subjects for economic experimentation. Our intervention is to propose a language of the *diverse economy* as an exploratory thinking practice, a weak theory of economy. This language expands our economic vocabulary, widening the identity of the economy to include all of those practices excluded or marginalized by a strong theory of capitalism. The landscape we describe does not ignore relations of power between economic practices, but neither does it presume that they are structured in any necessary or inherently reproducible manner. The rules of syntax and grammar of our language are loose to the point of nonexistence, allowing for empirical encounters and creative expressions of the new, the unthought, the unexpected. We approach economic relationships as something to be contingently rather than deterministically configured, economic value as liberally distributed rather than sequestered in certain activities and denied to others, and economic dynamics as proliferating rather than reducible to a set of governing laws and mechanical logics. We are not overly concerned with the chaotic and noncomprehensive aspects of this language experiment as our objective is not to produce a finished and coherent template that maps the economy "as it really is" and presents (to the converted or suggestible) a ready-made "alternative economy." Our project is to disarm and dislocate the naturalized hegemony of the capitalist economy and make the space for new economic becomings—ones that we will need to work at to produce.[18]

We begin constructing our language by convening some of the radical diversity of economic relations and conceptualizing it in terms of three practices[19]:

- different kinds of *transaction* and ways of negotiating commensurability (Figure 13)
- different types of *labor* and ways of compensating it (Figure 14)
- different forms of *enterprise* and ways of producing, appropriating, and distributing surplus (Figure 15)

The following discussion focuses on unpacking and clarifying Figures 13, 14, and 15.

TRANSACTIONS

Formal market exchange, in which calculations of commensurability and thus "rules" of exchange are believed by mainstream economists to abide by immutable laws, accounts for only one subset of transactions that circulate the goods and services that support livelihoods. Perhaps the most prevalent form of exchange is the huge variety and volume of *nonmarket* transactions that sustain us all. Goods and services are produced and *shared* in the household, nature provides abundant goods that are *taken* as well as stewarded, people and organizations *give away* goods and services, some people rightfully or illegally *steal* goods, taxes and property are *appropriated* and goods and services *allocated* by the state, and goods and services are traded within and between communities according to traditions of *ritual exchange*.[20] In these transactions there are no rules of commensurability and there may be no formal calculation of how much is shared, taken, given away, stolen, or allocated, but cultural rules and norms are reflected in how these transactions are conducted. These *nonmarket* transactions are shown in Figure 13 as a major contributor to the diverse economy along with *market* and *alternative market* transactions.

TRANSACTIONS	RULES OF (IN)COMMENSURABILITY
NONMARKET	**INCOMMENSURABILITY**
Household flows	Intra-household negotiation
Gift giving	Cultural norms of reciprocity
Indigenous exchange	Ritual practice
State allocations	Citizen entitlements
State appropriations	State entitlements
Gleaning	Traditional right
Hunting, fishing, gathering	Negotiation of stewardship
Theft	Illegal right
Poaching	Right of the have-not
MARKET EXCHANGE	**ECONOMIC COMMENSURABILITY**
"Free"	"Laws" of supply and demand
Naturally protected	"Natural law"
Artificially protected	Social agreements or state policy
Monopolized	Monopoly corporate power
Regulated	State policy
Niche	Social agreement
ALTERNATIVE MARKET	**SOCIAL COMMENSURABILITY**
Sale of public goods	State policy
Ethical "fair-trade" markets	Producer-consumer agreement
Local trading systems	Producer-consumer agreement
Alternative currencies	Community agreement
Underground market	Trader agreement
Co-op exchange	Inter–co-op agreement
Alternative credit	Financier-borrower negotiation
Barter	Trader agreement
Informal market	Trader agreement

FIGURE 13. Transactions.

If we examine the diversity of formal *market* transactions we see a variety of socially, naturally, and governmentally constructed contexts for commodity exchange. For mainstream economists, market transactions involve the exchange of equivalents (and are, thus, without obligation beyond the transaction). "The market" is a space in which commensurability is established according to the laws of supply and demand that arise from the actions of rational self-interested producers and consumers. In its mythical representation within the hegemonic discourse of capitalocentrism, the market is represented as "free." But we know that this is rarely the case. Markets are naturally and artificially protected, monopolized, regulated, and niched and, in all these cases, transactions are governed by context-specific power relations, rather than abstract and universal logics.

There are many forms of *alternative* market transactions in which goods and services are exchanged and commensurability is socially negotiated and agreed upon. They include the vast number of transactions that take place in the informal and underground markets in which goods and services are traded according to very local and personalized agreements;[21] the exchange of commodities between and within worker cooperatives, where prices are set to enhance the sustainability of the cooperative; the ethical or "fair" trade of products, where producers and consumers agree on price levels that will sustain certain livelihood practices; local trading systems and alternative currencies that foster local interdependency and sustainability; and the marketing of public goods and services produced by the state that are "sold" under conditions where profit maximization is not the prime arbiter of viability.[22] Barter is another prevalent form of transaction in which goods deemed to be equivalent in value by their producers or traders are exchanged without recourse to money.[23]

In its singular, normal, and lawful guise, "the market" is usually identified with capitalism, and as such it is imbued with expansiveness, authority, and force. "The capitalist market" has powers to penetrate and subordinate, to create subjects and desires. But not all markets are where capitalist commodities are exchanged and not all commodities transacted in formal markets are produced by capitalist firms. Seen in the context of the plethora of exchange transactions that persist in making up our economic world (shown in Figure 13) it seems absurd to think that such a small part of the transactional whole, and one that is so aridly abstract in its theorization, has such power to colonize and obscure.[24]

LABOR

The labor that supports material well-being is performed in many different contexts and is compensated in many different forms, as shown in Figure 14. The most prevalent form of labor the world over is the *unpaid* work that is conducted in the household, the family and the neighborhood, or the wider community. While this work is unremunerated in monetary terms, many would say it does not necessarily go uncompensated. The rewards for this labor may come in the form of love, emotional support, protection, companionship, and a sense of self-worth.

LABOR	COMPENSATION
UNPAID	
Housework	Nonmonetary
Family care	Nonmonetary
Neighborhood work	Nonmonetary
Volunteer	Nonmonetary
Self-provisioning labor	Food and other goods
Slave labor	Food and lodging
WAGE LABOR	
Salaried	Negotiated salary + benefits
Unionized	Protected wage + benefits
Nonunionized	Unprotected
Part time	Un/Protected wage
Temporary	Unprotected
Seasonal	Unprotected
Familial	Personally set wage
ALTERNATIVE PAID	
Self-employed	Living expenses + savings
Cooperative	Cooperative wage + share
Indentured	Food, lodging, and stipend
Reciprocal labor	Reciprocated labor
In-kind	In-kind payment
Work for welfare	Dole payment

FIGURE 14. Labor.

They also come in the consumption or enjoyment of what has been produced—a clean house, washed clothes, meals, cared-for children, gardens, a clean neighborhood, or care for the poor, sick, or disabled. The nonmonetary nature of this compensation does not disqualify this work from assuming a central role in the functioning of any economy. Other forms of unpaid labor include the work of self-provisioning or subsistence (for example, gardening, gathering, hunting, fishing, making clothes) that is compensated by the goods and services that are produced. To include all of this work in a conception of a diverse economy is to represent many people who see themselves (or are labeled) as "unemployed" or "economically inactive" as economic subjects, that is, as contributing to the vast skein of economic relations that make up our societies. It is also to recognize the multiple forms of work that most of us (and especially those, often women, who work the "double day") engage in.

We have become increasingly aware that the unpaid labor of slaves is still prevalent in many contemporary economies. In the United States, for example, (largely nonwhite) prison labor manufactures car license plates and furniture for state institutions (such as universities), and performs call center services (Bair 2004). In the United Kingdom, forced prison labor provides packing services for manufacturing and retail companies.[25] Current international attention has been drawn to the persistence of child debt bondage in many developing countries and growing forms of sex slavery and people-trafficking all over the globe (Bales 1999). All these forms of unpaid, unfree labor represent modern-day slave labor.

Paid labor also takes many forms as different groups negotiate the power relations that structure the employment relation. There are the highly paid professionals and other salaried workers who are able to exert power in the workplace and exact compensation for their labor that far exceeds the amount needed to cover the costs of a socially acceptable standard of living. There is the dwindling unionized workforce, whose ability to control entry to a labor market enables them to exact higher wages and benefits. There is the growing number of nonunionized, part-time, temporary, and seasonal laborers, whose wage payments are more likely to be unregulated and low. For those who work for family members or friends, something like a market wage is usually paid, but is slightly adjusted up or down, according to personal negotiation.

The usual image of wage labor is of workers who do not own any means of production but sell their labor power to a capitalist employer in return for a monetary wage set at a level that allows them and their dependents to buy the commodities necessary for subsistence. There are, however, many other forms of labor that are "paid" but can be distinguished from capitalist wage labor. We have listed these as *alternative paid* in Figure 14. Worker cooperatives employ a labor force that is paid a living wage set at an amount decided by the cooperators. This may or may not be equivalent to market-set wages for similar labor. In addition, workers may receive capital payments that accrue on the basis of their ownership stake in the enterprise. Individual self-employed workers are in the position of paying themselves a wage. They can decide their own wage level and benefit entitlement. Some, such as doctors or lawyers or tradesmen in a buoyant building boom, might make a good living and can periodically distribute portions of profit to increased consumption. But often self-employed business people find that they cannot reward their labor at anywhere near the monetary rate it would be awarded in the general labor market.[26]

Many other people labor in return for payments in kind (sometimes mixed with monetary payments). A share farmer performs labor on someone else's land in return for a portion of the harvest, or with the proviso that some of the landlord's land can be used to generate a family income. A live-in migrant domestic servant works for a contracted period as an indentured laborer in someone's home in return for room and board and a small allowance of spending money that does not amount to a living wage. A pastor performs caring labor in a community and is often supported by in-kind payments—access to a house, car, gifts of food, and a small stipend. Residents of a community offer their collective labor to others at times of high labor demand (harvest, house renovation, or moving) in return for a reciprocal claim on labor when the time arises.[27] Welfare recipients must sometimes perform labor in the community sector in return for their welfare checks.

This elaboration of different kinds of labor and compensation has a number of political effects. First, it expands access to economic identities that fall outside the limited scope of valorized identities, such as employer, employee, and entrepreneur. Second, it draws some attention to the different degrees of freedom workers have to negotiate the amount they receive as a payment to meet "subsistence" or other needs.

ENTERPRISE

The diverse economy is made up of many kinds of enterprise in which ownership and production are differently configured. In this exercise of reading for difference, our use of the term *enterprise* diverges from popular understandings and focuses on the ways in which different production units (including businesses, government institutions, farms, and households) generate and deploy produced

ENTERPRISE	APPROPRIATION OF SURPLUS
NONCAPITALIST	
Communal	Cooperators
Independent	Self
Feudal	Landlord/household head
Slave	Slave owner/leaser
CAPITALIST	
Family firm	Family
Private unincorporated firm	Business owners
Public company	Board of directors
Multinational	Board of directors
ALTERNATIVE CAPITALIST	
State enterprise	State
Green firm	Board of directors
Socially responsible firm	Board of directors
Nonprofit	Board of directors
Producer and consumer cooperatives	Producers, consumers

FIGURE 15. Enterprise.

wealth. We apply our interest in class *as a process* to the task of generating a language of economic diversity, highlighting the many different ways that enterprises organize the production, appropriation, and distribution of surplus labor.[28] In Figure 15, enterprises are distinguished only in terms of who appropriates the surplus produced. In the following discussion, we include a more complex consideration (difficult to represent schematically) of production and distribution issues that also contribute to enterprise diversity.

In the Marxian view, one of the major contributors to social wealth is "surplus labor."[29] The notion of *surplus* labor or *surplus* product above and beyond what is *necessary* for reproduction has long figured in classical political economic thought. Marx was the first to produce an economic theory of society that hinged on the distinction between necessary and surplus labor. As he defined it, necessary labor "is the quantity of labor time necessary to produce the consumables customarily required by the producer to keep working," while surplus labor is "the extra time of labor the direct producer performs beyond the necessary labor" (Resnick and Wolff 1987, 115). Marx proposed that "surplus labor in some form must always remain, as labor beyond the extent of given needs" (1991, 958, quoted in Resnick and Wolff 2002, 46).[30] In any society, some kind of surplus is produced and used to support the nonproducing members of the society, as well as to build the distinctive social and cultural institutions that create social meaning and social order. In most societies, "unpaid" or "unremunerated" surplus labor is appropriated (often in product or value form) by someone other than the producer.[31] The "accounting" distinction between necessary and surplus labor provides one analytical frame for highlighting the different ways in which this significant portion of wealth is collected and dispersed.[32]

Many producers have no control over what happens to their surplus labor— it is appropriated by nonproducers who claim a right to the products produced on a variety of grounds. In capitalist firms, workers can be seen to have relinquished the right to their surplus as part of the wage contract and it is appropriated by their capitalist employers (Marx 1977). In family-run capitalist firms, workers' and family members' surplus is appropriated by the family owners and distributed to all the activities that support production (interest on borrowed finance, taxes, advertising costs, management, etc.), perhaps to business expansion and any remainder to the family itself. In private unincorporated capitalist firms it is the capitalist or board of directors who are the appropriators and first distributors of surplus. In public companies the board of directors are in charge of appropriating surplus and distributing it to the banks, governments, realtors, advertising agencies, and management staff who provide supports for the enterprise and make competing claims on appropriated surplus. Business expansion and dividend payments to the shareholders must also be paid out of this fund. A multinational firm operates in a similar manner, though here the surplus may be appropriated from workers in one global site and distributed to shareholders who are more likely to be in the "developed" world.[33]

There are many other enterprise forms coexisting with capitalist business in which the surplus of producers is appropriated by nonproducers. In feudal agricultural establishments in many parts of the "developing" world, access to land for subsistence is granted on the condition that tenant farmers perform surplus labor on the landlord's land or produce surplus product that is appropriated by the landlord. In many households in which a traditional gender division of labor prevails, domestic work is performed by women and could be seen to be appropriated and distributed by a patriarchal household head.[34] Slaves produce surplus labor that is appropriated by their owners or those who lease them from slaveholders. In all these cases, the capitalists, landlords, household heads, and slaveholders/leasers have first claim on distributing the appropriated surplus. As with capitalist enterprise, not all of this surplus is available for consumption or accumulation, but must be used to pay for all the activities that support production.

In some businesses, producers do control their own rate of surplus production and appropriation and are the ones who decide how distributions out of surplus should be allocated. Independent, self-employed producers set the distinction between their wage (the necessary labor payment) and a surplus and decide how the latter is to be distributed. In worker cooperative enterprises, producers set their own wage and appropriate and distribute a communal surplus.

Not all capitalist firms are driven to distribute their surplus only toward expansion or to shareholders and managers. Difference *within* the category of capitalist enterprise is as important to recognize as the difference *between* enterprise forms and class processes.[35] Increasingly there are "alternative" capitalist firms that market themselves as "green" or "socially responsible." What distinguishes these firms from their mainstream capitalist counterparts is a commitment to ethical practices in addition to profit making. "Green capitalist" firms, for example, might agree to introduce environmentally responsible production technologies or might distribute part of their appropriated surplus to environmental concerns (for example, clean-up, investment in recycling technology and environmental monitoring). "Socially responsible" capitalist businesses might commit to increasing workers' ownership of the firm or distribute appropriated surplus to social and community projects (for example, scholarships for local youth or provision of community infrastructure or services).[36]

State capitalist enterprises employ wage labor and appropriate surplus but have the potential to distribute surplus funds to public benefit. Nonprofit enterprises similarly employ wage labor and appropriate surplus, but by law they are not allowed to retain or distribute profits. In general, these organizations barely make enough to cover expenses and are dependent on input from funders.[37] Producer cooperatives, such as those in various farming sectors, include independents and larger businesses who produce and appropriate their own surplus and market their product via a central marketing division that employs wage labor and is funded out of a cooperatively controlled distribution from surplus.

By distinguishing all these different ways in which a large proportion of social wealth is generated and deployed, we are able to represent an "economy" as something more extensive and less concentrated than our usual, common sense understanding of capitalism. A focus on surplus suggests analytical tools for harnessing social wealth in new ways and directing it toward the building of different kinds of economies (see chapters 4, 5, and 7). Figures 13, 14, and 15 are but three ways of beginning to map out in broad and contestable categories the complex diversity of some of the economic relations that make up economies. Clearly there are intricate interdependencies between each of these strands as they are woven together in the economic fabric of our lives. Our list-like figures are poor representations of this vision, resembling, as they do, the pulling of just three threads from a complicated weave. For the power of the diverse economy to be grasped, for its representation to motivate the kinds of affective responses that will begin to dislocate capitalocentrism's hegemony, we turn to other kinds of visualizations.

A SHIFT IN FOCUS

Representations of the diverse economy have the potential to provoke a figure/ground shift both in visual and conceptual perception and in the emotional grasp of possibility. In our action research we have used a number of different visual portrayals of the diverse economy to promote a perceptual shift. For those who are interested in an empirical "take" on the diverse economy, a pie graph representation of the economy provides a useful starting point.

Figure 16 represents hours worked in one week in the United States in 1990 broken down into those devoted to commodity production and those to noncommodity production in households and the government (Bowles and Edwards 1993, 99). A first impression is that commodity production claims only half of the total hours worked and that household and state work are thus hugely significant economic activities. A second impression concerns the size of the capitalist economy. Remember that commodities are just goods and services produced for a market, and that not all commodities are produced in capitalist enterprises. If we had the data more appropriately disaggregated, we could divide the commodity sector into hours worked by the self-employed, by members of cooperatives, and by those in the slave sector (for example, by the two million prisoners in United States prisons). Figure 17 shows a hypothetical and probably exaggerated breakdown of these amounts transposed onto the original chart. When we subtract the hours worked by those in the noncapitalist commodity-producing sectors from the general category of "commodity production," we see that hours worked in *capitalist* commodity production are substantially less than 50 percent of total hours (probably 40 to 45 percent at most). This vision of economy in terms of hours worked is one way of showing the capitalist economy in a less extensive role.[38]

Another figure that we have used to get across the diversity of the economy

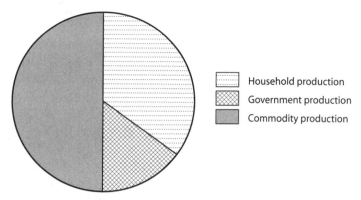

FIGURE 16. Hours worked by sector of production in the U.S. economy, 1990. From Bowles and Edwards (1993, 99).

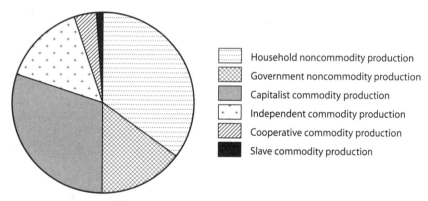

FIGURE 17. Hypothetically modified pie graph of Figure 16.

is the iceberg (see Figure 18). This image is one way of illustrating that what is usually regarded as "the economy"—wage labor, market exchange of commodities, and capitalist enterprise—comprises but a small subset of the activities by which we produce, exchange, and distribute values. It honors and prompts us to express our common knowledge of the multifarious ways in which all of us are engaged in economic activity. In the submerged part of the iceberg, we see a grab bag of activities, sites, and people. The chaotic, laundry-list aspect has an inclusive effect, suggesting an open-ended and slightly arbitrary process of categorization.

The iceberg figure is an explicitly pedagogical version of what we have called our diverse economy framework (Figure 19). In this summary table, all of our axes of economic difference—the columns of transactions, labor, and enterprise—are included together in one framing. As many have pointed out to us, this arrangement, with the activities theoretically associated with capitalism lined up in the top row, visually reflects (and perhaps reinstates?) the capitalocentrism we are trying to dislocate.[39] The point of this framing is really

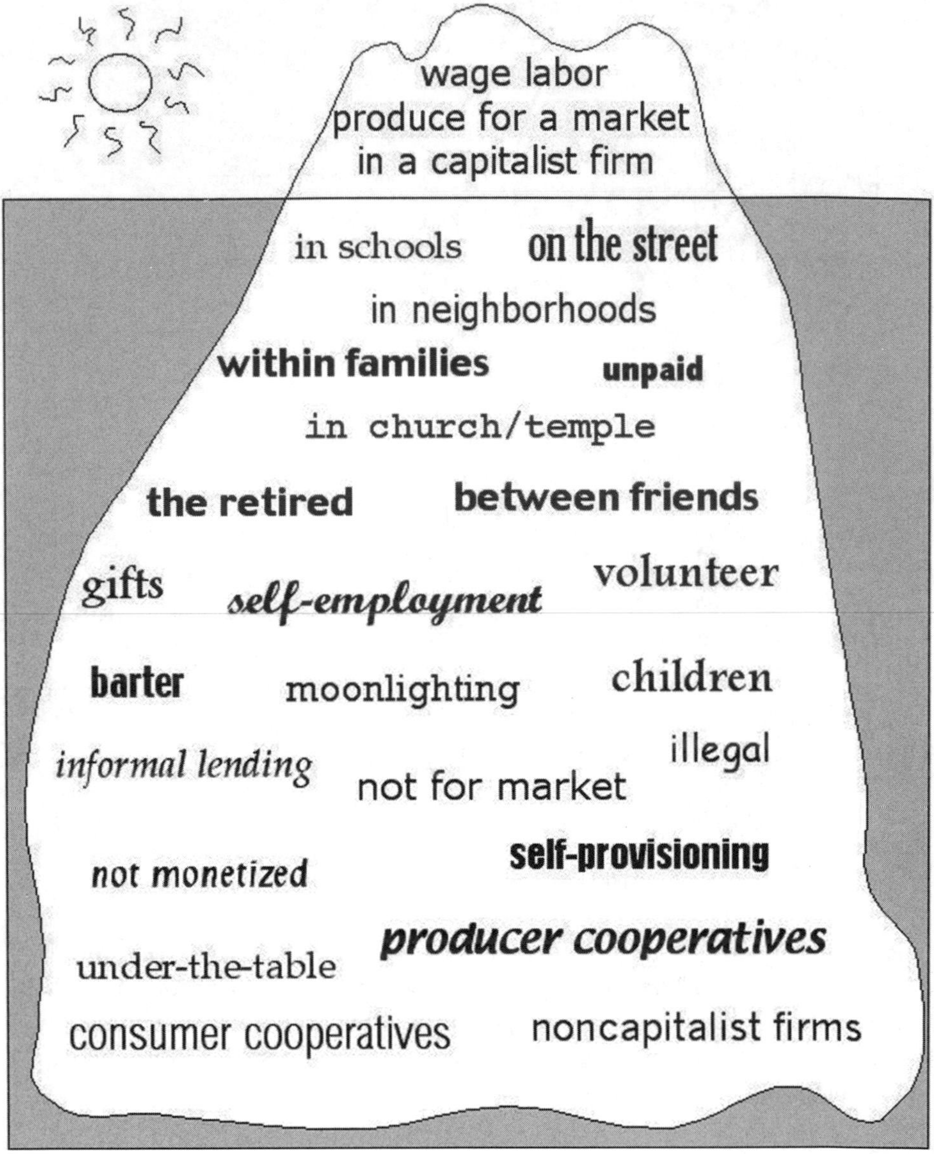

FIGURE 18. The iceberg. From Community Economies Collective 2001; drawn by Ken Byrne.

to highlight our deconstructive move. By marshaling the many ways that social wealth is produced, transacted, and distributed *other* than those traditionally associated with capitalism, noncapitalism is rendered a positive multiplicity rather than an empty negativity, and capitalism becomes just one particular set of economic relations situated in a vast sea of economic activity.[40]

TRANSACTIONS	LABOR	ENTERPRISE
MARKET	WAGE	CAPITALIST
ALTERNATIVE MARKET	**ALTERNATIVE PAID**	**ALTERNATIVE CAPITALIST**
Sale of public goods	*Self-employed*	*State enterprise*
Ethical "fair-trade" markets	*Cooperative*	*Green capitalist*
Local trading systems	*Indentured*	*Socially responsible firm*
Alternative currencies	*Reciprocal labor*	*Nonprofit*
Underground market	*In-kind*	
Co-op exchange	*Work for welfare*	
Barter		
Informal market		
NONMARKET	**UNPAID**	**NONCAPITALIST**
Household flows	*Housework*	*Communal*
Gift giving	*Family care*	*Independent*
Indigenous exchange	*Neighborhood work*	*Feudal*
State allocations	*Volunteer*	*Slave*
State appropriations	*Self-provisioning labor*	
Gleaning	*Slave labor*	
Hunting, fishing, gathering		
Theft, poaching		

FIGURE 19. A diverse economy.

The rereading for difference we have presented offers a weak theory of economy, "little better than a description" (Sedgwick 2003, 134, quoting Silvan Tomkins; see chapter 1), or in this case simply a set of categories and concepts. It proliferates difference in the economic landscape and at the same time calls into question the hegemonic capitalocentric dynamics—mechanistic logics of reproduction, growth, accumulation, commodification, concentration, and centralization—on which capitalism's naturalness (and naturalized dominance) are grounded. A weak theory of economy does not presume that relationships between distinct sites of the diverse economy are structured in predictable ways, but observes the ways they are always differently produced according to specific geographies, histories, and ethical practices.[41] This kind of theory does not shy away from the exercise of diverse forms of power (including co-optation, seduction, capture, subordination, cooperation, parasitism, symbiosis, conflict, coexistence, complementarity) that might influence the relationships between different economic practices. Instead it encourages us to explore their complex spatialities and temporalities.[42] The issue of theorizing economic power within a diverse economy will be revisited in chapters 5 and 7 when we discuss the development pathways of alternative economic projects.

The question remains of how the alternative economic language that we have convened might constitute a challenge to the hegemony of neoliberal global capitalism, the latest, and most potent form of capitalocentric discourse. Can this language liberate us from domestication and integration *within* this hegemonic discourse? Our answer is, only if we can learn how to speak the language of the diverse economy in a more active sense. This involves practicing our new lexicon, rehearsing our anticapitalocentric reading and speaking skills, and experimenting with how to express the weakly theorized "dynamics" of contingency, overdetermination, and ethical practice. The following section offers some examples and food for thought for those whose appetite for language games is not already sated.

ANTICAPITALOCENTRIC READINGS

To illustrate the use of our language of the diverse economy, we offer preliminary analyses of an industry sector, an enterprise, and an individual worker. We "map" the economic identities of each onto the diverse economy framework and discuss the implications for economic dynamism that arise from our representations.

Our anticapitalocentric readings are premised on the following insights:

- Economic sectors, enterprises, and subjects occupy multiple sites in the diverse economy.
- Each site has the potential to offer one or more economic identities (subject positions).
- Each economic relation offers different realms of economic freedom as well as opportunities for exploitation and oppression depending on circumstances.
- Economic dynamics are overdetermined and thus the relationship between activities in different sites cannot be predicted but is open to politics and other contingencies.
- Political struggles have the capability to diversify the economy and change relations between activities within it.
- Capitalist enterprise is as diverse as noncapitalist enterprise.

THE DIVERSE ECONOMY OF THE CHILD-CARE SECTOR

Let us consider the many ways and contexts in which the labor of child care is practiced and how this diverse economic landscape has been produced. Figure 20 shows the incredible range of transactions, forms of labor, and kinds of enterprises by which the work of child care is performed around the world. We have made no attempt to ascertain the volume of child care being performed by each practice, as this would be different in every geographical and cultural context.

A capitalocentric reading of this sector might emphasize its role in the "re-

TRANSACTIONS	LABOR	ENTERPRISE
MARKET	**WAGE**	**CAPITALIST**
Domestic service market	Hired housekeeper	Body-hire agency, e.g., Dial
Child-care market	Worker in corporate child-	an Angel Inc.
	care center	Work-based child-care center
		Capitalist child-care center
ALTERNATIVE **MARKET**	**ALTERNATIVE** **PAID**	**ALTERNATIVE** **CAPITALIST**
Local trading systems	*Cooperative*	*Environmental ethic*
Child care offered on LETS	Child care cooperative	Steiner kindergarten
network	worker	*Social ethic*
Alternative currencies	*Self-employed*	Religious kindergarten
Baby-sitting club (hours	Family day-care mother	*State enterprise*
calculated)	*Indentured*	Government funded child-
Underground market	Domestic servant who is an	care center
Cash-in-hand to	overseas contract worker	*Nonprofit*
neighborhood teens	(paid in cash and kind)	Community-based child-care
Barter	*In-kind*	center
Direct and equivalent	Live-in student who does	
exchange of child-care	child care in return for	
hours	room and board	
NONMARKET	**UNPAID**	**NONCAPITALIST**
Household flows	*Family care*	*Communal*
Parents sharing child care	Care at home by parents and	Child-care cooperative
Gifts	grandparents	Communal household
Family and friends offer to	*Volunteer*	*Independent*
baby-sit	Child care by friends and	Family day care
Indigenous exchange	neighbors	Parent-carer household
Child "given" to kin to raise	Volunteer-provided care at	*Feudal*
	church, meetings	Extended family with
	Slave	obligatory child care
	Children in debt bondage	

FIGURE 20. The diverse economy of child care.

production of the capitalist labor force," and highlight the logic of commodification that seems to be changing the child-care landscape and restructuring the provision of this service. When we look, however, at the many diverse ways that child-care services are performed, and the significant number of noncapitalist sites of provision, we could be tempted to theorize a set of dynamics that captures the continued generation and regeneration of forms of child care in which market mechanisms play no dominant role.

Note the variety of locations in which the "work" of child care is performed outside the traditional household where parents and grandparents care for children (unpaid, unregulated, and undervalued).[43] Many of these sites have arisen as a result of feminist political interventions. In Australia, for example, different kinds of feminist politics enacted at the community, state, and national scales have given rise to the community cooperative child-care movement, successful agitation for government-funded child care, and community trade networks and baby-sitting clubs. The corporate sector has, in recent years, responded to the feminization of the paid workforce by establishing capitalist child-care and domestic-service agencies. It is reasonable to argue that the diversity of economic relations that currently characterize Australian child care reflects the unparalleled success of a transformative feminist economic project focused on providing child care in a range of ways suited to varied economic circumstances. This politics has multiplied the options for women and men raising children in Australian society, as well as achieving other interests and objectives.[44]

ENTERPRISES IN THE DIVERSE ECONOMY

Enterprises are multiply inserted into the diverse economy. Within any one business, a range of market and nonmarket transactions are enacted, various kinds of labor are deployed, and different class processes of production, appropriation, and distribution can coexist. For example, a noncapitalist cooperative enterprise engages in formal as well as alternative market transactions, and a capitalist enterprise might participate in a local trading system and employ labor that is partially paid in kind. Capitalist enterprises might even incorporate elements of communalism into their business structure with representation by workers on the company board, and a system of cooperatives might establish some of the operations in its network as noncooperative capitalist enterprises. What such attention to diversity highlights is the contingent nature of any enterprise. It helps us locate the ethical decisions that are made within the organization that produce multiple or hybrid identities and the way that enterprise dynamics are motivated by these relationships and choices, rather than by mechanistic logics.

In Figure 21 we illustrate the diversity of a quasi-fictitious multinational capitalist mining and metals manufacturing company. In this case, mapping the many different transactions that constitute the company, including the state allocations that have ensured its "market success," provides one way of deconstructing the company's private capitalist status. It suggests the basis for a reexamination of the exclusively private claim on surplus generated within the company by its board and shareholders. And it gives us some framework by which to gauge the veracity of advertising claims for the company's "social responsibility."

TRANSACTIONS	LABOR	ENTERPRISE
MARKET	**WAGE**	**CAPITALIST**
Monopoly national steel market	Salaried employees	Multinational mining and metals manufacturer
"Free" international market for coal	Unionized workers	
	Nonunionized workers	
ALTERNATIVE MARKET	**ALTERNATIVE PAID**	**ALTERNATIVE CAPITALIST**
Barter	*In-kind*	*Socially responsible firm*
Intra-company transfers of inputs, e.g., coal for steel girders	Subsidized housing for mining workforce	Scholarships and traineeships for children of workers and in communities adjacent to plant
	Cars and luxuries for executives	
	Work for welfare	
	Garden work at office complex	
NONMARKET	**UNPAID**	**NONCAPITALIST**
Gift giving	*Volunteer*	*Communal*
Corporate gifts to trading partners, to communities	Guides for visitors to company historic sites	Company shares distributed to long-term workers
State allocations		
Industry assistance		
Protected national market		
State appropriations		
Corporate taxes		
Royalty payments		
Theft		
Private mining on Aboriginal land		

FIGURE 21. The diverse economy of an enterprise.

THE DIVERSE ECONOMY OF AN INDIVIDUAL ECONOMIC SUBJECT

Any one economic actor participates in many kinds of economic relations in the diverse economy, no one of which can necessarily be designated as primary or essential.[45] We all have experience of participating in a range of *transactions*, each with their own distinctive quality, in the family, in the community, at our local farmer's market, at big-box stores, and, for some of us, in the stock market. Similarly, most of us perform different kinds of *labor* in the course of a day, at least as we move between the workplace and the home. We are probably less conscious of the different class processes we participate in as we work in a variety of enterprises over the course of our days and lives. For example (see Figure 22), a worker in a capitalist enterprise might produce surplus value that is appropriated in a capitalist class process, but in her "nonwork" hours, she may run a small T-shirt business out of her basement in which her children are compelled to work after school.

Our "worker" is here appropriating her children's surplus labor in a quasi-feudal or slave class process. In addition, she may participate in an egalitarian sharing of domestic work between family members and do some self-provisioning in the garden and thus be seen as engaging in a household communal class process.[46] On the weekends she may do voluntary work in a nonclass process in which her labor contribution is a gift that supports the initial development of a

TRANSACTIONS	LABOR	ENTERPRISE
MARKET	**WAGE**	**CAPITALIST**
Consumer	Wage worker	Employee in capitalist firm
ALTERNATIVE MARKET	**ALTERNATIVE PAID**	**ALTERNATIVE CAPITALIST**
Underground market Cash-in-hand employment of children's friends *Barter* Eggs and vegetables for fruits *Informal market* Sale of commodities produced by small business	*Self-employed* Small business run "after hours" *Reciprocal labor* Baby-sitting club	*Nonprofit* Involvement in community enterprise
NONMARKET	**UNPAID**	**NONCAPITALIST**
Household flows Sharing household labor *Gift giving* To community *Hunting, fishing, gathering* Seasonal berrying and mushrooming	*Housework* Contribution to household *Family care* Contribution to family *Volunteer* In community enterprise *Self-provisioning labor* Vegetable patch and chickens	*Communal* Household *Independent* T-shirt business *Feudal* Uses child labor

FIGURE 22. An individual in the diverse economy.

community-based enterprise that may eventually become the site of a communal class process.

The richness of individual subjects' economic lives is something that is rarely appreciated, especially when theorizing political projects. When it comes to economic identity in contemporary society, there are a limited number of subject positions to occupy and identify with—consumer, worker, self-employed, unemployed, capitalist entrepreneur, investor, to mention the most obvious. The language of the diverse economy can be used to explore the multidimensional nature of economic existence and the possibilities this creates for political acts of economic transformation. To come back to our child-care example, the work of parents setting up a baby-sitting club might rarely be seen as a form of economic activism, especially as this organization could include people from very different income and occupational groups who identify differently with one or more of the above subject positions. Yet as we will see in the following chapter, this act of recognizing and creating interdependence can be an important contribution to a counterhegemonic politics of strengthening the community economy. This kind of "work" can also be seen as an important dynamic of self-organization that has multiple effects, even on the so-called "center" of the economy, the capitalist workplace.[47]

DISLOCATION AND POLITICS

By speaking a language of the diverse economy, we can begin to unravel the dense knots of meaning that sustain the hegemonic identity of "*the* capitalist economy." Working against the condensations and displacements that structure the discourse of capitalocentrism, we have produced an unruly economic landscape of particular, nonequivalent meanings. Our objective has been to dis-order the capitalist economic landscape, to queer it and thereby dislocate capitalocentrism's hegemony. In the space thus produced, we see opportunities for new economic becomings—sites where ethical decisions can be made, power can be negotiated, and transformations forged.

A counterhegemonic politics involves dis-identification with the subject positions offered by a hegemonic discourse and identification with alternative and politically enabling positions. In the economic realm today we are confronted with no one set of possible alternative identities. Certainly the historic identity of the communist worker no longer presents itself as an imagined counter-identity. Instead, as we have shown, the terrain is littered with half-hearted and defensive "economic" identities that are largely acknowledged as *social* identities— houseworker, giver of gifts, volunteer, cooperator, petty trader, home producer, artisan, member of a kin network, indigenous hunter, migrant, public servant, community worker, peasant, social entrepreneur. This ragtag group has no shared sense of economic right from which it might launch an articulated attack on a neoliberal global capitalist order.[48] Rather, the discourses that occupy roles as capitalism's outside or "other" seem to independently but effectively shore up its hegemony.

To follow through with the project of constructing a counterhegemonic politics (according to the guidelines proposed by Laclau and Mouffe), we need to identify an alternative fixing of economic identity around a new nodal point. To propose a new nodal point is no small task and one that we are somewhat ambivalent about, given the absence, or at least uncertain status, of subjects who might be able to identify with such a counterhegemonic fixing of meaning. Yet our concern for creating an environment for the cultivation of new economic subjects leads us on to tentatively propose the *community economy* as an alternative.[49] In chapter 4 we introduce the community economy as a potential convening signifier for many different forms of economic difference, constituting a chain of equivalences through new acts of identification.

4

THE COMMUNITY ECONOMY

Through compiling and speaking a language of economic diversity, we are working toward destabilizing the economy as it is usually known and performed, and attempting to reveal a space of political decision. Out of the deconstruction and multiplication of economic identities a number of questions arise: What are the contours of the decision space that has been opened up? How might economic politics now be pursued? And what might an ethical practice of economy be? In this chapter, we develop a political discourse of the *community economy* that articulates a set of concepts and practices concerned with economic interdependence. These concepts and practices, we believe, offer potential coordinates for counterhegemonic projects of constructing "other" economies.

We are not alone in calling for a new political discourse grounded in visions of sociality and conviviality and in the "wisdom emerging from the movement of movements" (De Angelis 2003). Indeed, many alternative economic movements and practices are explicitly about resocializing economic relations. One has only to think of the fair-trade networks that connect third-world producers with first-world consumers so that in the buying and selling of coffee or bananas or craft products, the act of commensuration is not disembodied, but is ethically negotiated in a quasi face-to-face manner (mirroring the once-vital international socialist trading blocs). Or the farmers' markets and farm-share arrangements that have sprung up in cities around the industrialized world to bring fresh produce to consumers at (higher) prices that allow farmers to stay in business. Here we see attempts to eliminate middle markets and increase the proportion of product value returning to producers so they can raise their standards of living or at least maintain their farms. We can also look to employee buyouts in the face of corporate abandonment in the United States, and worker takeovers in the wake of economic crisis in Argentina. Here workers are becoming owners and self-managers and are learning to make decisions about the allocation of the value they produce. Or take the antisweatshop movement, which has raised awareness about high rates of exploitation and below-subsistence wage rates in industries producing commodities sold in wealthy countries (R. Ross 2004). We can look to shareholder movements that use their financial clout to promote ethical invest-ments and police the enforcement of corporate environmental and social respon-sibility. Or to the living wage movements in large North American cities (Pollin and Luce 1998; Harvey 2000, chapter 7) and newly invigorated discussions across Europe and the United States of a universal basic income (van Parijs 2001). Even mainstream economic policy has become interested in promoting social entre-preneurship in which nonprofit enterprises provide social services at affordable rates and commit to employing community members who are excluded from other labor markets (Amin, Cameron, and Hudson 2002). In all these move-ments, economic decisions (about prices of goods, wage levels, bonus payments, reinvestment strategies, sale of stock, and so forth) are made in the light of ethical discussions conducted within various communities. In some cases, these com-munities are geographically confined to the "local," while in others they span the "global."

There are, of course, already existing discourses of the community economy, and a range of existing practices of community economic development. Many of these advocate community self-reliance through reduction of dependency on global and national economic ties and the destructive influence of mobile capital (see, for example, Douthwaite 1996; J. Pearce 1993; Power 1996; Shuman 2000; Wildman 1993; and Williamson, Imbroscio, and Alperovitz 2003). Proliferating over the past thirty years, these approaches promote community-owned enter-prises focused on import replacement activities, the marshaling of local finance and its recycling within the locality, and increasing harmony with nature. Eco-nomic difference is tolerated within a range of community-oriented enterprises (locally owned businesses, nonprofits, cooperatives, community-development corporations, employee-owned businesses) and proponents differ on whether there is room for state-run business or state involvement, such as support for social enterprises, in their visions of self-reliance. The shared ethic that underlies these community economic development programs privileges care of the local community and its environment.[1]

The practices and enterprise forms embraced by all these (and other) move-ments are made visible by a language of economic diversity such as the one we de-veloped in chapter 3. But how do we multiply, amplify, and connect these differ-ent activities? How do we trace "the connections between diverse practices . . . to dissolve the distinctions between inside and outside the movement" (De Angelis 2003, 2) and thus actualize movement goals in a transformed social order? In the view of De Angelis as well as ourselves, a counterhegemonic discourse is required that can establish (some of the) contours of a shared political practice. Movements that are resocializing economic relations provide us with many opportunities to identify sites where ethical economic decisions can be made around recognized forms of interdependence, and where we can begin to perform economy in new ways. We are interested in convening all these openings/sites of decision and engaging in the prearticulatory conversations that might crystallize an alternative discourse of the community economy as the potential ground for a new hegemonic articulation.

Conceptualizing a discourse and practice of the community economy, one that could resignify and thereby connect a diverse range of existing activities, has involved stretching concepts originally used in one arena or project to apply to another. We engage in this process of extension (discussed in the Introduction) first with respect to Jean-Luc Nancy's resignification of communism and community as forms of "being-with," enlarging while at the same time specifying this notion to embrace the interdependence of *economic* subjects, sites, and practices. Second, we extend Marx's language of class (and especially the concepts of necessary and surplus labor) to supply ethical coordinates for negotiating interdependency in actual projects of economic construction. What we are in the process of elaborating (tentatively yet investedly) is a discourse that might promote self-recognition and foster connection among a plurality of movements, contributing to a counterhegemonic "postcapitalist" project of resignification and enactment.

THE "PROPER PLURAL SINGULAR CO-ESSENCE" OF BEING

Jean-Luc Nancy argues that Western metaphysics, since its origins in Greek city-states, has suppressed the original alterity, or what he calls the "being-together," in the concept of Being.[2]

> We compear: we come together (in)to the world. It is not that there is
> a simultaneous arrival of several distinct units (as when we go to see
> a film "together") but that there is no coming (in)to the world that is
> not radically *common*; it is even the "common" itself. To come into the
> world is to be-in-common. Everything takes place as if the constant
> diversion (*détournement*) of this truth (to say its repression would be
> too easy) were the permanent rule of Western thought (of philosophy).
> (1992, 373–74)

Nancy notes ironically that the very production of a common *logos* depended on the circulation and communication of meaning among people. Yet in the quest to establish the metaphysical grounds of Being, the many concrete singularities that constitute the inherent plurality of being have become, in Western philosophy, subordinated within an abstract singularity (2000, 34)—the "I," or "one," who "knows." Western philosophy is thus grounded on "the problem of the city," the problem of how to share meaning and find ways to be together in the world.

For Nancy, the question of Being is "the question of being-with and of being-together (in the sense of the world)" (2000, 35). And the problem of the city/world will remain as long as we refuse to face up to the ontological conversation necessary to the task of thematizing "the 'with' as the essential trait of Being and as its *proper plural singular co-essence*" (2000, 34, emphasis added).

> Philosophy needs to recommence, to restart itself from itself against itself, against political philosophy and philosophical politics. In order to do this, philosophy needs to think in principle about how we are "us" among us, that is, how the consistency of our Being is in being-in-common, and how this consists precisely in the "in" or in the "between" of its spacing. (2000, 25–26)

Given Nancy's vision of the foundational relationship between being-in-common and Being, it is interesting to reflect on the way the language of community and collectivity has been developed in a minor key, almost as an afterthought, and only ever paired with that of individualism and particularity. Indeed the idea of being-together has been largely approached as a challenge for political action, and not also as a *ground* for thought or politics.

To explicitly theorize the sociality of all relations is, according to Nancy, to refuse to suppress the togetherness implied in any singularity, any identity or concept of Being. How such a refusal might initiate a discourse of economy is not developed in his work, though he draws our attention back to "communism," a topic that many would claim has absolutely no purchase in this, the "post-communist" era. Nancy argues, to the contrary, that the fascination with communism "as an idea, as phantasm, as project, or as institution" has shaped (and continues to shape) history in our time (1992, 376–77). "Far from simply being a word voided of all substance by Sovietism," communism is "also the index of a task of thought still and increasingly open" (2002, 8). It is a task of thought that returns us to the "common" basis or ground of the "individual," encapsulating the quintessentially ethical concern at the heart of "society"—the question of how to live together. With this key concern in mind, we begin our project of constituting a new political discourse of the community economy, enrolling the unwitting Nancy as a fellow underlaborer.

SOCIALITY AND COMMERCE

When a meal is cooked for a household of kids, when a cooperative sets its wage levels, when a food seller adjusts her price for one customer and not another, when a farmer allows gleaners access to his fields, when a green firm agrees to use higher-priced recycled paper, when a self-employed computer programmer takes public holidays off, when a not-for-profit enterprise commits to "buying local," some recognition of economic co-implication, interdependency, and social connection is actively occurring. These practices involve ethical considerations and political decisions that constitute social and economic being.

It has long been seen as an advantageous quality of capitalist economic relations (a sign of their modernity) that their sociality and interdependence is mediated through the market in which the sticky ties of culture and social allegiance are banished and the scope for decision severely limited. For some analysts the rise of purely calculative economic relations from the muddy allegiances and obligations of feudal or traditional indigenous economic relations is represented as a "great transformation" that saw the more obvious aspects of economic interconnection replaced by an asocial economic atomism (Polanyi 1968). Others who reject the taint of historicism and yet are happy to transpose capitalist sociality onto human history at large have sought to represent all economic behavior in any contemporary or historical context as structured by the essentialized calculus of atomistic individualism (Adaman and Madra 2002).

In Michel Callon's (1998) analysis of technologies of economy, the market economy promotes what are called "cold negotiations," in which agreement is reached with minimal social interaction—the potentially "hot" sociality of exchange having been cooled down by the application of economic calculation (Barry 2002, 268).[3] For economic anthropologist Stephen Gudeman, who recognizes complex systems of commensuration that do not necessarily negate sociality at work in both market and nonmarket transactions, the market realm nevertheless "situates individuals and groups as *separate actors* who undertake short-term interactions and exchanges to achieve both material ends and gain" (2001, 10, emphasis added).[4] Antipolitical, asocial, individual, disembedded, rational, efficient, short-term, calculable, incontestable—these are the qualities associated with economic transactions mediated by the (capitalist) market.

It was these very qualities (or ideological fictions) of capitalism that Marx hoped to disrupt, arguing that capitalist economic relations did not eradicate sociality and interdependence, but merely obscured them. Contrasting the economic relations of "primitive communes" with those of capitalism, Marx comments on how the *particular* and *social* character of communal labor is exposed and never lost to view, yet when labor is bought and sold as a commodity within capitalist relations, it is rendered *abstract* and *universal*:

> [T]he product of labour [under the rural patriarchal system of production] bore the specific social imprint of the family relationship with its naturally evolved division of labour. . . . It was the distinct labour of the individual in its original form, the *particular* features of his labour and not its *universal* aspect that formed the social ties. . . . In this case, the *social* character of labour is evidently not affected by the labour of the individual assuming the *abstract* form of universal labour or his product assuming the form of a universal equivalent.[5]

One of the main points of Marx's work was to argue that community is not eradicated by the mediation of capitalist commodity relations, but takes on a different meaning and form. As Nancy puts it, "Community means here [in Marx's text on primitive communism] the *socially exposed particularity,* in opposition to the *socially imploded generality* characteristic of capitalist community" (1991a, 74, emphases added).[6] Rather than seeing the latter as businesslike, disconnected, and asocial while the former is a fecund site of social connection, Marx theorizes these differences, according to Nancy, in terms of two different forms of social connection.

We would go along with Nancy (and Marx) in seeing different ways of "being-with" embodied in the sites and practices of the diverse economy.[7] They point to what is for us a truly salient distinction, between whether interdependence is recognized and acted upon or whether it is obscured or perhaps denied. Many of the technologies for representing and constructing markets, for example, mask the interdependence of parties and products in exchange; and a hallmark of capitalism is the denial of its basis in an exploitative form of interdependence in which nonproducers appropriate surplus from direct producers. While each of these practices institutes a form of social connection, each also hides or attenuates aspects of economic interdependence. Making these visible again is a step toward rendering them objects of politics and ethics. The distinction between implicit or effaced being-with and explicit being-with is thus the keystone of our counterhegemonic project of "differently politicizing" the economy.

In our view, a discourse of the community economy could act to create and sustain the identity of a postcapitalist economy constructed around a knot of definite meanings associated with economic being-in-common. What stands in the way of advancing this strategic language politics is the resistance we have to the "task of thought still and increasingly open" (Nancy 2002, 8)—the difficulty of thinking the commerce of being-together, of thinking "communism" divorced from its historical referents. Also standing in the way and perhaps pressing on us more powerfully are existing meanings and practices of community, including practices of "community economy." It seems that resignification must work against not only the widespread aversion to communism, but also the very popularity and prevalence of discourses of community.

UNDER A NEW SIGN

It is an interesting irony that in the current neoliberal political and economic climate, in which individualism is promoted as an unquestioned social good, all over the world the term *community* has increasingly come to the fore.[8] As journalist Tom Morton notes in the Australian context:

> Community has become a cult, an object of warm-and-fuzzy ritual worship for politicians of all stripes, academics and the rapidly expanding new class of social commentators. Nobody can get enough of

the C-word: it's supposed to be a panacea for reducing crime, stopping youth suicide, getting the unemployed back to work, and improving your health. To borrow a line from the well-known social theorists [actually comedians] Roy Slaven and H. G. Nelson, we live in a society where too much community can never be enough. (2000, 1)

For Morton, the unthinking embrace of this term across the political spectrum is a worrying phenomenon. The "C-word," he writes, "is the camouflage behind which government has conducted a massive withdrawal from society" in terms of its economic responsibilities (11), while at the same time promoting conservative, moralistic "community values" that endorse greater public involvement in citizens' private lives (10).

Morton puts his finger on one of the interesting, or perhaps suspicious, aspects of the term *community*—the way in which it seems to be able to do good work across the political and social spectrum. It would appear that no matter what context it is used in—whether with reference to the global financial community, the gay community, or the gambling community—it has some purchase. Feminist political theorist Iris Marian Young sheds some light on the "ideal of community" when she writes that it

presumes subjects can understand one another as they understand themselves. . . . [I]t privileges unity over difference, immediacy over mediation, sympathy over recognition of the limits of one's understanding of others from their point of view. (1990, 302, 300)

As it has been used in Western thought, the term *community*, Young argues, expresses the desire to overcome individualism and difference, to produce social wholeness and mutual identification (1990, 302). But it is just this fuzzy warmness that critics like Morton find so chilling.

In *The Inoperative Community*, Nancy is eager to avoid the sense of community that is built on already constituted subjects who are brought together in a constructed oneness. He argues that the "failure of communal models is . . . linked to their embrace of human immanence, that is, of totality, self-consciousness, self-presence" (Van Den Abbeele 1991, xiv). He wants to revive a notion of community as "neither a community of subjects, nor a promise of immanence, nor a communion of individuals in some higher or greater totality (a State, a Nation, a People)" (xiv). For Nancy, there is no common substance, no identity, "no common being, but there is being *in* common" (1991b, 4). The association of community with a *being* that is already known precludes the *becoming* of new and as-yet unthought ways of being. Mirroring this thought, Giorgio Agamben writes in *The Coming Community* of an "inessential commonality, a solidarity that in no way concerns an essence" (1993, 19).[9]

It would seem that to liberate economic difference, we need also to liberate community from its traditional recourse to common being. In terms of economic activism, this means resisting equating community economic development *only* with growing the local capitalist economy *or* with attempts to establish "small-is-beautiful" green self-sufficiency *or* with achieving community self-determination through promoting homegrown, locally oriented community business. Whether explicitly or implicitly, these conceptions of the community economy draw on normative ideals of the community as a fullness and a positivity. At the center of these community economies is a *commonality of being*, an ideal of sameness, whether defined in terms of incubator capitalism, or a "natural holistic community," or self-reliant localism. Not only is economic difference suppressed (if only lightly), but any *ethic* of being-in-common, of coexistence with the other, is relegated to a remnant.

There are, of course, already existing discourses of the community economy (sometimes referred to as the "alternative economy") in which economic plurality/difference has been celebrated and allowed to exist. Yet despite vast differences within the field of community economic development, it seems that when "community" and "economy" are put together, the power, expansiveness, and universality of the latter are compromised and constrained; rendered as face-to-face, human, small-scale, caring, and above all local, the community economy is necessarily positioned as "other" to the so-called "real economy" of international markets, competitive dynamics, and agglomerative tendencies that operate at the global scale.

The terms in Figure 23 pepper the large and growing field of community economic development—a field that is eclectic and productively chaotic. But underlying the conceptual scatter are two uniting tendencies: the first is the privileging of geographic "commonality" or localism, and the second is the sense (not fully visible in the figure, but palpable in its sources) that a certain positive, shared way of being—a form of "common being"—is already given in the concept of "community economy." However loosely and attractively depicted, building a community economy is not simply a process of ethical decision making among people who are creating something uncharted and unpredictable, but rather the realization of an ideal—putting the cart of common substance, it would seem, before the ethical and political horse. It is this already specified content (of community) that Nancy has been so concerned to dislodge, and that we have tried to undermine with a vision (of economy) as an ethical space of decision, rather than a specified set of qualities, forms, and functionings.

In constructing a discourse and practice of the community economy, what if we were to resist the pull of the *sameness or commonness* of economic being and instead focus on a notion of economic *being-in-common*? That is, rather than thinking in terms of the common properties of an ideal economic organization or an ideal community economy, we might think of the being-in-common of economic subjects and of all possible and potential economic forms. We might specify coordinates for negotiating and exploring interdependence, rather than attempting to realize an ideal. How might this lead to a conception of a commu-

ECONOMY	*COMMUNITY* ECONOMY
a-spatial/global	place-attached
specialized	diversified
singular	multiple
large scale	small scale
competitive	cooperative
centered	decentered
a-cultural	culturally distinctive
socially disembedded	socially embedded
nonlocal ownership	local ownership
agglomerative	dispersed
integrated	autonomous
export-oriented	oriented to local market
privileges short-term return	values long-term investment
growth oriented	vitality oriented
outflow of extracted value	recirculates value locally
privately owned	community owned
management led	community led
controlled by private board	community controlled
private appropriation and distribution of surplus	communal appropriation and distribution of surplus
environmentally unsustainable	environmentally sustainable
fragmented	whole
amoral	ethical
crisis-ridden	harmonious
participates in a spatial division of labor	locally self-reliant
MAINSTREAM ECONOMY	*ALTERNATIVE* ECONOMY

FIGURE 23. Key words of economy and community economy. From Bernard and Young (1997), Crouch and Marquand (1995), Meeker-Lowry (1995), Ife (1995), Pearce (1993), Power (1996), and Wildman (1993).

nity economy that is versatile enough to inspire economic imaginings without fixing them on any one fantasy of completion or salvation?

Resocializing the Economy

We are proposing that a discourse of the *community economy* has the capacity to politicize the economic in new ways by resignifying

- economy as a site of decision, of ethical praxis, instead of as the ultimate reality/container/constraint; and

- all economic practices as inherently social and always connected in their concrete particularities to the "commerce of being-together." (Nancy 2000, 74)

Resocializing (and repoliticizing) the economy involves making explicit the sociality that is always present, and thus constituting the various forms and practices of interdependence as matters for reflection, discussion, negotiation, and action.

But where might we look for strategies for negotiating plurality and interdependence, the ethics of connection that make up the fabric of economy? How might we redress the positioning of "community" as an afterthought to the given of the "individual" in thinking about economic matters? And what might a nonfantastical, nonsingular vision of the community economy be? Here we are seeking the ethical coordinates for a political practice, not a model or a plan, nor "elements of a fixed ideology, a dogma that we have to subscribe to" (De Angelis 2003, 4).

Nancy reminds us that Marx and Freud were two of the few thinkers who have attempted to "redress the relegation of the 'plural', 'social' or 'communitarian' dimension to the status of an addition to that of a primitive individual given" (2000, 44). Marx's project of exposing the social nature of capitalist economic relations, especially the way in which exchange masked the social origins of surplus value, is central to our understanding of economic relations and thus to the task of resocializing the economy.[10] His theory of surplus labor and Resnick and Wolff's anti-essentialist Marxian analysis of the class process offer some conceptual tools for practically approaching economic being-in-common. A class process involves the production, appropriation, and distribution of surplus labor (in labor, product, or value form) and is but one way of representing and accounting for flows of labor in a society (Gibson-Graham, Resnick, and Wolff 2000a, 2001).[11] Whether or not we acknowledge it, our own existence at every level can be seen as the effect of the labor of others. For our purposes, then, labor has an *inessential commonality*—"a solidarity that in no way contains an essence" (Agamben 1993, 19)—that might give us some purchase on economic being-in-common.

If we wish to emphasize the *becoming* of new and as yet unthought ways of economic being, we might focus on the multiple possibilities that emerge from the inessential commonality of negotiating our own implication in the existence of others. An ethical praxis of being-in-common could involve cultivating an awareness of

- what is *necessary* to personal and social survival;
- how social *surplus* is appropriated and distributed;
- whether and how social surplus is to be produced and *consumed*; and
- how a *commons* is produced and sustained.

Negotiations around these key coordinates and the interactions between them could inform an ethics and politics of the community economy.[12]

NECESSITY

The distinction between *necessary* and *surplus* labor cannot be seen as grounded in the ostensible reality of the body's "basic needs" for subsistence, but reflects a socially embedded ethical decision. What is necessary to survival and what is surplus is not predefined or given, in some humanist or culturally essentialist sense, but is established relationally at the moment of surplus appropriation itself. The boundary between necessary and surplus labor is an accounting device, inscribed on the body rather than emerging from within it, and the desire to move this boundary can be seen to have motivated political struggles historically and to this day. The decisions about how much time to put into food gathering or into cultural and community practice, how much of a wage increase to bargain for, how much is a "living wage," how much of one's harvest can be set aside for household needs, are all decisions about what should be seen as "necessary" to subsistence. Whether forcibly imposed or taken voluntarily, these decisions take place in a social and cultural milieu in which what is reasonable and ethical is sometimes explicitly, but more likely only implicitly, debated.

Fixing the socially acceptable meaning of necessary labor (or the necessary labor payment, often in the form of a wage) has material social consequences that translate into the level of consumption directly accessed by the producer and her dependents, the volume of social surplus that is privately or socially appropriated, and thus the level of social consumption indirectly accessed by society at large. In the case of the self-employed, the fixing of the wage payment is a personal decision, albeit one often highly constrained by the limited amount of wealth generated and the costs of servicing debts and providing ongoing inputs into the business. The self-employed entrepreneur can "choose" to work long hours and possibly start to accumulate surplus, or he or she can "choose" a more flexible life in which paid work figures less prominently, material needs are curtailed, and leisure or household activities assume greater importance. The sense that self-employment allows greater freedom to set the level of the necessary labor payment and the boundary between necessary and surplus labor is one thing that continues to attract people to this form of economic activity (Hotch 2000). In other situations, wage fixing is a much less personal and more social and political act. Within an alternative economic enterprise like a worker cooperative, decisions about how much to pay out in wages and benefits are matters of ongoing debate and have a direct impact on how much surplus is available for weathering an economic downturn, expanding the co-op, or supporting a wider community. In the case of a feudal workforce, the decision about how much of the harvest is to be paid to the landlord in return for access to land, and therefore how much of the harvest is available to support the producer's livelihood, is often imposed by law or traditional agreements. Negotiation might only center on other peripheral rights that will enhance survival, such as permission to use some of the land for additional income-generating activities, over which the landlord might agree to exercise no right of appropriation.

In the case of a unionized workforce, wage decisions are often fiercely negotiated with employers, with the emphasis traditionally being on limiting the workday and driving the wage payment as high as it can go (that is, increasing the necessary labor payment extracted from a capitalist employer).[13] Increasingly, in countries like Australia any kind of ethical debate about what is socially (and environmentally) necessary to survival has been sidelined in the union movement in the interests of serving the membership's desire for greater material reward. In this regard, the unions are only reflecting a widely held social belief that to limit desire in this "lucky country" is decidedly un-Australian. Recently in the Australian building industry the struggle has turned inward as union officials have proposed that union members limit their hours of work (and thus their wage packet) in the interest of establishing family-friendly working hours. In this industry, workers were voluntarily increasing the length of their workdays to exact higher wages, putting themselves among the highest-paid employees in the Australian workforce. Concern for the survival of family units and the high incidence of industrial accidents among those performing increasing amounts of voluntary overtime have led to a debate among the membership that has highlighted the way in which what had come to be seen as a socially acceptable/ necessary/high wage was counter to survival. This might be seen as a resuscitation of ethical issues that have long been dormant, stifled under the weight of a time-honored and socially validated practice of maximizing income and thus consumption.

In a world in which the quantity of material goods that is seen as socially necessary to survival is vastly different across income strata, international boundaries, rural and urban contexts, suburbs and ghettos, it is hard to escape the implications of economic being-in-common. The ethos of economic individualism that promotes the right to want and get more and that sees this unchecked desire as a crucial motivating force behind economic health (that is, growth) obscures the social and environmental implications of such behavior for "us all." An ethical discourse of the community economy would highlight the inherent sociality of decisions made in defining necessity, and the various forms of interdependence (the trade-offs or flow-ons) that are enacted when such decisions are made. Making the time and space in which to engage in meaningful discussion and decision making about them could be part of enacting a "community economy."

SURPLUS

Surplus labor, as Marx defined it, is the time of labor a producer performs above and beyond the labor time necessary to reproduce herself as a worker (Resnick and Wolff 1987, 115). Whenever surplus labor is appropriated and distributed, whether in labor, value, or product form, Marx sees a class process taking place. This process may be exploitative in the case of appropriation by nonproducers (in, for example, a capitalist, feudal, or slave class process) or nonexploitative in the case of producer appropriation (in an independent or communal class process).

In a diverse economic context such as we have been presuming, surplus labor is produced in all types of enterprises and environments and takes heterogeneous forms. For our purposes, and despite the obvious impossibility of aggregating incommensurables, we are conceptualizing an imaginary, unquantifiable social surplus made up of all these surpluses combined. This social surplus may be used to support those who are currently nonproducing (such as infants and some very old people) as well as helping to build and sustain the material and cultural infrastructure of the social order.[14] It is thus the potential object of ethical decisions and political contestation.

Marx's most famous intervention was to represent the class process of appropriating surplus in terms of its exploitative and individualizing effect, that is, in terms of what was *taken* from producers, provoking the anger and resentment rightfully directed toward the act of theft. This representation became the basis of the working men's movement for reclaiming some of their surplus labor in the form of higher wages and the political motivation for an approach to communism that saw the direct producers as having the superior "right" to appropriate surplus (Madra and Özselçuk 2003). But Marx also offered another vision of the class process in terms of its socially potentiating effect, by focusing on the moment of surplus distribution rather than appropriation. When appropriated surplus labor is distributed—in the form of payment, gift, or other allocation— community is produced or at least potentiated.[15] Value over and above what is needed by the individual for sustenance enters into a social space where society at large is able to exert its claims on the social surplus and from which it is allocated to many different ends. Each allocation allows for a becoming, a new way of being. Marx was keen to show how the socially potentiating force of the *capitalist* class process was channeled in certain directions by the private nature of surplus appropriation and distribution.

In the capitalist class process, the worker performs labor in return for a wage, and this interaction is usually understood as a fair exchange of equivalents between free economic subjects. The fact that the worker produces more value embodied in commodities than is compensated by her wage is neither here nor there—in the commerce of the labor market, the flow of surplus value to the capitalist is ignored. In this sleight of hand, a "fair exchange" delivers a portion of social surplus that could support the community of "us all" into the hands of individual capitalists who see this surplus as rightfully and individually theirs.[16] Surplus appropriation by the capitalist/board of directors is a private and largely unacknowledged affair and the distribution of surplus to creditors, taxes, shareholders, advertisers, patent offices, and so forth is seen as the private business of the capitalist or company board, for which retaining any remaining profit as an accumulation fund or for private income seems a just reward.

Recall that it is the very capacity for a society to produce surplus that enables its viability or "reproduction." It is the ability of surplus-producing ("productive") workers to create a surplus that allows for the survival and sustenance of society's nonactive ("unproductive") surplus-using members—children, the aged, the disabled, the administrators, artists, clergy, and so forth. But in the capitalist class process, the surplus that could be available to build and maintain society at large is privately appropriated and flows to the capitalist. The interdependencies that connect producers of surplus and nonproducers in the being-social that is society are, within capitalist economic activities, violently effaced.

That the social environment of "capitalism" is nevertheless "reproduced" despite the private appropriation of a substantial fraction of social surplus by the capitalist class is a (miraculous) product of a multitude of factors. Prominent among these have been the historic interventions of state bureaucracies, whose powers of taxation and capacities for fiscal redistribution have waxed and waned as national economies have boomed and slumped.[17] The other less-acknowledged mainstay of social reproduction in the face of the private capitalist appropriation of surplus has, of course, been the diverse noncapitalist economic activities that mainly predated and continue to coexist with capitalist economic relations. Here we can point to indigenous and familial practices that form nongovernmental social safety nets composed of household labor and transactions; intergenerational redistributions and intracommunity reciprocity and sharing; the self-sufficient self-employed and self-provisioners; the livelihoods sustained by access to common or traditional land and resources that escaped the primitive accumulation of capital; and the collective and cooperative enterprises that have sprung up, especially in sites of capitalist collapse or abandonment. Many of these activities not only produce items of necessity, but generate and distribute surplus as well. Perhaps in inverse relation to its claim on public acknowledgment, we could also recognize the minor role that capitalist philanthropy has played in distributing surplus in the form of subsidies for hospitals, medical research, think tanks, sports, opera, and other cultural industries that contribute to social well-being. Despite the rhetoric of capitalist growth, generosity, and societal progress, it could be argued that economic community, "economic being-in-common," has been ensured in large part by state and nonstate economic activities operating in the "noncapitalist" sector.[18]

The processes of private *appropriation* and *distribution* of surplus are some of the most difficult economic processes to discuss, so repressed have they been in economic theory over the last century.[19] If social surplus is what builds communities and cultures, then the decision-making processes that configure surplus appropriation and distribution will play an important role in determining their ethical character. Can we conceive of mechanisms by which the surplus produced by one set of "us all" might be appropriated and distributed by a larger more encompassing "us all," thus acknowledging that the "co-implication of existing is the sharing of the world"? We propose that decisions around surplus production, appropriation, and distribution provide another focus of attention within a discourse of the community economy.[20]

At the core of ethical economic becoming would be the consideration of questions such as the following: Who is to be included in decision making over the rate of appropriation of surplus and its distribution? Is there a maximum size of enterprise or social grouping in which such hands-on involvement is not feasible? Under what conditions might surplus appropriation be seen as nonexploitative?[21] How might nonproducers of social surplus have a say in how surplus is generated, appropriated, distributed? And, of course, what are the social destinations to which surplus is to be distributed, and those to which it will not? There are no simple answers to these questions. In each particular context, their resolution will be differently configured. What is important is that questions such as these, which acknowledge economic being-in-common, are posed and discussed. The next chapter traces the unique pathway by which a particular community distributed its surplus and navigated the construction of an ethical economy.

CONSUMPTION

Both mainstream and Marxist economic visions have a conception of economic "health" in which key indicators figure prominently. We are all familiar, from the financial press and elsewhere, with discussions of investment/expenditure ratios, debt/savings ratios, ratios of luxury expenditure to necessity expenditure, and so forth. These economic diagnostics can be read as pointing to different kinds of consumption—of producer goods enrolled in "productive consumption," for example, and of luxury and basic consumer goods and services (including housing). In a longstanding parallel with analyses of the functioning of the human body, they depend on a conceptualization of the economy as a closed, self-reproducing, and potentially crisis-ridden system. Discussions of consumption tend to center on which types will be more decisive in maintaining, growing, or overheating the body economic.

A discourse of the community economy works with a very different conception of the economy as an open system populated by diverse and incommensurable activities in which path-dependent relationships rather than predictable logics contribute to economic dynamism. Nevertheless, in enacting a community economy we might be interested to address the effects of certain kinds of consumption compared to others on community economic sustainability. We have already touched on these kinds of decisions in the discussion of necessity. When it comes to the distribution of social surplus—whether to "production" and to increasing the capacity to generate surplus, or to social consumption, such as to the provision of services that benefit all, or to lifting levels of domestic and personal consumption by distributing bonus payments—decisions rest on an evaluation of what kinds of consumption will serve and strengthen a community economy. While the tools of analysis that the Marxian tradition brings to this task are problematic (as, it might be said, are any tools) it is useful to review the issues they raise, as a way of further delineating the decision spaces that are opened up by a discourse of the community economy.

One of the thorniest political issues to emerge from Marxian political economy has been the distinction Marx made between labor engaged in capitalist commodity production that is *productive* of surplus value, and labor that is *unproductive* of surplus value (in this category he might include workers in advertising and marketing departments of commodity-producing firms, workers in the financial sector, upper-level management, or workers like domestic servants, who sell their labor power but are not involved in capitalist commodity production). In Resnick and Wolff's account, unproductive laborers are paid out of surplus value if they are employed by capitalist firms engaged in commodity production (thus they are recipients of distributed class payments) and receive a nonclass form of remuneration if they are otherwise employed.

The distinction between productive and unproductive labor that Marx adapted from Adam Smith is not unlike many such distinctions that are used in non-Marxian economics to focus on the "driving forces," rather than the "dependent activities," of an economy. For Marx, who was interested in identifying the internal seeds of capitalism's destruction, the number and productivity of *productive* workers was crucial to the volume of surplus value produced and thus to expansion through investment in productive capital, better known as capital accumulation.[22] Our question is, what role might this distinction, which has so often been misinterpreted as referring to *socially* unproductive economic activities, or ones that make a less socially valued contribution, play in a discourse of the community economy?

Clearly surplus is produced in a range of contexts other than capitalist enterprises and this suggests a diverse range of specific situations in which decisions about the deployment of surplus to "surplus-productive" versus "surplus-unproductive" ends might be made. For example, in a worker-cooperative car repair business, the service manager coordinates all jobs and her work is crucial to organizational functioning, but her "unproductive" labor does not take the form of billable hours and is not, therefore, perceived as producing income for the business—this derives from the "productive" labor of the mechanics. The ratio between the unproductive and productive workers in such a business will have a major impact on the sustainability and surplus-generating capabilities of the business, as well as the wage compensation paid to all cooperators. To take another example, in a household the so-called "unproductive expenditure" (from the perspective of the mainstream analyst) of household income on a new washing machine might actually increase the productivity of communal clothes-washing and free up labor time. This might be allocated to leisure, or to additional self-provisioning in the garden, or it might enable one household member to seek employment as a wage worker. In contrast to this example of "productive consumption," in another household income might be expended on enlarging the house, thereby increasing the time spent on house decorating and cleaning. This might have the effect of diminishing the amount of surplus labor time the household has to devote to voluntary community work. Consumption in one household increases the potential availability of domestic surplus labor and decreases it in the other. Lastly, in a traditional rural community the decision made by households to "unproductively" consume the year's savings in a community-wide fiesta is also a decision not to invest in increasing the productive capacity of the community, or upgrading local services. Yet by allocating surplus to the "unproductive" practice of sharing food and entertainment, the sociality and religious beliefs of the community are publicly affirmed and a commons replenished.

By highlighting the sociality of all economic relations, the community economy approach seeks to recognize the interdependence of a broad variety of economic and so-called "noneconomic" activities. The discourse of the community economy thus questions the practice of singling out certain activities as necessarily or invariably more important, more independent, more determining of economic "health" and distinguishing them from those that are more expendable, dependent, and less determining or potentially destructive within the economy. We are interested in fostering the community-economy-building capacities of social surplus, the dynamic interaction of multiple and diverse economic relations, and the crucial interdependence of economic and "noneconomic" activities. This would suggest that there is a need for some kind of lexicon with which to focus ethical debate about possible community economy trajectories, but not a set of structural dynamics or established judgments about what is good or bad for you economically.

In a diverse community economy, it is the capacity to produce social surplus in a variety of forms, and not just surplus value, that is of interest, as it is this surplus that can be used to replenish and expand the commons and the productive base. When it comes to the decisions about how social surplus is to be distributed, the question of increasing the capacity to produce surplus by investment in those activities that are productive of social surplus must be weighed against whether to expand activities that deliver social well-being directly, that consume social surplus in replenishing the commons, or that allocate surplus to increasing the standard of living by redefining what constitutes subsistence or a socially necessary wage payment. The kind of society and culture that is built will depend on how noneconomic activities are valued and resourced.

COMMONS

As Stephen Gudeman simply and eloquently states, "A community economy makes and shares a commons. . . . Without a commons, there is no community, without a community, there is no commons" (2001, 27). In his view, Garrett Hardin's so-called "'tragedy of the commons' which refers to destruction of a resource through unlimited use by individuals, is a tragedy not of a physical commons but of a human community, because of the failure of its members to treat one another as communicants and its transformation to a competitive situation"

(28). For Gudeman, creating and maintaining a commons is by definition an ethical practice of being-in-common, one that informs material practices and social boundaries of community.[23]

In the work of groups like Reclaim the Commons, the commons is already being recognized as an ethical coordinate of an alternative politics, with the traditional definition expanded to incorporate all manner of (potentially) common "wealth":

> Traditionally, THE COMMONS was cropland, grazing land, or forest that belonged to the community as a whole and benefited all. Now, THE COMMONS includes everything needed to support life on earth: air, water, shelter, food, energy, biodiversity—as well as our multi-cultural heritage. Corporations, aided by the governments they dominate, are seizing control of these basic rights, and privatizing them for the profit of a few. Yet, public control of the commons is essential for true democracy; for racial, economic, and social justice; and for a diverse and sustainable society. (www.reclaimthecommons.net)

A central issue of the commons is the ever-present danger of "enclosure" or private seizure and restricted use of communal wealth. In volume 1 of *Capital*, Marx described the private enclosure of the traditional commons as a violent project of "primitive accumulation" that enabled the rise of capitalist enterprise (largely by creating a proletarian labor force bereft of land and therefore desperate for work).[24] Contemporarily, while most attention has been given to the destruction of physical environments and the privatization of resources and genetic stocks in many parts of the "developing" world, one of the most insidious inroads into the commons has been the "taking" of public enterprise promoted by neoliberal economic policy in wealthy countries. Thatcher led the way in the United Kingdom in the 1980s with her sale of public property and services to private interests at bargain prices, seen by the unconverted as "giving away the commons to her friends."

The commons—whether it be agricultural land, a gene pool, an atmosphere, a wilderness, a database, a fishery, the Internet, community facilities and support systems, or even the whole set of relationships comprising a community economy—provides direct input into social and physical well-being. What must be individually or communally done to exact survival is clearly related to what can be accessed directly from the commons—whether it be clean air and drinking water, a public health system, a forest or marine environment that yields a whole range of foods and materials, a network of community-oriented enterprises, a system of reciprocity that ensures access to basic food requirements, a working road system and communication network, land for livelihood, or the psychological support of a shared culture in which symbols, values, memories, and traditions can be freely drawn on to create meaning. Crucially linked to the issue of necessity, the availability of the commons is one determinant of the necessary and surplus labor required to sustain an individual and a community.

The commons can be seen as a community stock that needs to be maintained and replenished so that it can continue to constitute the community by providing its direct input (subsidy) to survival. Clearly there is a delicate relationship between nourishing and preserving this stock and placing pressures on it to provide higher levels of consumption or inputs into the surplus-generating machine of production. Whether to deplete, maintain, or grow the commons is a major focus of ethical decision making. Such an ethical practice of commons management is part of what defines and constitutes a community. It creates and reproduces the "common substance" of the community while at the same time making a space for raising and answering the perennial question of who belongs and is therefore entitled to rights of decision.

COMMUNISM: "A TASK OF THOUGHT STILL AND INCREASINGLY OPEN"

In chapter 3 we assembled multiple discourses of economy that highlight the sociality and interdependence of economic relations. These heterogeneous relations are convened on an uneven terrain that has the potential, as yet unrealized, to destabilize and even dislocate the hegemony of capitalocentrism. Drawing on articulation as "a practice that establishes a relation among elements such that their identity is modified as a result of the articulatory practice" (Torfing 1999, 298), in this chapter we have been developing a discourse of the "community economy" as a part of a political project to unify this discursive terrain. Articulating the multiple, heterogeneous sites of struggle, such a discourse could resignify *all* economic transactions and relations, capitalist and noncapitalist, in terms of their sociality and interdependence, and their ethical participation in being-in-common as part of a "community economy."

To engage in this project of discursive construction, we have stepped aside from those visions of community economies that draw on a set of prespecified values, such as localism, self-sufficiency, stewardship, or sustainability. We have also distanced ourselves from the way "community" is being drawn into neoliberal economic discourse via "third way" policies that focus on social capital and social entrepreneurship. But one movement that particularly speaks to us, in part because of its confluence with political currents in the World Social Forum and the movement of movements, is that of the "solidarity economy." Principles espoused by exponents of solidarity economies include the use of resources based on needs, management strategies involving democratic processes of cooperation and participation, value placed on collective knowledge and collective work, equal distribution of benefits, and making use of natural resources without depleting them.[25] This is a broad movement, the list of principles is very long, and most of them are things that we support, albeit in the unquestioning fashion of radicals who know the direction "we all" should take. What is disquieting for us is not our unquestioned commitment to certain principles—that emerges from our own situatedness and is something we can't easily dislodge—but the recognition of the emerging outlines of a positive economic ideal, however loosely defined. The solidarity economy offers not just an ethical space of decision, or even one configured around certain abstract coordinates, but a particular ethics—what Foucault might call a morality.[26]

Recognition of economic-being-in-common is a precondition for a politics aimed at building and extending community economic practices. But such a politics confronts the dangers of posing a positivity, a normative representation of the community economy, in which certain practices are valued to the exclusion of others.[27] For instance, the language of the diverse economy recognizes the contemporary prevalence of indentured labor as a form of remunerated labor, and theft as a mode of transaction. Each is a site in which the sociality and interdependency of economic relation is not hidden, but is violently and coercively present. It is difficult to imagine the place of these practices in a discourse of community economy. Yet if we must necessarily "start where we are" to build ethical economies, what is the usefulness of simply judging such practices for their divergence from certain values? It would seem more positive and practical to treat the *existing* situation as a (problematic) resource for projects of *becoming*, a place from which to build something more desirable in the future. Thinking in terms of the ethical coordinates we proposed above, for example, a community might decide that theft is a legitimate mode of redistribution when it involves reclaiming a commons that has been unlawfully taken, as in land, resources, or intellectual property. Likewise indentured labor, for the Migrant Savings for Alternative Investment program (discussed in the Introduction and in chapter 7), is not simply to be condemned and eradicated (though that is one of MSAI's goals) but is also a resource for generating surplus and mobilizing subjects to build community enterprises back home. On what basis might we preemptively exclude or include such activities in strategies of building community economies?

In approaching the task of thought of signifying communism, or for us the community economy, that Nancy sees as still and increasingly open, we must keep in mind that any attempt to fix the fantasy of common being, to define the community economy, to specify what it contains (and thus what it does not) closes off the opportunity to cultivate ethical praxis. Nancy warns that "being-with" lacks symbolic identification. He poses the question of "whether being-together can do without a figure and, as a result, without an identification, if the whole of its 'substance' consists only in its spacing" (2000, 47). This spacing, or space of decision as we have identified it, constitutes the very negativity at the heart of the community economy. It is what makes the practice of building a community economy a process of continual resignification, of repeated traversals of any fantasy that there is a perfect community economy that lies outside of negotiation, struggle, uncertainty, ambivalence, disappointment, one that tells us what to do and how to "be communal."

In her essay, "Recalling a Community at Loose Ends," Linda Singer writes:

> [C]ommunity is not a referential sign but a call or appeal. What is called for is not some objective reference. The call of community initiates conversation, prompts exchanges in writing, disseminates, desires the proliferation of discourse. When one reads the appeal to community in this way, as the call of something other than presence, the problematic posed by the prospect of community shifts to the economy of discourse and articulation. (1991, 125)

Singer is representing community as a call to becoming of something yet to be defined. In light of her view, it seems appropriate that the task of thought we have set ourselves is not that of laying out a normative vision, but in tracing potential coordinates of a space of decision, ones that might alert us to (at least something of) what is at stake in attempting to practice economic being-in-common. We have proposed as topics for conversation the inessential commonality of the community economy with its ad hoc focus on the ethical concerns of necessity, surplus, consumption, and commons. Our call to becoming is a call to begin conversing about that of which we know little, about that which appears at best vague, at worst noncredible, and at all times chimeric.[28] We can only take encouragement from Nancy, who concludes his essay, subtitled "From the Existence of 'Communism' to the Community of 'Existence,'" as follows:

> We have no model, no matrices for this tracing or for this writing. We even think that the novel or the unheard of can no longer come about. But perhaps it is precisely when all signs are missing that the unheard of becomes again not only possible but, in a sense, certain. Here is the historicity of our history and the oncoming of the suspended meaning of the old word "communism." (1992, 393)

5

SURPLUS POSSIBILITIES:
THE INTENTIONAL ECONOMY
OF MONDRAGÓN

We have used the term "intentional economy" to refer to projects that treat economy as a political and ethical space of decision. The term potentially embraces a wide range of actual projects, constituting yet another field of economic diversity. We could think of the planned economies of the state socialist era or the neoliberal projects of today in which the ideal of a naturally self-regulating market sits oddly alongside massive economic intervention. Our own contribution to this nascent taxonomy is the "community economy" of chapter 4, which we understand (somewhat tentatively) as placing the issues of *necessity, surplus, consumption,* and *commons,* in the foreground of ethical deliberation and decision. These abstract terms have a lengthy lineage in economic thought and have been variously specified by many thinkers including Marx, in whose tradition we first encountered them as semiotic forces to be reckoned with. But their saliency for us, their meaningful life, especially with respect to intentional economies, is grounded in our encounter with a concrete particularity—the Mondragón cooperative complex in the Basque region of Spain. It is in thinking about Mondragón that we have found ourselves using these concepts and giving them, if not new meanings, new emphases as ethical lineaments of a practical economic culture.

We are not alone, of course, in finding inspiration in the story of Mondragón's vigorous expansion in the face of both the historical persecution of the Basque people in Spain and a present-day economic orthodoxy that militates against collective experiments. From a social base in the late 1940s that was divided by ideological differences, with physical infrastructure destroyed or depleted by civil war, the Mondragón community, under the guiding philosophy of Catholic priest Father Arizmendiarrieta, has built perhaps the most successful and well-recognized complex of worker-owned industrial, retail, service, and support co-operatives in the world. Today the Mondragón Cooperative Corporation (MCC) is famed for its more than thirty thousand worker-owners, its flexibility and longevity, its cutting-edge technology, and its innovations in worker participation. The Mondragón "commons" involves over one hundred cooperatives, including a bank capitalized by the deposited surplus of the MCC and mandated to initiate and cultivate more co-ops.[1]

Like other actually existing "utopias," Mondragón has been subjected to considerable scrutiny, some of which seems to reflect the desire for an oasis of success in the bleak contemporary landscape of economic politics and some, more negative in tone, the terrible disappointment and consequent wariness engendered by the failed economic experiments of the twentieth century. There is a hypercritical, because deeply invested, attitude toward the evaluation of Mondragón, and a requirement of near-perfection (perhaps applied to all self-proclaimed alternatives?) that no actual instance can possibly meet. More consequential for our project, however, are familiar ways of thinking that render Mondragón inadequate or useless as a guide to local economic experimentation. Its failures and shortcomings are often read as inherent weaknesses of the cooperative form rather than reversible errors, and are frequently taken as evidence of the impossibility of establishing a truly noncapitalist intentional economy in a system dominated by global capitalism.[2] Explanations of the MCC's origins and successes point to circumstances of a unique place and time: in the immediate post–World War II period, Basque isolation and persecution, and particularly the fascist suppression of Basque language and culture, fostered intense group solidarity in the Basque community and prompted a search for noncultural forms of communality; the long boom of Fordist growth after World War II offered a hospitable environment for the consumer durables that Mondragón excelled at producing; and the protection afforded by the Spanish state allowed the small Mondragón firms to grow to maturity under a relatively nurturing trade regime, rather than being hurled into the international market from their inception. No matter what specific explanatory conditions are adduced, the hidden message is that the MCC experience is unique—to a region, to a people, to a historical period—and is therefore not replicable. Indeed, the fact that it hasn't been replicated is taken as evidence that it cannot be.[3]

We have attempted to keep this kind of thinking at bay in approaching Mondragón, exercising theoretical care to maintain its function as a source of inspiration and practical knowledge for building community economies. This has required walking a fine line—attempting to acknowledge what we find problematic in the MCC while refusing to generalize from its (in our view) contingent shortcomings to the necessary deficiencies of cooperatives, refraining from interpreting failure in one dimension (gender equity, for example) as failure of the whole. One might call our reading of Mondragón an ethical practice of weak theory—choosing to view the MCC not as predictably limited and shaped by a capitalist world order, but instead as the complex, surprising, unfinished outcome of innumerable contingent acts and decisions. In light of this choice, the conditions that are seen as fostering Mondragón's success can be read more agonistically as challenges facing the cooperators, ones that they turned to their advantage through considerable ingenuity and effort. Fascist persecution, for example, was attended by deep division rather than automatic solidarity among the Basque population, and the challenge of fostering community was met, in part, by engaging in a collective project of increasing material well-being; Spain's "protectionist" economic isolation was actually a by-product of the shunning of the Franco regime by other European states, and the resultant limited market was something the cooperators might rather not have encountered, despite their manifest ability to deal with it. All the "explanations" of Mondragón, in other words, can be read as challenges successfully faced, rather than as structural or circumstantial guarantors of success.

In the rest of this chapter, we pursue the project of reading Mondragón in terms of decisions taken and challenges undertaken. We offer our reading as a partial counter to a tradition of essentialist or structural (and thus largely negative) readings of cooperative experiments, treating the circumstances confronting the cooperators as they presumably did—as material to be worked with and negotiated, rather than intrinsic obstacles or advantages. At the conclusion of the discussion, we pull out the central themes of the community economy and highlight the contribution of the Mondragón experience to a place-based politics of subjectivation.

ETHICAL THINKING AND PRACTICAL ETHICS

Perhaps the theoretical move that most clearly characterizes our reading of Mondragón is the choice to privilege an ethical rather than a structural vision of economic determination. In this we follow the lead of the cooperators themselves and of Father Arizmendiarrieta, who nurtured the Mondragón project from its earliest days.[4] The many study circles that Father Arizmendi ran prior to the commencement of the first cooperative and that he continued to run throughout his life focused not on economic theory and dynamics, but on the history and practical philosophy of economic self-determination and the values and practices of association and cooperation. Arizmendi's understanding of economic possibility is grounded in a vision of structural indeterminacy, a vision that opens up the economy as a field of responsibility and decision (Laclau 1995, 93). And, indeed, he never stopped urging his fellows and followers to embrace that responsibility, to continually renew their existing projects, to look ahead and establish new ones, and "every day to make a greater commitment to . . . the future economic and social transformation of society" (Whyte and Whyte 1988, 251, quoting a founding cooperator).

Crucial to the enactment of an ethical vision of economy has been a commitment among Mondragón cooperators to ongoing debate and reevaluation of their economic choices in the light of a specified set of ethical principles. The cooperative principles that have guided Mondragón are based on those set out in 1844 by the Rochdale cooperators of Owenite fame. Modified over the years by the International Cooperative Alliance and through the MCC's own experiences (Morrison 1991, 11–12; Ormaechea 1993, 139–86), they incorporate the following values and objectives:

1. *Open admission.* Membership of the Mondragón cooperatives is open to all who agree with the basic cooperative principles.[5]

2. *Democratic organization.* All worker-owners *(socio-trabajadores)* are equal members of the cooperative. Each has one vote in the democratically controlled General Assembly of the enterprise and in the election of members to other governing structures.

3. *Sovereignty of labor.* Control of the cooperatives is in the hands of the worker-owners, and they have a primary role in the distribution of surpluses. There is no distinction made between so-called "productive" workers (direct producers of surplus) and "unproductive" workers (office and sales personnel, who do not produce surplus, but enable its realization and are paid out of distributed surplus). All are assured of the right to determine how surplus will be distributed within and without the cooperative enterprise.[6]

4. *Instrumental and subordinate character of capital (people over capital).* In all instances people are valued over capital, which is seen as "basically accumulated labor and a necessary factor in business development and savings" (Morrison 1991, 11). For example, while the cooperatives require a substantial personal investment by new members, the need for capital does not stand in the way of open admission.[7] This principle ensures that capital does not have an independent existence, imperative, or logic. Returns paid out on capital saved or reinvested in the cooperative system are "just but limited," "not directly tied to the losses or surpluses of the co-ops" (11).

5. *Self-management.* The collective enterprise is managed through democratic participation of all members, based on the free flow of information, access to training, internal promotion for management, consultation, and negotiation about all decisions that affect worker-owners.

6. *Pay solidarity.* Wages are set according to principles of solidarity between workers within each cooperative, between cooperatives, and between cooperators and workers in conventional capitalist enterprises in the region.

7. *Group cooperation.* Cooperation is fostered among individual cooperatives within the same group, among cooperative groups within the MCC, and between the Mondragón cooperatives and other cooperative movements throughout the world.

8. *Social transformation.* Cooperative activities should promote ever greater eco-

nomic and social reconstruction of a Basque society "which is more free, just and solidary" (Ormaechea 1993, 175) through, for example, expansion of employment in the cooperative system.

9. *Universality.* The cooperators act in solidarity with "all those working for economic democracy in the sphere of the 'Social Economy,' championing the objectives of Peace, Justice and Development, which are the essential features of International Cooperativism" (Ormaechea 1993, 180).

10. *Education.* The organization is committed to education about cooperative principles and their dissemination to members, especially among those elected to office in the social and management bodies of the organization, and crucially to young people, the cooperators of the future (Ormaechea 1993, 183).[8]

These principles have been deliberately debated and frequently reinterpreted over the past fifty years in the process of producing specific social and economic outcomes. In all instances, a commitment to the guiding principle of *equilibrio,* which entails seeking a balance between conflicting interests and forces, has come into play in adjudicating differences and difficult choices. In effect, the cooperative principles function as a cultural commons created and drawn upon by the Mondragón cooperators. Commitment to them is part of a practice of subjectivation, the cultivation of a distinctive economic way of being. Working to realize and concretize them is an ethical practice that simultaneously constitutes the cooperators as communal subjects and as members of the Mondragón community.

The title of Roy Morrison's 1991 book, *We Build the Road as We Travel,* suggests the central and active role of ethical decision making in constructing the community economy of Mondragón.[9] The process of construction has involved the making of many difficult choices that establish future pathways and crystallize community values.[10] Not only did the cooperators find themselves up against political and economic forces and circumstances that required continual creative negotiation; perhaps more importantly, they confronted influential traditions of thought and long-standing criticisms and doubts about cooperative practice and viability. In adopting their ethical vision of economy, they were displacing the structural and essentialist visions that have militated against economic experimentation and the exercise of economic freedom. These persist in arguably intensified form today, creating a reluctance to engage in economic experiments because of their perceived futility, or for fear of repression by the all-powerful economy. Respect for the economy's essentialized actors and structural dynamics has become a form of unfreedom, a discursive enslavement, a refusal to explore economic power as unstable and situated (Allen 2003) and as potentially reversible "strategic games between liberties" that are always at hand, if not readily recognizable (Foucault 1988, 19; Hindess 1997, 97–98).

What is particularly fascinating about Mondragón, then, is its success not only in the light of political and economic circumstances, but in the face of the obstacles posed by economic and political *thought* about the viability and sustainability of cooperatives. Revisiting the historical debate about the limits of the cooperativist "way" reminds us of the power to foreclose possibility that lies in reductive forms of thinking. It also provides a backdrop against which to perceive the counterpower of the "ethics of thinking" practiced by Father Arizmendi and his nascent community of cooperators as they worked in their study circles and cooperative enterprises to revive the tender shoots of cooperativism that had been so nearly eliminated in left labor politics and among progressive economic thinkers. Perhaps most important, it suggests, by extension, the importance of an ethics of thinking to the cultivation of political possibility in the economic landscape of today.

LEFT LABOR POLITICS VERSUS COOPERATIVISM

The early denunciation of worker cooperativism by both the trade union and the revolutionary socialist movements has had a dampening effect on ethical debates concerning the economics of experimentation among leftists engaged in a critique of capitalism. In resuscitating the constructive ethical impulse, it is interesting to take a look back at some of the historical debates that have raged among those interested in cooperative economic experiments, either as an antidote or a replacement to capitalist organization. On the contemporary scene, invocations of the "third way" and a "social economy" have given debates over cooperatives and other economic associations renewed social relevance and political purchase (Amin, Cameron, and Hudson 2002; Adaman and Madra 2002).[11]

Against the clearly defined "first way," that is, capitalist consolidation and development during the nineteenth century, there arose multiple resistances and critical currents. The prominent economic theorists and activists, Karl Marx and Robert Owen, stand out among others as inspirations for two divergent streams of thought and practice—revolutionary socialism as a route to communism (the "second way"), and worker cooperativism and community distributism (the original "third way").[12] Both Marx and Owen believed that the rights of the productive and useful persons in a society should be recognized over the inherited and assumed rights of the unproductive and useless aristocracy. Both were exercised by the injustices of "social theft," whereby the surplus labor generated by the "industrious" or working class was appropriated by the nonworking or "idle" class (DeMartino 2003; Geras 1985).

In the emerging working-class movement, the two political aims of challenging the distribution of "rights" and redressing "social theft" were interwoven in the struggles of working people. As Beatrice and Sidney Webb, the influential Fabian socialists and historians of trade unionism in the United Kingdom, point out, the origins of the British trade union movement in the early nineteenth century were closely tied up with demands not only for political democracy and the rights of working men to vote, but also industrial democracy and the rights of working people to cooperative ownership and the control of industry and its product:

> The chief political organisation of the working classes during the Reform Bill agitation began as a trade club. In 1831 a few carpenters met at their house of call in Argyle Street, Oxford Street, to form a "Metropolitan Trades Union," which was to include all trades and to undertake, besides its Trade Union functions, a vague scheme of co-operative production and a political agitation for the franchise. But under the influence of William Lovett the last object soon thrust aside all the rest. The purely Trade Union aims were dropped; the Owenite aspirations sank into the background; and under the title of the "National Union of Working Classes" the humble carpenters' society expanded into a national organisation for obtaining Manhood Suffrage. (Webb and Webb 1907, 140)

The Reform Bill was defeated and the failure to deliver manhood suffrage fueled support for trade union formation in the mid-nineteenth century. The organization of the first Grand National Consolidated Trades Union during 1833–34 was inspired by Robert Owen's vision of national manufacturing companies owned by their workers, all of whom would voluntarily belong to a national federation of lodges. Each lodge was to

> provide sick, funeral and super-annuation benefits for its own workers; and proposals were adopted to lease land on which to employ "turnouts" [laid-off workers] and to set up cooperative workshops. (Webb and Webb 1907, 119)

As the labor movement grew, antagonism increased between pragmatic "Trade Union aims" (defense of workers' standards of living by wage setting and factory legislation to limit working hours) and utopian socialist "Owenite aspirations" (cooperative ownership of industry) (1907, 140). While admiring the ability of Robert Owen to inspire a surge of solidarity for the Grand National Consolidated Trades Union (even among "regiments of agricultural laborers and women"), the Webbs were extremely scornful of the "Utopian side" of his labor policy. Marx expressed similar scorn for the "utopia" of the cooperativist social democratic aspirations influencing the European working-class movement (1972).[13]

Their criticisms were of four kinds. First, there was the lack of a plan for how to *replace* the system of competitive capitalist industry with a system of socialized ownership, cooperation, and voluntary associations of producers. The Webbs asked,

> How was the transfer of the industries from the capitalists to the Unions to be effected in the teeth of a hostile and well-armed Government? . . .

> It is certain that during the Owenite intoxication the impracticable
> expectations of national domination on the part of the wage-earners
> were met with an equally unreasonable determination by the govern-
> ing classes to keep the working men in a state not merely of subjection,
> but of abject submission. (1907, 147–48)

Even the philanthropic mill owners, they note, were utterly resistant to giving up
their despotic control over workers and factories (1907, 147).

The Webbs' critique of Robert Owen's economic politics ultimately rested
on their acceptance that the economy was already (and perhaps always to be)
capitalist:

> In short, the Socialism of Owen led him to propose a practical scheme
> which was not even socialistic, and which, if it could have been carried
> out, would have simply arbitrarily redistributed the capital of the coun-
> try without altering or superseding *the capitalist system* in the least.
>   All this will be so obvious to those who comprehend *our capi-
> talist system* that they will have some difficulty in believing that it
> could have escaped so clever a man and so experienced and successful
> a capitalist as Owen. (1907, 146, emphasis added)

In a somewhat similar vein, Marx takes the German social democratic movement to task in 1875 for their terminology, writing that what they call "present-
day society"

> is *capitalist* society, which exists in all civilized countries, more or less
> free from medieval admixture, more or less modified by the special
> historical development of each country, more or less developed. (Marx
> 1972, 394, emphasis added)

Marx's "scientific" analysis of capitalism's tendencies toward expansion led him
to see what was coming as already "there"—the identity of the economy was unquestionably capitalist. But he was also acutely aware that capitalism was not
yet securely consolidated in a social and demographic sense. In response to the
Lassallian-inspired social democratic call for the "establishment of producer cooperative societies *with state aid under the democratic control of the toiling people*"
(1972, 394, emphasis in the original), Marx rather scornfully notes: "In the first
place, the majority of 'toiling people' in Germany consists of peasants, and not of
proletarians" (393). Rejecting the proposal that all classes other than the working class are *"only one reactionary mass"* (1972, 389, emphasis in the original), he
points to the potential for support from the "artisans, small manufacturers, etc.,
and peasants" (1972, 389). There is an interesting disjuncture between Marx's
empirical understanding of the diversity and magnitude of noncapitalist economic relations coexisting alongside capitalist relations and his belief in systemic
capitalist dominance: "Restricted . . . to dwarfish forms . . . the co-operative sys-

tem will never transform capitalist societies" (Marx 1985, 2, quoted in Mellor, Hannah, and Stirling 1988, 22).[14]

For Fabian and revolutionary socialists alike, the system was unambiguously capitalist (even if yet to fully come into being) and the power of industrial capitalists was already entrenched. To topple it would require the superhuman efforts of a centralized state or a revolutionary movement.[15] Only then might there be a conducive environment for new economic relations. Certainly, in the face of the "realities" of capitalist power, Owen's belief in the transformative effects of pedagogy seemed weak and myopic.[16]

Second, there was faulty *economic analysis* in the view that workers could "raise wages and shorten the hours of labour" to the point where they would get back the "whole proceeds of their labour" (Webb and Webb 1907, 144). This stemmed, according to the Webbs, from the "erroneous theory that labour is by itself the creator of value," that prices could be fixed by labor input alone, and the mistake of overlooking "the more difficult law of economic rent which is the corner-stone of collectivist economy" (147). Here they are referring to the payments for land and other nonlabor requirements of the production process that influence the price/value of the industrial product. Despite their dismissal of Karl Marx and his labor theory of value at this point in the text (147), they inadvertently repeat the exact criticism that Marx makes of the German social democrats when he questions their assertion that workers have rights to the "undiminished proceeds of labor" (1972, 384). Marx is keen to outline the deductions from total social product that will always diminish the portion of surplus product that could be returned to labor—the proportion set aside for expansion of production, the reserve fund for insurance against accidents and other unexpected events, the general costs of administration of production, the social fund to support schools and health services, and the funds to support those unable to work. In the view of both the Fabian and revolutionary socialists, cooperative ownership of the means and output of production did not resolve many of the thorny issues associated with the operations of the economy, specifically distribution of the proceeds of labor.

Third, ownership of the instruments of production by the workers who use them (democracies of producers) brought with it the dangers and temptations of group *individualism*. The Webbs saw a conflict of interest between the workers in a worker cooperative who could act as a "peculiarly 'interested' oligarchy" at odds with the community at large (Webb and Webb 1921, 462–68). If the agricultural union took possession of the land and the miners union the mines, there was danger of sectoral and sectarian interests becoming preeminent. Without adequate governance of the interdependencies of the economy, each trade, which was "but a fragment of the community" (1907, 465), would deteriorate into a Joint Stock Union, no different from a Joint Stock Company, in competition with the others to increase profits. The Webbs mistrusted producers as such and advocated handing the direction of the economy over to the state (representing the com- munity) and to democracies of consumers and citizens (organized into consumer cooperatives) who would keep prices down, advocate ever more efficient produc- tion technologies, and be much more successful in ensuring the "distribution of the inevitable surpluses that we know of as rent and profit equitably among all consumers" (1907, 462).[17]

This set of criticisms has been less developed within the revolutionary so- cialist movement, in which a privileged productionism allows the working class to take precedence over the rest of the community in directing the economy. As Mellor, Hannah, and Stirling note, Marx "clearly saw cooperatives as shin- ing examples of the organization of life under socialism" and he had a "prefer- ence for producer rather than consumer cooperatives" (1988, 22). He was keen to assert the value of the "cooperative factories raised by the unassisted efforts of a few bold 'hands'" as "great social experiments" that concretely demonstrated that *slave, serf,* and *hired* labor were but "transitory and inferior form[s], des- tined to disappear before *associated* labor, plying its toil with a willing hand, a ready mind and a joyous heart" (Marx 1985, quoted in Mellor, Hannah, and Stirling 1988, 23, emphasis added). Issues of individualism and collectivism were traditionally seen through the lens of class struggle, and the collectivism of the workers, while privileged over the individualism of the capitalists, is only ever ambiguously related to that of "the community."[18] The reluctance to deal with the complex politics of class versus community has led to many problems for workerist movements in their relations with issue-based and community-based social movements. It is in this realm of economic politics that the Mondragón case is particularly instructive.

Fourth, there were the *empirical facts* about worker cooperatives—most notably that, in comparison to consumer cooperatives, they seemed not to last.[19] Between the heady days of the 1830s, when trade unionists "aimed at nothing less than the supersession of the capitalist employer" (Webb and Webb 1907, 322) and the institutionalization of trade unions in the latter half of the nineteenth century, a number of cooperative workshops were set up by trade unions "as a means of affording, to a certain number of . . . members, a chance of escape from the conditions of wage-labour" (320). These ventures largely ended in failure and the Webbs' analysis of their lack of success contributed to what became gener- ally known as the "degeneration thesis"—the claim that "over time a democratic, worker-owned firm will tend to fall into decay, chiefly because of declining eco- nomic efficiency but also because of a loss of social dynamism" (Cheney 1999, 17). The diagnosis implied an inherent systemic weakness of the cooperative and human weakness of the cooperator in the face of the "logic of the market and the motivations of capital" (Mellor, Hannah, and Stirling 1988, 67). Marx's comments to the effect that cooperative factories reproduced the defects of the capitalist system (1981, 571) imply that he shared the view that, while indicative of a new mode of production, they could not stand alone and independently "re-produce" themselves (see n. 14).

The historical antagonism between left labor politics and worker coopera-tives continues to have resonance in the present, as do the still prominent views that the cooperative sector is insignificant and unthreatening to the dominant economic order,[20] that cooperatives are unable to build sustainable interdepen-dencies, that they are economically flawed and not really distinguishable from capitalism, that cooperators are prone to the individualistic self-interest of the cooperative, and that cooperatives are short-lived as well as politically conserva-tive and disinterested in solidarity with the more political struggles of the left.[21] What is salient here is a tendency to argue from an essentialist conception of the nature of cooperatives or of workers themselves, and from a structural vision of economic dynamics and development. Essentialist ways of thinking constrict the ethical space of becoming, obscuring possibilities of (self)cultivation and the way that cooperative practice itself calls forth and constitutes its own subjects. Likewise, a structural understanding of economy closes off ethical and political options by offering a limited typology of organizations and practices that can survive and thrive in any particular moment. To these ways of "thinking limita-tion," the experience of Mondragón stands in apparent contradiction, offering the opportunity to counterpose an ethical vision of subject formation and economic eventuation to an essentialist/structuralist reading. Once again the Webbs afford us materials with which to conduct this discursive and political experiment.

ETHICAL PRACTICES OF COOPERATIVISM IN THE MONDRAGÓN COOPERATIVE CORPORATION

In *The Consumers' Co-operative Movement,* Beatrice and Sidney Webb set out specific reasons for "Why democracies of producers fail in organizing produc-tion" (1921, 462–68).[22] Their criticisms stem from a view that the cooperative ideal, as propounded by Owen, for example, called for a "character which had not been formed" (Potter 1891, 29). They had a firm belief that "no man can be trusted to be judge in his own case" (Webb and Webb 1921, 465) and thus pre-dicted that an inevitable conflict of interest would arise between the workers in a cooperative and the community they serve.[23] These arguments are extended from an existing human nature to cooperative organizations and stand as classic objections to worker cooperatives (see Figure 24).

In what follows we examine the seven allegations listed in Figure 24, read-ing each as an ethical issue or challenge that has been addressed by Mondragón cooperators, rather than as a fixed obstacle to cooperativism deriving from human, worker, or cooperative nature. Through examining the actual practice of cooperativism around these challenges, we narrate the development of an in-tentional community economy in Mondragón. In the conclusion to this chap-ter, we highlight the ways that questions of *necessity, surplus, consumption,* and

- The self-governing workshop is inevitably "led to regard its own *product* or its particular function as of more than average importance to the community." (465)

- "[T]he conflict of interest between each self-governing industry or vocation and the community as a whole may appear in the exaction of *pay* above the average, or hours and conditions of work less onerous than those of others." (465)

- It is "perpetually tempted to exact, like the capitalist employer, a *profit* on cost; that is to say, to secure for its own members whatever surplus value is embodied in the price for which it can dispose of its product or service; or to put it in another way, to retain for its own members the equivalent of the advantage of all differential factors in production (such as superiority of soil or site, of machinery or administrative skill) that it controls." (465)

- "[E]very democracy of producers . . . [is] . . . perpetually tempted to seek to maintain existing processes unchanged, to discourage *innovations* that would introduce new kinds of labour, and to develop vested interests against sections of workers." (466)

- The "invidious" problems with "discipline" and the hierarchy of *managers* and producers; "[n]o self-governing workshop, no Trade Union, no Professional Association, no Co-operative Society, and no Local Authority—and no office or industrial enterprise belonging to any of these—has yet made its administration successful on the lines of letting the subordinate employees elect or dismiss the executive officers whose directions these particular groups of employees have, in their work, to obey" (467); "it is a matter of psychology." (468)

- "*[D]isputes* among different vocations and sections of vocations (whether brain workers or manual workers) as to which of them were 'entitled' to particular jobs, have been specially characteristic of every form of association of producers." (466)

- "[T]he tendency to exclusiveness is inherent in any association based on vocation in production . . . [and] . . . just because they are necessarily producing almost entirely not for their own use but for exchange, [they] can normally increase their own incomes, apart from any increase in efficiency in production, by restricting their *membership* and limiting their output in relation to demand in such a way as to enable them to raise the aggregate exchange-value of their product." (466)

FIGURE 24. Extracts from the discussion "Why Democracies of Producers Fail in Organising Production" in Webb and Webb (1921, 462–68, emphasis added).

commons have been addressed in the construction of the Mondragón economy. How these questions are negotiated has implications not only for the form and qualities of the community being created, but for its chances of survival and pathways of reproduction.

PRODUCT

> [T]he self-governing workshop is inevitably "led to regard its own
> *product* or its particular function as of more than average importance
> to the community." (Webb and Webb 1921, 465)

When the first enterprises were established in Mondragón, the cooperators sought to set up the production of commodities not being manufactured in the region (or in Spain). Commitment to an ethic of regional business solidarity influenced the decision not to replicate (and therefore create heightened competition for) businesses already locally established. They began with one cooperative business manufacturing paraffin stoves and progressively established new enterprises producing space heaters and electrical appliances, targeting local and national markets. This strategy worked very well in the consumer-deprived days following the war, when the Spanish economy was both depressed and politically isolated. Prices were protected by the high tariffs on industrial imports that stayed in place until Spain's entry into the European Economic Community beginning in 1986 (Whyte and Whyte 1988, 132).

The commitment of the MCC to the *social transformation* of Basque society through increased employment has led to the proliferation of cooperatives. During the establishment phase, the Mondragón cooperatives developed their own internal markets building backward and forward linkages among cooperatives. As some enterprises became larger, sections of production were spun off as independent entities. The components produced by a new cooperative had an assured market with the old parent firm and the cooperative had the opportunity for expansion by developing new markets, selling to buyers outside the cooperative system.

Strength in the manufacture of domestic white goods thus translated into strength in other product markets, such as machine tools. Most recently a movement into retailing and services is fulfilling the goal of increasing employment. Committed to the principles of *open membership, universality,* and *education,* the hyper and supermarkets, Eroski and Consum, are run as both worker and consumer cooperatives.[24] Consumer members are represented on the governing councils of the cooperative, but are not paid a consumer cooperative dividend. Eroski concentrates instead on "low prices, healthy and environmentally-friendly products and consumer education and advocacy" (Mathews 1997, 12). These enterprises have managed to carve out a significant market niche by offering cooperative membership to all consumers who shop with them, and by utilizing the MCC's internal links to agricultural and commodity producers. Eroski now employs over thirty thousand workers[25] and the chain extends beyond Spain. The Mondragón cooperators have not sought to establish any one product or function as more than of "average importance to the community" (Webb and Webb 1921, 465). The extent of product diversification is remarkable, from agricultural products to capital goods, domestic appliances, and retail services, and has led to the strengthening of the regional economy as a complexly differentiated and networked whole.

PAY

> [T]he conflict of interest between each self-governing industry or vo-
> cation and the community as a whole may appear in the exaction of
> *pay* above the average, or hours and conditions of work less onerous
> than those of others. (Webb and Webb 1921, 465)

The setting of wages (called *anticipos* or an advance) is one of the spaces of freedom open to Mondragón cooperators that has been seriously debated and modified in line with changes in the economic environment.[26] While all members of any one cooperative are democratically involved in the decisions regarding the operations of the cooperative enterprise, decisions about wages are made by the cooperative community as a whole at the Cooperative Congress, the democratically elected governing body of all the cooperatives. This signifies the import placed by the cooperative system on setting the necessary labor payments that influence rates of appropriation[27] and thus the production of cooperative surplus.

A number of principles come to bear here. The identification first and foremost of the cooperatives as a Basque survival strategy meant that they were very conscious of not recreating or instigating divisions within the Basque region.[28] This imperative became institutionalized in the ethic of regional *pay solidarity*. Wages are pegged to a base wage, which is "roughly comparable to that of suitable workers in neighboring Basque industry" (Morrison 1991, 50). This decision reflects a community commitment to ensuring that the Mondragón cooperators do not become a new wealthy "social class" within the region. A similarly informed decision to minimize wage differentials within any cooperative to a ratio of 1:3 between the bottom worker and the top manager was instituted by all the cooperatives (Whyte and Whyte 1988, 44). This ratio has been modified a number of times throughout the history of Mondragón and is currently 1:6.[29]

The decision to set wage levels at the level of the community and not the individual cooperative establishes safeguards against any one group increasing the production of surplus labor in their cooperative by driving wages down below the community-wide level, or jeopardizing the production of surplus by raising wages above this level. The decision to limit the necessary labor payment (thereby maximizing the surplus labor produced) enhances the economic ability to proliferate cooperatives. It also indicates a commitment to valuing community sustainability over and above immediate personal consumption, a commitment evident in many of the aspects of the Mondragón economic experiment.

PROFIT

> [I]t is "perpetually tempted to exact, like the capitalist employer, a *profit* on cost; that is to say, to secure for its own members whatever surplus value is embodied in the price for which it can dispose of its product or service; or to put it in another way, to retain for its own members the equivalent of the advantage of all differential factors in production (such as superiority of soil or site, of machinery or administrative skill) that it controls." (Webb and Webb 1921, 465)

True to the *sovereignty of labor* principle, the cooperative members are owners and first distributors of their profits, or disposable surplus, that is, what is left of their appropriated surplus labor after meeting all the enterprise expenses (involving deductions from surplus for insurance, taxes, new investment in plant and equipment, etc). The members of the General Assembly of the individual cooperative are not, however, at liberty to retain the remainder for their own use, but are in charge of major decisions about how to distribute profits. Certain distributions are determined by the cooperative system as a whole, and one distribution is enforced by Spanish law—the allocation of 10 percent of annual profits to social or charitable institutions. These funds are spent on educational programs conducted in the Basque language, as well as community and public health projects, providing important support for cultural maintenance (Cheney 1999, 87).

In principle, the cooperators have the strategic power to determine how 90 percent of the profit is allocated and it is in this arena of decision making that the strong commitment to *people over capital* and community over individual has increasingly come to the fore. Early on the cooperatives distributed 20 percent of their disposable surplus to a permanent reserve fund of retained earnings to be used for machinery replacement and upgrade. The remaining 70 percent of the profit was distributed on a yearly basis directly as dividends to the cooperators, "who could spend or save it as they chose" (Morrison 1991, 159). It soon became evident that this arrangement would not allow for long-term expansion of the individual enterprise or the wider cooperative system. The decision was thus made to establish internal capital accounts whereby 70 percent (or less) "is distributed to the worker-owners' personal internal capital accounts, apportioned according to number of hours worked and salary grade" (Morrison 1991, 50).[30] The individual worker's capital account earns interest at an agreed upon rate and "(m)embers may draw on the interest accumulated in their accounts, or use the accounts as collateral for personal loans, but the principal cannot normally be touched until they resign or retire" (Mathews 1997, 11). This means that effectively 90 percent of the profit or disposable surplus generated is saved to be reinvested in enterprise development.

In effect, this allocation of funds to "forced savings" has been a crucial enactment of strategic power on the part of the cooperators that has subordinated personal economic gain to the goal of strengthening and diversifying the cooperative system. The individual producers cede their right to directly determine many of the distributions out of appropriated surplus by depositing their individual capital accounts with the Caja Laboral Popular (the Working People's Bank). This institution is a second-degree cooperative (a cooperative of cooperatives) that is controlled by its worker-owners and its members (other cooperative enterprises). The foundation of the Caja Laboral[31] was a key intervention that enabled the economic power of cooperatively produced surplus to be marshaled within the cooperative system as a whole and dispersed in a manner that proliferated the intentional economy of Mondragón:

> The slogan used by the Caja in the early stages of its development was "savings or suitcases," indicating that local savings were necessary in order for there to be local jobs. The Caja also provided a means for the cooperatives to manage the capital held in their permanent reserves and individual capital accounts, so enabling them to retain within the group all of their surpluses other than the 10 percent allocated by law to community projects. (Mathews 1997, 13)

The Caja operates as both a bank and a business development agency. Its Empresarial Division engages in a second-order redistribution of the worker-owners' surplus, deciding where and how to allocate its investments so as to protect and advance the cooperativist vision. It offers low-interest loans to cooperatives and provides business and financial support to new start-up cooperatives (Cheney 1999, 56). The surpluses deposited with the Caja Laboral have also been used to establish a network of other second-degree cooperatives and groups that have provided ongoing support to the "primary" producer cooperatives: Lagun Aro, the social insurance cooperative that provides health care, life insurance, and social security to cooperative members and their families;[32] the education and training cooperatives providing education from preschool to the university level; and Ikerlan and Ideko, the research and development cooperatives that undertake scientific and technical research both for the cooperative businesses and on contract for the noncooperative sector.[33]

The generation of cooperative profit and its deployment into job growth in additional first-degree and second-degree cooperatives and in the provision of social services has, in Mondragón, become a way of sharing the dividends, connecting cooperative members to the wider community, and expanding and strengthening the cooperative community economy.

INNOVATIONS

> [E]very democracy of producers . . . [is] . . . perpetually tempted to
> seek to maintain existing processes unchanged, to discourage *innova-*

tions that would introduce new kinds of labour, and to develop vested
interests against sections of workers. (Webb and Webb 1921, 466)

The Mondragón cooperatives began with modest production processes that were appropriate to the local demand for domestic appliances. But technical education and innovation has always been a keystone of the cooperatives since the early days when the first graduates of the Escuela Politécnica Profesional formed the first cooperative enterprise. MacLeod notes that "the theory as well as the practice [of the Mondragón model] is infused with an almost fierce attachment to the necessity of being on the cutting edge of the most advanced technology available" (1997, 92). He speculates that this commitment to the latest technology might have been influenced by Don José María's impressions of the Spanish civil war in which the idealism of those who came together to support the Republican cause "was no match for the precision and efficiency of Hitler's technology" when the German air force came in to help Franco by bombing the Basques' most ancient and sacred city of Guernica (1997, 94).

Significant investment has been allocated to keep at the developing edge of production technology and methods and this allowed the MCC to become by the mid-1990s

> Spain's largest exporter of machine tools and the largest manufacturer
> of white goods such as refrigerators, stoves, washing-machines and
> dishwashers. It is also the third largest supplier of automotive compo-
> nents in Europe—designated by General Motors in 1992 as "European
> Corporation of the Year"—and a European leader in the supply of
> components for household appliances. (Mathews 1997, 2)

Mainstream technology and production processes have for many years served the primary agenda of building community sustainability, but there is now a commitment to developing environmentally responsible production techniques.

Adherence to the principle of *the instrumental and subordinate character of capital* has meant that technical change is not posed as a threat to the individual cooperator's job. While there is no question that innovation must take place to remain competitive, the cooperatives are designed primarily to gainfully employ people and not only to make profitable returns. With the introduction of new "labor-saving" machinery, workers are deployed to other existing cooperatives or retrained to work in new production processes and paid a maintenance wage. The cost of upholding this principle is met by reallocations of distributed surplus at the level of the individual cooperative and is also supported by the Caja Laboral. During the recession of the 1980s, for example, certain cooperatives increased to 45 percent the distribution to retained earnings to allow for the cost of retooling and upgrading machinery and paying unemployment benefits to laid-off workers, thereby reducing the allocation to individual cooperator accounts. The commitment to keeping enterprises going or changing their purpose so that they can continue to generate a disposable surplus that can build and extend the community has led to an emphasis on efficiency, high productivity, market expansion, and new business growth and product development.

MANAGEMENT

> [T]he "invidious" problems with "discipline" and the hierarchy of *managers* and producers; "No self-governing workshop, no Trade Union, no Professional Association, no Co-operative Society, and no Local Authority—and no office or industrial enterprise belonging to any of these—has yet made its administration successful on the lines of letting the subordinate employees elect or dismiss the executive officers whose directions these particular groups of employees have, in their work, to obey." (Webb and Webb 1921, 467)

Given that the Mondragón operations adhere to the principle of *self-management*, many issues to do with the direction of work and compliance with shop-floor discipline are sidestepped. Indeed this is one of their competitive advantages over conventional capitalist corporations. As Morrison notes, the cooperatives are "not burdened by layers of supervisors and managers who act as enforcers" and who must be paid out of appropriated surplus. Instead, he says, they have "a talented, committed force of worker-owners who can successfully use the new flexible technologies" (1991, 214). Workplace behavior must abide by an agreed-upon disciplinary code that addresses issues of punctuality, absences, and violation of co-op rules, specifying "light, serious and grave" offenses and appropriate punishments (from fines to suspension or expulsion). In a largely self-managed work environment, enforcement of these codes is mainly up to the individual and the immediate work group.[34]

There is still the question of how worker-owners relate to a general manager of the whole enterprise. In Mondragón each cooperative is set up with a number of elected councils that see to day-to-day governance and carry out the decisions made by the annual General Assembly of all cooperators.[35] The governing or directing council is made up of general members elected to a four-year term and is considered to be the most powerful body in the cooperative. It appoints, supervises, and removes the co-op manager, and oversees membership, job classification, accounts, the distribution of profits or losses, financial commitments, and business plans (Whyte and Whyte 1988, 76). The cooperative manager is appointed for a four-year period and may attend governing council meetings as an advisor, but has no vote. The governing council normally meets every morning before the workday begins, and at the conclusion of the meeting the councillors resume their specific jobs within the enterprise (Mathews 1999, 199). In the larger cooperatives a separate management council made up of the top executives and directors of the cooperative meets to formulate policies and plans to be approved by the governing council (Cheney 1999, 59). In these larger enterprises an audit committee keeps watch over the cooperative's financial operations.

Managers earn much less than they would outside the cooperative system, so they are often drawn from within the cooperatives or are young business school graduates brought in from the outside who are keen to participate in the cooperative movement. Some are even hired from traditional capitalist firms. They are "aware that they must succeed in order to maintain their jobs" (Morrison 1991, 74) and that they have to justify their decisions to worker-shareholders, who are much more involved in the business than the conventional shareholder (Bradley and Gelb 1983, 62). "Co-op managers, however, do not live in terror of losing their jobs. It is not a tragedy for a manager to fail; those who are replaced are reintegrated into the co-ops with another assignment" (Morrison 1991, 74).

In addition to the hired general manager, each cooperative has an elected president who is an ex-officio member of the governing council and social council (see the following section on disputes) and is invited to attend the meetings of the management council when there is one. Cheney notes that this dual governance-management structure imbues vitality in the organization and a strong democratic awareness. In his research he found that the two leaders often act as partners in management, with the elected president "typically more conscious of his or her constituencies than is the selected general manager" (1999, 61).

The clear specification of the terms and conditions of management and the individual rights and collective responsibilities of the worker-owners has contributed to one of the most successful systems of worker management in the world. The MCC is host to many study groups from all over the world interested in efficient business and industrial management with a strong emphasis on worker participation.

DISPUTES

> [D]isputes among different vocations and sections of vocations (whether brain workers or manual workers) as to which of them were "entitled" to particular jobs have been specially characteristic of every form of association of producers. (Webb and Webb 1921, 466)

The process of determining working conditions, wage levels, and job classifications in the Mondragón cooperatives has always been pursued outside of the "normal" operations of the labor market or conventional collective bargaining. This is partly because when the cooperatives were first begun, the Franco dictatorship banned membership in trade unions and political parties, though clandestine organizations existed. The commitment to the principles of *pay solidarity, self-management,* and *group cooperation* could also be seen as contributing to an interest in ways of resolving conflicts that do not draw on the us/them ideology of mistrust that has traditionally characterized trade union struggles over industrial relations. Efforts to build a sense of economic community are aimed at transforming the usual class divisions and antagonistic affects that often pertain between management and workers.

Within the cooperatives, social councils are organized to allow the voices of worker-owners *as workers* to be heard. The social council stands alongside the governing council and focuses on monitoring personnel matters, salary grades and advances, health and safety issues, and administering the co-op social funds. It aims to evaluate and possibly counter decisions made by the governing council that might be more influenced by business considerations and, as such, it operates like a union.

Disputes over job classification and reevaluation have indeed occurred in the Mondragón complex of cooperatives, the most famous being the dispute that erupted as the 1974 Ulgor strike. At this time Mondragón was under attack from elements within ETA, the Basque political organization, who saw this "entrepreneurial adventure" as "a disguised form of capitalism, and therefore an obstacle in the way of the proletarian revolution" (Whyte and Whyte 1988, 92–93). Criticism of the social councils was particularly strong, which were seen by the militant left as none other than a "bourgeois parliament," a "faithful servant and legitimate child of the system which gives rise to it" (Whyte and Whyte 1988, 93, quoting Azurmendi). ETA agitation within the cooperatives saw attempts to mount strikes in the early 1970s and the response by the governing council at the Ulgor plant was to distinguish "sympathy strikes" in support of labor causes in the wider Basque region from "internal strikes" focused on issues that could be raised and resolved with the social council. The latter were defined as attacks on the cooperative and subject to penalties and discharge (92).[36] The Ulgor cooperative had grown into a large and bureaucratic organization with 3,500 employees and management had recently implemented job reclassifications and individual merit ratings for shop-floor workers. These moves were met with misunderstanding, resistance, and ultimately a strike, resulting in the expulsion of the ringleaders. The whole experience caused a major rethinking within the cooperative complex and prompted many changes. One was the decision to limit the size of future enterprises, where possible, to around five hundred, so that high levels of communication could be maintained among the workforce.

Job classifications and individual performance goals are important, as not only do they translate into particular wage levels, but this in turn affects the share of cooperative dividends paid to the worker-owner. It is not surprising, therefore, that maintaining the commitment to solidary principles has not always been easy for the cooperators.[37] The strength of Mondragón has been its willingness to openly and democratically discuss these issues, to reflect on past mistakes, and to constantly change to sustain the original vision.

MEMBERSHIP

> [T]he tendency to exclusiveness is inherent in any association based on vocation in production. . . . [and] . . . because they are necessarily producing almost entirely not for their own use but for exchange, [they] can normally increase their own incomes, apart from any in-

> crease in efficiency in production, by restricting their *membership* and
> limiting their output in relation to demand in such a way as to enable
> them to raise the aggregate exchange-value of their product. (Webb
> and Webb 1921, 466)

As the history of Mondragón shows, the cooperatives have not displayed exclusiveness on the basis of production or vocation. On the contrary, they have expanded into multiple production lines and industries, building connections between workers of all trades and skills across a diversified economy within the Basque region of Spain. Output has been expanded rather than limited in relation to demand, and prices of Mondragón-produced commodities have been kept competitive with those of commodities produced within capitalist firms. Until recently, membership has been available to all who worked in a cooperative enterprise and wage levels have been regulated in line with the principles of *open membership* and *pay solidarity*. Many of the dangers of exclusivism or group individualism have been mediated by the principles and ethical practices elaborated above.

Today, one of the pressing challenges facing the MCC is related to this question of membership and market competitiveness. Mondragón watchers have drawn attention to the phenomenal growth of the cooperative corporation in the late 1980s, when it was initially adapting to the international market, and during the 1990s, when it reorganized the corporation along sectoral lines and commenced aggressive strategies to defend and increase its market position by establishing production sites outside the Basque region and in international locations (Cheney 1999; Clamp 2000).[38] In the ten years between 1992 and 2003, employment grew from 25,322 to 68,260. Most of the new employees were non-cooperators (www.mondragon.mcc.es).

The expansionist strategy within Spain and especially within the Basque region has been accompanied by a vigorous program of education and conversion to cooperative membership. But in the growing number of joint ventures, acquired firms, and start-ups outside of Spain, the workforces are wholly or partly composed of contract-based or non-owning employees. Foreign plants have been acquired or established both to access and cater to overseas markets (for example, in Morocco and Argentina to produce and supply domestic appliances) and to access cheaper labor and remain competitive in international markets (for example, in the components sector by locating a plant in Thailand) (Clamp 2000, 566, 568). The expansion strategy is pursued primarily to protect cooperative employment and operations in the Basque country by maintaining markets and competitiveness. Indeed, where possible the research and development arm of the corporation aims to "develop substitute technologies that enable the MCC to return manufacturing operations from overseas to the Basque region," thereby sustaining employment locally (Clamp 2000, 562).[39]

Clearly Mondragón has reached a juncture where, as Cheney observes, "the cooperatives have now far exceeded their founders' expectations of financial success, resources, geographic reach, and power" (1999, 72). It is important to highlight that the success of Mondragón has not been bought by their "democracy of producers" at the expense of the community from which they are drawn, nor from the citizens and consumers, both local and international, that they serve. But it cannot be denied that today the cooperators are facing new ethical dilemmas that have to do with the scale and reach of the economic justice they are keen to promulgate.[40] While cooperative membership is restricted at present by the capacity of the production system to generate continuing positions (not for the purpose of limiting output and sending prices up, as the Webbs predicted) employment of wage workers in the MCC is rising. The questions currently being debated within the MCC with respect to internationalization, growth, membership, and its cooperativist identity are of the utmost importance.

True to its principles of *universality* and *social transformation,* the MCC has always operated within an international community of cooperativist solidarity *and* a locally emplaced Basque community, which it seeks to make "more free, just and solidary" (Ormaechea 1993, 175). It maintains a strong role in international education about cooperatives and solidarity with the international cooperative movement, as is evident in its outreach programs and substantial financial contributions to the International Cooperative Alliance. But the MCC is not yet involved in education and conversion in its foreign plants. In response to "frequently asked questions" about this issue, the Mondragón Web site offers the following explanations:

> [T[he lack of adequate co-operative laws in the areas into which we have expanded; the fact that many new companies have been set up as part of a joint venture with other partners; and, above all, the fact that the creation of co-operatives requires the existence of co-operative members who understand and are committed to the co-operative culture, something which is impossible to obtain over a short period of time and in such a wide variety of locations. (www.mondragon.mcc.es)

The MCC's commitment to sustainability has led to a privileging of the Basque community economy and an attempt to stay true to the guiding principle of *people over capital* in the Basque region (maintaining sustainable employment) while engaging in operations elsewhere along mainstream business lines (where capital rules over people). Having a clear sense of which community is being sustained by what economic practices inevitably involves facing up to exclusions and violences and debating their acceptability at any one moment. But Cheney argues that the interest in international expansion is somewhat unexamined on the part of the cooperators (1999, 78) and cautions that "[i]n an effort to engage the market completely on its own terms, they may be unduly sacrificing the long-valued 'buffer zone' between them and the turbulence of the international market" (79). What Cheney seems to be suggesting is that the cooperators may be failing to exercise their central principle of *equilibrio,* in this case the need to balance their commitments to *universality* and *pay solidarity* with the apparent dictates of the market. Like the rest of us, they may be falling into a view of structural economic imperatives that leave no room to move, rather than adhering to their long-standing practice of ethically negotiating the difficult challenges they encounter.[41]

For us, the issue of the growth of noncooperator employment within the Mondragón workforce (currently approximately 50 percent) is particularly salient because we have understood Mondragón as a successful example of the sustainability of noncapitalist class relations. Whereas capitalism involves an exploitative class process in which surplus (labor or product) is appropriated by nonproducers, Mondragón has historically been a site of a nonexploitative communal class process in which the surplus is appropriated and distributed by the community of producers. In appropriating the surplus of noncooperators as well as their own, some cooperators are participating in both exploitative and nonexploitative class processes; they are "becoming capitalist" as well as communal subjects, and their firms are becoming communal-capitalist hybrids (Levin 2003). They may see this as a choice to abridge their principles of the *sovereignty of labor, self-management,* and *pay solidarity* for some laborers, who are presumably temporarily employed. But we have tended to see this move as involving an extensive engagement in capitalist relations of exploitation, a hybridization that makes the MCC "noncooperative" as well as cooperative, and a shift that is threatening to the very identity of Mondragón.[42] Exercising some care in our thinking on this topic, we have had to acknowledge our identitarian investment in the noncapitalist "purity" of the MCC and our disappointment in this change, while at the same time recognizing that the change is neither total nor irreversible. Mondragón is still a complex of cooperatives and its future is still open. And though we may not like it, the MCC may have been strengthened through marshaling surplus from noncooperators as well as cooperators, and using that surplus to create more cooperative employment back home.

What we see here could be understood as the Mondragón cooperatives succumbing to "group individualism," one of the dangers of the cooperative form identified by the Webbs. But what it brings home to us is the importance of how we think about it, and indeed about all of the Webbs' and others' objections to cooperatives, whether or not they seem applicable to Mondragón. It is not that product, pay, profit, innovation, management, disputes, membership (and a host of other issues) are unimportant for co-ops. The point is simply that they are objects of struggle, rather than necessary points of weakness or failure.

The story of Mondragón's intentional economy offers important empirical evidence against the degeneration thesis that has plagued cooperativist experimentation, suggesting that there is no logical imperative toward cooperative failure. It demonstrates various ways that cooperatives can navigate the "perpetual temptations" of individualism that the Webbs pinned on the "self-governing workshop," suggesting that any such inevitability is likely to be a function of the absence of debate about what it means to act as communal or cooperative subjects. And while "group individualism" seems to have emerged in a major instance, its pitfalls have been avoided in many others, through active discussion and ethical commitment to principles of solidarity. The point is not that individualism poses no threat, but that it is a threat to be met by performing community. It seems that long-term success (even an excess of success) of a system of worker-owned co-operatives is indeed possible if economic practices are scrutinized and modified in the light of fidelity to the community, its principles, and its evolving forms.

ECONOMICS, POLITICS, AND THE MONDRAGÓN WAY

As an antidote to structural and humanist pessimism about the viability of co-operatives, we have offered an extended discussion of the ethical decisions taken by the Mondragón cooperators in their efforts to consolidate what arguably stands as the most successful cooperativist regional economy in the world. But what remains to be emphasized in this discussion are the specifically economic dimensions of Mondragón's success. Mondragón was our first and theoretically formative encounter with what we have come to call a "community economy," and it presented (and thus helped us to delineate) the core concerns of a sustainable economic community: necessity, surplus, consumption, and commons. Among these four dimensions, we have always found Mondragón's practices of surplus management particularly compelling.

Coming into being in the 1950s, Mondragón was captured by an industrial economic imaginary in which productivity growth in manufacturing and expanding markets for goods guaranteed the steady enlargement of output and income. Community well-being was to be assured through the expansion of employment and the payment of wages to cover the elements of worker consumption. All this did not distinguish Mondragón from capitalist models of industrialization. But the growth of surplus attendant upon successful industrial development had a different meaning for Mondragón, where the cooperators in each cooperative appropriated their surplus communally. This meant that they also took the first decision about how it was to be distributed. Rather than dispersing it to distant shareholders or paying out large bonuses to managers, as capitalist firms were likely to do, Mondragón cooperators distributed their surplus (after taxes and other deductions) to the cooperative in the form of retained earnings and to themselves in the form of dividends to worker-owners. They then deposited these dividends in the Caja Laboral, in effect marshaling distributed surplus over the entire community. The potentiating and proliferative force of this pooled surplus is starkly and inspiringly manifest in the rapid development of the cooperative complex.[43]

Choices made in the dimensions of necessity and consumption have supported the strategy of enlarging and pooling surplus to finance cooperative growth.[44] The decisions to peg wages at a socially acceptable but modest level and to keep wage differentials to a minimum have privileged surplus generation over individual consumption, increasing the freedom to construct a very different kind of economy.[45] Allowing the community to oversee the use of the cooperatives' distributed surpluses has created a generative commons, a source of funds for sustaining and expanding the community of cooperators while at the same time contributing to individual wealth through the payment of interest on personal accounts. And while industrial cooperative growth has been a priority, this goal has been balanced with that of increasing social well-being, not only through paying adequate wages, but through developing cooperatives in the areas of housing, health care, pension management, education, and social services.

The process of marshaling surplus and directing it toward the expansion of a cooperative economy is intricately connected with the becoming of ethical communal subjects. Indeed Mondragón's greatest achievement could be seen as the construction of communal subjects via methods that operate on a range of material, social, cultural, and spiritual levels, but especially through the experience of ethical decision making around issues of individualism and collectivity. This is one of the areas in which the Mondragón experience affirms Owen against the Webbs, who wonder "where, in the wide world, could Robert Owen discover a body of associates . . . who had inherited or acquired characters fit for the difficulties of associated life and self-government?" (Potter 1891, 29). Owen believed that people could remake themselves through education—a belief skeptically rendered by the Webbs as "boundless" (1907, 146)—and imagined a considerable amount of that education taking place through simply living and working together. In his early years as a Mondragón curate, Father Arizmendi brought this Owenite associative vision to life. Though the initial cooperative was not established until 1956, he spent the years after his arrival in 1941 setting up youth groups, a medical clinic, and athletics and soccer clubs; teaching in the apprenticeship program of the largest company in town, Union Cerrajera; setting up an independent technical school, Escuela Politécnica Profesional;[46] and conducting more than two thousand study circles on social, humanist, and religious topics (Whyte and Whyte 1988, 29-32).[47] As the MCC matured, the co-ops themselves became the central arena of self-cultivation, but they have never fully taken over from the formal and informal educational and associative infrastructure initially developed by Don José María.

It may seem that Father Arizmendi was an anomalous twentieth-century thinker, sequestered in Mondragón, drawing his inspiration from the previous century and lacking affiliation with any recognized movement. But a closer look at Catholic thinking and practice in the 1940s and 1950s reveals a widespread tradition of social Catholicism and a band of worker-priests who pursued the project of transforming industry from within. These individuals organized study groups to encourage workers to see themselves as agents of industrial, and ultimately social, transformation (Mathews 1999, 189). Though ostensibly isolated in Mondragón, and perhaps more radically transformative in his vision, Arizmendi was animated by this contemporary discourse and practice of economic possibility, which circulated worldwide through the church and its radical followers. He and the cooperators who emerged under his tutelage could be seen as part of a place-based global movement, one that shared a transformative social and economic vision. The power they were bringing to bear was situated, collective, associational—the power of mutual action (Allen 2003, 53, citing Hannah Arendt). The economies they were creating in place were animated by the co-constitution of communal subjects and organizations. The economic and political imaginary that grounded their efforts was ultimately pluralist, reflecting the desire to proliferate rather than foreclose possibility:

> In the mind of the co-operators is the idea that future society probably must be pluralist in all its organizations including the economic. There will be action and interaction of publicly owned firms and private firms, the market and planning, entities of paternalistic style, capitalistic or social. Every juncture, the nature of every activity, the level of evolution and the development of every community, will require a special treatment . . . not limited to one form of organization if we believe in and love man, his liberty, and justice, and democracy. (Arizmendiarrieta, quoted in Whyte and Whyte 1988, 239)

It is in this pluralist spirit that we have taken Mondragón as our inspiration (rather than model) for the intentional community economy and the political and ethical project of its institution.

6

CULTIVATING SUBJECTS FOR
A COMMUNITY ECONOMY

In the local action research projects in which we have attempted to awaken and implement different (noncapitalist) economic possibilities, we have ultimately found ourselves engaged in what might be called "a politics of the subject." What this means to us minimally is a process of producing something beyond discursively enabled shifts in identity, something that takes into account the sensational and gravitational experience of embodiment, something that recognizes the motor and neural interface between self and world as the site of becoming of both. If to change ourselves is to change our worlds, and the relation is reciprocal, then the project of history making is never a distant one but always right here, on the borders of our sensing, thinking, feeling, moving bodies.

History making signals itself through "changes in the way in which we understand and deal with ourselves and with things," in other words, how we "operate," holistically understood as a world-making process (Spinosa et al. 1997, 2). As Spinosa, Flores, and Dreyfus see it, history-making acts involve the emergence of new "disclosive spaces," that is, "organized set(s) of practices for dealing with oneself, other people, and things that produce a relatively self-contained web of meanings" (17). Their example of the impact of feminism is compelling and resonates with our conception of a politics of the subject, discussed in the Introduction:

> In the recent past, the feminist movement in the United States has been
> history-making. Watching a Marilyn Monroe movie made in the 1950s

underscores how our perception of women has changed. However little some things may have changed—full justice for women has not been achieved, patriarchy has not been eliminated, women are not commonly seen as exemplary representatives of as many skill domains as men—watching a woman defer to a man's authority simply because of his gender evokes distaste in most of the West, a distaste that generally crosses gender, class, and race lines.

We are not saying that feminism has been history-making because it has changed the reflective judgments we make about women, though it obviously has. Rather, feminism has changed the way we see women prior to our reflective judgments. (1997, 2)

For us a politics of the subject addresses not only the emptiness of the subject that is the ultimate ground of our ability to change, but also the fullness beyond the level of conscious feeling and thought: whatever enables us to act prior to reflection, the habitual, the embodied knowledge, the ways of being in the world that we almost never think about. This fullness presents a close-in if also unbounded "subject-world," and there is growing interest in how such worlds change, how people come to inhabit new "disclosive spaces" or "microworlds" (Varela 1992), how subject (re)construction takes place.

In previous action research with women in Australian mining towns, we had tried to generate a new discourse of mining town work to supplement or supplant existing discourses, ones that limited women to the identities of "country woman" or "miner's wife" and allowed little room to move politically (Gibson-Graham 1994b). Over the course of the project we jointly produced with the women co-researchers a discourse of "mine shift work" that enabled self-recognition of their problematic auxiliary role as domestic supports to over-scheduled male partners. This emergent discourse constituted a new right and possibility of intervening in the industrial decision-making process that was formerly reserved for companies and unions (Gibson 1992, 1993). Unfortunately the research process was limited in scope by time and access to the fieldwork site, so we did not engage in nurturing new political subject-worlds anchored in the identity of the "mine shift-worker's wife." We were therefore never forced to confront the limits of a poststructuralist politics of identification—that the body has a "mind" of its own, that there might be resistance to new identities, attachments to old ones, unconscious refusals to change, fears of symbolization. In our subsequent more long-term action research interventions, these challenges of the "reluctant subject" were to rise up to face us and to shape how we pursued and conceptualized a new politics of community economic development.

We were initially confident that subjects were not totally "subjected," but had some latitude to undertake new subject positions and entertain new modes of being. Certainly "the obviousness of social identities" that had been seen to be determined by social structures was called into question by poststructuralist theory:

If agents were to have an always already defined location in the social structure, the problem of their identity, considered in a radical
way, would not arise—or, at most, would be seen as a matter of people
discovering or *recognizing* their own identity, not of *constructing* it.
(Laclau 1994, 2)

But exactly what might the process of "constructing" a subjectivity entail? The
decisive role of alternative discourses and new opportunities for subject identification is clear, but so too are the limits to the discursive constitution of subjects.
And the mechanics of subject movement remain a matter for theoretical speculation. While Foucault is instructive about the importance of ethical practices of
self-cultivation, he is less so about the actual techniques that might be brought to
bear on the elusive project of changing the self.

In a series of essays that explore the "praxis of ethical learning," Francisco
Varela outlines two very different traditions that have been concerned with the
"pragmatics of human transformation"—the Western tradition of psychoanalysis
and the Eastern teaching traditions (1992, 63, 64). Both offer insights into what
the action research process can or might be. Importantly, they address the interface between discourse/mind and materiality/body, pointing to the fascinating
possibilities of working at this intersection. Focused on the self and on individual
transformation, psychoanalysis has pioneered techniques of working with the
unconscious, the ego, and the drives, prompted by and in relation to the analyst. In Varela's view, the analytic process explodes the "self into pieces" and,
in the therapeutic space of analysis, suspends the desire to reconstitute the self
in old ways (64). From a Lacanian perspective, the role of the analyst is to inter-
rupt the analysand's project of shoring up her fantasies, which lock her into fixed
structures of desire and identity. An interruption by the analyst can provoke the
analysand's curiosity and begin the exploration that unravels fantasy and reveals
it for what it is.[1]

What the analysand achieves in a "successful" analysis is not a truly postfantasmatic condition (since fantasy is the mode of integration of the subject
into the symbolic order and the anchor of identification), but a more distanced
and reflective relation to fantasy. Sometimes called "traversing the fantasy," this
new positioning brings a different relationship to both identity and desire—less
trapped and invested, more aware of and open to possibilities of change. Identity
becomes less something to be policed and maintained than a site of becoming
and potential connection.[2] Desire is set in motion again, though with somewhat
less force, and disappointment is distanced from disillusion.

The Lacanian subject of Laclau and Mouffe is energized by an emptiness
or lack that pushes it to identify and signals an ever-present openness to the
resignifying project of hegemonic politics. What we have drawn from psychoanalysis, however, is not only the empty subject, but a recognition that attachment to an identity, and to particular subject-worlds, is cemented by enjoyment

and frustrated desire. The pleasurable hold of an identity on the body/mind is what pushes back at any attempt to cultivate subjects for a community economy. It would seem that it is only if this grasp can be loosened and the function of identity as ego support can become virtually irrelevant that a politics of becoming (communal) can emerge.

The Eastern teaching traditions of Confucianism, Taoism, and Buddhism offer a different set of transformation practices, or disciplines of the self, in which embodied actions are undertaken so as to constitute new microworlds of affect and behavior. Buddhism, for instance, offers ethical training in disciplines "that facilitate the letting go of ego-centered habits and enable compassion to become spontaneous and self-sustaining" (Varela 1992, 73). Foucault's interest in "care of the self" resonates with these practices. As Agamben points out, Foucault "often states the apparently opposite theme . . . the self must be let go of" (2004, 117). This prompts Agamben to ask:

> What would a practice of self be that would not be a process of subjectivation but, to the contrary, would end up only at a letting go, a practice of the self that finds its identity only in a letting go of self? It is necessary to maintain or "stay," as it were, in this double movement of desubjectivation and subjectivation. (117)

If the "art of living is to destroy identity, to destroy psychology" in Agamben's paraphrase of Foucault, we can recognize here one of the paradoxical formulations of Buddhism. At the same time that Buddhist practice cultivates the emptiness of self, meaning freedom from ego and the pulls of desire and aversion, it also cultivates the positive capacities of the self to be virtuous—loving, compassionate, happy in the happiness of others, responding with equanimity to life's constant changes, however uningratiating.[3] These qualities are cultivated through awareness and reflection, patient practices that involve observing feelings and thoughts and letting go of the negative ones nonjudgmentally, while receptively fostering and nurturing the positive. As a discipline of the body/mind, for example, the practice of lovingkindness requires consciously abiding in the heart, extending friendly feelings first to oneself and then radiating them outward in ever widening circles to eventually embrace all sentient beings (Varela 1992). What Buddhist practice offers, then, is not unlike the fruits of psychoanalysis: less investment in the self of ego and identity, greater openness to change (in the self and world), and enlarged capacities for joy and connection.

We have recognized in both the psychoanalytic and the Buddhist traditions the attention paid to aspects of subjectivity that exceed the identities emphasized by poststructuralism, as well as their acknowledgment that self-transformation is both possible and problematic, requiring social spaces and ongoing practices devoted to self-development. In our action research projects, we have been interested in promoting different ways of inhabiting the economy, of being economic subjects in a community economy, of taking action with others to shape economic possibilities. But we have become very aware of the limitations that existing sub-jectivities, particularly those associated with economic subject positions, place on movement and transformation. As we have experienced both ambivalence and resistance in ourselves and our community co-conversants, consciously and unconsciously we have drawn on insights from the psychoanalytic and Buddhist traditions to create strategies that enabled opening to change.[4]

What is presented here is a processing after the fact. Any semblance of co-herence is a product of the writing process and does not reflect the ways that these methods and techniques, if they can be called that, were implemented. In that we were taken by surprise on numerous occasions by the unsayable, the bodily and the affective, the excesses of pleasure and experiences of pain, our reactions and reflections are those of novice practitioners of a post-poststructuralist practice, led on by our ignorance and naivete and the honesty and resilience of our co-researchers in the community.

OUR ACTION RESEARCH PROJECTS

Wary of producing a private language of diverse economies (which seemed a project of childhood or even of madness), we felt from the outset the need to enter into conversations with people who were willing to entertain the idea of a different economy. We found those people in different settings—the Latrobe Val-ley east of Melbourne in Australia (see chapter 2), the Pioneer Valley of western Massachusetts in the United States and, more recently, the southern Philip-pines islands of Bohol (Jagna Municipality) and Mindanao (Linamon Munici-pality) (see chapter 7). In our research interactions, we hoped to *speak* and *hear* richer, more vibrant economic dialects, to explore and develop our rudimentary language of economic difference, to construct alternative economic representa-tions, to cultivate subjects for a community economy, and ultimately perhaps to build a linguistic and practical community around new economic projects and possibilities. In each site, the action research process has followed a series of steps that reflect these concerns (see Figure 25).

In this chapter we draw on stories from the projects undertaken in the late 1990s and early 2000s in the Latrobe Valley in Australia and the Pioneer Valley in the United States.[5] Much of the work on both projects was performed by "com-munity researchers" who were local people, many of whom had no prior experi-ence with research of any kind. In the Latrobe Valley Community Partnering Project, we chose to work with those who were most marginal to the mainstream vision of an economically and socially "developed" region—retrenched electrici-ty workers, unemployed young people, and single parents—and the community researchers were recruited from these groups. After they responded to advertise-ments in the local press, four people were hired part-time for one year to work in the community with others to form community-based enterprises. The academ-ic research team was joined by Leanne, a twenty-one-year-old first-generation Italian-Australian woman who was working part-time in a video shop but wanted

Step 1. Tracking practical economic knowledge in each region by convening focus groups with key participants in the local economic development conversation—planners, government officials, labor and business leaders—and key participants in local community development—NGO workers, social workers, service providers, religious and community leaders.

Step 2. Acknowledging the positives and negatives of existing representations by documenting the stereotypes of the region and its people and days in the lives of people differently situated within the local economy. Presenting these findings in visual form (e.g., photo essays or PowerPoint presentations) to be used as conversation starters to highlight two different paths for mobilization—the half-empty, needs-based, victim pathway or the half-full, assets-based, enacter pathway.

Step 3. Generating new representations via a "community economic audit" of nonmainstream, traditional or undervalued economic activities. This stage is really the heart of each project. It is conducted in collaboration with community researchers drawn from the alternative economic sector or from economically marginal or undervalued populations (the unemployed, housewives/husbands, recent immigrants, welfare recipients, retirees, youth, etc.). The audit is not intended to be exhaustive, but to delineate the range of economic activities in the region and to provide a setting in which to reframe individual economic identities with the acknowledgment that all people make a contribution to the diverse economy. In each project we trained the community researchers to engage in individual interviews that formed the basis for alternative economic representations. These interviews and the training and debriefing workshops that preceded and followed them created the social space in which an alternative discourse of economy could emerge.

Step 4. Documenting inspiring examples of community economic enterprises or activities. The purpose of these short case studies is to illustrate the variety of ways of populating the community economic landscape and provoke the desire to be a part of it. The case studies also provide insights into the "how to" of building community economies and raise the issue of how to promote linkages and synergies between alternative projects. Types of activities and organizations studied include cooperatives, self-employed individuals, worker collectives, family businesses, progressive or alternative capitalist firms, households, intentional communities, a food bank and community farm, alternative currency and barter networks, volunteer and other community organizations.

Step 5. Creating spaces of identification in which community researchers, community members, local institutions, and the research group itself could begin to imagine becoming actors in the community economy, identifying with various economic subject positions such as cooperator, gift giver, alternative capitalist, and so forth. These spaces included field trips, social events, displays, community brainstorming workshops and specialized "how to" workshops, public presentations, large community conferences, and face to face conversations.

Step 6. Acting on identifications within the community economy in which various groups formed to begin to build enterprises, organizations and community economic practices. In all sites this stage was the longest lasting and is on-going at the time of writing. In the projects steps 1 through 5 were conducted over a period of from three to twelve months while step 6 was differently supported by the projects in each site. In the Latrobe Valley this step initially involved eighteen months of input from the project team and has continued for three years since the project formally ended. In the Pioneer Valley this step has largely been conducted in the years since the project formally ended and has involved a number of the original project workers in an independent and voluntary capacity. In the Philippines there is provision for this step to be overseen by the project for two to three years.

FIGURE 25. Methodological steps of the action research projects. The methodologies are documented in more detail in Graham, Healy, and Byrne (2002) for the Pioneer Valley and Cameron and Gibson (2001, 2004) for the Latrobe Valley. See also www.communityeconomies.org.

full-time employment; Yvonne, a thirty-four-year-old single mother with two school-aged daughters; and Stephen and Alan, two middle-aged unemployed ex-electricity industry workers, one of whom had been a union official.

In the Pioneer Valley Rethinking Economy project, we trained seventeen community researchers and paid them to conduct interviews with friends and acquaintances who participated in the noncapitalist sectors of the diverse economy over a period of a few months. The community researchers were recruited via a range of networks and included a local artisan, six high school students, a number of intermittently or self-employed individuals, two retired people, a high-school dropout, a maintenance worker, two social-service providers (one who works with drug users and one who assists recent immigrants), and people involved in volunteering. They were young and old, pale and colorful, gay and straight, Latino and Anglo, male and female, speakers of EFL and ESL, well-educated and less so, drawn from all over the Pioneer Valley.

The participatory action research was designed and directed by ourselves and our academic colleagues.[6] Invariably questions about power and research ethics have been raised in connection with the projects. Some have expressed concern that because of our partisan interest in alternative economies, the research design has involved "manipulation" or possibly "indoctrination" of research subjects. There is suspicion that our attempt to bring diverse economic practices into visibility and encourage construction of community enterprises has "engineered" the very responses that support our thesis. To this last accusation, we plead guilty. Our research interventions can be seen as a form of ethical political action.[7]

In its traditional guise, participatory action research tries to break down the power differential between the researched and the socially powerful by enabling the oppressed to become researchers of their own circumstances (Freire 1972). In our poststructuralist participatory action research, we accept that power can never be banished from any social process. Power circulates in many different and incommensurate ways and there are always *multiple* power differentials at play (Allen 2003). From the outset, we saw our projects as aimed at mobilizing desire for noncapitalist becomings. What we came to recognize is that desire stirs and is activated in embodied interactions and settings in which power circulates unevenly and yet productively across many different registers of being.

Early on in the training of community researchers in the Pioneer Valley we stumbled onto something that alerted us to the fickle nature of power and desire. In our initial attempt to engineer an "equal" interchange between the academics with "formal knowledge" and the community members with "embodied knowing," we never offered a textbook definition of the economy or of capitalism, but spent a lot of time demystifying the economy, showing the contradictions in mainstream representations and conceptions. In hindsight, we realized that this withholding on our part, rather than creating a pure space of equality, was contaminating the research process with power in interesting ways. It made us intriguing, attaching the community researchers to us and to the mysteriousness of our formal knowledge and desires.

Gabriela, one of the academic researchers who had been a Lacanian analyst in her native Bolivia, understood this in terms of the relationship between analyst and analysand. The goal of the analyst is not to become the analysand's equal, but to move the analysand away from the project of shoring up their fantasies and into the difficult process of analysis—producing "truth," in other words, a different, more distanced relation to fantasy. To get the analysand interested in this process, the analyst must come to inhabit the space of desire, which is what we were inadvertently doing in the project. Our refusal to define the economy or capitalism had the effect of making our knowledge desirable.

We began to see the "inequality" between academic and community researchers as constitutive of our work, rather than as a hindrance or detraction. The relationship between academic and community member was eroticized by inequality, in other words, by the way "they" invested our peculiar status and formal knowledge with power, and this is in part what made our conversations work. A seductive form of power drew them to us and our project, even as it prompted them to mock, berate, or belittle the university and those working within it. We realized that, far from attempting to achieve a pristine interaction untainted by power, our project needed to mobilize and direct power, and to make sure that it was used to foster rather than kill what we hoped to elicit—passionate participation in the project.

The brief summary of the steps of our action research contained in Figure 25 conveys little insight into the events in thought and the shifts in affect and subjectivity that our venture into "the field" produced. In what follows, we reflect on the complex and challenging process of cultivating new subjects in place, drawing on selected stories from both projects. Our reflections have been weakly theorized in the following terms:

- discursive destabilization;
- encountering resistance and nonrecognition;
- reframing and renarrativizing;
- producing positive affect; and
- creating spaces of identification and ethical openings to communality.

In each section, we highlight those moments when we observed the embodied and the discursive jointly producing possibilities for new ethical enactments. We present these as moments that signal the potential emergence of subjects of the community economy.

DISCURSIVE DESTABILIZATION AND ITS UNEXPECTED EFFECTS

In beginning to construct the diverse economy as a set of possibilities for economic subjects, in both the Latrobe and Pioneer Valleys we started with the familiar capitalist economy that was seen to hold hostage the economic and social fate of each region. Early on, we held focus groups that attempted to access and dislocate the local countenance of Economy. These focus groups offered the opportunity to familiarize ourselves further with the disciplinary rigidities governing the practice of economic development (the most visible form of economic activism in the regions); to enter an ongoing local conversation about the economy; and to begin the search for openings and fissures in the imposing edifice of capitalist development (and deindustrialization) that structured the economic imaginaries of the regions. In retrospect, it seems we were looking for two sorts of openings—the discursive "nonclosures" signaled by contradictory ways of thinking and speaking, and the ethical opening of persons to one another that conversation provokes and enables.

In an initial focus group in the Pioneer Valley in 1999, planners and business and community leaders were asked to speak about the strengths and weaknesses, problems and successes, of the regional economy. The Pioneer Valley of western Massachusetts stretches north-south along the Connecticut River and includes two subregions marked by different discourses of economy: "the Happy Valley" to the north, comprising Franklin and Hampshire Counties, which is usually represented as a thriving semirural area centered on higher education institutions, the arts, and a large alternative sector; and the cities of Springfield and Holyoke in Hampden County to the south, which are portrayed as deindustrialized and depressed, though enlivened by a culturally diverse small business sector and a large informal economy. In the focus groups, familiar stories emerged, couched within the anxiety-ridden discourse of development in which every region is found wanting (and thus in need of economic intervention). The prescription was familiar: attracting "good" jobs by recruiting major capitalist employers, via subsidies and other inducements, to locate in the region.

But the discussion took an unsettling turn as some participants reiterated several times that a requisite of economic development was a suitably educated and acculturated labor force and others pointed to the fact that the two-earner family, whether wealthy or impoverished, left no one at home to raise the children:

> I think one of the dilemmas is, looking at the interface between family structure and the structure of the economy, is that increasingly in order to make it according to the standard of living we have adopted in this country, the significant adults in the family have to be working. . . . You know, women are working now in order for the economy to work with the low unemployment. And children are not attended to and we are not committing to after-school programs. (Community Reinvestment Act officer from Fleet Bank)

Discussion circled around the unspoken, perhaps repressed fear that successful economic development might bring with it the possibility (or even likelihood) of social failure. That this was something entirely outside the control of these economic development specialists may partially explain why it repeatedly bubbled up out of the ambient low-level anxiety. Where was the appropriate labor force to come from if no one was fully engaged in producing it?

At one moment the labor leader in the group recounted with muted horror the story of Conyers, Georgia, an affluent suburb of Atlanta where the largest outbreak of syphilis in the United States in decades had occurred among junior high school students, some of whom had as many as fifty partners. In Conyers, it seemed, economic development had betrayed its promise of social well-being, and indeed was undermining itself as a process (Healy and Biewener 2000). The story broke the flow of discussion and caused a shift in the emotional tenor of the group. The confident stance and productive anxiety that had prevailed in discussions of "what the regional economy needs" gave way to a confused and even despairing fearfulness.

Clearly the participants were able to draw on a longstanding intellectual tradition and their own social roles to assert the sufficiency of capitalist growth to the goal of producing economic and social development. But it seemed that they also harbored untamed fears of society out of control, and a tacit shared recognition of the insufficiency of the capitalist economy (no matter how developed) to the task of sustaining a community—raising its children, reproducing its sociality. These fears and vulnerabilities erupted through the smooth surface of rational interchange and destabilized the explicit closures and certainties of development. We encountered an unspoken, embodied acknowledgment that capitalist economic development might be a dependent rather than a self-sufficient process, and that social well-being has multiple wellsprings and determinants. As the sufficiency of capitalist development to regional well-being unraveled before our eyes, a dislocation took place. We recognized a discursive nonclosure, a breakdown of sorts, an unsettling of the subjects of a capitalist economy. Over the course of the project, we would return to this moment as an emotional opening for a counterdiscourse of "the household-based neighborhood economy" and its contributions to social well-being and economic development (Community Economies Collective 2001).

The first focus groups held in the Latrobe Valley in 1997 were with business and community leaders.[8] When asked to talk about the social and economic changes that had occurred in the valley over the last decade, the participants produced a well-rehearsed story centered on dynamics in the formal economy—privatization of the State Electricity Commission (SEC) in the face of state debt and the pressures of globalization. Words such as "victimization," "disappointment," "pawns," and "powerless" anchored this narrative in a sea of negativity and the moods of the speakers ranged from energetic anger to depressed resignation.

But when they were later asked to consider the strengths of the region and the capacities of the community to cope with change, an unmatched set of stories emerged, conveyed in that halting manner of speech in which new thought gets articulated. Participants spoke of artistic ingenuity and enterprise, of contributions made by migrants from non-English-speaking backgrounds and intellectually challenged residents, of the potential to revalue unemployed people as a regional asset.[9] The authoritative voice associated with discussions of downsizing and restructuring gave way to a more speculative and tentative tone. Moods began to lighten, and expressions of surprise and curiosity displaced dour agreement.

Though the stories were initially slow in coming, one example sparked another and soon they were tumbling out. To our surprise and pleasure, these stories began to map the contours of a relatively invisible diverse economy. No longer simply abandoned by capital, the region became populated by numerous examples of community-based economic alternatives that held promise for a vision of regional potential. At the end of the session, one participant noted the shift that had occurred in his own understanding and sense of possibility—a shift that had resulted from being placed in a different relation to the formal economic "identity" and familiar downbeat narrative of the valley:

> The interesting thing and rather ironic is that a bureaucratic organization like the Council or like the state government or a welfare organization might organize a panel to sit around and discuss the sorts of things that we have discussed, and . . . they probably wouldn't have achieved as much as we have achieved today. Because the information that I've gained just from hearing everybody talk . . . it's been absolutely precious. And it hasn't come about as a consequence of some bureaucracy wanting to solve problems but rather as we are pawns in another exercise [i.e., our research project]. I'm actually going away from here with more than I came with. (Local government official)

While we were gratified that our theoretical preoccupations were surfacing in stories of a vibrant hidden economy, what took us aback was the dramatic change in affect that accompanied their telling. Over the course of a two-hour conversation, the participants had moved from an emotionally draining narrative of regional destruction at the hands of the SEC, to outbreaks of raw emotion occasioned by retelling this painful story in the sympathetic presence of witnesses/listeners, to open, even exuberant responses to our questions about counterstories and alternative activities. As the session advanced, participants appeared to momentarily relinquish hard-edged identities associated with predictable and entrenched political views and make overtures to each other in a mixture of relief, disbelief, and recognition.

These lapses in rigidity signaled discursive destabilization and perhaps something more that was born of the collective moment. They alerted us to "fugitive currents of energy" (Connolly 1999, 143) that were released by the process of collective reflection. As sometime participants in consciousness-raising groups and various self-help/improvement-oriented small group discussions over the years, we were not unfamiliar with the welling up of empathy and enabling feelings associated with the witness of strongly felt emotions and fears. Varela (1992) sees this kind of embodied opening to the experience and needs of others as a sign of "ethical expertise," the "other-directed" know-how that has been enacted into our bodies and minds via the experience of being cared for by family and friends. This ethical expertise, or skilled behavior, is often suppressed by the "street-fighter mentality of watchful self-interest" (66), in which the self is strong, independent, and knowing. But at certain hinge moments of "breakdown" (11) the self-contained subject reenters the microworld of ethical know-how and the energies of connection are released.

What we observed being unleashed by collective reflection and the tentative voicing of fears were energies that enabled empathic listening and non-judgmental speculation about other economic values and ways of being. Here were economic development practitioners, business people, union officials, and local government functionaries dropping their armor—what might this mean for other people and the ethical practice of connectedness? Could the momentary relinquishing of established identities be prolonged so that new subjects, or "beings-in-common," could emerge? Might we be able to harness these enabling energies and move with them in a more interventionist way toward a new practice of economy? These were the challenges we set for ourselves as our projects unfolded.

ENCOUNTERING RESISTANCE AND NONRECOGNITION

As part of a qualitative assessment of how life was seen in the Latrobe Valley at the beginning of the project, we asked each community researcher to create a photo essay that told "their story" alongside that of their friends and acquaintances. We felt it was important to acknowledge the dominant representations of the Latrobe Valley and how they were reflected in the self-perception of the groups we were working with. Again we were both surprised and confronted by the powerful effects of what was initially introduced as a simple team-building exercise. These photo essays were used at various points in the project by the community researchers as conversation starters and it was in the context of these interactions that the psychic difficulties of relinquishing established economic identities surfaced.

The essays provide insights into the very different lifeworlds of the retrenched worker, the young and unemployed, and the single parent. In "Jock's Story," the ghost footprints of an industrial worker track through scenes of abandonment—Jock stands waiting for his mates at the vandalized bus stop where electricity workers once boarded the SEC bus (see Figure 26). There are images of derelict industrial buildings, abandoned mining equipment, a vacated workers' parking lot at the power station, pawn shops, and empty premises in the main street of Morwell. The retrenched workers who contributed to designing the photo essay wanted to convey their anger at the empty promises of growth with privatization, and their outrage that the electricity industry is still producing coal and power but that the living, breathing labor that "made" the valley is

FIGURE 26. Jock's story.

now nowhere to be seen. Mixed with this indignation is also nostalgia, evident in the caption, "How green was my valley"—a reference not to the Welsh coal vales where the novel of that name was set, but to their counterpart Australian coal valleys during past periods of rapid expansion, employment growth, and rising wages. The photo essay embodies a melancholic longing for the romance of a solidary working-class community (constituted largely by Anglo-Australians and British migrants) and a militant trade-union identity. It also conveys a yearning for the lost sense of security provided by a paternalist state authority that cared for its employees, positioning them as productive and respected citizens of Victoria, privileged working-class consumers in a buoyant state-centered economy (see chapter 2).

In conversations the community researchers held with retrenched workers, the anger that surfaced was a constant reminder of the wounded attachment that prevented any easy identification with subject positions in the community economy.[10] Asked about the difficulties of talking to people in the community, Yvonne responds:

> The negativity. One particular gentleman in a literacy class was quite obviously very frustrated and pessimistic. He was quite vocal and kept presenting me with stumbling blocks. "Look what *they* have done. What are *they* going to do about it? What's the use? No one is going to be bothered [with community enterprises]. People will want to be paid." I tried to address his issues without being confrontational. I tried

to be sympathetic and understanding. We talked a bit about the problems in our community. I agreed with what he had to say and used
"Jock's Story" as an image to summon it all up. It was evident that we
had to almost exhaust that line of thinking before moving on.

Thinking back to that conversation at a later date, Yvonne reflected on the fears
such a person might experience if they were asked to assume a different identity,
albeit one with a positive valuation, in the community economy:

> YVONNE: Well, I'm thinking about Wayne, who's worked and then been kicked out and
> then told that he has to . . . the whole dynamics. You don't have any control.
> You have this Centrelink [dole office] dark cloud hanging over you all the
> time . . . so you do feel out of control. And his argument was "*They* won't let
> us do it." *They* . . . whoever they are. So you're totally powerless. To start to
> think that you've got something to offer is opening yourself up a bit.
>
> KATHIE: Opening up to being abused, somehow?
>
> YVONNE: Yeah. Exactly. Vulnerable. You could be hurt.

This conversation illustrates the psychic investment in remaining a victim,
staying with the identity of unemployed worker of an immoral capitalist order.
They keep you tethered to something that, while painful, is known and familiar.
Embracing the unfamiliar is a risk that is too hard to contemplate. By allowing
Wayne to voice his anger and repressed fear, Yvonne opened up the possibility that this could become a moment of grieving that could be moved through,
rather than an expression of static reluctance.[11]

"The Young Latrobe Valley" photo essay evinces a similar sense of abandonment among the valley's youth who have nothing to do—except to vandal-
ize the built environment, drink, smoke, gamble, eat at McDonald's, and visit
Centrelink and the courts (see Figure 27). There is no nostalgia in this picture,
only the overwhelming frustration of being trapped in place and a sense of having been betrayed. Included in the poster are examples of the predominant media
depictions of the Latrobe Valley as a blighted and desperate community, in the
words of newspaper headlines, "The Valley of the Dole" (Tippett 1997), or "Valley
of Despair" (Shaw and Munro 2001). Above all, there is the insistent anxious
questioning about the future for this generation and an implicit mourning for the
identity that once would have been endowed by the formal economy.

For the unemployed youth in the valley who have never had the opportunity to embrace a valued economic identity, anger is internalized as self-disregard.
As shown in this conversation reported by Yvonne, this presents an even stronger
barrier to the mobilization of an alternative subjectivity than retrenchment does
for the middle-aged:

> I had a conversation with a young man who is long-term unemployed.
> His negativity was very deep rooted and I was having no success in
> inviting alternative ideas. "What can I do? I can't do anything. People

FIGURE 27. Latrobe Valley for the young unemployed.

look at me 'cause I'm a dole bludger—a bum." His negativity was more directed at himself, where the gentleman I mentioned earlier was directed outward—"they."

Yvonne goes on to show how the anger and negativity is taken on and reinforced by others:

The young man's father was present during our conversation and became angry with his son. "Listen to yourself. If that's what you believe, then that's what you are. Listen to what she has to say." The father is a friend of mine and I know the frustration he has felt with his son. He has done a lot to try to encourage him to do something for himself but it always ends flat. He has even resorted to calling his son a bum and threatening to disown him. He loves his son very much but is at a loss. It seems that the young are particularly vulnerable. Very much dislocated from the community.

The youth of the valley have been brought up by parents with high expectations of their ability to get a job and look after themselves. It is as though retrenched parents are now projecting onto the young unemployed their anger and guilt for not providing a future for their children. This compounds the sense of dislocation that makes youth a particularly hard group to work with, as another community researcher, Leanne, notes:

> I think I found that youth tended to have really negative images of
> themselves and I guess that was a huge thing for me to work with them,
> like their imagination was there, and their inspiration was there, yet at
> the end of the day the thing that lacked was their motivation.

The photo essay that represents the life of a single parent in the valley stands in stark contrast to those of the retrenched worker and unemployed youth (see Figure 28). It portrays constant activity, connections to many others and a list of juggled occupations—teacher, veterinarian, mind reader, domestic director, entertainer, chef, nurse, referee. Here identity and value are provided by many of the unpaid, untraded, unrecognized activities of the diverse economy. Absent is the sense of victimization by the greater economy, or any sense of abandonment by a paternalistic institution. The overall image is one of meaningful occupation, fullness and busyness and limited time for rest. Indeed, the essay could be read as expressing a refusal among single mothers to be defined in terms of the negative identities offered by the dominant discourse of economy.

We noticed a similar refusal of negatively valenced identities among low-income, female-headed, single-parent households of the inner-city neighborhoods of South Holyoke in the Pioneer Valley. AnnaMarie, a feminist planner in the Holyoke planning office and one of the academic researchers on the project, was all too aware of the mainstream representations of these households:

> Planners portray them as economically deficient, or even as economi-
> cally depleting if the women are receiving government assistance. . . .

FIGURE 28. A single parent's Latrobe Valley.

The underlying mainstream assumption about low-income communities is that they are somehow outside "the economy," or are lacking an economy, and so an economy needs to be developed there. In our Rethinking Economy project, we assume that there is already an economy in low-income communities. In fact, we assume multiple and diverse forms of economic activity taking place—both legal and illegal, for pay and not for pay, capitalist and noncapitalist, involving barter, gift, theft, and market transactions. Furthermore, we assume that the households in these communities constitute important sites of (largely unpaid) economic activity. Where the mainstream sees absence or emptiness, we see presence and fullness.

In the focus group I conducted with neighborhood women, I did not encounter empty, deficient, or depleted subjects. The women were intellectually lively and full of playfulness. By most mainstream standards, these women would be considered poor. But as they talked about their lives they said they "didn't feel that poor."

When AnnaMarie's focus group participants say they "didn't feel that poor," they are not denying their experience, which includes working at low-paying jobs, receiving inadequate government assistance, or living in the dangerous environment of an illegal economy. Rather, they are simply unable to recognize themselves within the dominant identity of Economy. Unwilling to measure themselves solely by its standards, they are refusing to be positioned as subjects of insufficiency who need proper economic identities in the formal economy.

What these reflections show is that subjects are differentially positioned with respect to dominant discourses and that this influences their relationship to the possibility of identification with alternative discourses. The reluctance of certain subjects to be resignified was counterposed to the availability of others to be resubjectivated within novel discursive terrains. In the Latrobe Valley, middle-aged men and unemployed youth were initially resistant to resignification within the community economy; among them our project was met by expressions of grief, resentment, anger, and self-hatred. Women, who were already involved in practices of the community economy, were usually open to the project and enthusiastic about its aims, though they were often unable to participate.

LEANNE: The women really took to the project and the understanding of it real well. They could see that it was really tangible. Whereas the men tended to put up the obstacles. . . . And it's funny, too, because the projects that we're involved in or that we're running now, there's more men involved than women.

YVONNE: I think the women pick it up really quickly. There was one group we talked to, a women's writing group over at the neighborhood house, and they were just bubbling with it. . . . I think women pick up that whole idea of what community is quicker. Whereas the guys have got to do the whole stand-back stuff and loner thing. And then, I suppose, thinking about why more guys are involved

> [in the project], I think it was a case of wearing them down or something,
> convincing them. . . . I suppose the women are really busy, busy keeping
> homes or looking after kids or looking after husbands.

In the women of both the Latrobe and Pioneer Valleys, we glimpsed the possibility of not being fully captured by dominant forms of economic subjection. In the men and young people of the Latrobe Valley, we saw the disorientation of having lost or been denied valued identities in the mainstream economy. In these partially disinterpellated and disidentified states, subjects were visible as potential spaces of cultivation. Despite the resistance and negativity we initially encountered, we were encouraged by our conversations to pursue the project of destabilizing existing identities, prompting new identifications, and cultivating different desires and capacities. We began by reframing the economy and economic roles and renarrativizing economic experience.

REFRAMING AND RENARRATIVIZING

One of the goals of the action research projects was to flesh out, through a community inventory, a diverse economy in which capitalist enterprises, formal wage labor, and market transactions occupy only the visible tip of the economic iceberg (see chapter 3, Figure 14). By giving a place in the diverse economy to activities that are often ignored (collective enterprises, household and voluntary labor, transactions involving barter, sharing and gift giving, and so forth), we hoped to refigure the identity and capacities of the regional economy. And by recognizing the particularity of people's economic involvements, including their multiple economic identities (in addition to being unemployed with respect to capitalist employment, for example, a person can be employed in household, neighborhood, and other noncapitalist activities), we were attempting to reframe the identities and capacities of individuals. We undertook slightly different reframing exercises in each site, but central to each exercise was the involvement of community researchers. Initially it was they who were the subjects of reframing within a new discourse of economy and region.

Over a period of weeks in the Latrobe Valley, the academic research team facilitated an intensive training of the community researchers. Initially we discussed different ways of thinking about economy and introduced the representation of the diverse economy. For inspiration and illustration of the diverse economy we visited a number of community-based enterprises and craft networks in the valley and talked to the people running them. None of the community researchers had a prior knowledge of these "alternative" economic activities. All were familiar through work experience only with the formal economy and its institutions—the SEC, banks, retail outlets, and welfare support organizations. After exposure to the kinds of enterprises the focus-group participants had mentioned, the community researchers' perceptions of the valley and its potentialities began to change:

YVONNE: I didn't realize there was such an extensive web of community groups, organizations, and services operating in the Latrobe Shire—Woodworx, for instance.[12] There's almost a whole industry quietly working away and if you were an average worker or family person you might not even know they exist. Though I have really noticed a gap. There seems to be a need for someone to connect all these groups and individuals. Some of them may not even know that another exists. On a cornier note I've actually come to quite like being a part of the Latrobe Shire community. Yeah, I almost feel like I belong.

NICKI[13]: Working on the project has given me some hope that the valley will not become a ghost town. That it is possible for the valley to survive without all the emphasis on getting in business. That other forms of communities can and do work. I guess it is more of a personal discovery rather than a project discovery, but if I had not been working here [on the project] then it is a discovery that I know I would not have made.

For Yvonne and Nicki alike, the training and field visits provoked a discursive reframing that allowed for new feelings of hope and belonging; meeting real life subjects of the noncapitalist community sector generated a sense of possibility, through the recognition of the diversity and vitality of an existing economy. Now they would be asked to bring this new knowledge, this reframed valley, into interactions with the wider community.

We started with community conversations targeted at generating different, more enabling representations of the people of the valley and the place itself. Drawing on the techniques of Asset-Based Community Development (ABCD), the community researchers invited people to document their personal gifts and capacities. This introduced a new fullness into the representation of identity. No longer were subjects defined as lacking or victimized; instead they were invited to see themselves as skillful and competent.

The Asset-Based Community Development method pioneered by John Kretzmann and John McKnight (1993) in their work with community activists and organizers from inner-city neighborhoods of large North American cities is a simple and incredibly powerful tool for invoking a reframing of community members and a renarrativizing of community-development trajectories. It takes the familiar image of the half-empty glass and likens it to the (self)images of many communities who are defined by what they lack and what they therefore "need." The needs-based portrayal invites solutions from the outside—grants and assistance from government and nongovernment agencies. It perpetuates dependence on needs profiling to continue aid and trains community members as grant proposal writers rather than as self-managers.[14] Kretzmann and McKnight suggest another route of action by concentrating on the half-full vision of a community that emphasizes the assets and capacities of community members, associations, institutions, and infrastructure. They argue that communities are built on their assets, not on their needs. The assets-based portrayal invites communities to begin thinking about what they can do to mobilize what they already have. While assistance might be garnered from outside, it is sought as a second, not a first, resort and only after community members have decided how they can manage additional resources themselves. We saw in this approach a similar commitment to problematizing representations and an effective method of collaboratively producing more enabling visions of community futures.[15]

Generating new representations of the Latrobe Valley involved marrying the ABCD method of bringing to light people's assets and capacities with the language of the diverse economy. The community researchers began group interviews with those in employment, life skills, and social service programs, recording the skills and capacities that people were already exercising or that were underutilized—their "gifts of the head, hand, and heart." The aim was not to produce a complete inventory of skills, but to shift people's self-perception as lacking and not up to the task of creating different futures.[16] What was important was the process of working together to complete a joint Portrait of Gifts. During this exploration people invariably surprised themselves with the extent of their capacities, learned new things about each other, and found common areas of interest.

Psychologists and family therapists Michael White and David Epston (1990) have developed an interpretive method of therapy that focuses on the meanings people attach to experience and the effect of these meanings on behavior. Their "narrative means to therapeutic ends" privileges the alternative stories and new meanings that allow people to give up inadvertently contributing to "the 'career' of [a] problem" (1990, 3). They note that

> those aspects of lived experience that fall outside of the dominant story
> provide a rich and fertile source for the generation, or re-generation,
> of alternative stories. (1990, 15)

The Portrait of Gifts exercise provides qualitative information "outside of the dominant story" for generating new representations of the Latrobe Valley. In place of depictions of the valley as distressed and dysfunctional,[17] the portrait offers a shared representation of a "caring community" and a glimpse of a new kind of economic subject, one who is concerned for and connected to others.

The Portrait of Gifts focuses attention on the range of unpaid and nonmarket economic practices, like gifting and voluntary work, that supposedly economically inactive people are engaged in. This and other portrayals of the Latrobe Valley as a learning place made up of skillful people were put together in a small brochure that was widely distributed throughout the community and used in radio interviews about the project and its outcomes (see Figure 29). People, not coal and power, are foregrounded as the primary regional resource and this asset is presented as already contributing to development.

With this alternative story of the valley and its people in hand, the community researchers pursued further conversations with people about the possibilities

GIFTS OF THE HEAD

- nearly ¾ of the people who filled in a Portrait of Gifts listen to children reading aloud.

- ½ have shared a skill with someone else.

- over ¼ have creative writing skills.

- nearly ½ have shared computer skills with someone else.

- some skills people would like to learn are:
  furniture restoration   internet skills
  sewing   tv and computer repairs
  first aid   organisational skills
  creative writing   leadership skills

- some skills people would like to share with others are:
  woodwork   sewing and dressmaking
  photography   arc welding
  basketball   tai chi

The Latrobe Valley - A Learning Community

Everyone in the Latrobe Valley has skills, talents and ideas.

Over 50 people have filled out a Portrait of Gifts to tell us about their skills, talents and ideas. These include people from TAFE Numeracy and Literacy classes, Moe Lifeskills Group and Moe Men's Group.

The Community Partnering project aims to:
- *bring together the skills, talents and ideas of diverse groups of people; and*
- *build community-based initiatives.*

For more information contact Yvonne Joyce, Stephen Lister, Alan Riley or Leanne Vella on 5136 9270 or 5136 9293.

GIFTS OF THE HAND

- almost ½ the people who filled in a Portrait of Gifts have mechanical or electrical skills like fixing household appliances.

- ¾ have computer skills.

- over ¾ have construction and maintenance skills, ranging from housepainting to furniture-making to concreting.

- over ¾ have lawnmowing or gardening skills.

- over ½ have art and craft skills, like drawing, painting, ceramics, pottery and leatherwork.

- people's hobbies and interests include:
  restoring old film equipment
  dancing   basketball
  lead lighting   darts
  tai chi   fishing

The Latrobe Valley - A Skillful Community

GIFTS OF THE HEART

- over ½ the people who filled in a Portrait of Gifts give food, money or household items to families in need.

- over ½ run errands, shop or drive for people who need transportation.

- nearly ½ help with children's sports teams.

- over ¼ help out in school classrooms.

- nearly ¾ listen or give support to people who need help.

- nearly ½ have first aid skills.

- some of the things that people care deeply about are:
  opportunities for young people
  the environment   family histories
  care of the elderly   recycling

The Latrobe Valley - A Caring Community

FIGURE 29. Pamphlet representations of the "Portrait of Gifts."

of playing new roles in the local economy, rescripting themselves as active makers of a community economy. As White and Epston note:

> When unique outcomes are identified, persons can be invited to ascribe meaning to them. Success in this ascription of meaning requires that the unique outcomes be plotted into an alternative story or narrative. And in this process . . . "imagining" plays a very significant role. Various questions can be introduced that assist in engaging persons in this ascription of new meaning, questions that actively involve them in . . . the "re-authoring" of their lives and their relationships. (1990, 16)

These kinds of questions were posed at a community conference in which the Portrait of Gifts was presented and people were invited to participate in a brainstorming session to imagine the community-based projects they could be interested in building. Almost fifty ideas were recorded (see Figure 30), providing a concrete imagining of actual activities that might be undertaken by newly authorized subjects of the community economy.

A similar process of reframing and renarrativizing structured the Rethinking Economy project in the Pioneer Valley. At the outset of the project, the primary economic identification of the community researchers was with capitalism—they were actual or potential workers, entrepreneurs, consumers, investors—and their economic politics was structured by antagonism or positive attachment to capitalist development. Capitalism, in other words, was the master signifier organizing economic space as a space of identification and desire. The challenge was to produce a dislocation in this formation and create the conditions for the emergence of noncapitalist modes of economic subjectivity. During the training, the iceberg image (see chapter 3, Figure 18) was used to portray the economy, with the capitalist economy above the waterline and a diverse, largely noncapitalist economy forming the huge submerged bulk below. We invited the community researchers to collaborate with us in coming to know (and speak about) the dimly lit economic realms under the surface of the water. Here the reframing that was required for constructing a language and a vision of economic difference in the Pioneer Valley was initiated.

Over the next few weeks each community researcher conducted six interviews with their friends and other contacts about their daily activities. As one way to represent their findings, at the weekend debriefing retreat we asked them to situate activities from their interviews on a four-cell matrix taped to the wall (see Figure 31). Predictably, the examples were scattered into all the market, nonmarket, paid, and unpaid categories and people were impressed by the diversity captured in this distribution. When we asked them to affix red stickers to any activity they considered capitalist, to the amazement of everyone, only four of the more than fifty examples received stickers. This prompted a lively exploration

Making and Exchanging Projects

- Fixing old bikes
- Tool recycling and lending library
- Making wooden furniture without power tools (bodging)
- Lawn mowing for elderly people
- Learning exchange that uses "gray power"
- Furniture exchange
- Half-used paint bank and exchange
- Dress pattern exchange
- Fibre and fabric bank
- Sharing garden tools
- Book binding
- Handyman assistance for the aged
- Inventors' resource centre
- Community woodworking shop
- Inventory of skills
- Fixing broken furniture

Cultural Projects

- Community filmmaking workshop
- Photographic developing room
- Youth newspaper
- Matching social dancers with learners
- Music workshops and festivals
- Communal cooking kitchen
- SEC recognition day
- Community bush dances
- Documenting family histories and personal stories
- Music jam sessions
- Sheet music and or musical instrument exchange
- Book reading
- Matching people who play musical instruments with those who want to learn
- Street parties
- Collectors' directory
- Christmas street decorations
- Murals and painting spaces
- Designing trees

Environmental Projects

- Fixing gardens for elderly or others in need of assistance
- Cleaning up waterways for children's play
- Backyard seed banks for native plants
- Water recycling off roofs
- Backyard tank yabbie and fish farming
- Recycling demolition materials
- Community chook yard
- Garden produce exchange
- Community gardens
- Teaching young people bush appreciation
- Collection point for sawdust and manure for community composting
- Recycling center for clean industrial waste to be used by preschools, primary schools, etc., for art activities

Ideas for Specific Workshops

- How to set up a community garden
- How to set up a community toolshed
- Cooperatives—how do they work?
- Management options for community projects

FIGURE 30. Ideas for community and economic projects.

of definitions of capitalism, as people began to distinguish capitalist from other market-oriented business activity.

What unexpectedly emerged from the interviews was the extent of what we came to call an economy of generosity, overflowing with goods, money, and labor. Not only were their interviewees providing care for family, friends, and neighbors—this we expected, though we were overwhelmed by the number of hours and amount of emotional energy committed—but in unimaginably various ways (outside the institutionalized volunteer and charitable sectors) we found people donating time, money, materials, and affection (see Figure 32).[18] Interviews revealed that gifts of labor and goods are often intertwined with the market economy. For instance, there's the woman with the agricultural bookstore who sells everything from pastoral poetry to textbooks on farm accounting and gets most of her books as donations from individuals and other used-book sellers in the valley. There's the woman who makes quilts, selling them from her clothesline (visible from the road), using old clothes and scraps of fabric that people bring to her house.[19] There's the retired CEO, the ex-postal worker, and the World War II veteran, all in their seventies and close friends for years, who donate their Mondays to beer bottling at the Berkshire Brewing Company because they enjoy spending time with each other and with the multiply-pierced young people who join them on the bottling line. Everybody gets lunch and a case of beer, but it's basically volunteer labor, intertwined not only with a market-oriented but also a capitalist enterprise.

Palpable in our conversations was the transformative and energizing force of language and recognition. As the researchers became known to themselves

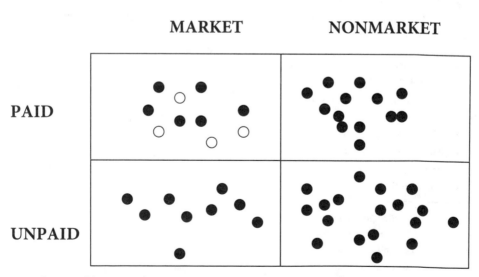

FIGURE 31. Four-cell matrix with economic activities categorized by market or nonmarket orientation of production and form of remuneration of labor. Clear circles are those considered capitalist by the community researchers.

the woman who tithes (meaning giving away fully one-tenth of her income) but not to the church—to friends and neighbors who need it

the depressed single mother who volunteers twenty-four-hour counseling and support services to drug addicts

the retired insurance adjuster who does dowsing as a gift, a way of opening people to their powers of intuition and connecting them to the environment (he is also a spiritual counselor and gives away counseling and writings on grieving)

the woman who raises "found" children (in other words, not her own), usually high-school-age boys

the fifty-two-year-old grandmother of fourteen who provides free advocacy services in her community and is writing a picture book about her many-colored grandchildren to show how much she appreciates them

the man who does professional quality videotapes of local concerts and gives the tapes to the performers

the lesbian couple who offer a place in their hardware store for people to sit by the fire and talk (not to mention opening it for community sings, with as many as two hundred people)

the sixteen-year-old aspiring artist who used to be on the streets and now takes care of her family, cooking and cleaning for her mother and father (they live separately) and mentoring her fourteen-year-old sister

the eighty-five-year-old woman who hosts weaving workshops to bring weavers together and keep them inspired (she also built a labyrinth on her property for those who are grieving and invites anyone to visit)

the mother who raises money locally for her son who does microenterprise lending in Southeast Asia

the middle-aged woman who makes lap blankets for nursing home residents as a way of thanking hospice for their care of her husband before he died

FIGURE 32. Examples of giving in the Pioneer Valley.

and to each other as participants in the gift economy, their experiences and desires poured forth, along with gratitude for a shared moment of visibility and validation.[20] This was another ethical moment in which the know-how of "authentic caring" (Varela 1992) was seen to be ubiquitous, providing both material and spiritual sustenance. The reframing and renarrativizing exercise allowed for what had been a relatively tacit, almost bodily source of joy and satisfaction, something that existed in the shadows of social and economic valuation, to be accepted into the symbolic language of economy. We saw the possibilities for an alternative discourse of economy begin to circulate productively and find its subjects.

At this point in the process it was clear that the poststructuralist contribution to action research could be a powerful tool. Coming to a new language and vision of economy turned out to be an affirmation not only of difference, but of economic capacity. The people engaged in our research conversations had a chance to encounter themselves differently—not as waiting for capitalism to give them their places in the economy, but as actively constructing their economic lives, on a daily basis, in a range of noncapitalist practices and institutions. Development possibilities became transformed by giving them different starting places, in an already viable diverse economy. Reframing individuals as subjects rather than as objects of economic development and renarrativizing the potential trajectory of regional development unleashed positive energies that we felt could be harnessed toward building community-based enterprises and mobilizing community economies.

PRODUCING AND SUSTAINING POSITIVE AFFECT

Our challenge was to work with the enabling feelings that had been released. As we came to understand, however, the process of becoming a different economic subject is not an easy or sudden one. It is not so much about seeing and knowing as it is about feeling and doing. As already noted, when we began working in the Latrobe Valley with those who had been marginalized by economic restructuring, we often encountered hostility and anger, anchored in a deep sense of powerlessness. Introducing our project of economic resignification seemed to reactivate the trauma of retrenchment (especially for men in their forties and fifties who had found it impossible to secure alternative employment) and to reinforce the bleak future envisioned by young unemployed people for whom the expectation of jobs in the power industry and related service sectors had been dashed. Rather than working mainly with language and discourse and counting on that to release and redirect affect, we found that with these groups we needed to directly address embodied, habitual, and emotional practices of being. To work against that which blocked receptivity to change and connectedness, we needed to move "beyond" identity and the insights of poststructuralism.

Political theorist William Connolly finds in the body and more specifically in the brain some of the factors that dispose us negatively (if unconsciously) to new situations and possibilities. He talks about "thought-imbued intensities that do not in themselves take the form of either conscious feelings or representations" (1999, 28) and finds one of their bodily locations in the amygdala, a small brain nodule at the base of the cortex. Triggered by "signs that resemble a past trauma, panic, or disturbance," the amygdala transmits fear along the pathways of the brain with considerable energy and intensity. Recognizing the barrier that such a bodily function poses to new becomings, Connolly proposes cultivating or educating the amygdala, resistant though it may be to cognitive manipulation. Since amygdalic panic arises not just out of corporeal predispositions but out of experience (of pain or disturbance), he suggests that counter-experiences issuing from experimental self-artistry and intersubjective arts might play a part in attenuating that panic. They might even create a space for the creativity that the amygdala unleashes (in Connolly's speculative imagination) through its frictional interaction with the relatively staid and reflective brains, the cortex and hippocampus (29).

As the project unfolded, we became more adept at creating ways to attenuate panic and promote positive affect. The community researchers were on the front line of this action, as much of the initial animosity was directed at them. Since the project was an initiative of Monash University (which has a regional campus in the valley) and the Latrobe Shire Council, the community researchers were initially identified with these regional institutions. For many in the valley, it was as though these powerful regional actors stood in for the SEC, drawing the projected anger that most felt toward the power authority. The community researchers found that they had to distance themselves from these institutions and work to identify themselves as ordinary community members who themselves had been marginalized by the economic crisis. As Leanne recounts:[21]

> In the end Yvonne would say, "Don't present yourself that you come from Monash." She would present herself as a single parent, and I would present myself as an unemployed person, and automatically you would have that rapport with someone, 'cause you're on the level that they're on. It would be until you'd say that the project is sponsored by Monash Uni and the Latrobe Shire—that's when you'd get the political stuff. But the political stuff to me tended to come, tended to be male driven.

The "political stuff" referred to here is the negativity and resistance couched in the language of us/them. Yvonne became quite skilled at dealing with the aversive reactions that emerged when the project was introduced, and with people's initial resistance when they were asked to portray themselves in terms of "assets and capacities," rather than needs and deficiencies. Her strategy was to avoid engaging with the angry energy that arose from the narrative of "our" victimization at the hands of "them."[22] She suspected that further exploration would lead back to the evils of the SEC, the conservative state government, and ultimately the Economy. And despite the promise of transformative enunciation that is said to arise from denunciation,[23] we all sensed that this exercise in debunking would be unlikely to inspire creative thoughts and desires for alternative economies. Our tactics, then, involved moving away from the narratives that triggered the amygdalic reaction and trapped local community members in fear and anger, making it nearly impossible to think about things differently.

To return to Yvonne's difficult conversation with Wayne:

> [I found out that] he is very good with his hands and knows a bit about cars. I asked, hypothetically, if there were a group of single parents

interested in learning about car maintenance, and if I could arrange a
venue and possible tools, would he be interested in sharing his skills
and knowledge? "Yeah, I'd do that, no worries," he said. I asked him
would he expect to be paid for his time. "No, I wouldn't do it for
money," he replied. I asked, "So do you think you'd get anything out of
it yourself?" "Yeah, I suppose I'd get some satisfaction out of it 'cause I
like to help people like yourself." So I really tried to turn it around and
have him answer or resolve his own questions and issues.

Where the man had felt pain and anger associated with past experiences
of Economy, under Yvonne's patient cultivation he moves toward pleasure and
happiness associated with a different way of being. Her questioning shifts his attention away from a narrative of impotence and victimization and into a hopeful
scenario that positions him as skillful and giving, endowed with an identity in a
community economy. The threat represented by our project, by Yvonne herself,
and by the formal Economy—all recalling the historic trauma of retrenchment
that prompts angry closing-off to emotional and social novelty—has been neu-
tralized through her affective tutelage. And in the place of anger at remembered
pain, there is a hint of joy in abilities seen in a new light, and a generosity of spirit
that surprises with its unfamiliarity. These feelings that attend creative moments
of becoming challenge and ultimately displace the more securely narrativized
emotions of reproach, defensiveness, blame, and resentment associated with established economic identities.

Varela writes that "[w]e are already other-directed even at our most
negative, and we already feel warmth toward some people such as family and
friends" (1992, 66–67). It is this quality of common ethical know-how that can
be worked with via extension to build new microworlds, new practical knowledges for a community economy. Such fleeting ethical moments as those related
above might appear to represent very minor shifts in the macropolitical scheme
of things. But they are a requisite part of the political process of enacting a different regional economy, where individuals from widely varying backgrounds
and life circumstances move beyond fear and hatred to interact in inventive and
productive ways.

The story of Kara, one of the community researchers in the Pioneer Valley,
exemplifies both Varela's notion of extension of familiar feelings to unfamiliar
situations and the role of self-cultivation as envisioned by Varela and Foucault in
fostering and stabilizing positive emotions. Kara initially was highly resistant to
the project's goal of bringing mainstream and marginalized economic actors into
conversation and collaboration, which she viewed as just a way of subsuming the
latter (and the project) to the agenda of the powerful. She saw the mainstream
people, whom she encountered through a video of our focus groups, as emis-
saries of the State, Capitalism, and Power, from which unholy trinity she was

hoping and indeed planning to entirely remove herself. Throughout the weekend training for community researchers, she nursed and vociferously communicated her antipathy. But at the last moment, during the evaluation of the training, she had a moment of self-evaluation and became open to the possibility of productive engagement with those she saw as (threateningly) different from her: "I don't want to be so us/them," she said, "or to live in a world that is set up that way, emotionally and politically." Suddenly the mainstream types were rehumanized, and the possibility of working with them became a political opportunity. It was as though in that very moment Kara was working on herself "to attenuate the amygdalic panic that often arises when you encounter . . . identities" (Connolly 1999, 36) that call the naturalness or sufficiency of one's own identity into question. By engaging in a "selective desanctification of elements in [her] identity" (146)—in this case, a highly charged oppositional stance with respect to power understood as domination—Kara was able to open herself generously: to the humanity of others, to the possibility of being other than she was, to participating with those most different from herself (in her own antagonistic worldview) in constructing a community economy.[24] By recalling her principles and returning to her store of skills and capacities, she was able to call up feelings of respect and connection, extending them to strangers and committing publicly to a positive emotional stance toward others.[25]

These stories of cultivation and self-cultivation illustrate practices that, if enacted on a daily basis, might translate momentary swerves from negative to positive affect into a more permanent state of being. Certainly taking up the challenge to revision "the economy" as a *community* economy involves sustaining positive affect so that desire can be mobilized toward building its new enterprises.

CREATING SPACES FOR NEW IDENTIFICATIONS AND ETHICAL OPENINGS TO COMMUNALITY

As a way of building on the dreams that emerged from initial conversations in the Latrobe Valley, we organized a range of events that drew people together in situations where crazy ideas and schemes could be freely thrown around without the pressure of a formal meeting regime and the expectation of concrete outcomes. Pizza-making and scone-baking events were particularly successful in getting people to meet, overcome the stultifications of shyness, begin to listen to one another, and build and transmit excitement. The focus on food production as an end in itself produced its own outcomes—a meal that was consumed by its producers and unwitting involvement in the practice of collectivity. Without any expectation that a group with a common goal should form, these events provided a space for a range of people from many different backgrounds to experience "being-in-common."[26]

Leanne described a moment of understanding prompted by these gatherings:

I guess the crunch came when Yvonne was doing her food events and things like that. And just the mingling and talking to people, to me that was like the breakthrough of . . . this is what it's about, it's working with other people and listening to other people and getting that opportunity to listen to their dreams and things like that.

She went on to consider how she herself had changed over the course of the project:

If I give myself the time, I can listen to anyone. I had only ever dealt with people over the counter [before involvement in the project]— with commercial transactions. I'm not as critical as I was. Working with people from various backgrounds and abilities—I'm more tolerant. I've learned to see the good in people. I had always been taught to be cautious and careful of people. My Dad always used to say, "The only friend you've got is yourself." But the project is a place where you can relax and take people as they come. It offers the security to trust people.

Reflecting here on the embattled sense of self that she had been brought up with, Leanne talks of the space afforded by the project for the transformative practices of listening and becoming.[27] Without rushing, by affording a context and open time, a generous spirit was coaxed out of researchers and community members alike. Across their many differences, people engaged with each other and came to identify together as activists in an emerging community economy. Leanne described this experience:

There's all these people with different backgrounds, different educational levels—but to me . . . they all wanted that one thing—they all wanted to belong or to have self-worth and to really get back that feeling of community in that I know my neighbors. And that just working with a group of people, I think, that was to me, that was the message, everyone's equal message—above all the differences, to me that was what I saw.

And to me that was what people were wanting to get back . . . a sense of self-worth and belonging because they tended to associate worth with money at the end of the day, so "If my skill can equal money, then that is self-worth." And I guess speaking to them and sort of the realization that "Ooh, I have got other skills I haven't used in a work practice before, that *they* are self-worth." I think that was the connection between everyone. At the end of the day it didn't matter if you were an intellect or were unemployed or had a part-time job. That was the bond at the end of the day.

Linda Singer suggests that we understand community "as the call of something other than presence" (1991, 125), the call of becoming, one might say. And the capacity for becoming is the talent we were perhaps most actively fostering—through individuals opening to one another, to the inescapable fact of their "own existence as possibility or potentiality" (Agamben 1993, 43) and to the opportunity to work together on building a community-based enterprise. Almost every meeting and event associated with the projects stimulated desires for alternative ways to be, and each of these desires operated as a contagion. In the face of this enthusiasm, however, there was still uncertainty about what a community enterprise actually was and how to build one. Most people had never been involved in community organizations or other enterprises that were not mainstream.

In the Latrobe Valley, we organized two how-to workshops in response to the interest in community gardens and worksheds that arose at the large brainstorming workshop. At each of the half day sessions, an invited speaker from an established organization (Gil Freeman from CERES, a community garden in inner-city Melbourne, and Joe America from the Mornington workshed) presented the story of how their enterprise operated. Yvonne's reflections written after these workshops highlight the difficulty of sustaining desires that are fleetingly mobilized:

> CERES was a great example to give to inspire people. It really highlighted that almost anything is possible. People are very disillusioned here and really need to be given plenty of inspiration and encouragement. People who feel they don't have much power or control, people who feel hopeless or helpless also feel fragile and valueless. And I think that's why we often find people who seem enthusiastic, who express their interest and then don't turn up to meetings, etc. It's not so much about commitment, but the idea that they won't be missed. A bus trip to CERES is certainly going to fuel people.

Two interested groups went on bus trips from the valley to inner-city Melbourne. While CERES itself made a strong impression on the visitors, it was the experience of the bus trip—of being cooped up together in a moving steel canister for hours at a time—that produced an atmosphere of enchantment that became the life force of the garden project that was soon organized.[28] As Jean recounts,

> [I] sat up the back of the bus, knitting very quietly, trying to mind my own business, but Claudio kept yakking in my ear all day. [Laughter.] . . . They're just a mixed group that if they're trying to do so much work, trying to do something, you've got to find where you fit, what they're trying to do, if it's such a good cause. To me it's like a giant big social club.

This "mixed group" of retrenched workers, retirees, housewives, people of non-English-speaking backgrounds, and unemployed youth obtained access to an abandoned caravan park in Morwell and began the Latrobe Valley Community and Environmental Garden (LTVCEG). For Jean, the bus trip and the CERES visit allowed her to see herself as part of the community garden project, though gardening is not her thing:

> Forget the gardening! . . . I'm taking a concrete square [where trailers used to be parked]. They all look at me as if I'm mad. "What am I going to do with a concrete square?" . . . I would like to bring my fairy garden from out of my backyard that I won't open to the public, and give it to the public, or leave it behind when I go.[29]

There was a feeling of hopeful surprise among the LTVCEG participants and a sense of astonishment that they had begun an enterprise with each other. A space had opened up for relations between people who thought they had nothing in common and an economy of interdependence had started to develop. Listening to Jean again:

> It wouldn't matter if you were ten in here, or a hundred and ten, everybody's equal. They're sharing their morning teas, their coffee, have a laugh, have fun, get ideas, the youngies can come up with things, too, you all learn from each other, you're coping with all types of people, from your hot-tempered stand-over bully, to your type that if you say something to them they scream straight back at you. You've got to learn to deal with every type. It's good learning, it's . . . I don't know, there's just something right about this whole thing.

Framing this process in Connolly's terms, we can see the project as fostering what he calls a "generous ethos of engagement between a plurality of constituencies inhabiting the same territory" (1999, 36) and, we should add, not in the habit of speaking to one another. Rather than asking people to mute their differences or rise above them, or to leave substantial parts of themselves at home when entering the public arena, the generous ethos is accepting of a range of beings and behaviors, including the socially unacceptable.

An ethos of engagement is an aspect of a politics of becoming (communal), where subjects are made anew through engaging with others. This transformative process involves cultivating generosity in the place of hostility and suspicion. But such unfriendly affective predispositions are not displaced easily, which means that the process involves waiting as well as cultivating. We found it necessary to give people numerous opportunities to encounter each other in pleasurable ways—creating multiple spaces of engagement, offering activities and events that promoted receptivity. What took place in these spaces was the awakening of a communal subjectivity and a faint but discernible yearning for a communal (noncapitalist) economy.

In the Pioneer Valley our growing sense that language was not enough inclined us similarly toward bodily practices of engagement as a supplement to the delights of wordiness. We tried to make our conversations and gatherings entirely pleasurable (food was one of their main ingredients) and also loose and light—not goal-oriented or tied to definitions and prescriptions of what a "left alternative" should be. Over the course of the project, without prompting, the community researchers and their interviewees began to express practical curiosity (as opposed to moral certainty) about alternatives to capitalism. We decided to take a week-long trip to Cape Breton to attend the Festival of Community Economics, a conference on worker cooperatives, where we would spend three days listening to stories of workers who appropriated the surplus they produced and distributed it to sustain community economies. Ten of us piled into a UMass Geosciences department van for the seven-day outing—including members of our university-based group, community researchers, activists, and local NGO workers.[30] Before our departure, the trip loomed in some of our minds as potentially difficult—a period of overexposure in the pressure-cooker environment of the van. But as we traveled, both exposure and pressure revealed their transformative qualities, and we found ourselves continually surprised by the unfolding pleasures of being together and traveling toward an unknown form of community.

Talk at the conference focused almost entirely on cooperatives. By contrast, the van was a conversational plurispace, with Jim, a community researcher, as conservator of spaciousness. A veteran of alternative enterprises who engaged nonstop—despite his need for solitude—in projects of constructing community, Jim feared that growing a community economy would become a practice of monoculture. "Are co-ops the only answer?" he asked, disturbed by the lack of alternatives (to cooperatives) discussed at the conference.

One afternoon on an outing we found ourselves at a dead end in a bog that must be one of the wonders of Cape Breton. Jim, our naturalist, became our guide, introducing us to the miniature laurels, roses, and irises that flowered there. Crowns low against the wind, roots seeking scarce soil for sustenance, these tiny ancient plants were fragile yet incredibly hardy. In a land both familiar and foreign, we had stumbled as lost travelers upon a thriving, yet barely visible ecosystem. What was this bog if not a groundportrait of a diverse economic community?

As an approach to life and to economic possibility, Jim offered a passionate tentativeness. "Not tentativeness in the sense of equivocating," Anasuya said, "but in the sense of really not knowing and allowing things to happen—being open, not fixating. It's like beginner's mind, Zen mind." Must there be only one way? Must we wrench sameness and singleness out of multiplicity? Throwing ourselves together in the van, embarking on a trip without a clear or single vision of what our goal might be, we found our desires dispersed and differentiated, yet activated by a quest for an alternative economy. The van became a traveling space of conversation and connection among different visions, projects, hopes, languages, experiences, and levels of involvement or commitment.

By the end of the trip, we had produced several fantasies of cooperative enterprises and the social life they might enable as a way of performing and acknowledging our temporary, satisfying collectivity. How are we to understand this unexpectedly pleasurable trip but as an experience of ethical self-formation, of working on the self, as Foucault would say (though without being aware of working)?[31] Through the conversations in the van, the discourse of economic interdependence and community we had ingested for three days became transmuted into bodily desires and flows of energy directed toward a fantasized communal economy.

What was striking was the affective stance of the van travelers. Their relation to the cooperatives they were disposing themselves to inhabit resembled that different relation to fantasy that has been called "traversal." There was no militant advocacy, no talk of struggle against a despised capitalism; co-ops were not the be-all and end-all, just an everyday (presumably problematic) place to nurture a community.[32] The passionate tentativeness we had first seen in Jim became the spirit of the van community. And the trip itself became an acknowledgment of the ways that we are all already in a space of communality.

REFLECTION ON SUBJECTS

The question remains: did subjects for a community economy emerge from the events in thought/feeling and bodily swerves reported above? Certainly new community enterprises were begun and people were enrolled in making them work. The struggles to become different kinds of economic subjects continued long after the action research ended and many people reported experiencing changes in how they understood and dealt with themselves and others. In this sense, the interventions achieved some form of "history making," at least at an individual scale (Spinosa et al. 1997, 2).

We end with a story from the Latrobe Valley of one subject who has continued to be involved in conversations and actions that are generating new community economic becomings. Ken, who was retrenched at the age of fifty-four after thirty years as an electricity worker in the valley, has been a stalwart who has kept one of the enterprises going. Since leaving the power industry, Ken had become well known for his house decorations at Christmas time—large painted wooden scenes lit up and mounted on the roof and in the garden. His example had inspired other neighbors to decorate their houses, producing in their neighborhood the largest concentration of decorations in the region. Ken wanted a job, but was convinced that his lack of qualifications and age stood in the way of ever being "economically active" again:

> KATHIE: It must have been a big thing to stop formal work.
>
> KEN: It was a big step.
>
> KATHIE: So did you look for work?
>
> KEN: Oh yeah, I used to go round and go down to CES [the Commonwealth Employment Service] and all that sort of stuff. I thought I was flogging a dead horse, in all honesty, 'cause nobody wants you at that age. And I don't have a trade. I was never an electrician or fitter or plumber or painter or anything like that—I didn't have a trade.

In the process of documenting the assets and capacities of residents of the valley, we found that Ken had many skills that he had taught himself. He was a concreter, a furniture restorer, a cabinetmaker, a gardener, and a builder. In addition, he was an avid model steam-train builder and a member of two local model railway clubs for which he regularly performed voluntary work as a train driver. As one of the enterprises to be developed as part of our action research, it was suggested that a community access "Santa's workshop" be set up in a former preschool as a site where people could create their own Christmas decorations under the tutelage of Ken and Stephen, one of the ex-SEC community researchers attached to the project:

> KEN: They wanted somebody to show people, to sort of guide them on—those that were interested in decorating their house and such—in the right direction. . . . So we got started on it and had one woman the first day . . . and then it gradually came until we had seventeen one day. . . . So [for] four weeks, two days [a week]. See, it wasn't bad. And we produced quite a bit of stuff, plus we did those decorations for Advance Morwell [the town's local business association] for their Christmas trees.

For the last six years, Ken has been a central member of the small group that runs the workshop, making decorations that are donated to nearby schools, nursing homes, and even local families.[33] Through the experience with Santa's Workshop, he has found a new economic identity. After the first year of operation, Ken had these reflections:

> KATHIE: What sorts of things did you observe?
>
> KEN: The help they gave each other was very good. Everyone seemed to get on fairly well . . . everyone got on well. The kids that were there were not a problem. . . . I suppose the biggest thing . . . was that nobody would clean up after themselves, not everybody, but there were some that didn't, they wouldn't clean the brushes properly and this sort of stuff. But overall it was great. And the core of people that came all the time and ended up on the last day to clean up and everything . . . they got on well.

Participating in Santa's Workshop is not always easy. Ken has found himself faced with the difficult challenges of balancing individuality with communality—people copying his designs, others not cleaning up, the difficulty of accepting complete strangers, of having kids being minded in the workspace, and of working mainly with women who lack skills as well as confidence. He and the others involved have risen to the challenge of accepting and working with difference, creating in the process new ways of "being together," cultivating forms of community that are not based on narrow town parochialism, but broader valley identification.

While Ken remains formally "unemployed," his work at Santa's Workshop has become recognized as suitable for the "work for the dole" payment from the state and he is now able to get a higher unemployment benefit. In the person of Ken, multiple subject positions coexist. On the one hand, he experiences the ignominy of finding himself on the employment scrap heap, having to regularly turn up at the dole office. On the other, he inhabits a new identity at Santa's Workshop:

> KATHIE: So had you ever seen yourself in the role of a teacher?
>
> KEN: No. Not really.
>
> KATHIE: Did you enjoy it?
>
> KEN: Oh yeah, it was quite good.

The process of disclosing new worlds involves complex movements between identification with new subject positions, exploratory acts of self-transformation, and the fixing of new "dispositional patterns of desire" that become part of what we experience as subjection (Connolly 1995, 57). At any point in the history-making process, an individual is caught in two places, experiencing the dissatisfactions and disappointments of what they know and habitually desire and the satisfactions and surprises of what is new, but hard to fully recognize and want. The individual needs nourishment and encouragement from without to sustain acts of self-cultivation, to see changing selves as contributing to changing worlds.

Since the Community Partnering Project ended, the main force providing a pull toward a new economic visioning has dissipated. In the valley as it currently exists there is no active "constitutive outside" that will support and connect individual experiments that are building a community economy.[34] In the absence of a collective presence that recognizes the potential future for enterprises such as Santa's Workshop and that continues to renarrativize the past and the present, it is very hard to foster new becomings. Our projects have demonstrated that it is possible to cultivate subjects for a community economy, but that disclosing and sustaining new worlds requires nourishment over more than a few years.

What gives us hope is the fact that individuals like Ken are continuing to do what they have come to love doing. Without fanfare or ambitious design, he and others are, in a very small way, creating a new commons—a space in which all can enjoy creative production, working communally and individually in full and sometimes joyful recognition of their interdependence.[35]

POSTSCRIPT TO THE ACTION RESEARCH PROJECTS

This chapter has chronicled, somewhat desultorily and nonsequentially, the cultivation of subjects for the community enterprises and initiatives that were to be created in the later phases of the action research projects. Four initiatives were begun during the life of the Community Partnering Project in the Latrobe Valley:[36]

1. Latrobe Valley Community Environmental Gardens was established in October 1999 as an incorporated nonprofit association to transform the three-hectare site of the old Morwell caravan park managed by the Latrobe City Council into a community and environmental garden.

2. Santa's Workshop initially opened in an unused preschool in 1999 from October to December as a community workshop space where people could make large outdoor Christmas decorations under the tutelage of an ex-SEC worker who decorated his house each year. Since 2000, it has been open all year, two days a week, with ongoing material support (insurance, electricity, rent-free premises) from the council.

3. Latrobe Community Workshed @ Newborough opened in 2000 as primarily a woodworking workshop located in an abandoned butcher's shop in Moe/Newborough.

4. Latrobe Cyber Circus started with a one-day circus workshop in June 2000 for young people, including those in drug rehabilitation and young unemployed people already active in the local techno-electronic music scene. Subsequently a one-week circus camp was held in 2001 to train the group in all aspects of circus skills and develop a performance for schools based on a Dr. Seuss story.

In the Pioneer Valley, the project finished in June 2001 with a community conference to which all project participants were invited (approximately one hundred people attended). During the "Where do we go from here?" brainstorming session that concluded the conference, an Alternative Economic Development Council for the Pioneer Valley was established to foster the development of the local alternative sector. The council involves activists, academics, and government officials. Since its establishment, the council has held monthly meetings and workshops in which local alternative entrepreneurs and activists discuss their problems and successes, and familiarize each other with projects around the valley. In particular, the council has supported the development of E2M (see chapter 7), sponsoring numerous public and classroom presentations to introduce this alternative business model to the local community. Currently the council is in the process of dissolving itself into the E2M board and Regional Economic Council.

7

BUILDING COMMUNITY ECONOMIES

While the previous chapter is grounded in the recognition that changing the world requires changing the self, this chapter acknowledges and explores the other side of the coin: to change ourselves, we must change the world. Both practices of change offer angles on, and different technologies for, the uneven and uncertain project of "disclosing new worlds" (Spinosa et al. 2001). Below we outline a number of projects in which people are taking decisions to build new kinds of economies, what we have called "intentional community economies" in which social interdependency (economic being-in-common) is acknowledged and fostered and new kinds of economic subjects are produced. We have conceptualized the construction of community economies under the rubric of *collective action,* a concept that rests on a reworking of familiar understandings of both agency and collectivity. The "collective" in this context does not suggest the massing together of like subjects, nor should the term "action" imply an efficacy that originates in conscious beings, or that is distinct from thought. We are trying for a broad and distributed notion of collective action, in order to recognize and keep open possibilities of connection and development in the economic projects we are describing. In our view, the collectivities involved in constituting these economies include ourselves and other researchers who are engaged (often collaboratively with the participants) in theorizing and analyzing individual projects, thereby making them available and transportable as models or inspirations; and the action involved is the effectivity and extension (in time and space) of the heterogeneous collectivity, including the performativity of the often tacit knowledge that it generates and brings to bear in world-changing experiments.[1]

Our stance here involves both resisting the attractions of any positive blueprint *and* proposing the *community economy* as a new and different kind of universal that might guide the process of building different economies (see chapter 4). Unlike the structurally configured Economy with its regularities and lawful relationships, the community economy is an acknowledged space of social interdependency and self-formation. Anything but a blueprint, it is an unmapped and uncertain terrain that calls forth exploratory conversation and political/ethical acts of decision.[2] The "emptiness" of the community economy, which awaits filling up by collective actions in place, is what distinguishes the project of building community economies from the related and more familiar project of economic development.

The practice of economic development has been dominated by the naturalized universal of the capitalist economy (as the model of economy, as the only true, viable economy, as something that effaces its particularist origins in the West, in certain forms of market, in certain types of enterprise). Development discourse centers on the problematic of bringing capitalist economic development to those spaces that are "lacking" its dynamic presence and allure of beneficence. Countless strategies are advocated that will engender (or more proactively "kick start") capitalist industrialization[3]—import substitution, export base development, direct industry assistance, cluster development, elimination of trade barriers that impede the global flow of industrial inputs and commodity outputs, deregulation of labor markets so that industrialization can be fueled by cheap labor, deregulation of financial markets so that investment will more readily flow into greenfield areas of industrial development, retraining of labor so that the demands of emerging industries can be met, and so on. All strategies are pursued with the promise that increased well-being will trickle down from the capitalist sector and its employees to the wider community. And all are beholden to the conviction that economic growth (variously measured in terms of GDP, levels of capital investment, levels of employment, etc.) is unquestionably desirable.

Underpinning the complex set of strategies, policies, and beliefs that constitutes development discourse is a particular ontological framing of economic dynamics that is rooted in the experience of Western European and North American industrialization. The relationships between production and consumption, investment and growth, proletarianization and material well-being, competition, technological change, and efficiency that ostensibly characterized these experiences have been reified as structural logics of economic functioning and elevated as universal principles (sometimes represented as natural "laws") of economic evolution. Different attempts to produce economic development ignore these laws at their peril, it seems.[4]

Notably, each of the projects we discuss in this chapter treats economic development as a (by)product of ethical debates and decisions, rather than of the working out of structural imperatives. We present the projects in terms of their challenges to the following tenets of mainstream development discourse:

- Communities and regions "need" some sort of engagement with the global capitalist economy in order to develop.
- Industrialization is the singular pathway toward economic well-being.
- Promoting capitalist enterprise will bring social and economic dividends to the whole community.
- In the current era of neoliberal global capitalism, regions must develop their export base to be economically viable.
- Growing the output of the capitalist commodity producing sector is good for all.

The examples are drawn from our own action research in the Philippines, the United States, and Australia, supplemented by insights from other projects around the world (see Figure 33). The eclectic selection of stories demonstrates that we can start where we are with *any site* within a diverse economy and at *any scale,* from the local to the global, to begin to build community economies.

To structure our discussion, we focus on the four coordinates of ethical decision making laid out in our exploration of community economies in chapter 4:[5]

1. We first examine the diverse economy of a community in place in which subsistence *needs* are being met by a variety of means. We ask how a project of building and enlarging a community economy might articulate with and sustain the strengths and assets already present in the community.

2. We then look at a number of different ways of generating, marshaling, and distributing *surplus*: by diverting migrant remittance funds into community-based production in the Philippines; by transforming women's neighborhood savings associations into worker-owned producer cooperatives in India; and by increasing community equity in all kinds of local businesses, thus generating a revenue stream for community distribution in western Massachusetts.

3. We next consider some of the decisions that particular communities have made to *consume* resources in ways that set them on unpredictable development pathways. We take up the story of the Anti-Displacement Project in western Massachusetts, which has chosen to maintain affordable housing and use it as a base for a vibrant community economy, and that of the Pacific island state of Kiribati, which is using trust funds to support subsistence and cultural regeneration.

4. Finally we examine a number of projects concerned with replenishing and enlarging the *commons* that provides a shared base of material, social, and spiritual sustenance for communities. Our examples include the building of community gardens in industrialized settings and a case of reclaiming and replenishing a commons devastated by rapid development in Mexico. We ask how enlarging the

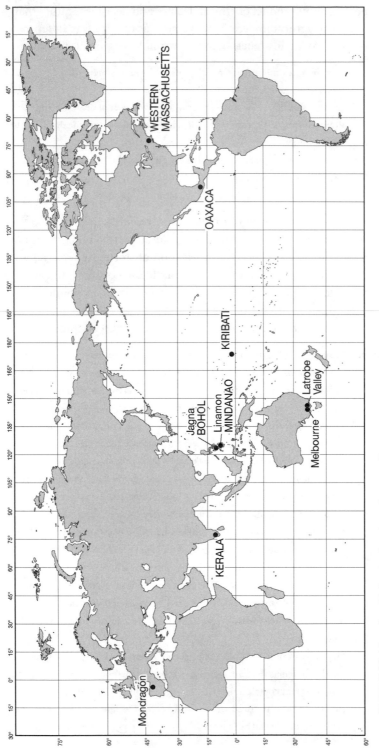

FIGURE 33. Map of world showing locations of case studies.

commons might both help communities to secure the necessities of life and at the same time provide opportunities for surplus generation and increased levels of well-being.

The infusion of specificities of place and pathway into development discourse is deeply destabilizing to economic certainty. Yet thinking of the economy as a contingent space of recognition and negotiation (rather than an asocial body in lawful motion) opens up for consideration the ethical practice of economic contingency. Describing the political space made available through current antinecessitarian thinking, Ernesto Laclau gives encouragement to the subjects it enables:

> [I]ncreasing the freeing of human beings through a more assertive image of their capacities, increasing social responsibility through the consciousness of the historicity of Being—is the most important possibility, a radically political possibility, that contemporary thought is opening up to us. (1991, 97–98)

The ethics of contingency, Laclau implies, involves the cultivation of ourselves as subjects of freedom—self-believing in our economic capacities, responsible to our political abilities, conscious of our potential to become something other than what we have heretofore "chosen" to be. If the economy is a domain of historicity and contingency, we can be actively involved in producing other economies, in a process that will transform us as economic subjects.

NEGOTIATING NECESSITY: APPRECIATING (NOT DEPRECIATING) ECONOMIC DIVERSITY

If constructing a community economy involves starting where you are and building on what you have, then some kind of inventory of existing local assets is a requirement for any initiative. What makes this task tricky rather than straightforward is the familiar development practice of devaluing what exists in place in favor of what is to be built according to universal specifications. Simply to perceive existing assets and capacities requires mobilizing techniques of rereading the local landscape—in this case, reading for absences (discussed in the Introduction) to restore visibility and credibility to what has been coded as backward, insufficient, or "nonexistent" as a contribution to development.

Development practice is imbued with the assumption that we all "need" development. Not surprisingly, it is capitalist development that is seen to provide what places and people "ought" to have. The absence of capitalist development is manifest in a whole set of unfulfilled "needs"—for jobs, wage income, health care, education, adequate housing and food.[6] The "basic needs approach" to development documents these in the attempt to determine the best ways of satisfying them through the allocative mechanisms of donor aid and development assistance (the latter favoring offers of "fishing rods rather than fish," so that the receivers can begin to self-provision).

The dominant needs approach to development focuses on what is missing, on the ways that basic requirements are not being met.[7] A solution is usually sought from outside the community. Decades of experience with the normative underpinnings of development discourse have led most people in both developed and developing nations to accept this representation of absence and negativity and to believe that outside assistance is necessary if needs are to be met. In our action research in the Philippines we have sought to challenge the presumption of lack as a way of starting to build a community economy in Jagna Municipality.

Jagna is a small, income-poor municipality of just over thirty thousand residents in the rural island province of Bohol. Around one-sixth of the population is dependent for their livelihoods on the remittances sent by household members who are overseas contract migrant workers (OCWs).[8] The majority of residents are farmers growing wet and dry rice, coconuts, bananas, and, in the higher areas, cooler climate vegetables and flowers. Along the coast are fishing settlements where people are struggling to make a living from the depleted near-shore fishery. Monetary incomes are low and economic development is squarely on the agenda of the new mayor of the municipality.

The glass-half-empty, "needs" representation of Jagna is well entrenched among local barangay (subdistrict) councillors and their immediate communities in the larger municipality. A recent exercise in participatory planning has seen each barangay compile a "development plan" that identifies strengths, weaknesses, opportunities, and threats (according to the familiar SWOT analysis favored by participatory rural appraisal practitioners). The "needs map" produced by these reports (see Figure 34) represents the locality as inferior, nonproductive, and ignorant (Santos 2004). From this knowledge base, the development plans outline requests for financial and infrastructural inputs that are way in excess of anything the municipal office can provide.

An alternative mapping of the diverse economy of Jagna produced as part of our action research project arrived at a very different representation of the assets of the community, one that includes dense networks of interaction between people that contribute to community resiliency, identity, and well-being (see Figure 35). While Jagna lacks a capitalist sector of any significant size, it is nevertheless the site of considerable economic activity (see Figure 36). The vast proportion of *enterprises* (in the righthand column) are independent agents— self-employed farmers, fishers, traders, drivers, and carpenters who produce and appropriate their own surplus, if indeed there is any available after meeting their own and their family's subsistence needs and the cost of inputs and machinery upkeep. A sizeable number of farmers are tenants working in a feudal relationship where the surplus is appropriated by a landlord and their labor is rewarded in kind with 50 to 75 percent of the harvest, depending on who pays for farm inputs. There are 220 businesses registered in Jagna, but most of these are very small family trading and merchandising enterprises that straddle the line between self-employment and use of family labor, with perhaps a handful of wage workers. Apart from the larger merchants and the one bank, there are no significant larger enterprises. The port is the largest and most capitalized enterprise in the area. It is state owned and run by the Port Authority with a few paid employees. The majority of port laborers are self-employed porters who are members of a labor association. There are no worker collectives and only one consumer cooperative water-supply business. The small number of nonprofit enterprises includes public schools and a handful of NGOs, including an alter-trade enterprise that organizes the export of bananas from Jagna growers to Japanese consumer cooperatives.

In Jagna *labor* is performed in many different ways (see the middle column of Figure 36). Wage workers are government employees and a small number of landless farm workers and general laborers. The range of forms of unpaid labor is large, particularly in the agricultural hinterland, where there is a culture of sharing and cooperation attached to the intensive hand labor of rice cultivation. Complex practices of voluntary labor exchange and gifting of labor are reflected in a rich language replete with specific terms and understandings of exchange, reciprocity, and interconnectedness, as documented in Figure 37.[9]

There is a complex mesh of *transactions* and exchanges involving goods, services, and finance that do not generally intersect formal markets (see the lefthand column of Figure 36). Barter between coastal communities and the rice-growing uplands is prevalent, with coastal people traveling to rural areas during harvest time to barter dried fish, wine, clay pots, salt, and cigarettes for rice. Rice farmers engage in a barter system called *tihap* in which they receive money or fertilizers before or during the land-preparation period and repay the donor in rice, with interest figured in, after the harvest. The alter-trade network negotiates exchange between the banana growers' cooperative in Jagna and Japanese consumer cooperatives, which guarantee a market and fair prices despite fluctuations in world banana prices. As with many cash-poor communities, there is a great variety of mechanisms for obtaining money outside of formal bank lending (see Figure 38). Notable among these practices are the communal forms of saving and borrowing for specific individual or household purposes—ceremonies and rituals like weddings, funerals, fiestas, or family livelihood projects like house building or land acquisition.

Jagna's diverse economy is made up of a thin layer of capitalist economic activity underlaid by a thick meshwork of traditional practices and relationships of sharing, borrowing, volunteering, and individual and collective work. These are the economic practices that are produced, in Santos's terms, as nonexistent or as "non-credible alternatives to what exists" by the monoculture of capitalocentric thinking (2004, 238). While the majority of people in Jagna are being supported and sustained by these hidden economic activities, there are still those for whom secondary education for children is a luxury that must be forgone when cash incomes are down, and for whom housing standards are basic, with no potable

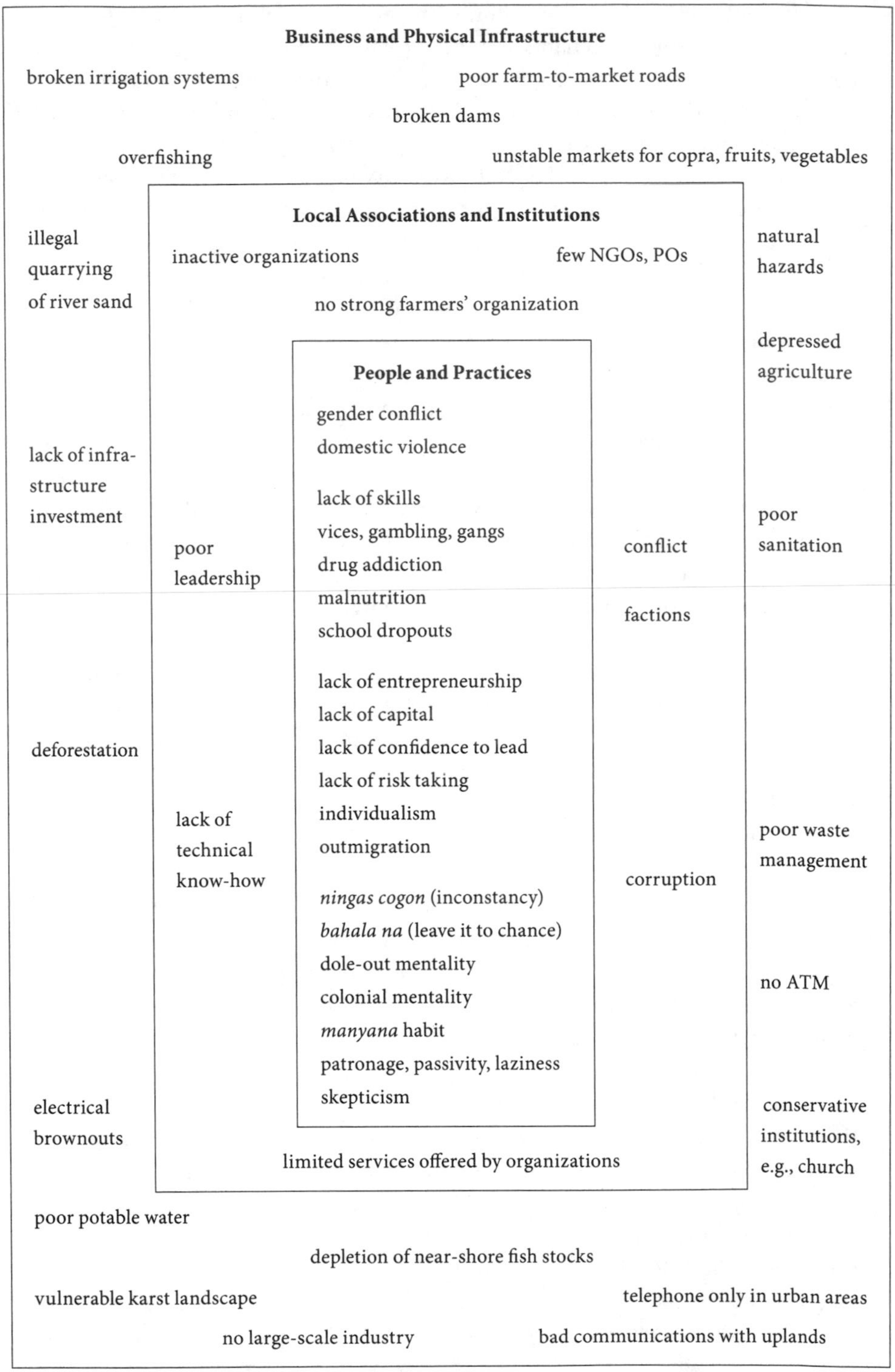

Business and Physical Infrastructure

broken irrigation systems

poor farm-to-market roads

broken dams

overfishing

unstable markets for copra, fruits, vegetables

illegal
quarrying
of river sand

natural
hazards

Local Associations and Institutions

inactive organizations

few NGOs, POs

no strong farmers' organization

depressed
agriculture

lack of infra-
structure
investment

People and Practices

gender conflict

domestic violence

lack of skills

vices, gambling, gangs

drug addiction

malnutrition

school dropouts

poor
leadership

conflict

poor
sanitation

factions

lack of entrepreneurship

lack of capital

lack of confidence to lead

lack of risk taking

individualism

outmigration

ningas cogon (inconstancy)

bahala na (leave it to chance)

dole-out mentality

colonial mentality

manyana habit

patronage, passivity, laziness

skepticism

deforestation

lack of
technical
know-how

corruption

poor waste
management

no ATM

electrical
brownouts

conservative
institutions,
e.g., church

limited services offered by organizations

poor potable water

depletion of near-shore fish stocks

vulnerable karst landscape

telephone only in urban areas

no large-scale industry

bad communications with uplands

FIGURE 34. Needs map of Jagna municipality.

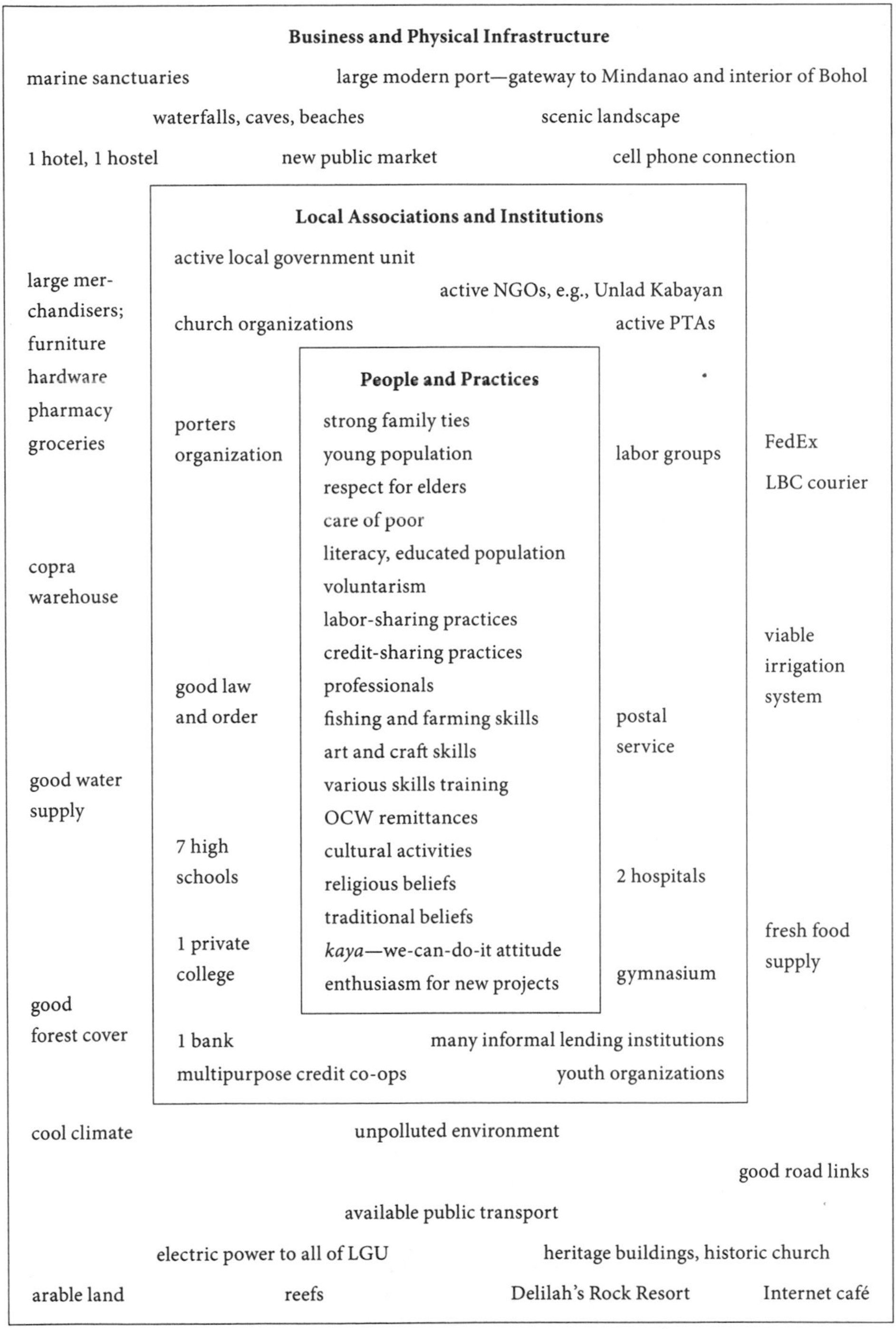

Business and Physical Infrastructure

marine sanctuaries   large modern port—gateway to Mindanao and interior of Bohol

      waterfalls, caves, beaches   scenic landscape

1 hotel, 1 hostel   new public market   cell phone connection

Local Associations and Institutions

active local government unit

      active NGOs, e.g., Unlad Kabayan

large mer-
chandisers;   church organizations   active PTAs
furniture
hardware
pharmacy   **People and Practices**
groceries

porters	strong family ties	labor groups
organization	young population	
	respect for elders	
	care of poor	
copra	literacy, educated population	
warehouse	voluntarism	
	labor-sharing practices	
	credit-sharing practices	
good law	professionals	
and order	fishing and farming skills	postal
	art and craft skills	service
good water	various skills training	
supply	OCW remittances	
7 high	cultural activities	
schools	religious beliefs	2 hospitals
	traditional beliefs	
1 private	*kaya*—we-can-do-it attitude	
college	enthusiasm for new projects	gymnasium

good
forest cover 1 bank   many informal lending institutions

    multipurpose credit co-ops   youth organizations

FedEx

LBC courier

viable
irrigation
system

fresh food
supply

cool climate   unpolluted environment

                     good road links

       available public transport

   electric power to all of LGU   heritage buildings, historic church

arable land   reefs   Delilah's Rock Resort   Internet café

FIGURE 35. Assets map of Jagna municipality.

TRANSACTIONS	LABOR	ENTERPRISE
MARKET	**WAGE**	**CAPITALIST**
Goods: furniture, agri-vet, hardware, pharmaceuticals, groceries, motorcycles Services: Internet, medical, telecommunications, rental properties Credit: First Consolidated Bank 2 percent monthly interest Seven lending institutions and pawnshops	Private business Farm laborers General laborers Port workers Municipal employees Provincial Government employees NGO employees	Merchants: Seventy-five retailers, six dealers, two trading, one wholesaler Bank: First Consolidated Bank Manufacturing: Six businesses (including welding, catering, dressmaking) Services: Fifty-nine (including private hospital, schools)
ALTERNATIVE MARKET	**ALTERNATIVE PAID**	**ALTERNATIVE CAPITALIST**
Local trading systems Sari-sari stores, *suki* relations *Ukay ukay* used clothing House-to-house and sidewalk vending *Alternative currencies* Rice paid for use of thresher and plough *Underground market* Drug trade *Co-op exchange* Alter-trade network *Barter* Upland rice for coastal fish, wine, cigarettes, pots, salt *Alternative credit* Multipurpose co-ops: porters, coconut growers *Kabaway*: households pool money to buy fiesta carabao and access funds for credit during year *Suking tindahan*: credit from sari-sari stores for basic goods *Repa-repa*: revolving credit associations used to access large amounts for housing, land, major appliances *Tampuhay*: savings group, funds divided at end of year	*Self-employed* Farmers, fishers, traders, drivers, producers, porters *Indentured* 781 OCW seamen and domestic helpers *Reciprocal* *Hungos*: group labor on rice lands *Badsanay*: exchange of individual labor services *In-kind* *Sagod*: landless perform weeding and harvest labor in return for one-sixth share of harvest Tenant farmers: paid with 50, 66, or 75 percent of harvest, depending on inputs Hired labor: harvest coconuts P70/day plus meals *Guno*: harvesting corn for farmer with entitlement to one-seventh of what is picked *Hagpat*: helping pick fish from fisherman's net in return for one-third of catch *Pension* Retirees	*Socially responsible firm* *Botica sa Barangay*: pharmacy run by political party that sells cheap medicine to less well off *State enterprise* Philippines Port Authority *Nonprofit* NGOs Schools Alter-trade organization

TRANSACTIONS	LABOR	ENTERPRISE
continued	continued	continued

NONMARKET	**UNPAID**	**NONCAPITALIST**
Household flows	*Volunteer*	*Communal*
Food sharing	*Tingub*: regular voluntary work	Pangdan Water Cooperative
Child-care sharing	on irrigation channels	Households
Care of house and animals	*Bayanihan*: communal work	*Independent*
Gifts	to help households or	Fishing enterprises
Charity to poor—house	barangay	Farms
built, water-sealed toilets	CIVAC: "citizen's voluntary	Trading business
constructed	action" led by barangay	Small-scale producers:
Suki-ay: one family supplies	captain to do road fixing,	carpenters, drivers,
another family with food	street cleaning	chainsaw operators, cock
and drink for fiesta	Parish Pastoral Council	breeding, video game rental
Dajong: neighborhood	JCW beautification projects	Households
mortuary assistance	*Housework/Family care*	*Feudal*
including money, food, and	Cooking, cleaning, child care,	Tenant farms
services	care of sick	Households
Gala 1: families give money,	Family work on farm	
rice, wood to family of	Family work in small business	
marrying son		
Gala 2: dances and money		
offered in honor of patron		
saint—fundraising for		
church		
Dory: credit for no-interest		
debt of gratitude		
Indigenous exchange		
Ritual offerings to spirits		
Gleaning		
Pamukak collecting fruits and		
vegetables after harvest		
Theft		
Stealing crops to settle		
gambling debts		
Illegal extraction of sand and		
gravel		

FIGURE 36. Jagna's diverse economy. Figures on business and employment from the Bohol Provincial Medium Development Plan 1998–2003; figures on numbers of people in various occupational categories from Barangay Development Plans and Unlad Kabayan's unpublished survey of OCWs.

Bayanihan: an indigenous practice of helping each other do voluntary community work, for example, moving a nipa house or making a school garden.

Hungos: a group of rice farmers who band together to do voluntary work on one person's farm, like preparing rice paddies for cropping, planting, or harvesting. The expectation is that this favor would be returned at some time. Mostly practiced by upland rice farmers.

Tingub: a group of barangay residents who regularly perform voluntary labor, such as maintaining irrigation canals, irrigating rice fields. This is often done on a district level at a certain time of the week or month.

Badsanay: a practice of exchanging individual labor services through verbal agreement.

CIVAC: stands for citizen's voluntary action, where everybody in the community renders voluntary labor services for road fixing, cleaning the residential surroundings and other community work. This is always spearheaded by the Barangay Captain or the Barangay Council.

Sagod: a labor arrangement introduced after agrarian reform whereby landless laborers perform weeding on another's land and are granted the exclusive right to harvest that same plot for a percentage of the crop, usually one-sixth if the crop is threshed and cleaned.

FIGURE 37. Local terms for forms of unpaid labor.

water or water-sealed sanitary toilets. These kinds of shortfalls in meeting what could be considered subsistence needs create an incentive for family members to seek employment overseas. It comes as no surprise to find that most of the remittances sent by overseas contract migrant workers to their families are spent on education costs and housing improvements—replacing natural fiber with iron roofing, building an indoor bathroom and toilet, and, for the longer term OCWs, a new concrete structure.[10] Many households look to overseas migration as their only option for obtaining what are seen to be necessities of life.

In mainstream economic discourse, the huge growth of global contract labor migration over the last few decades is viewed unproblematically as the coming into being of an international labor market in which some national economies participate as labor exporters and others as labor importers. The force driving this growth is seen to be the individual migrant decision-maker "rationally" maximizing her returns on a terrain that is becoming less obstructed by barriers to movement. Not surprisingly, a sense of economic being-in-common has been largely erased by this view.

An understanding of OCW migration from Jagna produced within a discourse of the community economy might focus on negotiated relationships among necessity, commons, surplus, and consumption, yielding an entirely different vision of the subjectivity, motivations, and choices of migrant workers. Filipina

Dajong: this is a vernacular term meaning "to carry together" and refers to the practice of mortuary assistance organized at a neighborhood level. Upon death of a neighborhood resident, member families donate money and or other services such as carrying the coffin, offering labor for digging the burial hole, preparing food for the members of the *dajong* who are required to attend during the burial ceremony.

Gala 1: a group, often composed of parents who have sons of marriageable age, which forms to lessen the financial burden of marriage preparation. Members of the *gala* contribute money, rice, wood, or anything that will assist the family of the marrying son.

Gala 2: an activity where people offer dances and money in honor of the patron saint who is celebrated at a particular time and place. This practice is usually performed during and after fiesta time. It is also a fund-raising scheme for any church-based celebrations and other activities.

Kabaway: a group of people that put together some agreed amount of money to procure carabaos to be slaughtered during fiesta time. The saved amount is extended for credit services to members with interest payable a month or two before fiesta celebration.

Repa-repa: a revolving credit group in which members regularly contribute a set amount of money which is pooled and drawn upon by one member selected at random using a raffle. All members get to draw on the pool within a certain period. This practice is used to access money for big projects such as house improvements, buying major appliances or land.

Tampuhay: a savings group in which members put away an amount of money and then divide it among their group at the end of the year.

Suki-ay: A practice of giving some goods or money to families celebrating fiesta. The families that receive these goods will return the favor during the fiesta of the donors.

FIGURE 38. Alternative market and nonmarket ways of accessing money.

contract migrants working as domestic helpers or live-in caregivers are seeking to fund the necessaries of life that are elsewhere provided as part of a commons. Most of their host countries—Hong Kong, Singapore, Canada—guarantee universal access to public education and public housing at reasonable standards for low-income earners. State allocations and redistributions of wealth replenish and sustain these commons, reflecting hard-won community decisions that underwrite a generalized standard of living. What citizens of host countries are availed as a commons is for Filipina migrants something to be purchased individually, out of the proceeds of their labor (the necessary labor fund). A discourse of the global community economy might highlight national differences in the commons that supports subsistence levels. The growing interdependence between national economies at the household level provides the opportunity for some interesting community economic conversations on this and related topics.

The relationships among necessity, surplus, and consumption are no less interesting and ethically provoking. It is ironic that legal employment as an indentured laborer in households in host nations entitles the migrant worker to be paid less than what is considered a living wage in that social context (partly because housing, often in the kitchen itself, is supplied). From their paltry incomes, migrant workers nevertheless regularly decide to save a portion that they define as surplus to their immediate requirements. Their savings are usually gifted as remittances, to be used by families back home for necessities and also to procure consumption goods that are not universally recognized as socially necessary to subsistence in the Philippines. Currently some migrants are working with the Asian Migrant Centre (AMC) in the Migrant Savings for Alternative Investments (MSAI) program. They are rethinking what to do with portions of their surplus, forming savings groups to pool it with others to fund alternative enterprises back home (see Introduction). This often requires difficult negotiations with families who have been counting on an increased consumption fund, asking them to settle for somewhat less than they expected.

From the perspective of mainstream development discourse, Jagna would be well advised to deal with its deficiencies by exporting more labor or promoting a shift to export agriculture as a way to generate more cash income in the community to meet subsistence needs. From the perspective of building a community economy, the options open out in many different directions. A full audit of livelihood practices, including the contribution of nonmarket transactions and unpaid labor, allows for reflection on what the community is nourished by (rather than what it lacks) and for public discussion of which of these practices could be strengthened or extended. There is the opportunity to review and decide what to do about the more oppressive aspects of some of these practices, such as how they might maintain and heighten status and power hierarchies within the community or how they might foster exploitative flows of labor. And there is the chance to locate where and for whom real shortfalls in meeting subsistence needs are taking place and to discuss community-wide strategies (other than watching energetic and educated young people leave to take up menial jobs as OCWs) to address these.[11] By starting first with an appreciation of the diverse ways in which the Jagna community economy *already* produces a culturally rich and largely sustaining lifestyle for the people of the municipality, a new decision space is opened up—the choice can be made to build on this present base and ensure that it is not inadvertently depreciated (or even destroyed) by mainstream development interventions that offer the fantasy of a future sufficiency.

GENERATING, MARSHALING, AND DISTRIBUTING SURPLUS

At the base of the development dream is faith in the incredible productive capacity of capitalist enterprise to generate wealth that can then "float all boats," supporting higher standards of living and increased levels of well-being. What is rarely a part of this dream, however, is the mechanism by which these benefits will be distributed (let alone redistributed) to all *beyond* those who actively participate in capital investment or labor markets. The "us all" that constitutes the majority of society not directly participating in these markets (where some "return" can be expected) is left out of the picture.[12] The ethical dimensions of surplus generation, its distribution and role in building society, are not up for discussion in mainstream development discourse, despite ample evidence that the disparities wrought by capitalist development are not disappearing, either within many national economies or on a global scale. The many projects world-wide in which the marshaling and distribution of surplus is explicitly built into a community economy intervention offer a challenge to the belief that capitalist development is the best or only way of generating wealth for all.

Mondragón provides an inspirational model of a community economy built around the production, marshaling, and distribution of surplus (see chapter 5). At the heart of Mondragón's success in generating local employment and increasing standards of living is a strong base of worker-owned industrial co-operatives in which the workers appropriate the surplus they produce (rather than having it go to the capitalist, or to the board of directors of a capitalist firm). The cooperatively produced commodities are marketed locally, nationally, and internationally. Much of the surplus produced and appropriated by the coopera-tors is distributed to their individual capital accounts, which must be deposited in the central Mondragón bank until they retire. Through this arrangement, the cooperatives marshal their surplus in a centrally administered investment fund that is used to create more co-ops and employment. Over its fifty years, the Mondragón community economy has created not only many industrial co-ops, but also retail and service co-ops providing social security, education, health care, and housing to the whole community.

Any examination of the Mondragón experiment must be struck by the con-tingent conditions prevailing in the Basque region that presented the cooperators with their particular challenges and opportunities. This model cannot be simply transported to other sites in the world and be expected to work without modi-fication. In each site, the existing conditions will present their own challenges and will shape the decisions made and the pathways followed. The insight that surplus *is* generated and that wealth *can be* shared equitably and democratically is what Mondragón offers.

As part of our action research project in the Philippines, we are collabo-rating with Unlad Kabayan Migrant Services Foundation Inc., an NGO pio-neering community enterprise development that takes some of its inspiration from Mondragón. One of the differences is that this organization is working in noncontiguous communities around the Philippines where migrant savers are involved in the MSAI program and investing in surplus-generating businesses. The finances marshaled for these enterprise experiments are savings set aside by contract migrant workers from what might normally be remitted to families for consumption expenses. These workers can be seen as choosing to constitute and appropriate a surplus by demarcating the portion of their wage that goes to consumption (and thus reflects necessary labor) and the portion available for investment.[13] Savings groups formed overseas in Hong Kong, Singapore, and Japan and among merchant seamen across Europe are investing in organic chicken farms, ube (aromatic yam) processing and confectionery making, and a coconut coir manufacturing plant. Unlad is currently concentrating their efforts in a few regions of the Southern Philippines in Bohol and Mindanao. Working in a political climate in which cooperatives have lost their meaning through state co-optation and the corruption of most of the growers' cooperatives during the Marcos era, the form of enterprise development is a matter for discussion.

With the transfer of administrative power and budgetary responsibility that accompanied decentralization in the Philippines, local governments are now in the front line of responsibility for development agendas (Legaspi 2001). Many are interested in working with Unlad to develop local enterprise capacity. In the municipality of Linamon an abandoned agricultural training college has become the site of a joint NGO-council-sponsored center for the Social Entrepreneur and Enterprise Development Scheme (SEEDS). Migrant savers are funding the technical development of new commodities made from local agricultural products (camote/pumpkin, coconut coir) to be sold in local and national markets. Our project is working alongside this intervention with community researchers, mobilizing interest in collective enterprise development and enrolling local people in a newly emerging community economy. One of the inspirations we are looking to in this intervention (in addition to Mondragón) is an emerging cooperative economy in Mararikulam.

Mararikulam is one of the poorest areas of the coastal Indian province of Kerala. Currently the community is engaged in what they call the "Mararikulam experiment"—an adventure in generating local income and employment for the poorest of the poor inspired by the Mondragón experience. The Mararikulam experiment builds on decades of struggles for social justice in Kerala and most recently the province-wide 1996–2001 Kerala People's Campaign for Decentralized Planning, which lifted literacy levels and engaged people in planning processes through innovative grassroots initiatives carried out in each village (Thomas Isaac and Franke 2002). Today in the province literacy rates are above 90 percent, infant mortality is low, and life expectancy exceeds seventy years—a situation that is closer to what we would expect in a wealthy country, rather than in one of the poorest places in India (Franke 2003, 8).[14]

In the spirit of self-reliance associated with Mahatma Gandhi, the Mararikulam experiment involves over 1,500 neighborhood savings groups, each made up of twenty to forty women, that are transforming themselves from credit associations to production cooperatives. The exclusive emphasis on women's involvement is a way of addressing issues of gender equity in Kerala, developing women's productive power to enhance their social and political power. The first step has been to generate capital by organizing groups of women to redefine some of their meager earnings as a surplus to be saved and invested, rather than as part of the necessary consumption fund. Even very small amounts, when saved by seventeen thousand women, have yielded enough to capitalize a number of small cooperatives (Franke 2003, 9).[15] The co-ops initially started producing soap, an ideal product not only because it can be made using coconut oil, an abundant local input, but because Kerala consumes more soap per capita than the rest of India. At a meeting held in 2002, thirty thousand women took the Maari soap pledge to buy Maari soap rather than imported brands, in a conscious act of resistance to corporate globalization, as well as an affirmation of local self-reliance (see www.mararidevelopment.org/the_pledge.htm).

The goal of the Mararikulam experiment is to generate up to twenty thousand jobs "paying enough to bring households above the poverty line" (Franke 2003, 8) by creating a big federation of small co-ops. In each cooperative, any surplus the women produce is reinvested for product improvements or other company costs. By 2003, the second stage was underway, with co-ops producing semiprocessed foods, umbrellas, school notebooks, school bags, and kits. The third, more ambitious stage will develop Mararikulam's food-producing potential, including fish farming and processing the ocean catch of fish, shrimp, and mussels. It will also develop more technologically advanced employment in the manufacture of coir (coconut fiber) products, like geotextiles and packaging. Here the cooperatives will become exporters, producing food and manufactured products beyond the local capacity for consumption.

Local governments and the worker-owners themselves supply 42 percent of the investment funds for this experiment with additional funding coming at this stage from provincial and international agencies. The small worker cooperatives are supported by a centralized marketing and capital management corporation that runs on commercial principles and provides services to all the microenterprises across the larger community.[16] Purchasing these services involves a distribution of surplus generated in the small enterprises, but it is a distribution that ensures a greater likelihood of enterprise success and the sustainable generation of an income for the poor women involved.

The basic idea of the Mararikulam experiment is that local "wealth" can be collectively marshaled to bring people out of poverty. Through constructing the capacity to generate surplus in cooperative enterprises that are supported by community-wide organizations, the chance that benefits will be widely distributed and shared is maximized.[17] Rather than relying on the promise of a trickle-down of benefit from the development of capitalist enterprise, the women of Mararikulam are using their own savings to leverage funds from community-based organizations and building self-reliant worker cooperatives in which they are the first receivers and distributors of their own surplus.

Our final story about marshaling surplus involves alternative capitalist enterprises. An Economic Model for Millennium 2000 (E2M) was founded by Michael Garjian, an inventor and social entrepreneur who was formerly a successful businessperson in western Massachusetts. E2M emerged from Garjian's disaffection with being on the growth treadmill of maximizing profits and working for shareholders at the expense of workers and communities. As a business model, E2M is very simple: to qualify as an E2M company, a business must donate at least 5 to 20 percent of their equity to their workers and 5 to 20 percent to the local community, represented by a regional economic council. This creates a revenue stream to a community fund administered by the council, which is made up of representatives of the different demographic groups in the region. The council distributes the fund to finance new enterprises, social services, or other community projects.

E2M companies make the decision to commit to the community for many different reasons, including personal ones. Garjian argues that some older entrepreneurs are tired of business as usual and want to make a contribution, while some young entrepreneurs are yet to be wholly captured by "the system." There are also other more business-oriented motives. An E2M-certified enterprise is eligible for low-interest loans and low-key venture capital from the regional economic council. Traditional venture capitalists look for returns of ten to twenty times their investment, if not more. The E2M council is happy to see an enterprise create jobs and achieve sustainable growth. In addition, companies have an advantage in being locally recognized as E2M-certified companies, qualifying for local purchase agreements and attracting loyal consumers.

From the community point of view, E2M represents a way to garner equity in local business and divert a portion of the surplus generated in the region toward strengthening the local community, all within a predominantly capitalist economic environment. As the E2M fund grows, the regional economic council can not only create more E2M companies, but can even begin to buy out existing companies and convert them to E2M-certified businesses, potentially wholly owned by their workers and the community. The regional economic council could also potentially invest in building affordable housing, or providing adequate health care and social services.

In western Massachusetts, the E2M business model has been launched (see www.e2m.org) and a regional economic council formed, composed of representatives of local labor unions, community groups, churches and educational institutions, community development funds and agencies, government, and private business. This venture is in its early days. At this stage, we can see it as an innovative concept that builds on the realization that decisions can be made within any enterprise (whether capitalist, self-employed, or cooperative) as to how to structure equity and distribute surplus. There are no laws or regulations that determine how these decisions are to be made and herein lies the opportunity to insert ethical choices that reflect economic being-in-common. Garjian's E2M model invites enterprise owners to consider making business decisions that reflect their commitment and debt to their workers and their communities. It allows for greater community involvement in the economic activities of the region without prescribing what kinds of enterprises best suit the goal of marshaling surplus for community economic strengthening.[18] Most important, this intervention helps to redefine the economic community by distributing surplus and enlarging a commons that can be drawn on to meet local needs for social services and subsistence goods, as well as to expand local business. In its structure and scope for decision making, E2M acknowledges the contributions made by entrepreneurs, employees, and the community alike to the workings of a community economy.

With the exception of Mondragón, the projects discussed here are in their early phases, raising all the questions about viability and sustainability that the beginning stage of any project is unable to address. Moreover, the distance we are taking in these overviews makes them appear seamless and unproblematic. From this vantage point, we cannot see the close work of stitching (and undoing and restitching) that is the daily ethical practice of building a community economy. Suffice it to say that in all these instances, conflict, failure, and discouragement are part of the process of coming into existence. As nascent efforts, they are especially vulnerable to loss of confidence and the waning of commitment of early enthusiasts.

Interestingly, all of these projects are oriented toward building local community economies but are "replicable" on a global scale. Mondragón offers an inspiring vision that can take root in any locale, whereas E2M has actually created the institutional infrastructure for chartering regional economic councils worldwide. Despite their potential replicability, each of them is also defined by the contingencies of project and place. Mondragón and E2M, for example, function independently of state involvement, while Mararikulam and Linamon are sponsored, respectively, by provincial and municipal governments. In each case an ethical decision has been taken about whether, and which level of, government should be part of the project. There are no simple rules to follow and no one-size-fits-all model available for building community economies; thus the examples function more as goads and inspirations than as blueprints for replication.

CHOOSING HOW TO CONSUME:
DECISIONS ABOUT DEVELOPMENT PATHWAYS

Given the discursive dominance of neoliberal globalization, there appears to be some agreement between both opponents and advocates of capitalist development that we have seen the end of economic self-determination for localities. Communities, it is argued, must adjust to the demands of the global economic system or consign themselves to economic backwardness and deprivation. Neoliberal versions of development discourse offer no options other than growing your export base and competing with other communities to get a piece of the global pie. The unchallenged assumption is that economic growth comes from exports that bring in dollars from outside the region; those dollars fuel local economic growth via the mechanism of the famous "multiplier effect." Every job created in an export industry, whether it be high-tech manufacturing or higher education, means more local employment in other sectors.[19] The workers spend their wages with local retailers and consume local services, thus creating private sector jobs; they pay taxes and create jobs in the public sector.

It makes sense, then, that localities are competing with each other to build their export and employment base, either by fostering an industrial cluster characterized by dynamic growth and backward and forward linkages among a number of local firms or by recruiting large enterprises to invest in the region to create new jobs. These might be multinationals, like Toyota, or they might be federal prisons, a growing industry in the United States. To attract businesses, local and state officials will commonly offer large subsidies and tax breaks, often paying far more per job than that job can possibly yield in tax revenues over a period of many years. Many academics and policy makers have documented the problems with this approach: companies frequently deliver many fewer jobs than they promise; the jobs may go to people outside the local area who commute from a long distance and spend their wages where they live (contributing to a multiplier effect there, but leaking wealth away from the community where the plant is located); the profits of the company are generally not reinvested in the local area; the company may not buy its inputs locally; businesses induced to locate in the region may pick up and move well before the subsidies they receive are recouped by the local government. Yet the hopeful vision remains: if we create job growth in export industries, local wealth will increase and so will the standard of living and quality of life. The following stories represent two very different challenges to this singular narrative, showing how well-being can be created directly, without resort to the circuitous pathway of export-led trickle-down development.

The first story concerns an organization that has generated jobs not from an export base, but by tying social services together with income-generating projects in the Pioneer Valley of Massachusetts. The Anti-Displacement Project (or A-DP) is based in Springfield, the largest city in western Massachusetts, with a racially mixed population of African-, Italian-, and Irish-Americans and, more recently, Spanish- and Russian-speaking immigrants. From the 1960s to the 1980s, publicly sponsored but privately owned housing had been built for low-income tenants, but as mortgage periods came up, owners "opted out of the affordable housing business" and allowed the housing to deteriorate or sold it off or started to rent at market rates (Hogan 2003, 83). In the face of this destruction of what we might call a partial commons, the A-DP was formed in 1988 to organize tenant buyouts of apartment complexes and maintain low-income housing in the region. By accessing funds from the Department of Housing and Urban Development and forming tenant-owned housing cooperatives and tenant associations, the A-DP proceeded to purchase and renovate five apartment complexes, preserving them for use by low-income tenants. Currently their real property is distributed from Springfield in the south to Greenfield in the north of the Pioneer Valley and they have over fifteen million dollars in assets. They have raised more than sixty million dollars in leveraged funds and have "preserved, purchased, rehabilitated, and managed as affordable housing" over two thousand at-risk units (Hogan 2003, 88). The organization now represents over fifteen hundred families and is led by "a core of over 300 seasoned leaders" (85) trained in the Saul Alinsky method of community organizing and activism.

The A-DP's commitment to innovative organizing and community building does not end with housing. They offer youth, education, and leadership programs, support computer rooms and community kitchens in every housing complex, and are the largest single distributor of free food from the regional food bank. They recently started a worker center and hiring hall where the tenant-owners can find jobs, circumventing the temporary employment agencies that are notorious for underpaying workers. Since job creation is part of the A-DP's mandate, they have also started a for-profit worker-owned cooperative business, United Landscaping Company (ULC), with the apartment complexes as their first customers. In the past, maintenance, landscaping, and snow removal—a major expense—have been contracted out. Now ULC does the work and also takes on contracts to maintain non–A-DP properties. While ULC has created jobs for tenants where they have control over the workplace and revenues, the co-op sees its commitment as not only to its worker members, but to the greater A-DP community.

In 2002, the A-DP began a campaign at Whiting Farms, one of their housing projects in Holyoke, to build more low-income housing units on adjacent vacant lots. This plan has brought them into conflict with the city of Holyoke, which is hoping to develop an industrial park in the same location. A-DP members argue that it is an open question whether an industrial park would do more than a housing project for the city's economy. They point out that Whiting Farms residents paid a lot of real estate taxes to the city last year; an expansion of the housing project at Whiting Farms would be certain to expand the residential tax base, whereas an industrial park would cost the city tax revenue in the form of tax abatements or infrastructure subsidies. Moreover, industries in the park might create employment but not necessarily for Holyoke residents. In contrast, building A-DP housing would create jobs for local construction workers (including A-DP tenant-owners), and would address an immediate social need for more affordable housing.[20]

The A-DP's suggestion that Holyoke collaborate with them to satisfy the local demand for low-income housing points toward a different development strategy, one that aims at improving social well-being directly, rather than expanding the export base and waiting for the "multiplier effect" to trickle down or across. It also highlights the decision space that many local governments occupy and the difficulties elected officials may have in deciding between competing projects in the light of the "laws" of economic development. For Holyoke officials to allow the A-DP access to land for the "unproductive" activity of providing additional housing for local consumption *and not* to grant access to private corporations for the "productive" activity of generating value added in export industries, they must go against mainstream economic thinking and their own advisors and planners, who are trained in the vision of a "correct" development pathway.[21] From this story we can see that local governments may not only have a decisive role in the local economy, but also ethical options and opportunities for building community economies.

Another story that highlights decisions over the consumption of public funds and implications for development pathways takes us to a Pacific island nation. The Republic of Kiribati is a Micronesian island state of just under one hundred thousand people scattered over thirty islands in the Central Pacific.[22] Prior to independence in 1979, Kiribati was part of the Gilbert and Ellice Islands Colony, a British territory. Its small land area and generally unproductive coral soils mean that today most of the nation's wealth is derived from fishing, plus a limited amount of copra and seaweed production.

Kiribati is a low-income country with an estimated GDP in 2000 of about US$79 million, or about US$800 on a per capita basis (Gibson and Pretes 2004). The country has what has been called a MIRAB economy—one maintained at higher than expected levels of economic performance by migration (MI), remittances (R), foreign aid (A), and bureaucracy (B) (Bertram and Watters 1985). To conceive of a MIRAB economy as "viable" and "sustainable," it is necessary to re-imagine economy in its anticapitalocentric diversity and to consider the economic space of Pacific island states as including Pacific islanders resident overseas (Bertram and Watters 1985). Almost all the resident populace is engaged in aspects of the noncapitalist economy. Only about 20 percent of the resident working-age adult population is formally employed, and most of these hold jobs in the public sector. The remaining 80 percent depend for their livelihood on a combination of subsistence (fishing and agriculture) and family support (from both resident and nonresident family members, especially those employed abroad as sailors or working in New Zealand).

The Republic of Kiribati is in the fortunate situation of having at its disposal a windfall capital fund originally based on royalty revenues derived from mining the extensive phosphate deposits once found on the island of Banaba (Ocean Island).[23] The Revenue Equalisation Reserve Fund was established as a publicly owned "trust fund" in 1956 when Kiribati was still a British colony.[24] This trust fund has transformed nonrenewable phosphate resources into renewable fiscal resources. From 1956 to the mine's closure in 1979, 25 percent of phosphate revenues was deposited into the fund and all income generated by the fund was saved and reinvested. The fund has grown considerably since its inception and in 2000 it reported a balance of US$508 million. At present, all fund assets are invested offshore by two London-based fund managers in an equal balance of equity and fixed-income investments. The fund itself is administered by a committee consisting of the minister of finance and five other senior officials. Parliamentary approval is needed for all drawdowns.

The use to which this source of public revenue has been put is of particular interest to us in thinking about options for consumption, in this case of the revenues deriving from a commons. Mainstream imaginings of development argue that to be sustainable, a country must be "underpinned by productive activity within the territorial boundaries of the island economy itself" (Bertram 1993, 248), preferably activity that generates exports and foreign currency income. For Kiribati, now that mining has been exhausted, the only option for export-led development is to further exploit its ocean resources. The republic has taken the bold step of forgoing this pathway to development and refusing to invest trust fund revenues in expanding export-oriented fishing activity. Instead the country's trust fund has been put to use in stabilizing the economy, supplementing income flows from remittances and development aid, and supporting the viability of subsistence activities. While aid is still sought for large capital projects, like building new roads and hospitals, trust fund incomes are also used periodically to supplement government revenues, especially at times when copra prices and fishing revenues are low. At these times, the government is authorized to make drawdowns against fund income.

The fund allows the Kiribati government a degree of self-sufficiency unmatched by most other developing countries. It does not need to borrow from abroad to finance deficit budgets, levy heavy taxes on the population, overexploit natural resources (like fish), or turn to corrupting activities like offshore banking or passport dealing to bring in foreign exchange. Having the additional cushion of fund earnings also allows the Kiribati government to subsidize services in the outer islands, which are remote and expensive to service. An inter-island airline, as well as freight services, communications, power, and health-care delivery, are among the public goods supported in part by fund income. In Kiribati, noncapitalist productive industry (fishing and agriculture) sustains a diverse subsistence base and a distinctive cultural identity; it is to the end of supporting this activity that fund managers play the stock markets of the developed world, maintaining the trust fund revenues that underpin a distinctive development pathway.[25] By deciding not to try to develop an export base, the Republic of Kiribati is maintaining and replenishing its commons, constituting an economic community made up of resident islanders, remote migrants from Kiribati who dream of returning at retirement, and the even more distant fund managers in global financial markets.

RECLAIMING AND ENLARGING THE COMMONS

Mainstream imaginings of development argue that to be sustainable, a region must have at its economic base some core productive activities that are capable of generating and expanding wealth. The task of development is to discover the best options for "adding value" in a region and to see these activities grow. The assumption is that, by fostering productive activity, the population of the whole region will benefit from the multiplier effects of increasing employment, increased demand for goods and services, and the attraction of additional investment that will guarantee their supply. This vision of economic development is an abstracted extension of the particular pathway of European and North American industrialization, an extension that has been universalized as "the model of development" and forced on countless places with the expectation that its contingent dynamics can be easily reproduced. The crucial role of what Marx called *primitive accumulation* in the "successful" realization of this particular model of development has never been fully acknowledged.

The expropriation of the commons that fueled Western industrialization involved private theft of common lands, restriction of access to resources and culturally meaningful sites, and destruction of traditional and agricultural livelihoods. The success of this expropriation is reflected in the almost total disappearance of the term "commons" from mainstream public discourse in the West. Today there is a revival of interest in reclaiming and enlarging the commons in the industrialized countries, and protecting the yet-to-be completely destroyed or expropriated commons in the "developing" world. In this section we examine the role of enlarging the commons as one of many potential pathways toward building community economies.[26] Stories of the commons drawn from the United States, Australia, and Mexico offer another challenge to the representation of industrialization as *the* pathway to increased economic well-being.

Nuestras Raices (Our Roots) is a network of community gardens located in the deindustrialized city of Holyoke in the Pioneer Valley of western Massachusetts, where one-third of the city population is Puerto Rican. Since 1993, this nonprofit community organization has been converting vacant lots scattered throughout downtown Holyoke into community gardens, reclaiming urban space for the people's use. With active community involvement, Nuestras Raices' mission is to build on what people already know (agriculture, for instance, which many of them have practiced from their youth in Puerto Rico) and to deliver what they specifically need, like food security and a place for young people to learn skills and stay off the streets. The gardens currently involve over one hundred families and each garden plot produces up to one thousand dollars' worth of produce each year, adding a substantial amount to the food budget of a family below the poverty line.[27]

Nuestras Raices supports an active youth program in which kids learn marketing skills and sell garden produce at the local farmers' market. They also coordinate workshops in nutrition, commercial food preparation, organic farming, and leadership skills. Over the past few years, Nuestras Raices has been renovating an abandoned building sold to them by the city of Holyoke, transforming it into a multi-use community facility. Largely built by volunteer labor and the generous gifting of time, materials, and expertise from people and organizations across the Pioneer Valley, the Centro Agricola includes a greenhouse, a business incubator, a commercial kitchen, and a restaurant that uses foods produced from the greenhouse and from a brick-oven bread bakery located in the incubator.

By reclaiming and enlarging an urban commons, Nuestras Raices is encouraging productive activity that meets local needs directly (in the form of food and income support), that has multiplier effects (spinning off numerous small and potentially employment- and surplus-generating community-based enterprises), and that provides greater well-being and social interconnection within an expanded economic community that is identified with both Holyoke Puerto Rican immigrants and the wider Pioneer Valley.

CERES, a nonprofit environmental and community garden in inner-city Melbourne, is a similarly impressive organization that has reclaimed and enlarged the commons, demonstrating over a long period how access to a commons can proliferate community economic activity. Located on what was originally a dump site on the banks of the Merri Creek, CERES began over twenty years ago as a small volunteer community garden that was pioneering raised garden beds as a way to provide productive growing space on a polluted site. Initially CERES catered to the largely Mediterranean immigrant community living in the surrounding high-density urban environment who wanted garden plots. Over the past two decades, CERES has been transformed into a multidimensional enterprise. It currently houses commercial activities, including a café, plant nursery, educational program, and solar electricity–generating plant that sells electricity to the national power grid, as well as a host of volunteer and alternative market initiatives. CERES is now a well-established community business with an annual budget of over $A1.6 million and twenty-five full-time equivalent employment positions (see www.ceres.org.au).

It was this garden that provided the inspiration for a group of volunteers to begin the Latrobe Valley Community and Environmental Gardens Inc. (LTVCEG) as part of our action research interventions discussed in chapter 6. The story of the LTVCEG illustrates some of the challenges and setbacks that face those attempting to create a new commons. This experiment is located in a rural resource region where private land, in the form of suburban house lots, is abundant, but community connections and identifications are in need of rebuilding after the swift and devastating effects of privatization of the state industrial commons. The LTVCEG was granted access to an abandoned and derelict trailer park site situated near the center of Morwell on Crown land[28] and overseen by the Latrobe City Council. A committee of management was formed, made up of people who were unemployed, retired, from non-English-speaking backgrounds, of varying ages, and with intellectual and physical disabilities, none of whom had participated in a community organization of this sort before. They were keen to create a new kind of community among themselves that could be extended to all who were interested. Indeed, for key members of the group the social connections being built were what were most important. A field trip to CERES had been a magical experience and the CERES vision was what motivated and focused their energies.

The group stepped onto a steep learning curve as they set out to transform the vast three-hectare site into a community and environmental garden. The initial phases involved a considerable amount of off-site activity. They applied for planning permission and then sought grant funding for water reconnection and fencing (a requirement of the planning permit),[29] held regular barbecues to raise funds for public liability insurance, and organized working bees to clear the site of rubbish, old vegetation, and the concrete pads from each trailer site. They obtained funds to commission a landscape architect to help design the layout of the site; this exercise came up with a beautifully illustrated plan that was a minor replica of the combination of activities the group had seen at CERES.

In hindsight the decision to engage an outside "expert" who transposed an inner-city model of a community garden to a very different rural site set the group on a problematic development pathway. Here we can recognize the ease with which any group jumps at a model (whether of industrialization or community gardens) that seems to have been successful elsewhere. Listening for what is really needed and creatively modifying an initial idea to suit local conditions is a difficult and time-consuming process. But so, too, is trying to make an inappropriate model work, as the LTVCEG found.

With each of the preparation tasks, a range of skills had to be acquired, for example, occupational health and safety training, food handling, managing finances and sales taxes, and meeting and group skills. The bureaucratic and physical work of site preparation seemed interminable. A composting and worm-farm system modeled on the CERES example was established and crops of vegetables (mainly broad beans) were planted, some of which were donated to the local food bank. By the end of 2003 (almost four years after the group had started working together) only two major crops of vegetables had been produced and many of the initially very enthusiastic members had lost interest or become discouraged. Exhausted by their efforts and cautious about investing further energy into trying to reignite interest, the committee of management made the decision to close down the gardens. Upon reflection, the former president of the committee wished that they had thought to explore the possibility of specializing earlier on with growing food for the food bank, and not sticking to the plan of the landscape designer.[30] And yet he had this to say when asked to comment on the closure:

> But I still think that some of the positives that came out of it were people—there were young people who had never been involved in an organization and they have had that opportunity of working in those relationships and they learned quite a deal from that and that is always a positive. And maybe there will be things that they have learned from this that they can utilize at another stage.
>
> I wouldn't call it a failure—I would call it as something where people attempted a vision which they felt was very worthwhile. They have gained a lot from what they have done and they can utilize that in the future. Maybe down the track it could work. I don't think you can always say that because this one didn't work that another won't.

While a new commons has yet to be established in the Latrobe Valley, it is clear that the experience of attempting to build the LTVCEG had the effect of creating new subjects more attuned to the possibilities of community economic development. This story reminds us that building community economies will always be a process of experimentation, choices, and failures, as well as successes, and indeed that success and failure are subject to interpretation (like the rest of life experience).

From the very different context of Bahias de Huatulco in the state of Oaxaca on the southern Pacific coast of Mexico, David Barkin argues for the importance of listening to people (including children) and starting with what is at hand to begin to replenish and enlarge the commons (2004). In the face of massive destruction of the watershed of the Sierra Madre del Sur by illegal logging, agricultural practices, and tourist hotel development, a local NGO has worked with the indigenous people of the hinterland to reconstitute native forests and address the damage to the river basins and the diminution of the aquifer supplying water to the coastal areas. Resisting a proposed Mexican government plan to designate this area as a protected reserve, they argued that this would further disenfranchise the seventy thousand indigenous residents and make them more dependent on outside aid. Pursuing instead a community resource management strategy, they took the decision to embark on a large-scale silviculture project that saw the individual planting and care of fifteen million trees of twenty-six tropical dry-forest varieties (including one million rosewoods) over an eight-year period. High-tech drip irrigation techniques were matched with indigenous practices of care (including burial ceremonies for any trees that did not survive) and an unprecedented 98 percent survival rate for new seedlings was achieved (Barkin and Pailles 2000).

An innovative feature of this major reclamation project was the way that it was integrated with other aspects of building a community economy, including meeting the subsistence needs of people engaged in the reforestation project during the lengthy period before the forest became harvestable. Various ways of connecting local resources with international markets were pursued. Having been alerted by an entrepreneur to the international value of rosewood, an endangered species, the community, in partnership with the NGO, devised a plan to harvest and use the prunings of the rosewood trees. They obtained a fair-trade contract for eight million director's chairs to be sold in Europe over ten years, for which 25 percent of the proceeds were paid out up front and used to cover the cost of the seedlings and the irrigation system, and to provide income for the people planting and maintaining the forest. Another enterprise based on forest prunings was initiated when a fourteen-year-old boy came up with the idea of making baseball bats signed by well-known Mexican ballplayers on major league teams in the United States. The boy and his younger brother got the players to send signatures on metal plates so that each bat could be "signed" and workers were trained in woodworking and taught to make the bats to the specifications of the major leagues. These local products have been sold for fifty dollars each to Mexican immigrants and others all over the United States to raise funds for commons reclamation.

Over the course of these projects, the five rivers running to the coast off the Sierra Madre del Sur have been rehabilitated and restored, endangered forest species have been reestablished, and income-producing activities have been generated for the local residents.[31] By choosing to reclaim and replenish the commons (and to deny continued access to loggers and international tourist chains), this regional community has secured the base that provides its necessary subsistence, while also creating opportunities for surplus-generating activities to be developed. "Alternative" international markets have been accessed to support this "local" project, and in the process a new economic community that transcends the local area has been created.

Barkin (2004a) notes that the reforestation project is tied in with a larger vision of economic self-determination and with practices of freedom among economic subjects. The indigenous people of Huatulco consciously maintain themselves on the margins of the global economy, picking and choosing when and where to work in a proletarian setting. In this way, they are constituting migration for wage work as a resource to support local projects of livelihood and commons maintenance, rather than as an imperative of globalization or of individual and family survival. They organize their ethical practices of being-in-common around four reiterated principles: autonomy (the rallying cry of the Zapatistas, connoting self-governance and self-management); self-sufficiency; productive diversification (necessary to make self-sufficiency viable); and local ecosystem management. These principles dictate a particular regional scale for the community economy that is under construction: it must be coextensive with the watersheds of the rivers and aquifer, with a sufficiently large population and political strength to demand self-government, and with a range of habitats, settlements, and skills to support productive diversification and specialization. In the practice of building the community economy, individuals and small collectives are engaging in surplus generation and accumulation, yet they are doing so in a context of shared rules and principles through which individual processes are collectively guided. This has inspired Barkin to articulate a vision of the expanded reproduction and replication of regional economic communities that offer greater "degrees of freedom" while at the same time acknowledging interdependence and building upon natural and human being-in-common.

Building Community Economies
As a Practice of (Post)-Development

In this chapter we have briefly documented a variety of paths toward differently imagined forms of social and economic development. Each has been treated as a project of building a "community economy," understood as an ethical and political space of decision in which negotiations over interdependence take place.

Though there will be many other ways of framing the issues for decision, we have specified four coordinates that can be (and are being) used to orient the development of community economies—*necessity, surplus, consumption,* and *commons.* In the examples we presented, communities are pursuing alternative routes to development by various means:

- choosing to meet local *needs* by delivering increased well-being directly (rather than relying on the circuitous route of capitalist industrialization) and recognizing and building on the diversity of practices that support subsistence and sustain livelihoods
- using *surplus* as a force for constituting and strengthening communities—defining the boundary between necessary and surplus labor, monitoring the production of surplus, tracking the ways in which it is appropriated and distributed, and discussing how it can be marshaled to sustain and build community economies
- recognizing *consumption* as a potentially viable route to development rather than simply its end result, and defining and making decisions about consumption versus investment on a case-by-case basis, rather than privileging the latter as the "driver" of development
- creating, enlarging, reclaiming, replenishing, and sharing a *commons,* acknowledging the interdependence of individuals, groups, nature, things, traditions, and knowledges, and tending the commons as a way of tending the community

What is striking, from our perspective, is the way that ethical decision making around the four coordinates is operating as a force for development. This has prompted us to imagine that what we are seeing here is the emergence of an alternative set of "dynamic principles of development" or, more accurately, the beginning of an alternative way of thinking about development dynamics.

One of the most powerful ways that alternative languages of economy have been subordinated to that of capitalism has been through the theorization of economic dynamics that, while associated with the historical rise of competitive capitalism, have become naturalized as universal logics of economy in mainstream economic discourse. These logics privilege the (uni)linearity and dominance of capitalist development achieved through and manifest in commodification (marketization),[32] the concentration and centralization of capital, capitalist expansion (capital accumulation), labor-saving technological change, and the extinction or subordination of "precapitalist" forms. Their discursive dominance is evident in the ways that alternative economic dynamics are devalued and demoted as ineffective contributors to economic development. The vast extent and persistence of self-employment over millennia, for example, is afforded no independent role in the shaping of contemporary development (Gibson-Graham 1996), nor is the creative transformation and proliferation of indigenous economies in codevelopment with marketization.[33] Given the capitalocentric thinking that dominates the field, how might we unhinge notions of development from those of growth and capitalist expansion and loosen the discursive grip of unilinear trajectories on narratives of change?

In line with our interest in fostering ethical relationships rather than activating structural logics as an approach to development, we have been looking for new languages of dynamics to support our vision of the possibilities of building community economies. In this quest, we have been drawn to the metaphors of complex open systems, nonlinear histories, path dependency, nonreproductive adaptations, emergence, and self-organization that are increasingly being employed to help understand processes of interdependent codevelopment in many different fields.[34] What is enabled by these conceptual ruminations is the possibility that novel economic interventions, in the absence of dominant (linear) pressures for extinction by capitalism, have the power to initiate potentially major changes. While the injunction to "start where you are" suggests that one's region, sector, or social group is as good a place as any other to begin, the new languages of dynamics offer a sense that the scope and scale of a project's effectiveness are not limited by its starting place.

WHERE DO WE START?

If we embrace the implications of overdetermination, mutual constitution, and path dependency, we are left with a "weak theory" of economic dynamics that continually poses the questions—what might economic development be and become? How might we enter into processes of economic experimentation and reevaluation? Fortunately, the epistemology of alternative dynamics involves not knowing, or not knowing very much, about the path any particular intervention will lead us down. And in the absence of clear instructions about where to start, we are afforded the ubiquitous starting place of *here* and *now*. What the "start where you are" orientation offers is not only the potential fruitfulness of any particular location and moment, but the requirement to treat obstacles and local deficiencies as resources rather than (merely) as barriers to projects of economic construction. Approaching the existing conditions in a spirit of experimentation and generosity, we are encouraged to view them as conditions of possibility as well as of impossibility.

In any setting we confront difficult circumstances that are potentially generative, if only we can engage them productively. Communities confronting the WTO have been moved, for example, to engage in "fair trade," and the Basque people facing fascist repression of their language and culture were inspired to create a cooperative complex as a way to sustain their communities. What is visible in these and similar examples is a postfantasmatic relation to power. Starting where they are, these communities are up against many things—including themselves. While they do not accord themselves the power to create everything they might desire, they refuse to give their opponents the power to destroy everything they create.[35] The evaluative framing of action is likewise forgiving; success and failure are situated on a continuum and the positioning of any project on that continuum is ever-changing as the path unfolds.

For us, however, "start where you are" refers not just to the geographic and social place of origin, but to the conceptual starting place, and here the ground is slippery and problematic. The conventional conceptual origin of economic development is a local space of deficiency within a global capitalist economy, a starting place that offers very few possibilities. One of the goals of our "language politics" has been to replace this impoverished conceptual ground with a rich diversity of economic practices and organizations—a heterogeneous set of transactions, forms of labor and remuneration, types of enterprise and modes of surplus appropriation and distribution (see Figure 19, "A Diverse Economy," in chapter 3). The language of the diverse economy brings into visibility a great variety of economic sites and practices in any particular location, constituting them as a resource for building community economies.

The diverse economy framework poses an active challenge to the dominance of any one set of organizing principles or determining dynamics. Decentering the economy and deconstructing the dominance of a singular "capitalism" simultaneously de-essentializes economic logics. Including the full range of noncapitalist and alternative capitalist organizations and practices in the economy widens the scope of motivating drives to encompass more than calculative rationality and competitive individualism. Expanding the economy to legitimately include such things as feudal enterprises, informal markets, self-provisioning labor, and gift giving undermines hierarchical valuations of cultures and economic practices. The field of economic intervention is radically shifted and the space and scope of decision enlarged.

Indeed, this language is our principal technology for "repoliticizing the economy." Like any language, it offers concepts that are not initially embedded in organizing frames (like narratives or models).[36] It provides a fragmentary and incoherent starting place, an ontology of disarray that both invites and necessitates political decision. In the set of disarticulated elements that constitutes a diverse economy, we find conceptual resources for a politics of building community economies, creating new relationships and synergies among different types of transactions, property, labor practices, and organizations. The development project no longer entails simply (painfully) submitting to the demanding logic of global capitalism, but becomes instead an ethical and political engagement—a sometimes difficult and conflictual process of experimenting with, fostering, exploring, connecting, expanding, and reworking the heterogeneous and scattered elements of a diverse (becoming community) economy.

Finally, "start where you are" suggests that there is no privileged social location from which to embark on building a community economy. For us this means that our academic location is no less or more suitable as a starting place than our other social locations as women, citizens, middle-aged adults, yoginis, local residents, workers, and bearers of racial privilege. The extended and complex collectivities engaged in building community economies cannot be recognized in simple relational oppositions like academy/community. While the capabilities we bring to bear may be shaped by our academic training, and some of the networks we are embedded in may be constituted through our academic activities, these particularities distinguish us within, but do not separate us from, the communities we are working with. Instead they enable us to connect in particular ways.

REPRISE

We began this book by invoking an emerging political imaginary that has inspired us to engage in a postcapitalist politics here and now. This (feminist) imaginary allows for modest beginnings and small achievements without restricting their effectivity in time and space. It prompts an open and experimental orientation to action and a resilient (even humorous) attitude toward inevitable setbacks and obstacles. It recognizes that changing the self is a path toward changing the world, and that transforming one's environment is a mode of transforming the self. Perhaps most powerfully it offers a vision of global transformation through the accretion and interaction of small changes in place.

This new imaginary gives us a larger world in which to start where we are. Bolstered by an imagined connection—with the movement of movements, with people in every local setting and circumstance—we sense our wider engagement in collective action. This action takes place in a landscape of potentially articulated projects and practices, connecting them imaginatively as well as practically.

It takes a world to create a locality, and an imagined world to transform ourselves in place. Perhaps this is one way that (counter)hegemony is enacted.

NOTES

INTRODUCTION

1. The World Social Forum is, according to Wallerstein (2002, 36–37), the "new claimant for the role of antisystemic movement," one that "seeks to bring together all the previous types—Old Left, new [social] movements, human-rights bodies, and others not easily falling into these categories." It is not surprising, therefore, that it incorporates a range of positions on strategies for social change.

2. Notes from Nowhere (2003); title of the economic alternatives track at the Boston Social Forum, July 2004; Kingsnorth (2003); title of a 2004 conference in New York.

3. Quoted in Solnit (2004, 105). Solnit notes that Jordan was a founding member of Reclaim the Streets (see http://rts.gn.apc.org/) and is now involved in the global justice movement.

4. Exercising power rather than "taking" it, the Zapatistas are operating in the present and in place to make domination impossible (Osterweil 2004). In the words of Subcomandante Marcos, "It is not necessary to conquer the world. It is sufficient to make it new" (Klein 2002, 220).

5. Maria Hynes, Scott Sharpe, and Bob Fagan (2005, 3) recount, for example, the actions of the Yes Men, who announced to a Sydney meeting of chartered public accountants on May 21, 2002, the dissolution of the World Trade Organization, effective September 30, 2002, and its replacement "by a new Trade Regulation Organisation (TRO), which 'Will have as its basis the United Nations Universal Declaration of Human Rights, with the aim of ensuring that the TRO

will have human rather than business interests as its bottom line.'" They note that "[s]ome of the audience at the CPA meeting in Sydney were, after their initial shock, more receptive to the proposed changes, offering suggestions on how to make the new organization benefit the poor. 'I'm as right wing as the next fellow,' said one of the accountants, 'but it's time we gave something back to the countries we've been doing so well from.'" (This action is reported at http://www.gatt.org/home wto.html and http://www.rtmark.com/yestro.htm.) Hynes, Sharpe, and Fagan understand the political value of such actions, in Arendtian terms, as producing an "event in thought," a digression not from "things as they are but from what *we take to be given*" (19).

6. Marcos traces his privileging of poetry and humor to his own literary upbringing, noting that by the time he "got into Marx and Engels, [he was] thoroughly spoilt by literature" (2001, 78).

7. Rebello (2004), following Deleuze.

8. And as developed in two volumes on antiessentialist class analysis and class politics coedited with Steve Resnick and Rick Wolff (Gibson-Graham, Resnick, and Wolff 2000a, 2001). See chapter 3 for an extended exposition of class as a process of surplus production, appropriation, and distribution.

9. From these ways of thinking, capitalism emerged as the necessarily and naturally dominant form of economy and as an object of transformation that could not be transformed (Gibson-Graham 1996). We were invoking economic representations that narrowed the field of economic intervention, constituting a "depoliticized" way of thinking about economy; this is not to deny that the creation of a self-contained economic object, and the truth of that object, was and is a political project (Mitchell 2007).

10. While we can but gesture toward these diverse and growing literatures here, we refer throughout the book to the work of those we are indebted to and connected with in many of these fields. See also the Preface for individual acknowledgments and attributions.

11. One of the principal moves we have made to denaturalize capitalist dominance is to define capitalism clearly and relatively minimally. In our understanding, derived from Marx, capitalism involves the production of commodities for a market by free wage labor. It also involves an exploitative class process in which surplus labor is appropriated from the direct producers in value form by nonproducers—an individual capitalist, say, or the board of directors of a capitalist firm (see Gibson-Graham, Resnick, and Wolff 2000a, 2000b, 2001). These practices take place in sites (enterprises) scattered over a landscape rather than constituting an economic system coextensive with the social space of the nation or the world. By refusing to define capitalism as a system, we have attempted to level the conceptual playing field, so to speak, placing capitalism on the same footing as other forms of economy that lack systemic embodiment, "laws of motion," and "logics of development." In this way, capitalist dominance becomes something that must be argued for and demonstrated rather than presumed. The

problem with most structural and systemic conceptions, of course, is the performativity of economic representation. Once we have created a theoretical monster and installed it in the social landscape, our thinking and politics will tend to orient themselves around its bulk and majesty and our emotional outlook will reflect the diminished likelihood of displacing it.

12. After writing *The End of Capitalism* we were often chastised for our optimism. In our eagerness to expose the bizarre imperviousness of "economy" to the widespread recognition of the discursivity of social experience, we unwittingly gave the message to some that the materiality of discourse could be imagined away. This misunderstanding led to some intriguing and, at the time, exasperating interchanges—one of the most memorable being a challenge to prove our point by walking through the wall of the conference room where we were presenting!

13. Though hardly proximate, the choice of this last field site was made possible by KG's move to the Research School of Pacific and Asian Studies at the Australian National University, where Asia-Pacific fieldwork is required and supported.

14. Arturo Escobar has pointed out to us that we could have turned to other social movements for similar inspiration.

15. We recognize that we are risking the charge of naïve optimism here while simultaneously courting its perverse pleasures.

16. The most far-reaching changes may be the most difficult to perceive because they are "prior to reflection," according to Spinosa, Flores, and Dreyfus (1997): "However little some things may have changed—full justice for women has not been achieved, patriarchy has not been eliminated, women are not commonly seen as exemplary representatives of as many skill domains as men—watching a woman defer to a man's authority simply because of his gender evokes distaste in most of the West, a distaste that generally crosses gender, class, and race lines. . . . We are not saying that feminism has been history-making because it has changed the reflective judgments we make about women, though it obviously has. Rather, feminism has changed the way we see women *prior to* our reflective judgments" (2).

17. While global women's movements have devoted much energy to "engendering" global development processes through international conferences and commissions, feminists have not fixated on the global as the ultimate scale of successful activism (Harcourt 2005). In confronting imperial globalization, they are continuing their orientation to the local, the daily, the bodily, recognizing that transforming the world involves transforming sites, subjects, and practices worldwide. That this place-oriented activism may involve them in global movements (of migrant workers, for example) is not a contradiction, but simply a confirmation that places are constituted at the crossroads of global forces (Massey 1999a, 2005).

18. We have been provoked to think in this way through engagement in a

project called Women and the Politics of Place, which we are involved in with Arturo Escobar, Wendy Harcourt (editor of the journal *Development*), and a number of other feminist activists and academics around the world. The idea of the project is to narrate and theorize a globally emergent form of localized politics—one that is largely *of* if not necessarily *for* women—and thus bring this politics into a new stage of being. The vision is that women are both threatened and mobilized by the contemporary wave of globalization, and that they are already everywhere engaged in constructing and revitalizing places, in response to the exigencies and possibilities of their everyday lives. What the project hopes to do is foster this tenacious, dispersed, and barely visible "movement," creating connections (networks or "meshworks"), sharing information and inspiration through academic and nonacademic channels, and developing local experiments into a collective knowledge that will spawn and support more projects and ideas. Representing this movement and connecting its participants, the project will create a recognized (self)identity for something that already exists, thereby empowering and expanding it (Gibson-Graham 2005a; Harcourt and Escobar 2002, 2005).

19. Reflections on the Alliance are prompted by an article by Arjun Appadurai, "Deep Democracy," published in *Public Culture* in 2002 and those on the MSAI come from our own research support work with the Hong Kong–based NGO Asian Migrant Centre and the Philippines-based NGO Unlad Kabayan Migrant Services Foundation Inc., which have together developed this program (see Gibson, Law, and McKay 2001).

20. Since a lot of policies and bureaucracies exist to deal with the slums, knowing who, where, and what the conditions of slum dwellers actually are is a matter of practical urgency and strategic advantage (Appadurai 2002, 36).

21. Appadurai describes the membership in the savings groups as "akin to a spiritual practice" with a "profound ideological, even salvational, status" (2002, 33).

22. In this sense, these initiatives understand the inherent spatiality of power and are able to locate spaces that afford the freedom to act, indeed the room to exercise their own localized forms of power (Allen 2003).

23. The MSAI program has organized savings groups all over the world wherever Asian contract migrant workers are employed (Hong Kong, Singapore, Japan, Taiwan, South Korea, Italy, the Netherlands) and, in partnership with other NGOs, it has facilitated MSAI-funded enterprise development in the Philippines, Thailand, and Indonesia. As a member of the Migrant Forum of Asia, the AMC is currently debating and exploring the MSAI model with migrant organizations interested in its applicability to other countries, such as Nepal and Bangladesh.

24. For our alternative imaginary of a global politics grounded in ubiquity rather than unity, another ontological inspiration comes from Teilhard de Chardin,

who once wrote about God as "infinitely profound and punctiform" (quoted in Dillard 1999).

25. Allen argues that power is not a "thing-like" substance that can be possessed and is capable of extensive and undiluted control over space, nor does it have the totalizing reach of "an undifferentiated quality, constituted through a multitude of practices which in true immanent fashion serve to govern our conduct" (2003, 190–91). He notes that "the fantasy of power as something which is *either* centred *or* decentred allows us to believe that, if it does not overstretch itself, it remains a force to be reckoned with, or, alternatively, if it is a force so pervasive and all encompassing in its reach it leaves little room for manoeuvre. Either way, the effect is potentially disarming" (195). Compellingly, Allen maintains that "we have lost sight of the particularities of power, the diverse and specific *modalities* of power that make a difference in how we are put in our place, how we experience power" (2). He says we need to identify what kind of power we face in any situation and "how power in its more provisional yet spatially nuanced guises exercises us" (196). He distinguishes, for example, the powers of domination, authority, manipulation, coercion, and seduction.

26. Harvey (2000) cites a similar "dialectical conception" central to Roberto Unger's work: "Only by changing our institutional world can we change ourselves at the same time, as it is only through the desire to change ourselves that institutional change can occur" (186).

27. Torfing (1999, 304), paraphrasing Laclau and Mouffe.

28. In volume 2 of *The History of Sexuality*, Foucault distinguishes two elements of every morality: the first is the code, or the principles, but the second and often more important element is the cultivation of the ethical person (1985).

29. In our own history, the advent of poststructuralism marked a crucial transition in the remaking of our theorizing selves, prompting us to become more conscious of practices of thinking and their potential impacts on ourselves and the world. The recognition of the performative power of discourse—something we had always counted on yet never fully conceptualized—provided both inspiration and ongoing support for the project of rethinking economy in order to enact different economies. Once we had fully accepted the previously marginalized view that ideas had effects (rather than representational accuracy), we could begin to think about the effects we wanted to produce, and the techniques of thinking that would allow us to produce them.

30. Sara Ahmed (2004, 170) speaks of the majority position as concealing "the emotional and embodied aspects of thought and reason."

31. Because we are "interested in the things we disclose and not in the disclosing" (Spinosa, Flores, and Dreyfus 1997, 30), we may be even more unconscious of these than we are of the affective stances we adopt when we think. To refuse to recognize this is to fail to bring to one of the paths of history making the amplifying boost of consciousness and intention.

32. We address the emotions associated with a traditional imaginary of revolutionary politics in chapter 1.

33. See Gibson-Graham (1996, chapter 2): "Althusser's overdetermination can be variously (though not exhaustively) understood as signaling the irreducible specificity of every determination; the essential complexity—as opposed to the root simplicity—of every form of existence; the openness or incompleteness of every identity; the ultimate unfixity of every meaning; and the correlate possibility of conceiving an acentric—Althusser uses the term 'decentered'—social totality that is not structured by the primacy of any social element or location" (27).

34. See, for example, the nonresemblance between the virtual and the actual in Deleuze, making "difference primary in the process of actualization" (Rebello 2004, 3, quoting Deleuze).

35. The vision of the local as internal to and constrained by the global becomes untenable through the lens of what Law and others have called a "baroque" reframing, by which each social space becomes infinitely complex and incommensurable with the others. Baroquely framed localities cannot be theorized as "adding up" to a global economy or simply subsumed to a global regime like Empire or neoliberalism.

36. Eve Kosofsky Sedgwick is our principal instructor and inspiration here, and we have watched in awe and delight as she takes apart heterosexuality, for example, scattering its shards around her devil's workshop (1990, 1993).

37. In the realm of economy, this involves "valorising alternative systems of production . . . which have been hidden or discredited by the capitalist orthodoxy of productivity" (Santos 2004, 240). What is hidden, of course, is much more than the wealth and strengths of the excluded and marginalized—it is also the failures and disappointments of the powerful. In the critical literature on multinational corporations, for example, there are no thoroughgoing studies of their failures and stumblings. Who documents how seldom they achieve their goals? Who catalogs their mistakes, setbacks, terrible years, lengthy periods of decline, and internal disarray? In the absence of a knowledge of failure, we are left with a concoction of success—a sense that multinational corporations alone among actors are able to shape the world in accordance with their agendas. Perhaps this sense, to the extent that we embody it, is one condition of our economic powerlessness.

38. Connolly invokes Nietzsche's seasonal metaphor in *Thus Spake Zarathustra* to make a similar point. A winter doctrine understands the freeze of winter as a law of nature ("at bottom everything stands still"), while a spring reading restores fluidity and possibility, rescuing thinking "from the undertow of structuralism and its tragic consequences" (Connolly 1999, 53; 2002, 54–55).

39. This is the subject that Žižek brought to Laclau and Mouffe's project of radical democracy (1990, 251).

40. Ethan Miller has helped us to see this, in one of his always clarifying and motivating summaries of our work.

41. This quote is from Ernesto Laclau or Judith Butler—we would gratefully accept help with attribution.

42. An MTD member visiting western Massachusetts in late 2003.

1. AFFECTS AND EMOTIONS FOR A POSTCAPITALIST POLITICS

1. We acknowledge Sara Ahmed's discussion of the notion of "impression," which captures the productive and at times painful mix of feelings, sensations, and thoughts that our critics have induced in our bodies/brains (2004, 6).

2. Ahmed identifies the emotional content of what we have called a "stance": "Emotions are intentional in the sense that they are 'about' something: they involve a direction or orientation towards an object. . . . The 'aboutness' of emotions means they involve a stance on the world, or a way of apprehending the world" (2004, 7). We would like also to include in our definition of stance an *affective* as well as an emotional element. Following Massumi (2002, 27) we distinguish affect from emotion, seeing emotion as a consciously narrativized and personalized feeling, and affect as a passionate, shared, and embodied intensity that erupts beyond the register of consciousness (28–33; see also Connolly 2002, 64–77).

3. In an insightful paper that covers a much more extensive literature on the subject of affect than canvassed in this chapter, geographer Nigel Thrift (2004) provides a comprehensive review of affect theories and their relevance to contemporary urban politics.

4. Both are interested in countering the ways in which the political right has been able to work so successfully on the emotional and affective registers beyond rational thought and are keen to warn progressives of the dangers of ignoring the influence of these on political sensibilities (Massumi 2002, 44; Connolly 2002, 65). Their warnings resonate with those of George Lakoff (2004), who points to the way the framing of issues by the right taps into and fans people's deep-seated fears, making them susceptible to policies that appear to offer protection, but often go against their presumed interests.

5. This view has received a major injection of theoretical energy with the publication in 2000 of Hardt and Negri's *Empire,* heralded as the communist manifesto of our time. These authors see a politics of difference, for example, as "pushing against an open door" (138) and postmodernism and postcolonialism, to the extent that they espouse fluidity and hybridity, as offering something the enemy thrives upon. They characterize place-based (identity or locality) politics as reactive and defensive, constituting a nostalgic retreat to the small and manageable in the face of the daunting challenges of global capitalism and Empire. Working as we were with people in local communities to multiply economic identities and construct different economic futures, we read *Empire* as yet another attempt to say that our projects were always within and never alternative to the dominant.

6. Of course not all reactions were of this kind. There were also the encouraging minority reactions from people who were engaged or interested in

local economic alternatives and politics—the minister who had visited Mondragón, the Buddhist couple who had gone to Nicaragua with Witness for Peace, audiences who somehow got captured by the wealth of examples in certain presentations. They wanted to talk about how to avoid the dangers, or how to deal with them as they arose, and offered additional examples to support our arguments. This forced us to realize that the negativity we were encountering was only one aspect of a political culture, and only part of the emotional range of any individual.

7. Sedgwick draws attention to Freud's discussion of the striking similarity between paranoid delusions and the systems of philosophers "among whom he included himself" (2003, 125). She comments that although Freud may have found the "putative congruence between paranoia and theory" unpalatable, it is no longer regarded as such, indeed "to theorize out of anything *but* a paranoid critical stance has come to seem naïve, pious, or complacent" (125, 126). Perhaps this is because of the longstanding theoretical interest in structure, a place where, according to Massumi "nothing ever happens, that explanatory heaven in which all eventual permutations are prefigured in a self-consistent set of invariant generative rules" (2002, 27).

8. Sedgwick's designation of strong theory is taken from Silvan Tomkins, who distinguishes between strong affect theory and weak affect theory. Strong theory accounts for a "wide spectrum of phenomena," accumulating power as it orders more and more of the world, training the theorist to be ever more anticipatory of "contingencies before they actually happen," paradoxically producing and increasing negative affect as it attempts to alleviate the fear and humiliation that accompanies surprise. Weak theory, by contrast, is "little better than description." Insofar as it welcomes surprise and fails to establish "necessary" connections between phenomena, weak theory liberates the positive affects of freedom and ameliorates the negative affects of fear and shame (2003, 134). Sedgwick is keen to point out that not all strong theory carries negative affect. One could construct a "wide-ranging and reductive" strong theory that is not "organized around anticipating, identifying, and warding off the negative affect of humiliation" (145). In this chapter we could be seen as constructing a strong theory of a culture of thinking with the motive (that we hope has a positive affect) of highlighting freedoms and choices of how to think.

9. Here we are borrowing the language of Connolly, who notes, "Consummate narratives invest theory, explanation, and interpretation with more certainty and sufficiency than they warrant. They express the hubris of theory in a world too complexly intermeshed to fit the strictures of either lawlike explanation or deep interpretation" (2002, 16).

10. Özselçuk argues that mourning can involve articulating a loss "in a way that opens it up to productive transformation" (2003, 4). Her research on the privatization of state-owned industry in Turkey identifies the opportunity ex-state workers took to reclaim their state worker subjectivity, "not solely as a

sectarian identity or a melancholic preoccupation," but as a nodal point representing community and household stakeholders "around which a multiplicity of social demands were articulated" (6).

11. The moralistic stance of the left is in this view a compensation, a seizing of ground by those deprived of more worldly forms of power (W. Brown 1995, 44); powers of adjudication are taken as recompense—though they are bitter tasting, a "complaint against strength" (44), blaming rather than creating.

12. Connolly's explicit project is to thicken a "series of fragile connections between thinking, freedom, care of the self, and care of the world" (2002, 113). Latour is interested in a different role for the critic and in generating associations for the word *criticism* with "a whole new set of positive metaphors, gestures, attitudes, knee-jerk reactions, habits of thought" (2004, 247). Sedgwick wants to explore "some ways around the topos of depth or hiddenness, typically followed by a drama of exposure, that has been such a staple of critical work of the past four decades," and to get some distance from the "bossy gesture of 'calling for' an imminently perfected critical or revolutionary practice that one can oneself only adumbrate" (2003, 8).

13. This outline for a program of self-cultivation shares much with the Buddhist religious tradition in which belief in the capacity to be good and practices that cultivate goodness are inextricably linked. Sedgwick describes the experience of assenting to Buddhist teachings as "an exchange of recognition—at best, of surprising recognition. As if the template of truth is already there inside the listener, its own lineaments clarified by the encounter with a teaching that it can then apprehend as 'true'" (2003, 165). We share with Sedgwick, Connolly, and Varela, among others, an interest in what Buddhist practice can teach us about doing thinking and politics.

14. This is reminiscent of the Argentine Movement of Unemployed Workers' inversion of the value placed on knowing, honoring "not knowing" as a political strength (Chatterton 2005, 28).

15. Weak theory can be strong politics—it opens up social options that would be inaccessible to a theorist intent on eliminating surprise (by exploring the unknown rather than extending and confirming the known). It widens the affective possibilities of politics (who knows what emotions will arise in an experimental, only partly mapped space?) and allows for the possibility of maximizing positive affect (something we all want to do, which means that participation in politics would not be limited to the stoical cadre of the already politicized). "No one way of thinking" is the companion motto to the World Social Forum's "another world is possible." And we might add, "no one way of feeling."

16. To use the language of Nancy Fraser.

17. Latour, echoing Donna Haraway, similarly calls for a form of thinking whose import "will no longer be to debunk but to protect and care" (2004, 232).

18. Our reading of tentative micropolitical movements in *The Full Monty* has aspects of a weak theory approach, but because we are enrolling disparate

phenomena into a narrative of class becoming, it could be argued that we are producing a strong theory analysis (forcing the text to "mean what we want it to," as one reviewer put it). Either way, we are producing this reading with a reparative motive in mind that is carefully attentive to all the slight openings to the new that we can discern.

19. We first saw *The Full Monty* in 1997, the year it came out and the year following the publication of *The End of Capitalism*. Watching this film in an art-house cinema in Eugene, Oregon, we felt as if we were watching our book, soaking up its message in visual imagery, hearing its insights spoken in working-class northern English accents, feeling its affect ripple through the audience as laughter exploded and bodies moved. Here in a fantasy imaginary realm our political project was being made concrete—new identities in a community economy were being constructed for workers discarded by the formal economy. It seemed that writer Simon Beaufoy and director Peter Cattaneo were our filmmaking alter egos, identifying and elaborating the political potential of our book in one eighty-eight-minute-long bite. When, at a later date, we saw *Brassed Off,* which had been made in 1996, we suffered a similarly powerful sense of recognition, this time of the emotions and affects we wanted to leave behind.

20 Žižek finds in the evacuated place of revolutionary politics two left "attitudes" or orientations: (1) symbolic recursion to the old ways, buttressed by excoriating attacks on postmodern cultural politics (our melancholic stance); or (2) complete abandonment of left discourse and acceptance of global capitalism as "the only game in town." The latter leads to an accommodation with respect to capital, mitigated by efforts to soften the local impacts of globalization.

21. Divergent readings of *The Full Monty* are equally apparent among those that focus on masculinity. Sharyn Pearce (2000, 235) finds that "the film's ending reasserts the status quo as the men, who appear likely to re-enter the work force now that Gerald has obtained another job in management, are no longer on the scrap heap. Masculinity has been shored up once more, to the exclusion of the women, who have been returned to their proper place." This reading stands in stark contrast to that of Judith Halberstam (2001, 439), who sees the film as productive of a "new model of maleness centered upon masculine display and vulnerability" and as a film in which masculinity is "precisely welded together from a collectivity of minority masculinities" (440). Far from returning women to their place, Halberstam's *Full Monty* presents "women with power" who "do not simply behave like men" (439).

22. See Gibson-Graham, Resnick, and Wolff (2000a, 2000b, 2001).

23. Much of the text that follows was part of an oral presentation interspersed with film clips delivered at the Marxism 2000 conference at the University of Massachusetts Amherst. We have changed the text only slightly and have retained its rather colloquial style. Many of the points made have been introduced in the earlier sections of the chapter, so we are hoping that this looser rendition with its visual prompts will complement and illustrate the preceding text.

24. Perhaps we can also see the affective crisis of modernist oppositional politics in terms of a jouissance crisis. The old modes of getting off politically are not giving us the same kicks as before, but there is no real desire for change. Indeed, just as the analysand enters into analysis not looking for change but to reclaim the old sense of enjoyment, to renew the satisfaction in dissatisfaction, so the melancholic left looks to a reinvigoration of old political movements and identities, though it recognizes their failures, instead of to new forms of postmodern politics. Rather than distancing ourselves from such attachments as optimistic future makers, we see ourselves embedded in the same painful recognition and resistance to change as the rest of the old/new left.

25. This is clearly a paranoid reading of *Brassed Off.* As an audience member at one of our talks once commented, we could easily read the two films as portraying different stages in the grieving process. This line of analysis would produce a much more reparative reading of *Brassed Off* than the one presented here.

26. Bennett's description of enchantment has much in common with Massumi's rendition of the event: "Nothing is prefigured in the event. It is the collapse of structured distinction into intensity, of rules into paradox. . . . The expression-event is the system of the inexplicable: emergence, into and against regeneration (the reproduction of a structure)" (Massumi 2002, 27).

2. RELUCTANT SUBJECTS

1. Governmentality, as Foucault conceptualizes it, refers to a "mentality" formed by an ensemble of "institutions, procedures, analyses and reflections, the calculations and tactics that allow the exercise of [government]" (quoted in Miller and Rose 1990, 2). Allen (2003) understands governmental power as above all entailing the "government of oneself" (77), and as distinct from disciplinary forms of control by virtue of the latitude and agency conferred on the subject: "The diffuse social and political arenas in which the art of government is exercised allow for the possibility of negotiation and even rejection of prescribed ways of acting and conforming" (77). In this chapter we follow Allen in emphasizing the way that power is always constituted in particular places and lacks an abstract being or transcendental location.

2. In separate but related action research projects in the United States and Australia we are engaged in community conversations about economic diversity and alternative regional development strategies based on diverse representations of economy. Our interest is in releasing economic identity from the "law" of the (capitalist) Economy and generating new economic identities that reflect the diversity of economic relations (in households, voluntary organizations, and collectivities, as well as in self-employment and small and large capitalist businesses) that constitute our economies. In the Community Partnering Project discussed here, Jenny Cameron played a major role as the research fellow who orchestrated day-to-day action research activities (Cameron and Gibson 2001, 2005a, 2005b,

2005c). The academic research team also included Katherine Gibson and Arthur Veno as chief investigators.

3. The commission is referred to as both the SEC and the SECV by official documents and community members.

4. This genealogical interest in deactualizing the (capitalist) Economy has much in common with recent work by Susan Buck-Morss (1995), Timothy Mitchell (1998, 2002), and William Walters (1999). We are focused here on the local and regional scale (not the national or societal level) and have a specific interest in the co-creation of spatial entities such as the region.

5. We include an examination of a set of tables and graphs in an engineering report commissioned by the Victorian government in 1908; the rhetoric of the charter of a Statutory Authority, the State Electricity Commission of Victoria (SEC), established in 1919; and a series of maps and panoramic pictures contained within planning reports commissioned by the SEC and the Victorian government in 1947 and 1949. These tables, graphs, texts, and maps offer snapshots of the "discontinuous and contingent re-territorializations of the economic" that occurred over time in the valley (Walters 1999, 315; see also N. Rose 1999; Miller and Rose 1990; Robson 1992; Rose and Miller 1992; P. Miller 1994). The technologies we discuss are linked to their authors—engineers Charles Merz and John Monash, and planners Frank Heath and W. E. Gower. Though not economists, these men can be seen as having animated dominant economic logics of their time, translating them into practices and tokens that have been handed on to be reenergized by countless other actors in a chain of meaning production over the years (Latour 1986).

6. Two focus groups were held and videotaped in 1997. One group brought together "economic" and the other "community" spokespeople from the region (see Gibson, Cameron, and Veno 1999 for a detailed account of these focus groups). All names used are pseudonyms in accordance with Monash University's research ethics protocol.

7. Harry's statement reminds us that *region,* a key word of geographic discourse, derives from both *regionem*—direction, boundary, district—and *regere*—to direct or to rule (R. Williams 1983, 264–65).

8. Mary Poovey (1998) traces this sort of commonsense acceptance of numbers to the successful separation and elevation of numerical representation over rhetoric during the prehistory of the Enlightenment in the early seventeenth century, when new systems of double-entry bookkeeping ushered in the modern fact.

9. Merz was all too aware that the struggle between rationality (exemplified by efficient mass production) and irrationality (displayed by disorganized, small-scale utility providers) produced a constant destabilizing force, and that the power of "rational technical argument" was highly contingent. Only three years before he had been bitterly disappointed when the London Supply Bill became bogged down in local political struggles and was not passed. Technical

issues to do with the economics of small-scale and large-scale supply "developed into a dispute on the merits of public versus private enterprise," fanned by the Fabians and their interest in municipal socialism (Hughes 1983, 255). Merz's attempt to try again in 1914, this time at the request of the London County Council, was similarly thwarted (256). In England, it seems, the process of naturalizing a discourse of economic centeredness was more contested at this time.

10. The new Latrobe Shire Council that was elected in 1997 replaced five smaller councils that were forced to amalgamate in 1995 as part of a statewide rationalization of local administration. Despite references to the Latrobe Valley as a "region" that date from the 1940s when an explicit language of regionalism entered into practices of governmentality (Auster 1987; Ryan and Taylor 1995; Gibson-Graham 1994a), it took until the end of the twentieth century for the valley to come under the jurisdiction of one regionwide local governing body.

11. "Interpellation" is Althusser's word for the process of identification or subjectivation, in which the subject is "hailed" by the social/symbolic order (discourse or ideology, in his terms) and in responding to the address accepts and assumes a particular subjectivity—for example, housewife, criminal, third world, mother.

12. Wherever possible, we avoid reference to the "state" as a thing in itself, as this representation of a monolithic identity is at odds with the governmentality approach we are employing. We use "state" to refer to the state of Victoria or the Victorian state government, a very specific place or set of institutions and practices. A state capitalist enterprise refers to an economic institution that employs wage labor and participates in appropriating surplus value from its workers (i.e., exploitation), but is involved in distributing surplus and accessing resources in ways that usually differ markedly from those of private capitalist firms.

13. The newly formed commission had no experience of large-scale mining operations or the generation of electricity from brown coal, so it was decided to ask Lieutenant-General Sir John Monash, who was based in London overseeing the repatriation of Australian troops, to "mount an intelligence operation" to Germany to find out how it was done (Serle 1982, 436). Some twelve months later, Monash, the prominent Melbourne engineer, recent corps commander of the Australian Infantry Force in Europe, and son of Prussian Jewish immigrants, had been appointed general manager of the State Electricity Commission.

14. This name was derived "from the native words, Yalleen (meaning brown), and Lourn (meaning fire)" (SECV 1921, 11) and is the only direct indication that the land under discussion might have had other owners or that there existed a resident indigenous population in the valley.

15. In many ways Yallourn operated like the "company towns" that were built near remote mines by multinationals during Australia's resource boom in the 1960s and 1970s (Gibson 1991). In its day, however, it differed quite markedly from other towns that were single industry/company dominated. In comparison to the townships associated with the New South Wales black coal mining

industry, the civic facilities and quality of housing were far superior and were seen by many residents as important and valid industrial "gains." Our thanks to Graeme Byrne, who grew up in Yallourn, for this insight.

16. Some textile and clothing firms relocated to the region in the post–World War II period with the assistance of direct subsidies offered by the state government, but these operations mostly closed when those sectors went through major rationalization in the 1980s.

17. Heath had been favorably impressed with Russia's small city planning schemes and was envious of the system of land ownership that placed no obstacles to reconstruction and development of the country. These views were expressed in an account of "Town Planning in the Soviet Union," which was attached as an appendix to the 1944 volume *We Must Go On: A Study in Planned Reconstruction and Housing,* which he coauthored with F. Oswald Barnett and W. O. Burton, founding members of the Victorian Housing Commission (N. Brown 1995, 57).

18. No explicit recommendation regarding Yallourn is made, though the implication of its unfortunate placement on top of some of the best coal reserves is obvious. See Read (1996) for the story of Yallourn's removal in the 1970s.

19. State-owned industry never had credibility as part of a commons that the unions could and should have defended against privatization. The idea of generating a sustainable commons from the nonrenewable resource base in the valley, through levying a resource tax on coal mined and creating a community fund, was never pursued. When one government official raised the possibility in the focus group, Harry nixed it as making the valley's electricity uncompetitive nationally. In this response, we recognize once again his subjection to the Economy. See Gibson-Graham (1994a) for further discussion of economic politics and regions in Australia.

20. Indeed, genealogy can be seen as an ethical practice of thinking, "rereading" for historical contingency to open up future possibilities.

21. In Foucault's words, "Three domains of genealogy are possible. First, an historical ontology of ourselves in relation to truth through which we constitute ourselves as subjects of knowledge; second, an historical ontology of ourselves in relation to a field of power through which we constitute ourselves as subjects acting on others; and third, an historical ontology in relation to ethics through which we constitute ourselves as moral agents" (1983, 237). All can be seen to have been present, in uneven admixture, in this discussion.

22. Submission to the SEC involved not only passivity and dependence, but also a sense of mastery over the form and direction of development in the valley. The realization that continued economic efficiency no longer requires people and that the state no longer requires cooperation and compliance since it has sold off the industry has contributed to a deep-seated and almost unshakable feeling of abandonment. In the absence of employment with the SEC, a sense of mastery has been lost, as has a sense of inclusion. For men, the repetitive practice of turning up at work and submitting to the subjection of the SEC has ceased,

to be replaced only partially by the ritual fortnightly call at Centrelink (the federal government's employment agency, where dole payments must be secured). Of course, other ritual practices—the sports meetings, club and pub attendance, union meetings, and general performance of manhood in the valley—all could be seen as shoring up the ghost economic identities of workers. But these activities cannot hide the fact that an absence is present—an opening, a rupture has occurred in the repetitive practices that articulated SEC identity and subjection. What might emerge from this constitutive absence?

23. Writing about such a legacy, Addelson (2005) offers the notion of an embodied collective memory. This memory is not understood as a single narrative or community consensus, but as the shared enactment and reenactment of experiences and feelings in place.

24. See Özselçuk (2003) for an example of a similar situation in Turkey in which privatization called forth a discourse of a public or "community" economy that "emerged only in the aftermath of loss" (10) but formed the potential basis for a new economic politics.

3. Constructing a Language of Economic Diversity

1. For many on the left, it seems, the debate about what kind of socialism or communism we might desire has been replaced by resigned discussion of what kind of capitalism we can support.

2. Mitchell points to the instrumental role of a range of technologies developed in the 1920s and 1930s—Keynesian economics, econometric modeling, dam building, hydroelectric systems, national electricity grids, and communication systems—in the construction of this image: "The forms of technical calculation, distribution and the control of flows, addressing, accounting and billing, and much more helped to constitute the world that would later take shape and be identified as 'the economy'" (forthcoming). The historical geography of the Latrobe Valley discussed in chapter 2 provides an illustration of the contingent technologies that produced an abstracted "regional economy."

3. It is interesting to note that in 1994, the Organisation for Economic Co-operation and Development organized a workshop to discuss "putting the economy back in its place . . . reintegrating it in things political" (Sauvage 1996, 11). Inspired by Braudel's three-tiered economic typology of subsistence, local trade, and world trade, this workshop discussed "generative metaphors" of a plural economy as an alternative to the "dominant, market-based" paradigm of economy (11). Our diverse economy intervention has many overlaps with this project, but takes a more disaggregated approach to the task of economic re-visioning.

4. Arturo Escobar has argued that our project of making the invisible visible, or seeing (in his terms) "different economies always on the rise," requires a different "politics of reading on our part as analysts, with the concomitant need to contribute to a different politics of representation" (2001, 158). This reading

project enrolls and builds on the work of many others (such as Ferdinand Braudel, Stephen Gudeman, Karl Polanyi, and Teodor Shanin) who have produced representations of economic diversity.

5. Laclau and Mouffe draw on the work of Saussure, Althusser, Derrida, Foucault, Freud, and Lacan to develop their theory of hegemony. For those unfamiliar with their work, Jacob Torfing's book (1999) provides an excellent introduction.

6. Strong theorizing, as discussed in the Introduction, cultivates the capacity to be expansively relevant to all situations, to have a way of framing everything, to make all phenomena bear on a core thesis. Laclau and Mouffe's theory of politics is a form of contingent structuralism, a strong theory that does not involve reduction, but rather the constitution of a totality (hegemony) that is never finally fixed. We have found this theory to be a helpful tool for understanding the dominance of capitalist economic discourse without getting drawn toward a paranoid affective stance. To think hegemony, one must allow for dominance, but at the same time read for the openings and unfixings that can be worked on by a counterhegemonic politics.

7. It is remarkable that with the relegation of class politics, the economy has, in many ways, dropped out of the picture of Laclau and Mouffe's project of radical democracy. While Mouffe (2000) calls for the need to "foment a plural economy where the associative sector would play an important role alongside the market sector and the state sector" (126) and advocates a politics of redistribution from salaried workers, an unconditional minimum wage, and support for nonprofits, these strategies are proposed without any serious challenge to the hegemony of the neoliberal capitalocentric discourse that stands as an effective barrier to the widespread mobilization of an economic counterpolitics.

8. We first coined the term "capitalocentrism" in *The End of Capitalism* (Gibson-Graham 1996, 6). This "straw man" of our own creation is the strong theory of capitalism that pushes back at us, provoking us to think differently. While we have never conducted an extended genealogy of this discourse, we have very much appreciated the significant contributions others have made to such a project (without recourse to this particular naming). See, for example, Mitchell (1998, 2002, forthcoming), Poovey (1998), and Buck-Morss (1995).

9. Braudel calls for something similar when he writes: "[W]e should not be too quick to assume that capitalism embraces the whole of western society, that it accounts for every stitch in the social fabric . . . that our societies are organized from top to bottom in a 'capitalist system.' On the contrary . . . there is a dialectic still very much alive between capitalism on one hand, and its antithesis, the 'non-capitalism' of the lower level on the other" (1984, 630, quoted in De Landa 1997, 46).

10. Karl Polanyi's theory of different forms of economic integration is another way of representing a diverse economy (1944/2001). His focus was explicitly on the historical coexistence of different types of exchange—reciprocity, redistribu-

tion, householding, and market exchange. Polanyi proposed that these systems existed in both "co-determining and hierarchical" interrelation, but that in any historical period one became the "dominant or integrating form" (Stodder 2002, 29). The great transformation that Polanyi described involved the disembedding of market exchange, which had been "common since the later Stone Age," from its social context and its ascendancy in the modern era to dominance as the "primary organizing principle of social-economic life" (1944, 57, quoted in Stodder 2001, 33). Our representation of a diverse economy builds on aspects of Polanyi's typology of exchange, situating redistribution not as a type of exchange but as an allocation of surplus, and sidestepping the duality and implicit capitalocentrism of his disembeddedness theory.

11. As Adaman and Madra (2002) point out, many of the activities that draw on these behaviors, such as "voluntary contributions made to charities, services donated to self-help organizations, gifts and counter-gifts, inheritance, domestic work, childcare, and intra-community support networks" (1045) are lumped by mainstream economic theory into the "third sector." Here they are reduced to manifestations of self-interested maximizers operating in environments that are variants of, or supports to, market exchange where contracts are implicit but sometimes unenforceable, or they are seen as pathological practices that should be eliminated in the interests of economic efficiency and development.

12. See, for example, the work of Brandt (1995); Delphy (1984); Folbre (1987, 2001); Henderson (1991); Luxton (1997); Matthaei (2001); and Waring (1988).

13. For example, the changes in household size and the organization of household economies that have been identified as the "demographic transition" are still linked in a dependent relationship to capitalist growth.

14. For accounts of the interdependence of household practices and capitalist economic activities that do not employ a capitalocentric framing, see Gibson-Graham (1996, chapter 9); Parr (1990, 1999); and C. Williams (2005). Ethan Miller (2004, personal communication) has alerted us to examples of independent economic dynamics emanating from community-based economic activities such as that described by Raddon (2002, chapter 5) on the practice of "generosity competition" within a local economic trading system that drove "prices" down while strengthening community, and by Primavera (2002) on events that led to an economic "crash" within the barter networks of Argentina.

15. See, for example, Crewe, Gregson, and Brooks (2003); Emery and Pierce (2005); Gershuny (2000); Grabiner (2000); Godbout (1998); Lee (1996); Mingione (1991); Sauvage (1996); Pahl (1984); Redclift and Mingione (1985); Renooy (1990); Shanin (1990); Williams and Windebank (1998); and van Geuns et al. (1987).

16. Belief in the contribution of social capital to economic prosperity is not limited to analysis and policy concerned with the developing world. Indeed, as Fine's (2001) genealogy of the term demonstrates, through its migration into economics and political science (via the championing of Gary Becker and

Robert Putnam) from the divergent sociologies of Pierre Bourdieu and James Coleman, social capital was first established as a key concept of analysis in the developed world.

17. This is not to denigrate the significant contributions of many Marxists who have attempted to theorize economic difference and transition in ways that eschew this teleological and capitalocentric representation. See, for example, the early debates about articulations of modes of production (Wolpe 1980; Gibson-Graham 1996, 39–43), or the more contemporary debates about transitional and "hybrid" economies (Chakrabarti and Cullenberg 2003; Gibson-Graham and Ruccio 2001; Kayatekin 2001; Pickles and Smith 1998; Resnick and Wolff 2002; Yang 2000).

18. This project of constructing a language of the diverse economy is open-ended, unfinished, and collectivized. It is continually being modified, clarified, and complicated as new inputs of various kinds come to light. The language is an intellectual commons that we invite all to sustain and gain sustenance from.

19. The three strands are separated for pedagogical purposes and their discussion is pitched at the generalist reader. These economic practices exist in complex combination with each other and with the many more dimensions of difference that could be added to this discussion, for example, "property and resource ownership." As yet we have not developed any of the implications of the diverse economy for theorizing relations with the environment and would greatly appreciate input on this issue. The suggestion by Ethan Miller (2004, personal communication) of the inclusion of human/nonhuman transactions is one welcome extension.

20. See Altman (1987) for a detailed account of the interaction of multiple nonmarket transactions, including ceremonial exchange, and market transactions in a hunter-gatherer Aboriginal community in northern Australia. While the vast extent of the literature on gift giving and ritual exchange has focused on these practices in "traditional" societies (see, for example, Gudeman [2001] for an overview and a more complex consideration of obligation, equivalence, and reciprocity), recent research in "the west" has highlighted the huge significance of gift giving, sharing, and obligatory allocations between extended kin networks and other networks, such as church groups and locality-based communities (Godbout 1998; Community Economies Collective 2001; Vaughan 1997).

21. Recent United Kingdom research on cash-in-hand and in-kind transactions in the underground market by Williams (2004, 2005) uncovers the extent and variety of these transactions, showing how both low-income and high-income groups are involved in them in different ways. Attempts to stem tax avoidance by cracking down on cash-in-hand transactions have led some governments to represent the informal sector as lawless, parasitic, and not civic-minded. Williams's research provides a useful antidote to this representation.

22. The rise of a neoliberal economic orthodoxy in most nations has delegitimated the state sector of the economy in which transactions have not been

governed by market forces alone, but by considerations of public good, equity, and redistribution. The pressure to commercialize the provision of what were once treated as public goods (postal services, power, telecommunications, health, education, public transportation, etc.) has seen the alternative economic ethics associated with state involvement in the economy overridden by those of individualism and competition. Whether we are thinking about the remnants of experiments with centrally planned economies, welfare or social democratic states, or the much-heralded neoliberal state, all involve nonmarket transactions (welfare payments, direct or indirect industry subsidies, public goods such as education or health, etc.). These allocations are governed by policies that reflect a multitude of social values, including national development, class transformation, economic justice, environmental sustainability, and so on.

23. Barter is one way to conceptualize the internal transactions of goods and services that take place *within* capitalist firms between different divisions. In some companies these internal transactions are audited and accounted as each division must be seen to be independently making a profit. Reducing "transaction costs" by taking over suppliers and distributors and thus partially withdrawing from the market has often been seen as a way of increasing returns.

24. North comments, "It is a peculiar fact that the literature on economics . . . contains so little discussion of the central institution that underlies neoclassical economics—the market" (1977, 703–16, quoted in Callon 1998, 1). As if taking up this call, Michel Callon (1998), Andrew Barry (2002), Hassan Zaoual (2002), and others are pursuing analyses of markets that illustrate their contingencies and the diverse and uncertain forms of economic power they wield and enable.

25. See the Campaign Against Prison Slavery Web site, www.againstprisonslavery.org.

26. This discrepancy might be understood in many different ways—as the price "paid" by the sole entrepreneur for freedom from a boss, as the freedom to be compensated in nonmonetary terms (more open time or access to the business's raw materials or output) (Hotch 2000) or, especially in the third world, where many people scrape together a living through self-employment (for example, as rag pickers or small store owners), as all that is available in the absence of job opportunities in the formal labor market.

27. In many societies there is a rich language of terms for different kinds of reciprocal labor claims and in-kind labor payments. See chapter 7 for some examples from the southern Philippines.

28. Attempts to recoup and develop Marx's economic analysis of surplus production, appropriation, and distribution have rekindled an interest in an antiessentialist economic language of class (as opposed to a language of social distinction) (Resnick and Wolff 1987; Gibson-Graham, Resnick, and Wolff 2000a, 2001). This language is nonsystemic in that it offers the possibility of theorizing the complex coexistence of multiple (capitalist and noncapitalist) class processes

in the constitution of contemporary societies and subjects. It is also nonlinear in that it is released from a teleology of economic development, where feudalism gives way to capitalism, and capitalism to socialism (or to the end of history). In other words, it allows a reinstatement of history and contingency in the domain of economy.

29. By social wealth we refer to all the stocks of real and monetary assets and flows of value added in any time period.

30. Hindess and Hirst (1975) clarify this point when they state: "Surplus labour . . . exists in all modes of production because the conditions of reproduction of the labourer are not equivalent to the conditions of reproduction of the economy" (26).

31. Resnick and Wolff (2002, 81) note that neoclassical economic theory's "insistence that all labor in capitalism is equivalently necessary masks the necessary/surplus distinction that Marxists stress in their analysis of capitalism." They add, "Nor is that surprising, given the history of neoclassical economic theory's emergence after 1870. It gives ample evidence of an evolution shaped significantly by the project of theoretically negating Marxism by refusing to admit the concept of surplus" (2002, 81n13).

32. Surplus labor is produced and appropriated in many sites in the economy, not just in the formal business enterprise. In sites usually not associated with "business" activities, such as churches, trade unions, or universities, for example, workers may be employed within a capitalist class process in which surplus value (the capitalist form of surplus labor) is appropriated and distributed (Curtis 2001). These workers may not identify at all with the subject position of the exploited worker, especially if, as in the case of church or union work, there is a strong ethic of laboring for the greater good of the membership. In private and public colleges and universities today there is, however, a growing recognition that the speed-up and job restructuring experienced by many faculty is producing higher returns for their employers and the term "exploitation" has entered the lexicon of academia.

33. The geography of surplus-value production, appropriation, and distribution is another dimension of enterprise diversity that much of the economic geography literature of the 1980s was concerned with (see, for example, Massey [1984], and Graham, Gibson, Horvath, and Shakow [1989]). This interest in global flows of surplus value built on a rich Marxian literature on uneven development that highlighted the historical precedents of the internationalization of capital and global surplus flows within slave and colonial economies.

34. A reading of feudal class processes in the household is presented by Fraad, Resnick, and Wolff (1994). Cameron (2000) builds on this work and argues, however, that much of what might look like a patriarchal gender division of domestic labor and a feudal class process could also be read as an independent class process in which a woman appropriates her own surplus labor and distributes it to family members as part of the performance of gender identity.

35. A failure to be attentive to this difference blinds us to the potential for there to be capitalist firms/employers who recognize and value (whether for altruistic or advertising reasons) their interdependence with communities and environments.

36. The "race to the top" to institute environmentally sustainable and socially responsible best practices need not jeopardize the maintenance and success of a capitalist class process. Company "profitability" may be maintained by favorable publicity, or by government "rewards" for pursuing a politically prominent clean-up agenda. Our point here is that "profitability" is overdetermined by many factors and cannot be reduced to a limited set of determinations (Gibson-Graham and O'Neill 2001; Vlachou 2001).

37. This is not to deny the recent exposure of ways that some large nonprofits have sequestered surplus within their organizations in ways that do not comply with the overall ethic of service to the community or warrant continuation of their tax-exempt status.

38. Enid Arvidson (2000) has produced a geography of economic diversity for Los Angeles that similarly shows capitalism as less extensive. Drawing on a reinterpretation of census data, she has mapped employment by class process for Los Angeles census districts. Using the same method, Dwight Billings and Matthew McCourt (2002) have produced a representation of the regional economy of Appalachia that highlights class diversity.

39. Capitalist economic relations are still portrayed *on top*; this top row is the only one in the framework where the cells can be read as *fitting together* across the row.

40. In previous work (and in Figures 13, 14, and 15) we have queered these dominant terms, making capitalism different from itself (Gibson-Graham 1996, chapter 8; Gibson-Graham 1997; Gibson-Graham and O'Neill 2001). If we were not aiming to highlight the deconstructive move of rendering "noncapitalism" a proliferative positivity against the seeming singularity of "capitalism," but were marshaling all the queering moves we have made, we might produce a diverse economy representation that included the many forms of market exchange, wage labor, and capitalist enterprise shown in Figures 13, 14, and 15. In this representation, the distinctions between market/alternative market, wage labor/alternative paid and capitalist/alternative capitalist enterprise would be blurred, and the "capitalist economy" would disappear as a unified category.

41. Recent research in economic geography is exploring the way that theories of economic dynamics, such as those governing trade or industrial growth, were born of specific geographies and transported around the world, becoming "universalized" and "naturalized" in the process (see, for example, Sheppard [2005]).

42. Our thanks to Ethan Miller (2004, personal communication) and John Allen (2003) for this expanded vocabulary of power and for alerting us to the exciting potential of theorizing different of forms of economic power within diverse economies.

43. Feminist geographers have produced some of the most insightful empirical analyses of many of these sites in which caring labor is performed. See, for example, Gregson and Lowe (1994); Hanson and Pratt (1995); and England (1997).

44. This is not to ignore the significant threats currently posed by so-called family-friendly governments to the viability of this diversity, especially where community-based and cooperative child care are concerned.

45. For another illustration of this point, see the fictitious account of the characters Bill and Sue (Gibson-Graham 1996, 59–63).

46. For those interested in a more elaborated discussion of class processes in the household, see Fraad, Resnick, and Wolff 1994; Cameron 2000; Rio 2000; and Pavlovskaya (2004).

47. In previous research, we have shown how interventions in the "domestic sphere," such as the formation of baby-sitting clubs, has had a politicizing effect on women and families that has reverberated in the capitalist workplace in terms of resistance to un-family-friendly shift work schedules (Gibson 1993; Gibson-Graham 1996, chapter 9).

48. Individual groups included in this ragtag collection, e.g., housewives, petty traders of the global south, and indigenous people, have, however, been able to successfully claim political or moral rights/entitlements in certain contexts.

49. Others have proposed the *solidarity economy,* the *popular economy,* the *labor economy,* and the *social economy* as new foci for economic activism. As will be discussed in chapter 4, our concept of the community economy shares a lot with, and is also distinguished from, these alternative visions.

4. THE COMMUNITY ECONOMY

1. Ethan Miller points out that community self-reliance visions are often situated within larger global analyses of resource overconsumption and motivated by a strong sense of "extra-local" solidarity (2004, personal communication).

2. The "being-together" is also expressed as the "being-with," "being-social," "being-in-common," "co-appearing," or "compearance."

3. Andrew Barry notes that "[t]hose involved in the market do not worry about morality or politics, not because they are immoral or apolitical, but because enormous efforts have been made to make morality and politics calculable, and make them happen in other places" (2002, 273). These prior evaluative calculations become registered in the pricing system, which in turn governs the calculations of commensurability in exchange.

4. Gudeman (2001) advances a position that is somewhat at odds with the tendency within anthropology to see market exchange as starkly differentiated from gift exchange, the former involving the reciprocal exchange of "objects of equivalent exchange value," and the latter involving a "relationship between subjects in which the actual objects transferred are incidental to the value of the relationship established" (Schrift 1997, 2; Gregory 1982). For Gudeman, mar-

ket exchange does not have an exclusive claim on relations of reciprocity and equivalence.

5. From *A Contribution to the Critique of Political Economy*, quoted in Nancy (1991a, 74, emphasis added).

6. Nancy goes on to aver that "[i]f there has been an event in Marxist thought, one that is not yet over for us, it takes place in what is opened up by this thought" (1991a, 74).

7. Though we would step aside from the dualistic framing and the tendency to conflate capitalism and markets.

8. This is not a first, of course. Larry Grossberg reminds us that the United States in the 1960s was another time and place of the foregrounding of "community" (2004, personal communication). Miranda Joseph (2002) asks what accounts for the "extraordinary power and persistence of a dominant discourse of community" (xxx). Her disappointing (and even to her, depressing) answer is that community supplements capital, shoring it up and facilitating its flow (xxxii).

9. Joseph (2002) reads the criticisms made by both Nancy and Agamben of the "violently universalising tendencies of community" and their belief in the "impossibility of community" as an invitation to "political passivity" (xxix, xxx). We interpret their criticisms, including those of political projects that have relied on notions of community (Nazism, fascism, communism, third-wayism), as an incentive/invitation to imagine politics (and community) differently, in its nonfantasmatic guise.

10. As Nancy notes: "[W]e have a pressing need once again to take up the thought of economy—and not only a questioning of the 'economic' in the name of the 'political' or 'ethical.' To the contrary, the latter should be worked over via a reinterrogation of the former, through an 'ontological' reinterrogation (bound up with an ontology of being-with). Marx's deepest inspiration was of this order. Value must be rethought" (2002, 7).

11. Flows of labor represent only one kind of social value that circulates in a society. We propose an approach to theorizing community economies through the entry point of social labor, not because we agree with Marx that it is *the* calculus of value, but because it provides us with a basic language for thinking more concretely about economic being-in-common.

12. The term "coordinates" comes from De Angelis, who argues for the "development of a new political discourse based on two main coordinates, commons and communities" (2003, 1). We have enlarged his set of coordinates to reflect our own interest in developing a new discourse of *economic* politics, but we share with De Angelis the commitment to adopting coordinates that can help us orient our practices and thinking in different concrete contexts (rather than attempting to specify an ideal economy/society out of context).

13. The sociality of labor remuneration has, of course, long been politicized through the struggles of unions, which have highlighted the social effects of wage setting on standards of living and the economic implications of wage levels for

profit making. When we think about politics and the economy, it is largely to wage struggles that our attention is directed. Even then, these struggles are often represented as "out of place," as an imposition of a political agenda onto a largely apolitical technical terrain—the "level playing field" of the economy.

14. DeMartino defines social surplus as "the residual that arises from the fact that those who perform the labor necessary to provision society produce more than they themselves consume" (2003, 8). For a discussion of the importance of social surplus to the project of building community economies, see Gunn and Gunn (1991, 3–6).

15. This representation constitutes a creative and reparative reading of class.

16. Yahya Madra (1999) offers a profound insight into the subjectivity effects of this transaction. The trauma of exploitation, he argues, involves not the violation of the rights of a pregiven individual, but the very constitution of the subject as an "individual" and the concomitant rupture with a possible community and communal subjectivity. He argues that the wage payment restricts the worker to her necessary labor, imposing an imaginary completeness as a self-contained individual. Though connected to the larger community through the distributions of her surplus that sustain and nourish it, she is not aware of her connectedness; though sustained and reproduced by that larger community, she is not aware of her incompleteness (in the dimension of labor, at least).

17. It is notable that the redistributive fiscal policies of the modern state have focused more on taxing incomes than taxing profits, allowing the surplus appropriated by capitalists to be exempt from social redistribution mechanisms. Economic interdependency has been constituted as a relationship between the "well off" and the "less well off," often with the effect of setting social groups against each other. The form of economic being-in-common fostered by the social democratic state has enabled the view that social redistribution to "us all" stymies individualism and produces a dependent welfare class. In the face of this vision of economic being-in-common, it should not surprise us that the task of invigorating a discourse of the community economy might be an uphill battle. Luckily some are willing to take it on. Pointing to the successful right-wing framing of taxes as something you need "relief" from, Lakoff, for example, suggests a progressive campaign to reframe taxation as an "investment in the future" or a way of "paying your dues" (2004, 24–25).

18. Evoking aspects of this representation, A. S. Byatt writes in *A Whistling Woman*: "Sometimes I think the whole human world is a vast pool of carers caring for carers caring, creeping through a jumble of capitalists, exploiters, masters and oppressors whom we don't see, and automatically loathe, another SPECIES" (2002, 62).

19. As Gunn and Gunn (1991) note: "Confronted with the most productive economic system yet known to humankind, we are left with the question of what happened to social surplus. It certainly exists, but it is hidden from view by a mix of economic theory and carefully structured ideology" (17).

20. George DeMartino (2003) makes a similar proposal in his inspiring discussion of class justice, where he distinguishes productive, appropriative, and distributive justice. Questions he sees as important to consider include ones that concern the production of surplus, like "Who should be encouraged or required to contribute to the social surplus? What mechanisms are legitimate for securing these contributions? And how much should be asked of each contributor?" (8). With respect to appropriation he suggests: "Which arrangements of appropriation are just, and which are unjust? Who should enjoy appropriation rights and just what authority should these rights entail?" (9). In the area of distributive justice, he is particularly concerned with questions of need and methods of need assessment as the basis for distributions.

21. Though we might think of the so-called communist system of the former USSR as nonexploitative, Resnick and Wolff (2002) theorize it as involving the appropriation of surplus labor from the direct producers by the central government in a form of "state capitalism" that is no less exploitative than the private capitalism of the so-called capitalist economies.

22. It should be acknowledged that this portrayal presents Marx in only one of his guises. The Marx who is preoccupied with the systemic dynamics of capital accumulation is definitely not the Marx of Resnick and Wolff (1987) or of Norton (2001), who argue that the accumulation of productive capital is only one among many destinations of distributed surplus value, and certainly not one to be privileged a priori.

23. Kevin St. Martin points out that the categories of community and commons are generally presumed to be the ontological foundation of systems of resource use in the third world whereas in the first world there's a focus on the preferences and behavior of individual actors (2005). With St. Martin, we are hoping to render both concepts applicable in every social setting.

24. In a fascinating paper that revisits some of the Scottish sites of expropriation documented by Marx in *Capital,* volume 1, Mackenzie (2002) recounts efforts by local communities to rebuild the commons through community investments of labor and love.

25. See www.globalexchange.org and www.awid.org for articles exploring and explaining the emerging discourse of the "solidarity economy."

26. From our perspective, the solidarity economy and other positive economic ideals comprise locally specific valuations and practices elevated to a high level of generality (even universality) where they seem somewhat overspecified, and not easily applicable to the full range of diverse economic and political conditions. Referring back to Figure 23, it would seem premature and "out of place" to suggest that community economies could only be constructed to include enterprises that privileged the long over the short term, or were small scale, or oriented to the local market, or locally owned. To stipulate in advance the characteristics or the spatiality of community economies by, for example, privileging the local at the expense of other scales is to foreclose areas of ethical decision making and

the ongoing negotiation of community boundaries. This brings us back to our insistence on what we have called (in the Introduction) the negativity of place, that vision of place as presenting an opening to the contingencies of ethics and politics, and to the community economy as an empty signifier whose ability to unify a heterogeneous discursive field rests on its never achieving a complete or fully specified meaning.

27. Lepovsky reminds us of the active "unworking" of unity that is necessary if a "community without unity" is to be possible (2003, 64).

28. Our call for conversations about necessity, surplus, consumption, and commons among academics, activists, and communities configured at various geographical scales is one step in a process of enactment. In the chapter that follows, we trace the contours of these kinds of conversations and the particular ethical decisions that have constituted a community economy in Mondragón, a place that has provided inspiration for countless community economic activists for half a century. We are also interested in the micropolitics of identification, and in cultivating affective conditions that will foster the emergence of communal subjects. Our research practice is concerned with actually building community economies and community economic enterprises, making material interventions and finding subjects who can identify with community economic projects. We hope that perhaps this will contribute to a new political discourse and practice of community.

5. SURPLUS POSSIBILITIES

1. The publication of a book by Robert Oakeshott in 1978 and the BBC documentary about Mondragón in the late 1970s enabled the message of this cooperativist project to spread throughout the English-speaking world, at a time when the increasing internationalization of production appeared to be heralding the latest "stage" of capitalist economic dominance. Early studies in English provide histories of the establishment of the cooperatives and descriptions of the changing organizational structure and activities of the group (Oakeshott 1978; Gutiérrez-Johnson and Whyte 1977). Later research has explicitly compared the performance and practices of the Mondragón cooperatives with the experience of workers and enterprises in the capitalist sector (Thomas and Logan 1982; Bradley and Gelb 1983; Hacker 1989; Kasmir 1996). Some studies have focused on the way the cooperatives negotiated the difficult period of recession and rationalization during the late 1970s and 1980s, when the Spanish economy was becoming more open to international market forces via admission to the European Economic Community, and the effects of globalization in the 1990s (Weiner and Oakeshott 1987; Whyte and Whyte 1988; Morrison 1991; Cheney 1999; Clamp 2000). Finally, a number of authors have discussed Mondragón as an inspiration for community and regional economic development in their respective contexts (Morrison 1991; MacLeod 1997; Mathews 1999).

2. Positive representations of Mondragón are driven by the desire to high-

light the utopian otherness of the alternative, but they are also haunted by the fear of uncovering failures that undermine these differences, rendering the alternative no more than the "same." Much of the Mondragón story has thus been told within a *capitalocentric* framing (Gibson-Graham 1996, 40–41). The figures of the capitalist enterprise and the capitalist economy shadow the representations of Mondragón's cooperative businesses and work practices and they are positioned with respect to capitalism as either different from, the same as, beholden to, or dominated by its forces and relations.

3. Actually a number of communities have taken Mondragón as a model and are adapting its strategies to their own circumstances and requirements (see, for example, the discussion of Mararikulam in Kerala, India, in chapter 7).

4. Usually referred to as Father Arizmendi (or Don José María), this Basque priest was posted to Mondragón in 1941 straight after his ordination, having had his request to study sociology in Belgium turned down by his Monsignor (Whyte and Whyte 1988, 28). He was interested in seeking "democratic economic and social arrangements that might benefit all in the community and give a strong footing for postwar society" (Cheney 1999, 39) and was well read in the social and political economic theorists of the nineteenth and early twentieth centuries. He admired the experiments of Robert Owen and the Rochdale Pioneers, and was familiar with the agricultural co-ops and anarchist worker co-ops that flourished in Spain prior to and during the civil war. His readings and observations led him to value "institutional autonomy and identity as two of the most important characteristics of alternative organizations" (39).

During the 1950s, Father Arizmendi set himself the goal of promoting unity in a society fractured by civil war and political division. In his view, the economic strategy of setting up cooperatives was a step toward building a cohesive community and enabling Basque cultural survival and regeneration. Under the repressive Franco regime, Basque language had been outlawed and ownership of production facilities denied Basque communities. Working within and against these constraints, the Mondragón cooperatives began to grow and foster an economic basis for renewed expression of Basque cultural identity. Community coherence and preservation has remained an underlying commitment guiding many of the strategic economic decisions taken by cooperators (interview with José Ramon Elorza, human resources director, Ikerlan, April 22, 1997).

5. According to Whyte and Whyte (1988, 255), approximately 25 percent of cooperators were non-Basque at the end of the 1980s.

6. In the terms proposed by DeMartino, this reflects a "weak definition of appropriative justice" in that those who "directly produce the surplus (Marx's productive workers) are not excluded from fair and meaningful participation in its appropriation," but are joined by other members of the cooperative and in a less direct way by other members of the wider community (2003, 18).

7. The 2004 entry fee was €11,773 (www.mondragon.mcc.es). According to Mathews, the fee represents "roughly 10 percent of the estimated average capital

requirement for the creation of a new job" and the "(p)ayment can be made on the basis of a 25 percent initial contribution, followed by monthly installments" (1997, 11). These can be paid through deductions from the worker's earnings.

8. Whyte and Whyte summarize Mondragón's values, objectives, and principles slightly differently, including "basic values" of equality, solidarity, dignity of labor, and participation; agreed-upon "objectives," such as job creation, human and social development, autonomy and self-governance, and economic progress; and "guiding principles," which include balance (often called "equilibrio"), openness, and future orientation (1988, 257–61).

9. It also communicates the open-endedness of a process for which there are no economic models that can be pulled down off the shelf to ensure success. Cheney reports one of the founders of the original Mondragón cooperative as saying: "Although there was much talk about a 'third way,' we weren't entirely sure what exactly we were embarking on. From the perspective of the 1990s, of course, everything that came to pass in the past forty-some years all looks much clearer" (1999, 40).

10. A similar point is made by Mutersbaugh (2002) in his fine-grained analysis of production cooperatives in highland Mexico.

11. Giddens claims that the phrase "third way" "seems to have originated as early as the turn of the century, and was popular among right-wing groups by the 1920s. Mostly, however, it has been used by social democrats and socialists" (1998, 25). As a major inspiration for Tony Blair's (1998) embrace of a contemporary "third way" politics that navigates a middle path between a rapidly dismantling "welfare state economy" and a rapidly consolidating "free market economy," Giddens offers a sleek rendition of "third (cooperativist) way values." The third way for him looks "for a new relationship between the individual and the community, a redefinition of rights and responsibilities" that has well and truly "abandoned collectivism" (65). In the war of words that makes up political debate, reference to what we might consider the original "third way" has been lost or blurred. Deploying terms like "trust," "mutual obligation," and "reciprocity" that hail from the cooperative support systems of the early nineteenth century, contemporary third way politics offers a language that softens the impact of a neoliberal economic agenda, obscuring and even rendering desirable the withdrawal of state benefits.

12. The basis of distributism was "the belief that a just social order can only be achieved through a much more widespread distribution of property. Distributism favours a 'society of owners' where property belongs to the many rather than the few, and correspondingly opposes the concentration of property in the hands either of the rich, as under capitalism, or of the state, as advocated by some socialists. In particular, ownership of the means of production, distribution and exchange must be widespread" (Mathews 1999, 2).

13. Engels' wonderful description of Owen as "a man of almost sublime, childlike simplicity of character, and at the same time one of the few born leaders

of men" (1972, 613) was matched with genuine admiration for his achievements, but did not diminish a harsh dismissal of the "mish-mash" of his and other utopians' mode of thought (616). Martin Buber (1958) offers a thorough and inspiring critical reading of Engels and Marx's anti-utopianism, showing how it rested on a conception of "utopian" thinking as voluntaristic, in contradistinction to the scientific understanding of capitalist development and the form of revolutionary replacement it would necessarily require.

14. It is interesting to note that Marx saw "cooperative factories run by workers themselves" *both* as evidence of the emergence of a new mode of production "within the old form" that was made possible by the historic innovations (the factory and credit systems) associated with capitalist production, *and* as bound up in the reproduction of "all the defects of the existing system," i.e., capitalism (Marx 1991, 571). His theoretical and political project led him to foreground capitalist dominance in almost every instance.

15. Or, given the inherent progressivism of much socialist thinking, the full-blown development of capitalism to the point where transition would be inevitable. Beatrice Potter (later Webb) writes in 1891: "Robert Owen's Co-operative ideal . . . was an ideal which required for its realization a science which *had not arisen,* a character which *had not been formed,* economic and legal conditions *existing nowhere* in the purely aristocratic societies of Europe. Above all, unless it were to be subjected to an iron-bound tyranny, such a community would necessitate the development of an administrative system, of the nature of which even Owen himself had formed no conception, and which could only originate in a pure and enlightened [capitalist?] democracy" (1891, 29, emphasis added).

16. Today, in the light of recent strategies and successes of identity and other politics that foreground the subject, it seems rather prescient and grounded in actual practices of transformation. Write the Webbs, "He [Owen] had a boundless belief in the power of education to form character; and if any scheme promised just sufficient respite from poverty and degradation to enable him and his disciples to educate one generation of the country's children, he was ready to leave all economic consequences to be dealt with by the 'New Moral World' which that generation's Owenite schooling would have created" (1907, 146).

17. In favoring the "community of consumers and citizens" as "directors" of the economy over the working class, the Webbs configured the role of consumption differently from the mainstream socialist tradition (1921, 482). In their words: "We are, in fact, habitually misled by our too narrow view of the social function of consumption. It is necessarily the consumer who, according to his tastes and desires, determines the demand and 'sets the fashion,' and thereby decides the kinds and qualities of the commodities and services, high or low, material or spiritual, that shall be produced. 'Consuming goods . . . is the creation of a type of life.' In the social organization of the world, the act of consumption 'is directive: it is constructive'" (1921, 482–83).

18. This ambiguity can be seen in Marx's exchanges with anarchists such

as Bakunin and Proudhon, who were concerned that in a postrevolutionary state "government by the working people" would reproduce structures of domination, with "human nature" leading the representatives of the workers to look down on "ordinary workers from the heights of the state" (1978, 546). Marx's somewhat weak response (which contradicts other pronouncements) is that once the economic foundations of classes have been destroyed, wage workers will have abolished the specificity of their class character and the privileging of true proletarians will no longer hold. With a reference to actually existing cooperatives, Marx asks for it to be taken on trust that the threat of individualism overriding collectivism will be avoided, asserting that "If Herr Bakunin knew one thing about the situation of the manager of a workers' cooperative factory, all his hallucinations about domination would go to the devil" (1978, 546).

19. This criticism is susceptible to the obvious rejoinder that most capitalist firms fail in the first year, with only a very small percentage lasting more than five years.

20. Cooperatives, for example, have been "stereotyped as small ('dwarfish'), labor-intensive, underfinanced, and poorly managed" (Ellerman 1984, 5) and having no power with respect to the dominant structure of capitalism.

21. Of course there is another story to be told of the waxing and waning of support by the labor movement for cooperative development. Movement involvement with co-ops has ranged over time from the building of trade union consumer cooperatives in the early part of the twentieth century, to experiments with worker-owned production in the 1970s, to worker buyouts and employee stock ownership plans (ESOPs) in the 1980s (Alperovitz 2005). This point highlights the rhetorical violence of referring to a unity called the "labor movement" when its historical and geographical differences have been so great.

22. These criticisms were first propounded by Beatrice Potter (Webb) in her 1891 book, *The Cooperative Movement in Great Britain,* and then incorporated into her 1921 book with Sidney Webb.

23. Potter (Webb) displays a certain elitism in the observation that those who were attracted to cooperativism were the unemployed, "workers already degraded by starvation or idleness, or restless or discontented spirits" who were, in her estimation, "incapable of the most elementary duties of citizenship" (1891, 29). With such a low opinion of the masses, it is not surprising to see Webb and her husband enshrine a mistrust of the worker's capacity for motives other than greed at the center of their evaluation of worker cooperatives.

24. Consum left the MCC in 2003.

25. Including many noncooperators.

26. The issue of hours and working conditions will be taken up under "management" and "disputes."

27. In that this act of appropriation is undertaken by the workers themselves, it seems more realistic to use this terminology, rather than the more well known "rate of exploitation."

28. During the Spanish civil war the Basque community had been split by Republican, socialist and anarchist loyalties, as well as having been decimated by outmigration and the targeted bombing of Guernica, the spiritual and governmental center of Basquedom.

29. In many of the technologically advanced enterprises, there are no workers receiving the base grade pay. The move to the greater ratio was instigated by the need to permit salaries of the top managers to rise to 70 percent of established market equivalents (Cheney 1999, 49). The wages issue has been complicated in recent times with the employment of non-worker-owners *(eventuales),* who will be included as full cooperative members when new full-time jobs are generated, and non-worker-owners with fixed-term contracts *(socios temporales).* Cheney notes that these non-*socios* make around 80 percent of the wages of the *socios* and receive no dividends (86). In 2003 approximately half of the MCC workforce of 68,260 were non-worker-owners (www.mondragon.mcc.es).

30. Cheney notes that in recent times it has been reported that some *socios* have voted to reduce the reinvestment of their dividends into the collective capital fund to 30 percent, that is, to what is required by statute. His informant attributes this shift to a demise of the "culture of sacrifice" (or giving) that characterized the first forty years of cooperative development and the rise of consumerism in Basque society (1999, 80). It is also possible that with the growth and consolidation of the MCC there is less pressure within the organization to rely on this fund for business expansion.

31. In setting up this bank, the cooperatives took advantage of a clause in Spanish law that allowed a cooperative credit union to offer 1 percent higher interest than other financial institutions (Mathews 1999, 206). It was able to quickly attract the savings of local people and channel them into financing further development of the cooperative system.

32. Under Spanish law the cooperators (as self-employed) were excluded from normal social security taxes and benefits and so they formed their own system to provide social benefits to themselves and their families (Whyte and Whyte 1988, 19).

33. Mathews summarizes the implications of this economy of surplus distribution for the diverse forms of property ownership that coexist, including ownership of common property: "[M]embers of the co-operative have property of four kinds: firstly, ownership of their jobs; secondly, direct personal ownership of the balances held for them in their capital accounts, which earn additional income for them through interest to which they have regular access; thirdly, a shared ownership of the assets of their co-operatives, such as buildings, equipment and reserves, the governance and management of which they are directly responsible for; and, finally, a further shared ownership—albeit less direct—of the secondary support co-operatives in which the primary co-operatives are major stakeholders" (1999, 232).

34. One cooperator explained to us how her job was to plan the flow of work

in the factory for the week. As long as this plan was ready to be operationalized on the shop floor on Monday morning, it did not matter when she did her work. Sometimes she came in on the weekend to complete it if she had spent her time on other things (she was active in local government) during the preceding week. She was appreciative of the considerable freedom to organize her work time; at the same time, she expressed a strong sense of responsibility to the cooperative enterprise and had a well developed work/service ethic. This account points to the reduced need for managers to police behavior or give orders. As an employee of the worker-owners, the manager is free in turn to look to the smooth running of production and the commercial side of the business.

35. At the General Assembly, position papers and business plans are presented, debated, and approved. The meeting is preceded by smaller "preparatory chats" for groups of thirty to forty *socios* to review and modify the plans and strategies to be presented (Cheney 1999, 58).

36. A move which Father Arizmendi was said not to have supported (Morrison 1991, 154).

37. With reorganization of work into teams, there are current moves to reward output with team-based pay, which is producing more controversy within the group (Cheney 1999, 130).

38. Clamp records that "foreign subsidiaries generated 9 percent of the international sales in 1997" (2000, 564). By 2003, thirty-eight production plants and seven corporate offices were located in Argentina, Brazil, China, the Czech Republic, France, Germany, Holland, India, Iran, Italy, Mexico, Morocco, Poland, Romania, Russia, Thailand, Turkey, and the United Kingdom (www.mondragon .mcc.es).

39. The components plant acquired in Thailand employs one hundred Thai workers. Clamp notes that by 1998 "MCC's engineers were able to redesign the component. They can now manufacture the same component with fifteen workers once again in Mondragón. The plant in Thailand will be maintained since they anticipate that there will be other components, which will encounter similar labour cost challenges" (Clamp 2000, 568).

40. Supportive critics like George Cheney (1999) are worried that their success will undermine the values that have provided organizational strength in the past. We see this as a realistic and sympathetic concern.

41. This is not to say that Mondragón has avoided the issue of noncooperator employment. Indeed, it is definitely on the agenda, and positive moves have been made to address it: "Being aware of this problem, the . . . Co-operative Congress (General Assembly of all MCC co-operatives), which was held in May 2003, approved a resolution regarding 'Membership Expansion' which urged the organisations responsible for this area to study and develop formulas which would enable non-member employees to participate in the ownership and management of their companies, similarly to that which occurs in co-operatives" (www .mondragon.mcc.es).

42. This is not how they see it, however. The Mondragón Web site offers the following response to the frequently asked question, "Do you consider cooperativism to be an alternative to the capitalist production system?": "We have no pretensions in this area. We simply believe that we have developed a way of making companies more human and participatory. It is an approach that, furthermore, fits in well with the latest and most advanced management models, which tend to place more value on workers themselves as the principal asset and source of competitive advantage of modern companies" (www.mondragon.mcc.es).

43. Not surprisingly, the Mondragón cooperators seem very aware of the benefits of this strategy of marshaling surplus, as opposed to allowing it to drain away in payments to shareholders or to workers to increase personal consumption. One of the responses to the "frequently asked question" about the secrets of Mondragón's success stresses "re-investment of practically all resources generated" (www.mondragon.mcc.es).

44. In thinking about the lessons that might be learned for development of community economies, two important politics built around ethical economic decisions come to mind—that of the living-wage movement, an intervention to pressure city governments to pay minimum wages to their workers in areas of the labor market that have traditionally remained unorganized by trade unions (Pollin and Luce 1998), and the simplicity movement, a self-conscious interest by communities in voluntarily minimizing consumption levels, particularly in regions where an ethos of environmental stewardship has taken root (Pierce 2000). One focuses on ethical principles affecting the lower level and the other focuses on those affecting the upper level of wage payments. Unlike in Mondragón, these movements are separated from a politics that might address the implications of decisions and choices regarding wage levels for surplus generation and distribution. This disjuncture might well have the effect of undermining the strategic developmental power of these forms of economic politics, while not in any way diminishing their moral force.

45. Supporting these particular decisions are those to do with the social relations of cooperative work—the decision to develop sophisticated methods of self-management and techniques of nonconflictual dispute resolution. Decisions made about other economic issues might be viewed as more conventional or undifferentiated from those taken by capitalist enterprises. For example, with respect to the choice of products produced, market development, and the introduction of new technologies, the cooperatives have opted for intense product diversification, expanding national and international markets and cutting-edge computerized technology. Their decisions to participate in commodity markets at the top end have ensured market success, but more importantly have supported the continued growth of cooperatives.

46. The school was to provide the technical and organizational base from which the producer cooperatives grew (Whyte and Whyte 1988, 30).

47. "We were disciples . . . who year after year educated ourselves, thanks

to the teachings of Don José María, along lines of social concern and toward a translation of religious ideas into something that would link up with our real world" (Mathews 1999, 189, quoting Gorronogoitia). The Mondragón Web site offers, as the first in a series of answers to the frequently asked question about the secrets of Mondragón's success, the "vital role played by Arizmendiarrieta, the driving force behind the Experience, with his grand vision of the future and his influence over both students and disciples when putting his ideas into practice" (www.mondragon.mcc.es).

6. CULTIVATING SUBJECTS FOR A COMMUNITY ECONOMY

1. An interruption of familiar ways of dealing with economic experience was one of the things that our action research projects were trying to produce. Just as the analyst intervenes at moments in the ongoing flux of words emitted by the analysand, we as academic and community-based researchers hoped to stop the "conversation" at moments, fixing attention on certain events and elements, and over time to use these to construct a new narrative of a community economy. Such a narrative does not originate in the past as it was (for that past is no more), but in the past as it shall have been for what the community is in the process of becoming (paraphrased from Lacan, Écrits, as quoted in Lee 1991, 78). Like the Lacanian analyst, then, we recognized that a new future requires a new past.

2. For Butler, the psyche "exceeds the imprisoning effects of the discursive demand to inhabit a coherent identity, to become a coherent subject" (1997, 94) and the psychoanalytic setting is one place to look for the energy that has the potential to transform subjects.

3. These are the four Brahmaviharas. Ever the oral tradition, Buddhism is nothing if not excellent at listing and enumerating.

4. One could see our personal involvement in these practices of the self as having bled into our academic and community research practice, inadvertently enacting creative extensions and events in thought.

5. The Australian projects included "Economic Citizenship and Regional Futures," 1997–99 (Australian Research Council Large Grant No. A79703183); and "Building Sustainable Regions: Testing New Models of Community and Council Partnership," 1999–2000 (Australian Research Council Strategic Partnerships with Industry Research and Training Scheme Grant No. C79927030). The U.S. project was "Rethinking Economy: Envisioning Alternative Regional Futures," 1999–2001 (National Science Foundation Grant No. BCS-9819138).

6. In Australia the academic research team included Katherine Gibson, Arthur Veno, and Jenny Cameron, who was project coordinator and responsible for most of the on-the-ground work in the Latrobe Valley. In the United States, the project led by Julie Graham involved a large and shifting group of paid and volunteer academic researchers (Community Economies Collective 2001).

7. Both projects were approved by our respective university research ethics committees. It is interesting to note that local economic activists are rarely

questioned on the grounds of their ethical positioning. Perhaps the reluctance to view research as a political act leads to the expectation that somehow it can be power-neutral if the correct ethical procedures are followed.

8. These are reported in more detail in Gibson, Cameron, and Veno (1999) and drawn on in chapter 2.

9. One participant gave the example of Whyalla, South Australia, where many people had been retrenched by the steel industry. Local planners came to see the unemployed as their major regional asset (rather than seeing them as a drain on the community), since unemployment benefits tended to be spent locally, rather than on holiday travel out of state or on trips to the hairdresser in Adelaide.

10. The term "wounded attachment" is drawn from W. Brown (1995). A counterpart to the anger of those who were contacted by the community researchers was the depression of those who kept to themselves. Stephen, one of the ex-SEC community researchers, explained the difficulties of meeting up with his former mates: "It's not necessarily that I have a network of retrenched workers . . . in fact I haven't . . . 'cause the ones who are retrenched are sitting at home. I've lost touch with them because they were only pessimists or they were at the wrong end of the spectrum. I'm optimistic that I'll find some more work when I'm finished here, whereas they've gone home and said 'Well, I'll never get another job and that's it.' I avoid getting involved with them because of getting dragged down to the common level."

11. John Forester reminds us of the importance of acknowledging current representations and understandings, no matter how uncomfortable this may be. In a chapter entitled, "On Not Leaving Your Pain at the Door," he argues that participatory processes are likely to fail if planners ignore or dismiss "the self-perceptions and deeply defining experiences, of the citizens involved" (1999, 245). In the case of Wayne, perhaps our project of economic resignification reactivated the trauma of retrenchment and the uncertainties it provoked. At the same time it called forth an expression of feeling that many men in the valley had been unable to voice.

12. Woodworx is a not-for-profit woodworking business. See http://www.communityeconomies.org/stories/workfocus.pdf.

13. Nicki joined the project at the start as the community researcher who was also an unemployed young person. After a few months she was offered full-time employment at another job and Leanne took her place.

14. The performative effect of these representations is reminiscent of the effect of development discourse, through which the majority of the world's population came to see themselves as illiterate, underemployed, and in need of development.

15. We have been drawn to the reframing that the ABCD method effects, and particularly the reassessment of power relations that occurs for those who engage with it. It is possible to use this technique without subscribing to the

relatively nostalgic and normative vision of community that appears to underpin the Kretzmann and McKnight approach.

16. Initially the Portrait of Gifts exercise was seen by many as "just another research exercise to get information out of people without being of any relevance to them" (Jenny Cameron's research journal). It took some time for the research team to find a way to use this tool in a more collective and exploratory manner that foregrounded the shift in self and collective perception that such an inventory exercise could promote.

17. Not long before the commencement of our project, a particularly bad case of child abuse that ended in murder had received much national attention in the press, further compounding a prevalent metropolitan view of the valley as not only economically depressed but socially dysfunctional.

18. Most of these involve women, invoking the stereotype of the female volunteer and caregiver, but there were many men interviewed whose lives revolve around giving. See Community Economies Collective (2001).

19. Recently her daughter got a scholarship to Berkeley and made her mother a Web page. Now she sells quilts not only with an honor box in her garage, but to people in other countries.

20. A flow of passionate energy accompanied the voicing of these roles in the gift economy. When Lucy outlined her six interviews with retired people, highlighting their extraordinary gifts of time and labor, Coral, with her full-time job, three children, and tough-guy persona, wept to think that it would be thirty years before she could devote herself fully to volunteering.

21. Leanne reflected on her strategies to create an axis of shared identification as a way of diffusing this amygdalic reaction: "I guess that was one thing I brought to the group was that when people would speak to me I could sympathize because my family had worked in the SEC since [the year] dot and when Dad left he was unemployed for two years and couldn't get a social security benefit and things like that. We as a family struggled." KATHIE: "What did it mean to you that your father was unemployed?" LEANNE: "Personally it meant a lot, things were fine for a while, but then Dad got moody, and he had trouble finding a job 'cause he didn't have great writing skills 'cause he left school at a young age. It was hard. Things that I saw as being simple, like go and get a job, apply for a job, or go and get this certificate, it wasn't easy for him to do that and he still struggles with that today. And yet I see him as a man who very much underestimates his own abilities, and I don't know why he is like that, maybe it's because of his lack of education."

22. Antipathy and ressentiment are the common emotions of modernist politics—the fuel of revolutionary consciousness and action. But the political effectiveness of such emotions is questioned by many today. Wendy Brown, for example, notes that the subject of this kind of affect becomes "deeply invested in its own impotence" and is more likely to "punish and reproach" than "find venues of self-affirming action" (1995, 71).

23. In, for example, Paulo Freire's "pedagogy of the oppressed" (1972).

24. Our examples here appear to confirm Foucault's observation that contemporary ethical practices of self-formation are addressed primarily to feelings. Feelings are the "substance" of modern ethics; they are what we endeavor to form and transform. For the Greeks, by contrast, acts linked to pleasure were the substance of ethics; for the Christians the substance was desire (Foucault 1997, 263–69).

25. The practices of recall and extension invoke the therapeutic methods associated with the couch and cushion instituted by the psychoanalytic and Buddhist traditions.

26. Or what Alphonso Lingis (1994) describes as the "community of those who have nothing in common" except that they die (and eat).

27. White and Epston (1990, 31) describe the space of the therapeutic environment in a similar fashion: "Insofar as the desirable outcome of therapy is the generation of alternative stories that incorporate vital and previously neglected aspects of lived experience, and insofar as these stories incorporate alternative knowledges, it can be argued that the identification of and provision of the space for the performance of these knowledges is a central focus of the therapeutic endeavour."

28. For an exploration of enchantment that has enchanted and inspired us, see Bennett (2001).

29. Jean's fairy garden is inhabited by garden sculptures (gnomes, flamingos, etc.) set up in scenes and distributed about the lawn.

30. Carole Biewener raised most of the money for the trip, making it possible to offer subsidies to those who needed them.

31. The spaces of self-cultivation are often the spaces of the community economy itself. As Jaime, a community gardener in the Pioneer Valley, once said, reflecting eloquently on his own practices of cultivation, "the garden is the community." He continued: "It is necessary to strengthen new leaders, for them to do what I'm doing, so they continue forward, making a call to this community, so that . . . this, instead of being a community garden, that the whole city be a garden, and that the flowers be the people" (Community Economies Collective 2001, 26).

32. Recently, some four years after the trip, three van travelers have started a cooperative cosmetics business with others in the valley.

33. Since 2000 the workshop has been open two days a week throughout the year, making decorations that are sold to private businesses, town committees, and individuals. The nonprofit community enterprise operates largely outside of formal market relations, drawing on volunteer labor, barter exchange with local business, payments in kind, and donations. Proceeds from sales go directly into a special account at a local hardware store to pay for materials supplied to the workshop at cost. The surplus funds that have accumulated during the year are then made available to the community in the form of free timber and paint for local residents to make their own decorations closer to Christmas.

34. See Cameron and Gibson (2005c) for a discussion of our attempts to get the shire to assume aspects of this role and some insights into why they foundered.

35. The video, "It's in Our Hands: Shaping Community and Economic Futures," made by Jenny Cameron (2003) documents many of the stages of the action research and permits us to glimpse the joy of Ken and another community member associated with Santa's Workshop. See www.communityeconomies.org/action/Film_Order_Form.pdf.

36. See Cameron and Gibson (2005a, 2005b, 2005c) for further discussion of these enterprises and their life histories.

7. BUILDING COMMUNITY ECONOMIES

1. We are indebted to Callon (2005) for important aspects of this conceptualization.

2. This decision space might also be understood as calling forth the performativity that constitutes the community economy as a seeming substance in the same way that Butler views the constitution of gender: "[T]he performance of gender creates the illusion of a prior substantiality—a core gendered self—and construes the effects of the performative ritual of gender as necessary emanations or causal consequences of that prior substance" (1990, 29).

3. Industrialization refers not just to resource extraction, agriculture, and manufacturing, but to the production of services (or what used to be called "tertiary" industry).

4. Of course mainstream development discourse has its critics and disbelievers. But even attempts to outline alternative economic pathways have failed to completely disengage from the economic determinism and logical dynamism of capitalocentric discourse. Projects of communist and socialist construction enacted many of the key aspects of what we now know as "development," viewing industrialization as the motor of the economy and appropriating surplus from agricultural and other enterprises for investment in industrial development. Projects of community economic development that replace the growth imperative with local self-reliance often fix on import substitution and pin their hopes for sustainable economic development on its purportedly generative properties. Other explicitly alternative experiments set up their blueprints in opposition to features associated with the capitalist economy—growth, accumulation, private ownership, exploitation of the environment, global integration, markets, and so forth. Economic prescriptions are thus negatively dominated by capitalocentric discourse and the alternative only gains coherence through defining what it is not.

5. We have categorized each example in terms of one of the four coordinates for purposes of clarity and focus, though each of them could be discussed in terms of all four.

6. Development interventions in the "third world" have gone from pro-

moting large projects of infrastructure and industry development to addressing more directly the basic requirements of living—potable water, immunization, health care, food security. With the recognition that the long-term impacts of earlier large-scale interventions (such as dam building for irrigation or hydro-electricity, land reallocation, introduction of technology-intensive, export-oriented agriculture) have increasingly been manifest in the destruction of traditional economies with their indigenous "social safety nets," the call for aid to meet "basic needs" has accelerated.

7. This point is forcefully made by Kretzmann and McKnight (1993), who have explicitly tackled the needs (or glass half-empty) representation and the ingrained belief in dependence on outside help in cities across the United States.

8. The Republic of the Philippines has avidly promoted the export of contract labor as a primary development intervention, along with the somewhat less successful strategies of attracting overseas investors into export-processing zones and supporting export-oriented agriculture.

9. These terms and their definitions were compiled from Barangay Development Planning reports, community discussions, and the research and local knowledge of the Jagna research team—Joy Apag, Maureen Balaba, Amanda Cahill, Nimfa Lloren and Deirdre McKay. For further discussion of these terms and their meanings, see McKay (2005).

10. That is, after the debts incurred from arranging the migration contract and travel have been cleared—which often consumes all savings from the first two-year contract period.

11. The AMC, Unlad Kabayan Migrant Services Inc., and the Jagna CPP have made a space for these discussions, which are ongoing.

12. The assumption is that all of "us" have access to these markets via membership in a household in which someone is participating in them.

13. Gibson, Law, and McKay (2001) make the point that the decision to set aside this surplus marks a transitional moment in class subjectivity. The migrant worker who has been the indentured and exploited subject of a slave or feudal class process takes on an additional class position as a self-appropriating subject of an independent class process.

14. Most of the sources that we have used in this discussion of Mararikulam are the work of two social scientists, T. M. Thomas Isaac, who is a professor of development as well as a member of the Kerala State Legislative Assembly, and Richard W. Franke, professor of anthropology at Montclair State University in the United States. These and other social scientists are an important part of the collectivity that has brought the Mararikulam experiment into being, not only by chronicling its progress and disseminating this information worldwide, but by providing assessment and reflection that contributes to its ongoing development.

15. This is where the Mararikulam experiment is both building on and going beyond the development approach of the Grameen Bank of Bangladesh,

which has demonstrated the benefit that savings and small-scale loans can have on women's livelihoods. In Mararikulam the lending structure is organized and controlled by elected committees of the women's neighborhood groups rather than an outside bank bureaucracy. Members of the savings groups are linked not just via the social monitoring of saving and loan repayment, but also as collective worker-owners of income-generating microenterprises. The usual projects that target savings and microcredit involve women working alone in self-employed microenterprises, and the level of marketing, technological, and quality-control support is minimal, thus increasing the vulnerability of the enterprise and diminishing its chances of growing beyond a certain small size. Rankin (2001) has also pointed out the dangers of programs that rely on collective disciplining of individual repayment behavior, resulting in an undermining of existing communal aspects of the economy such as traditional sharing practices. In the Mararikulam case, the emphasis on micro-cooperative enterprises attempts to address the individualism of such initiatives.

16. Using public campaigns like the Maari soap pledge, the marketing firm works on establishing brand-name loyalty, but will also "arrange economies of scale where practicable, will oversee product quality to facilitate out-of-region markets, will assure consistent health and safety standards in all the local units" (Mararikulam Experiment Project Web site, page 2).

17. The construction of local health-care clinics, for example, is part of the accompanying project of improving public health, health care and nutrition.

18. In this sense it proposes a different pathway toward "building socially controlled assets at the community level" than that proposed by Gunn and Gunn (1991, 81–82). In their pathbreaking and inspirational book *Reclaiming Capital*, Gunn and Gunn identify nonprofit corporations, community land trusts, community development corporations, and consumer and worker cooperatives as "alternative institutions of accumulation" that "bring more social surplus under democratic control" through ownership or control of assets by the community. As we hope is clear from the preceding discussion, we see all these alternative institutions as playing a crucial role in building alternative economies. Gunn and Gunn do express some concern for the inclusion of mainstream business in the community economic vision when they discuss the support by CDCs of for-profit activities and suggest that "CDCs may end up providing apprenticeships for members of chambers of commerce" (94). We are particularly interested in the hybrid option that the E2M model presents, which allows capitalist enterprise also to be a contributor to a community economy. The equity interest held by the regional economic council and the employees would have the effect of maintaining an influence on the practice of business within the putative mainstream, while the association with E2M would mark a capitalist business as definitely "alternative."

19. It may be difficult to see higher education or tourism as an export since

the service is consumed locally, but the commodity produced by each of these industries (educational or tourist services) brings in dollars from outside the region.

20. Oddly enough, it's called economic growth and development if we build prisons to warehouse human beings, but not if we build housing for local people—because the latter doesn't enhance the export base.

21. And who usually have little contact with the social and community development branches of local government and cannot comprehend the magnitude, or the development implications, of the economy these branches deal with.

22. See Pretes (2006) for the research on which the following discussion is based.

23. Phosphate mining began in 1900 and continued until 1979, even after the removal in 1945 of all Banabans to a new home on the island of Rabi in Fiji (at that time another British colony).

24. It began with A$555,580 provided by the colonial administration (Toatu 1993).

25. Pretes (2006) makes a similar argument with respect to the support the Alaska Permanent Fund provides to the still vital subsistence sector in Alaska via the payment it makes each year to every Alaska resident.

26. Our definition of the commons accords with that of Gudeman, who sees "shared interest or value" forming the base of a community and being inseparable from it, as opposed to the more narrow definition of an open-access or common-pool material resource that is separable from a human community (2001, 27).

27. Community gardening is being developed in many disadvantaged areas of the industrialized world and represents a re-emergence of self-provisioning in urban economies. Sauvage (1996) reports on the benefits of production for one's own consumption in community gardens in the Aquitaine region of France: "For those receiving the guaranteed minimum income (RMI), the produce from their gardens is the equivalent of an extra month's income per year, but most of all it enables them to avoid the poor nutrition that often goes with poverty and to eat a healthy diet, which is becoming increasingly difficult in our cities. There is also a multiplier effect, since . . . an average of nine people benefit from the produce of a plot either on a regular or occasional basis; this multiplier effect reflects the communal aspect of this activity. Gardening provides an opportunity for mutual help and exchange; it is entirely natural for those involved to give and receive gifts, which encourages social relations" (197).

28. A form of Australian national ownership.

29. In accessing grant funding they were very successful. A Federal Government Family and Community Networks Initiatives Grant, a Latrobe City Trust–Gambling Impact Fund Grant, and a Latrobe City Council Community Grant were used to pay for infrastructure and training, site fencing, water reconnection, the purchase of gardening equipment, health and safety training, and leadership training.

30. Another factor that may have been important in the path-dependent trajectory of the LTVCEG was the absence for many years of a "leader" or "mentor" figure, someone with some community experience perhaps, who could help the group think through issues and encourage them to take creative and possibly radical decisions. The president who presided over the closure of the gardens was such a person, but had joined the organization too late to make the interventions that might have kept the core group together. In contrast, CERES has been guided over its more than twenty-year trajectory by an inspirational figure who was initially a school principal in the area and who, after retirement, continued to offer mentorship to the organization. In Mondragón (see chapter 5) Father Arizmendi provided inspiration and education from well before the inception of the first cooperative until his death several decades later. Though never a leader and never involved in any cooperative enterprise, he functioned as a teacher, mentor, and "idea person," starting more than two thousand study groups on issues related to cooperative and community development and prompting innovation through his many suggestions (including ones that were initially perceived as crazy, but later became central to the success of the cooperative complex, like the idea of starting a bank in 1959). Of concern here is the role and importance of key individuals and also the question of appropriate governance structures for nascent organizations that are in need of considerable hands-on attention accompanied by far-reaching vision and energy.

31. As an alternative form of payment for "environmental services," the international hotels on the coastal plain have offered loans to highland communities to establish bungalows in model ecotourist villages in the hinterland and have guaranteed a tourist market by selling short-stay packages to their own clients. Again a new kind of economic being-in-common has been established across the usually conflicted indigenous people/tourist divide.

32. Colin Williams's recent book (2005) offers a strong empirical rebuttal of the commodification thesis.

33. Although this type of work is being done. See, for example, Chakrabarti and Cullenberg (2003) and Curry (2003).

34. See, for example, the work of Anderson et al. (1988); Kauffman (1993); Stengers and Prigogine (1984); and Varela (1984). For applications to the fields of economic development and urbanization, see De Landa (1997) and Jacobs (2000), and for a review of the interest in complexity within geography, see Thrift (1999). Within economic geography, Sheppard and Plummer (2005) are taking up the challenge of alternative dynamics in exciting ways.

35. In Callon's terms, "Force is acquired through weakness or, rather, by successive compositions of small weaknesses, reversed one by one and not in one fell swoop. Strength is the outcome of a long process of accumulation, weaving of alliances and relations, from micro-positions constructed first as little gaps or differences lodged in the interstices of existing configurations. The examination

of these small differences is consequently theoretically important and practically strategic" (2005, 18).

36. The diverse economy is an attempt to represent, to use the language of Law (2004), following Chunglin Kwa, an open system that is patchy, only partially coherent, heterogeneous, continuous, limitless, and thus unable to be modeled into an emergent whole. The diverse economy is a representation born of a "baroque sensibility," that is, "an imagination that discovers complexity in detail or (better) specificity, rather than in the emergence of higher level order" (Law 2004, 19).

BIBLIOGRAPHY

Adaman, F., and Y. Madra. 2002. "Theorizing the 'Third Sphere': A Critique of the Persistence of the 'Economistic Fallacy.'" *Journal of Economic Issues* 36, no. 4: 1045–79.

Addelson, K. 2005. "Foresight and Memory." Unpublished book manuscript. Leverett, Massachusetts.

Agamben, G. 1993. *The Coming Community.* Trans. M. Hardt. Minneapolis: University of Minnesota Press.

———. 2004. "'I am sure that you are more pessimistic than I am. . . .' An Interview with Giorgio Agamben." Trans. Jason Smith. *Rethinking Marxism* 16, no. 2: 115–24.

Ahmed, S. 2004. *The Cultural Politics of Emotion.* Edinburgh: Edinburgh University Press.

Allen, J. 1999. "Spatial Assemblages of Power: From Domination to Empowerment." In *Human Geography Today,* ed. D. Massey, J. Allen, and P. Sarre, 194–218. Cambridge: Polity Press.

———. 2003. *Lost Geographies of Power.* Oxford and Malden, Mass.: Blackwell Publishing.

Alperovitz, G. 2005. *America beyond Capitalism: Reclaiming Our Wealth, Our Liberty, and Our Democracy.* Hoboken, N.J.: John Wiley & Sons.

Althusser, L. 1972. *Politics and History.* London: New Left Books.

Altman, J. 1987. *Hunter-Gatherers Today: Aboriginal Economy in North Australia.* Canberra: Australian Institute of Aboriginal Studies.

Alvarez, S., E. Dagnino, and A. Escobar, eds. 1998. *Cultures of Politics, Politics of Cultures.* Boulder, Colo.: Westview Press.

Amariglio, J., and D. Ruccio. 1994. "Postmodernism, Marxism, and the Critique of Modern Economic Thought." *Rethinking Marxism* 7, no. 3: 7–35.

Amin, A., A. Cameron, and R. Hudson. 2002. *Placing the Social Economy.* London: Routledge.

Anderson, P., K. Arrow, and D. Pines, eds. 1988. *The Economy as an Evolving Complex System.* Redwood City, Calif.: Addison-Wesley.

Appadurai, A. 2002. "Deep Democracy: Urban Governmentality and the Horizon of Politics." *Public Culture* 14, no. 1: 21–47.

Arvidson, E. 2000. "Los Angeles: A Postmodern Class Mapping." In *Class and Its Others,* ed. J. K. Gibson-Graham, S. Resnick, and R. Wolff, 163–89. Minneapolis: University of Minnesota Press.

Auster, M. 1987. "Origins of the Australian Regional and Metropolitan Planning Movement 1900–1940." *Journal of Australian Studies* 21: 29–39.

Bair, A. 2004. "An Economic Analysis of Prison Labor in the United States." Unpublished PhD dissertation, University of Massachusetts Amherst.

Bales, K. 1999. *Disposable People: New Slavery in the Global Economy.* Berkeley and Los Angeles: University of California Press.

Barkin, D. 2004a. "Incorporating Indigenous Epistemologies into the Construction of Alternative Strategies to Globalization to Promote Sustainable Regional Resource Management: The Struggle for Local Autonomy in a Multiethnic Society." Proceedings of the conference, "Bridging Scales and Epistemologies: Linking Local Knowledge and Global Science in Multi-Scale Assessments," Alexandria, Egypt, March 17–20. http://www.millenniumassessment.org/documents/bridging/papers/Barkin.david.pdf.

———. 2004b. "Sustainable Resource Management: A Strategy to Create New Beneficiaries from World Trade." Paper presented to the Department of Economics, University of Massachusetts Amherst.

Barkin, D., and Pailles, C. 2000. "Water and Forests as Instruments for Sustainable Regional Development." *International Journal of Water* 1, no. 1: 71–79.

Barnes, T. 1996. *Logics of Dislocation: Models, Metaphors, and Meanings of Economic Space.* New York: Guilford Press.

Barnett, F. O., W. O. Burt, and F. Heath. 1944. *We Must Go On: A Study in Planned Reconstruction and Housing.* Melbourne: Book Depot.

Barry, A. 2002. "The Anti-political Economy." *Economy and Society* 31, no. 2: 268–84.

Benediktssen, K. 2002. *Harvesting Development: The Construction of Fresh Food Markets in Papua New Guinea.* Ann Arbor: University of Michigan Press.

Bennett, J. 2001. *The Enchantment of Modern Life.* Princeton, N.J.: Princeton University Press.

Bernard, T., and J. Young. 1997. *The Ecology of Hope: Communities Collaborate for Sustainability.* Gabriola Island, B.C.: New Society Publishers.

Bertram, I. G. 1993. "Sustainability, Aid, and Material Welfare in Small South Pacific Island Economies, 1900–90." *World Development* 21: 247–58.

Bertram, I. G., and R. Watters. 1985. "The MIRAB Economy in South Pacific Microstates." *Pacific Viewpoint* 26: 497–519.

Billings, D., and M. McCourt. 2002. "Representing Class and Economies in Appalachian Kentucky." Paper presented at the Subjects of Economy conference, University of Massachusetts Amherst.

———. 2003. "Representing Class and Economy in Appalachia." Paper presented at the conference on Subjects of Economy, University of Massachusetts Amherst.

Blair, T. 1998. *The Third Way: New Politics for the New Century.* Fabian Pamphlet 588. London: Fabian Society.

Botsman, P., and M. Latham. 2001. *The Enabling State: People before Bureaucracy.* Sydney: Pluto Press.

Bowles, S., and R. Edwards. 1993. *Understanding Capitalism: Competition, Command, and Control in the U.S. Economy.* 2d ed. New York: Harper Collins.

Bradley, K., and A. Gelb. 1983. *Cooperation at Work: The Mondragón Experience.* London: Heinemann Educational Books.

Brandt, B. 1995. *Whole Life Economics: Revaluing Daily Life.* Philadelphia: New Society Publishers.

Brassed Off. 1996. Directed by Mark Herman. UK, Miramax and Channel Four Films.

Braudel, F. 1984. *The Perspective of the World.* Vol. 3 of *Civilization and Capitalism: Fifteenth–Eighteenth Century.* London: Collins.

Brown, N. 1995. *Governing Prosperity: Social Change and Social Analysis in Australia in the 1950s.* Cambridge: Cambridge University Press.

Brown, W. 1995. *States of Injury.* Princeton, N.J.: Princeton University Press.

———. 1999. "Resisting Left Melancholy." *Boundary 2* 26, no. 3: 19–27.

———. 2001. *Politics Out of History.* Princeton, N.J.: Princeton University Press.

Buber, M. 1958. *Paths in Utopia.* Boston: Beacon Press.

Buck-Morss, S. 1995. "Envisioning Capital: Political Economy on Display." *Critical Inquiry* 21: 434–67.

Butler, J. 1990. *Gender Trouble: Feminism and the Subversion of Identity.* London: Routledge.

———. 1993. *Bodies That Matter: On the Discursive Limits of "Sex."* London: Routledge.

———. 1997. *The Psychic Life of Power: Theories in Subjection.* Stanford, Calif.: Stanford University Press.

Byatt, A. S. 2002. *A Whistling Woman.* London: Chatto and Windus.

Callari, A. 1991. "Economic Subjects and the Shape of Politics." *Review of Radical Political Economics* 23, nos. 1–2: 201–7.

Callon, M., ed. 1998. *The Laws of the Markets.* Malden, Mass.: Blackwell.

———. 2005. "Why Virtualism Paves the Way to Political Impotence: A Reply to Daniel Miller's Critique of *The Laws of the Markets.*" *Economic Sociology European Electronic Newsletter* 6, no. 2.

Cameron, J. 2000. "Domesticating Class: Femininity, Heterosexuality, and Household Politics." In *Class and Its Others,* ed. J. K. Gibson-Graham, S. Resnick, and R. Wolff, 47–68. Minneapolis: University of Minnesota Press.

Cameron, J., and K. Gibson. 2001. *Shifting Focus: Pathways to Community and Economic Development. A Resource Kit.* Monash University and Latrobe City. www.communityeconomies.org/action.php.

———. 2005a. "Alternative Pathways to Community and Economic Development: The Latrobe Valley Community Partnering Project." *Geographical Research* 63, no. 3: 274–85.

———. 2005b. "Participatory Action Research in a Poststructuralist Vein." *Geoforum* 36: 315–31.

———. 2005c. "Building Community Economies: A Pathway to Alternative 'Economic' Development in Marginalised Areas." In *Community and Local Governance in Australia,* ed. P. Smyth, T. Reddel, and A. Jones, 172–91. Sydney: UNSW Press.

Cameron, J., and J. K. Gibson-Graham. 2003. "Feminising the Economy: Metaphors, Strategies, Politics." *Gender, Place and Culture* 10, no. 2: 145–57.

Chakrabarti, A., and S. Cullenberg. 2003. *Transition and Development in India.* New York: Routledge.

Chakrabarty, D. 2001. *Provincializing Europe: Postcolonial Thought and Historical Difference.* Princeton, N.J.: Princeton University Press.

Chatterton, P. 2005. "Making Autonomous Geographies: Argentina's Popular Uprising and the 'Movimento de Trabajadores Desocupados' (Unemployed Workers Movement)." *Geoforum* 36, no. 5: 545–61.

Cheney, G. 1999. *Values at Work: Employee Participation Meets Market Pressure at Mondragón.* Ithaca, N.Y.: Cornell University Press.

Clamp, C. A. 2000. "The Internationalization of Mondragón." *Annals of Public and Cooperative Economics* 71, no. 4: 557–77.

Cole, G. D. H. 1953. *Socialist Thought: The Forerunners, 1789–1850.* London: Macmillan.

Colectivo Situaciones. 2004. "Causes and Happenstance (Dilemmas of Argentina's New Social Protagonism): Research Manuscript No. 4." *Commoner* 8 (Autumn/Winter), http://www.thecommoner.org.uk/previous_issues.htm#n8.

Community Economies Collective. 2001. "Imagining and Enacting Noncapitalist Futures." *Socialist Review* 28 (3–4): 93–135.

Connolly, W. 1995. *The Ethos of Pluralization.* Minneapolis: University of Minnesota Press.

———. 1999. *Why I Am Not a Secularist.* Minneapolis: University of Minnesota Press.

———. 2002. *Neuropolitics: Thinking, Culture, Speed.* Minneapolis: University of Minnesota Press.

Copjec, J. 1994. "Sex and the Euthanasia of Reason." In *Supposing the Subject,* ed. J. Copjec, 16–44. London: Verso.

Crewe, L., N. Gregson, and K. Brooks. 2003. "Alternative Retail Spaces." In *Alternative Economic Spaces,* ed. A. Leyshon, R. Lee, and C. Williams, 74–106. London: Sage Publications.

Crouch, C., and D. Marquand, eds. 1995. *Reinventing Collective Action: From the Global to the Local.* Cambridge, Mass.: Blackwell.

Curry, G. 2003. "Moving beyond Postdevelopment: Facilitating Indigenous Alternatives for 'Development.'" *Economic Geography* 79, no. 4: 405–23.

Curtis, F. 2001. "Ivy-covered Exploitation: Class Education and the Liberal Arts College." In *Re/Presenting Class: Essays in Postmodern Marxism,* ed. J. K. Gibson-Graham, S. Resnick, and R. Wolff, 81–104. Durham, N.C.: Duke University Press.

De Angelis, M. 2003. "Reflections on Alternatives, Commons, and Communities, or Building a New World from the Bottom Up." *Commoner* 6 (Winter), http://www.commoner.org.uk/previous_issues.htm#n6.

De Landa, M. 1997. *A Thousand Years of Nonlinear History.* New York: Zone Books.

Deleuze, G. 1986. *Foucault.* Trans. and ed. S. Hand. Minneapolis: University of Minnesota Press.

———. 1995a. "Control and Becoming (Interview with Toni Negri)." In *Negotiations, 1972–1990,* 169–76. New York: Columbia University Press.

———. 1995b. "Postscript on Control Societies." In *Negotiations, 1972–1990,* 177–82. New York: Columbia University Press.

Delphy, C. 1984. *Close to Home: A Materialist Analysis of Women's Oppression.* Trans. D. Leonard. London: Hutchinson.

DeMartino, G. 2003. "Realizing Class Justice." *Rethinking Marxism* 15, no. 1: 1–31.

Dillard, A. 1999. *For the Time Being.* New York: Alfred A. Knopf.

Dirlik, A. 2001. "Place-based Imagination: Globalism and the Politics of Place." In *Places and Politics in an Age of Globalization,* ed. R. Prazniak and A. Dirlik, 15–51. New York: Rowman & Littlefield.

———. 2002. "Women and the Politics of Place: A Comment." *Development* 45, no. 1: 14–18.

Douthwaite, R. 1996. *Short Circuit: Strengthening Local Economies for Security in an Unstable World.* Dublin: Liliput Press.

Ellerman, D. 1984. *The Mondragón Cooperative Movement.* Harvard Business School Case No. 1-384-270. Boston: Harvard Business School.

Emery, M., and A. R. Pierce. 2005. "Interrupting the Telos: Locating Subsistence in Contemporary U.S. Forests." *Environment and Planning A* 37: 981–93.

Engels, F. 1972. "Socialism: Utopian and Scientific." Reprinted in *The Marx-Engels Reader,* ed. R. C. Tucker, 605–39. New York: Norton & Company Inc.

England, K., ed. 1997. *Who Will Mind the Baby?* London: Routledge.

Escobar, A. 2001. "Culture Sits in Places: Reflections on Globalism and Subaltern Strategies of Globalization." *Political Geography* 20, no. 2: 139–74.

———. 2004. "Other Worlds Are (Already) Possible: Self-organisation, Complexity, and Post-capitalist Cultures." In *The World Social Forum: Challenging Empires,* ed. J. Sen, A. Anand, A. Escobar, and P. Waterman, 349–58. New Delhi: Viveka Foundation.

Fernandez, J. R. 1996. *Mondragón: Forty Years of Cooperative History.* Mondragón: Mondragón Cooperative Corporation.

Fine, B. 2001. *Social Capital Versus Social Theory: Political Economy and Social Science at the Turn of the Millennium.* London: Routledge.

Fink, B. 1999. *A Clinical Introduction to Lacanian Psychoanalysis: Theory and Technique.* Cambridge, Mass.: Harvard University Press.

Folbre, N. 1987. "A Patriarchal Mode of Production." In *Alternatives to Economic Othodoxy: A Reader in Political Economy,* ed. R. Albelda, C. Gunn, and W. Waller, 323–38. Armonk, N.Y.: M. E. Sharpe.

———. 2001. *The Invisible Heart: Economics and Family Values.* New York: New Press.

Forester, J. 1999. *The Deliberative Practitioner: Encouraging Participatory Planning Processes.* Cambridge, Mass.: MIT Press.

Foucault, M. 1983. "Afterword." In *Michel Foucault: Beyond Structuralism and Hermeneutics,* ed. H. L. Dreyfus and P. Rabinow, 208–52. Chicago: University of Chicago Press.

———. 1985. *The History of Sexuality, Vol. 2: The Uses of Pleasure.* New York: Pantheon.

———. 1988. "The Ethic of Care for the Self as a Practice of Freedom." In *The Final Foucault,* ed. J. Bernauer and D. Rasmussen, 1–20. Boston: MIT Press.

———. 1997. *Ethics: Subjectivity and Truth.* Ed. P. Rabinow. New York: New Press.

Fraad, H., S. Resnick, and R. Wolff. 1994. *Bringing It All Back Home: Class, Gender, and Power in the Modern Household.* London: Pluto Books.

Franke, R. W. 2003. "The Mararikulam Experiment: Women-owned Cooperatives in Kerala, India—A People's Alternative to Corporate-Dominated Globalization." *GEO: Grassroots Economic Organizing* 57 (May–June): 8–11.

Fraser, N., and A. Honneth. 2003. *Redistribution or Recognition? A Political-Philosophical Exchange.* Trans. J. Golb, J. Ingram, and C. Wilke. London: Verso.

Freestone, R. 1989. *Model Communities: The Garden City Movement in Australia.* Melbourne: Thomas Nelson Australia.

Freire, P. 1972. *Pedagogy of the Oppressed.* Harmondsworth, UK: Penguin.

The Full Monty. 1997. Directed by Peter Cattaneo. UK, Fox Searchlight.

Geras, N. 1985. "The Controversy about Marx and Justice." *New Left Review* 150 (March–April): 47–85.

Gershuny, J. 2000. *Changing Times: Work and Leisure in Post-Industrial Society.* Oxford: Oxford University Press.

Gibson, K. 1984. "Industrial Reorganisation and Coal Production in Australia 1860–1976: An Historical Materialist Analysis." *Australian Geographical Studies* 22: 221–42.

———. 1991. "Company Towns and Class Processes: A Study of the Coal Towns of Central Queensland." *Environment and Planning D: Society and Space* 9: 285–308.

———. 1992. "'Hewers of Cake and Drawers of Tea': Women, Industrial Restructuring and Class Processes on the Coalfields of Central Queensland." *Rethinking Marxism* 5, no. 4: 29–56.

———. 1993. *Different Merry-Go-Rounds: Families, Communities and the Seven-Day Roster.* Pamphlet. Ipswich: United Mineworkers Union.

———. 2002. "Women, Identity, and Activism in Asian and Pacific Community Economies." *Development: Journal of the Society for International Development* 45, no. 1: 74–79.

Gibson, K., J. Cameron, and A. Veno. 1999. *Negotiating Restructuring: A Study of Regional Communities Experiencing Rapid Social and Economic Change.* Australian Housing and Urban Research Institute Working Paper 11, AHURI, Brisbane, Queensland. http://www.ahuri.edu.au/pubs/work_paps/workpap11.html.

Gibson, K., L. Law, and D. McKay. 2001. "Beyond Heroes and Victims: Filipina Contract Migrants, Economic Activism, and Class Transformation." *International Feminist Journal of Politics* 3, no. 3: 365–85.

Gibson, K., and M. Pretes. 2004. "Openings in the Body of 'Capitalism': Trust Funds, 'Marginal' Places, and Diverse Economic Possibilities." Paper presented at the Annual Meeting of the Association of American Geographers, Philadelphia.

Gibson-Graham, J. K. 1994a. "Reflections on Regions, the White Paper and a New Class Politics of Distribution." *Australian Geographer* 25: 148–53.

———. 1994b. "'Stuffed If I Know': Reflections on Post-Modern Feminist Social Research." *Gender, Place, and Culture* 1, no. 2: 205–24.

———. 1996. *The End of Capitalism (As We Knew It): A Feminist Critique of Political Economy.* Oxford, UK: Blackwell Publishers.

———. 1997. "Re-placing Class in Economic Geographies: The Political Implications of an Alternative Conception of Class." In *Geographies of Economies,* ed. R. Lee and J. Wills, 87–97. London: Edward Arnold.

———. 1999. "Capitalism Goes the 'Full Monty,'" *Rethinking Marxism* 11, no. 2: 62–66.

———. 2000. "Poststructural Interventions." In *A Companion to Economic Geography,* ed. E. Sheppard and T. Barnes, 95–110. Oxford, UK: Blackwell Publishers.

———. 2002. "Beyond Global vs. Local: Economic Politics outside the Binary Frame." In *Geographies of Power: Placing Scale,* ed. A. Herod and M. Wright, 25–60. Oxford, UK: Blackwell Publishers.

———. 2003. "An Ethics of the Local." *Rethinking Marxism* 15, no. 1: 49–74.

———. 2005a. "Building Community Economies: Women and the Politics of Place." In *Women and the Politics of Place,* ed. W. Harcourt and A. Escobar, 130–57. Bloomfield, Conn.: Kumarian Press.

———. 2005b. "Economy." In *New Keywords,* ed. T. Bennett, L. Grossberg, and M. Morris, 94–97. Oxford, UK: Blackwell Publishers.

———. 2005c. "Surplus Possibilities: Postdevelopment and Community Economies." *Singapore Journal of Tropical Geography* 26, no. 1: 4–26.

Gibson-Graham, J. K., and P. O'Neill. 2001. "Exploring a New Class Politics of the Enterprise." In *Re/Presenting Class: Essays in Postmodern Marxism,* ed. J. K. Gibson-Graham, S. Resnick, and R. Wolff, 56–80. Durham, N.C.: Duke University Press.

Gibson-Graham, J. K., S. Resnick, and R. Wolff, eds. 2000a. *Class and Its Others.* Minneapolis: University of Minnesota Press.

———. 2000b. "Introduction: Class in a Poststructuralist Frame." In *Class and Its Others,* ed. J. K. Gibson-Graham, S. Resnick, and R. Wolff, 1–22. Minneapolis: University of Minnesota Press.

———. 2001. *Re/Presenting Class: Essays in Postmodern Marxism.* Durham, N.C.: Duke University Press.

Gibson-Graham, J. K., and D. Ruccio. 2001. "'After' Development: Negotiating the Place of Class." In *Re/Presenting Class: Essays in Postmodern Marxism,* ed. J. K Gibson-Graham, S. Resnick, and R. Wolff, 158–81. Durham, N.C.: Duke University Press.

Giddens, A. 1998. *The Third Way: The Renewal of Social Democracy.* Cambridge, UK: Polity Press.

Gilligan, C. 1982. *In a Different Voice.* Cambridge, Mass.: Harvard University Press.

Godbout, J. 1998. *The World of the Gift.* Trans. D. Winkler. Montreal: McGill-Queen's University Press.

Grabiner, Lord. 2000. *The Informal Economy.* London: HM Treasury.

Graham, J. 2002. "Women and the Politics of Place: Ruminations and Responses." *Development* 45, no. 1: 18–22.

Graham, J., K. Gibson, R. Horvath, and D. Shakow. 1989. "Restructuring of U.S. Manufacturing: The Decline of Monopoly Capitalism." *Annals of the Association of American Geographers* 78, no. 3: 473–90.

Graham, J., S. Healy, and K. Byrne. 2002. "Constructing the Community Economy: Civic Professionalism and the Politics of Sustainable Regions." *Journal of Appalachian Studies* 8, no. 1: 49–60.

Greenwood, D. J., and J. L. G. Santos. 1992. *Industrial Democracy as Process: Participatory Action Research in the Fagor Cooperative Group of Mondragón.* Stockholm: Arbetslivscentrum.

Gregory, C. A. 1982. *Gifts and Commodities.* London: Academic Press.

Gregson, N., and M. Lowe. 1994. *Servicing the Middle Classes: Class, Gender, and Waged Domestic Labour in Contemporary Britain.* London: Routledge.

Gudeman, S., ed. 1998. *Economic Anthropology.* Cheltenham, UK: Edward Elgar Publishing Limited.

———. 2001. *The Anthropology of Economy: Commodity, Market, and Culture.* Oxford, UK: Blackwell Publishers.

Gunn, C., and H. D. Gunn. 1991. *Reclaiming Capital: Democratic Initiatives and Community Development.* Ithaca, N.Y.: Cornell University Press.

Gutierrez-Johnson, A., and W. F. Whyte. 1977. "The Mondragón System of Worker Production Cooperatives." *Industrial and Labor Relations Review* 31, no. 1: 18–30.

Hacker, S. 1989. *Pleasure, Power, and Technology: Some Tales of Gender, Engineering, and the Cooperative Workplace.* Boston: Unwin Hyman.

Halberstam, J. 2001. "Oh Behave: Austin Powers and the Drag Kings," *GLQ* 7, no. 3: 425–52.

Hanson, S., and G. Pratt. 1995. *Gender, Work, and Space.* New York: Routledge.

Harcourt, W. 2005. "The Body Politic in Global Development Discourse During the 1990s: A Women and Politics of Place Perspective." In *Women and the Politics of Place,* ed. W. Harcourt and A. Escobar, 32–47. Bloomfield, Conn.: Kumarian Press.

Harcourt, W., and A. Escobar. 2002. "Women and the Politics of Place." *Development* 45, no. 1: 7–14.

———, eds. 2005. *Women and the Politics of Place.* Bloomfield, Conn.: Kumarian Press.

Hardt, M. 2002. "Today's Bandung?" *New Left Review* 14 (March–April): 112–18.

Hardt, M., and Negri, A. 2000. *Empire.* Cambridge, Mass.: Harvard University Press.

———. 2001. "Adventures of the Multitude: Response of the Authors." *Rethinking Marxism* 13, no. 3–4: 236–43.

———. 2004. *Multitude: War and Democracy in the Age of Empire.* New York: Penguin Press.

Harris, H. L. 1948. "The Implications of Decentralization." In *Decentralization,* ed. H. L. Harris, 1–13. Sydney: Angus and Robertson, in conjunction with The Australian Institute of Political Science.

Harris, H. L., H. S. Nicholas, F. A. Bland, A. Manerd, and T. Hytten. 1948. *Decentralization*. Sydney: Angus and Robertson in conjunction with The Australian Institute of Political Science.

Harter, L. M., and K. J. Krone. 2001. "The Boundary-Spanning Role of a Cooperative Support Organization: Managing the Paradox of Stability and Change in Non-traditional Organizations." *Journal of Applied Communication Research* 29, no. 3: 248–77.

Harvey, D. 2000. *Spaces of Hope*. Berkeley and Los Angeles: University of California Press.

Harvey, D., and E. Swyngedouw. 1993. "Industrial Restructuring, Community Disempowerment, and Grass Roots Resistance." In *The City and the Factory*, ed. T. Hayter and D. Harvey, 11–26. London: Mansell.

Harvie, D. 2004. "Commons and Communities in the University: Some Notes and Some Examples." *The Commoner* 8 (Autumn/Winter), http://www.thecommoner.org.

Healy, S., and C. Biewener. 2000. "Development Discourse: A Genealogical Analysis." Paper presented at the Marxism 2000 Conference, University of Massachusetts Amherst.

Heath, F., and W. E. Gower. 1947. *Latrobe Valley Development: Interim Regional Survey and Report*. Melbourne: State Electricity Commission of Victoria.

Henderson, H. 1991. *Paradigms in Progress: Life beyond Economics*. Indianapolis: Knowledge Systems Inc.

Hindess, B. 1997. *Discourses of Power: From Hobbes to Foucault*. Oxford, UK: Blackwell.

——. 1998. "Neo-liberalism and the National Economy." In *Governing Australia: Studies in Contemporary Rationalities of Government*, ed. M. Dean and B. Hindess, 210–26. Melbourne: Cambridge University Press.

Hindess, B., and P. Hirst. 1975. *Precapitalist Modes of Production*. London: Routledge and Kegan Paul.

Hogan, J. P. 2003. "Ladders to Success: The Anti-Displacement Project, Springfield, Massachusetts." In *Credible Signs of Christ Alive: Case Studies from the Catholic Campaign for Human Development*, 83–100. Lanham, Md.: Rowman and Littlefield Publishers.

Hotch, J. 2000. "Classing the Self-Employed: New Possibilities of Power and Collectivity." In *Class and Its Others*, ed. J. K. Gibson-Graham, S. Resnick, and R. Wolff, 143–62. Minneapolis: University of Minnesota Press.

Hughes, T. P. 1983. *Networks of Power: Electrification in Western Society 1880–1930*. Baltimore: The Johns Hopkins University Press.

Hui, P. K. 2004. "In Search of a Communal Economic Subject: Reflections on a Local Community Currency Project in Hong Kong." In *Remaking Citizen-*

ship in Hong Kong: Community, Nation, and the Global City, ed. A. Ku and P. Ngai, 480–502. London: Routledge.

Hynes, M., S. Sharpe, and R. Fagan. 2005. "Laughing with the Yes Men: The Politics of a Practical Joke." Unpublished paper, Sociology Department, School of Social Sciences, The Australian National University.

Ife, J. 1995. *Community Development: Creating Community Alternatives—Vision, Analysis, and Practice.* Melbourne: Longmans.

Ironmonger, D. 1996. "Counting Outputs, Capital Inputs, and Caring Labor: Estimating Gross Household Output." *Feminist Economics* 2, no. 3: 37–64.

Jacobs, J. 2000. *The Nature of Economies.* New York: Vintage Books.

Jessop, B. 2003. "From Thatcherism to New Labour: Neoliberalism, Workfarism, and Labour Market Regulation." In *The Political Economy of European Unemployment: European Integration and the Transnationalization of the Employment Question,* ed. H. Overbeek, 137–53. London: Routledge.

Joseph, M. 2002. *Against the Romance of Community.* Minneapolis: University of Minnesota Press.

Kaplan, C. 2004. "The Death of the Working-Class Hero." *New Formations* 52: 94–110.

Kasmir, S. 1996. *The Myth of Mondragón: Cooperatives, Politics and Working-Class Life in a Basque Town.* Albany, N.Y.: State University of New York Press.

———. 1999. "The Mondragón Model as Post-Fordist Discourse: Considerations on the Production of Post-Fordism." *Critique of Anthropology* 19, no. 4: 379–400.

Kauffman, S. 1993. *Self-Organization and Selection in Evolution.* New York: Oxford University Press.

Kayatekin, S. A. 2001. "Sharecropping and Feudal Class Processes in the Postbellum Mississippi Delta." In *Re/Presenting Class: Essays in Postmodern Marxism,* ed. J. K. Gibson-Graham, S. Resnick, and R. Wolff, 227–46. Durham, N.C.: Duke University Press.

Kingsnorth, P. 2003. *One No, Many Yeses: A Journey to the Heart of the Global Resistance Movement.* London: Free Press.

Klein, N. 2002. *Fences and Windows: Dispatches from the Front Lines of the Globalization Debate.* New York: Picador.

Kretzmann, J., and J. McKnight. 1993. *Building Communities from the Inside Out: A Path toward Finding and Mobilizing a Community's Assets.* Evanston, Ill.: Assets-Based Community Development Institute, Institute for Policy Research, Northwestern University.

Laclau, E. 1990. *New Reflections on the Revolution of Our Time.* London: Verso.

———. 1991. "Community and Its Paradoxes: Richard Rorty's Liberal Utopia."

In *Community at Loose Ends,* ed. The Miami Theory Collective, 83–98. Minneapolis: University of Minnesota Press.

———. 1994. "Introduction." In *The Making of Political Identities,* ed. E. Laclau, 1–10. London: Verso.

———. 1995. "Time Is Out of Joint." *Diacritics* 25, no. 2: 86–96.

———. 1996. *Emancipation(s).* London: Verso.

———. 2000. "Identity and Hegemony: The Role of Universality in the Constitution of Political Logics." In *Contingency, Hegemony, Universality: Contemporary Dialogues on the Left,* ed. J. Butler, E. Laclau, and S. Žižek, 45–89. London: Verso.

Laclau, E., and C. Mouffe. 1985. *Hegemony and Socialist Strategy.* London: Verso.

Lakoff, G. 2004. *Don't Think of an Elephant: Know Your Values and Frame the Debate.* White River Junction, Vt.: Chelsea Green Publishing.

Larner, W., and R. Le Heron. 2002. "The Spaces and Subjects of a Globalising Economy: A Situated Exploration of Method." *Environment and Planning D: Society and Space* 20, no. 6: 753–74.

Latour, B. 1986. "The Powers of Association." In *Power, Action and Belief: A New Sociology of Knowledge?* ed. J. Law, 264–80. London: Routledge and Kegan Paul.

———. 2004. "Why Has Critique Run Out of Steam? From Matters of Fact to Matters of Concern." *Critical Inquiry* 30 (Winter): 225–48.

Law, J. 2004. "And If the Global Were Small and Noncoherent? Method, Complexity, and the Baroque." *Environment and Planning D: Society and Space* 22, no. 1: 13–26.

Leadbeater, C. 1997. *The Rise of the Social Entrepreneur.* London: Demos.

Lee, J. S. 1991. *Jacques Lacan.* Amherst: University of Massachusetts Press.

Lee, R. 1996. "Moral Economy? LETS and the Social Construction of Local Economic Geographies in Southeast England." *Environment and Planning A* 28: 1377–94.

Legaspi, P. E. 2001. "The Changing Role of Local Government under a Decentralized State: The Case of the Philippines." *Public Management Review* 3, no. 1: 131–39.

Lemke, T. 2001. "The Birth of Bio-politics: Michel Foucault's Lecture at the Collége de France on Neo-liberal Governmentality." *Economy and Society* 30, no. 2: 190–207.

Lepovsky, J. 2003. "Towards Community without Unity: Thinking through Dispositions and the Meaning of Community." *Disclosure* 12: 49–75.

Levin, K. 2003. "Enterprise Hybrids and Alternative Growth Dynamics." Unpublished PhD thesis, Department of Economics, University of Massachusetts Amherst.

Leyshon, A., R. Lee, and C. Williams, eds. 2003. *Alternative Economic Spaces.* London: Sage Publications.

Lingis, A. 1994. *The Community of Those Who Have Nothing in Common.* Bloomington: Indiana University Press.

Lipton, M. 1982. *Development and Underdevelopment in Historical Perspective.* London: Methuen.

Luxton, M. 1997. "The UN, Women, and Household Labour: Measuring and Valuing Unpaid Work." *Women's Studies International Forum* 20, no. 3: 431–39.

Mackenzie, F. 2002. "Re-claiming Place: The Millennium Forest, Borgie, North Sutherland, Scotland." *Environment and Planning D: Society and Space* 20: 535–60.

MacLeod, G. 1997. *From Mondragón to America: Experiments in Community Economic Development.* Sydney, Nova Scotia: University College of Cape Breton Press.

Madra, Y. 1999. Untitled paper presented at the conference of the Association for Economic and Social Analysis, Hancock, Massachusetts, July.

———. 2001. "Class, the Unconscious, and Hegemony." Unpublished paper presented at the University of Massachusetts Amherst.

Madra, Y., and C. Özselçuk. 2003. "Class, Hegemony, and the Real." Paper presented at the conference on the Desire of the Analysts: Psychoanalysis and Cultural Criticism in the Twentieth-First Century, Columbia, South Carolina, February.

Mararikulam Experiment Project. *"Mararikulam Experiment."* http://www .mararidevelopment.org/the_pledge.htm.

Marcos, Subcomandante. 2001. "The Punch Card and the Hourglass." Interview by G. García Márquez and R. Pombo. *New Left Review* 9 (May–June): 69–79.

Marx, K. 1972. "Critique of the Gotha Program." Reprinted in *The Marx-Engels Reader,* ed. R. C. Tucker, 383–98. New York: Norton & Company Inc.

———. 1977. *Capital.* Vol. 1. Trans. B. Fowkes. New York: Random House.

———. 1978. "After the Revolution: Marx Debates Bakunin." Reprinted in *The Marx-Engels Reader,* ed. R. C. Tucker, 542–48. New York: Norton & Company Inc.

———. 1985. "Statements to the International Working Men's Association." In *Working Together,* Greater London Council Economic Policy Group. Pack No. 5.

———. 1991. *Capital.* Vol. 3. London: Penguin Books.

Massey, D. 1984. *Spatial Divisions of Labor: Social Structures and the Geography of Production.* New York: Methuen.

———. 1999a. *Power Geometries and the Politics of Space-time.* Heidelberg: University of Heidelberg.

———. 1999b. "Spaces of Politics." In *Human Geography Today,* ed. D. Massey, J. Allen, and P. Sarre, 279–94. Oxford, UK: Blackwell Publishers.

———. 2005. *For Space.* London: Sage Publications.

Massumi, B. 2002. *Parables for the Virtual: Movement, Affect, Sensation.* Durham, N.C.: Duke University Press.

Mathews, R. 1997. "The Mondragón Cooperative Corporation: A Case Study." Paper presented at the International Communications for Management Conference on Executive Remuneration, Sydney, April.

———. 1999. *Jobs of Our Own: Building a Stake-holder Society.* Sydney: Pluto Press Australia.

Mathie, A., and G. Cunningham. 2002. "From Clients to Citizens: Asset-Based Community Development as a Strategy for Community-driven Development." Occasional paper, The Coady International Institute, St. Francis Xavier University. http://www.stfx.ca/institutes/coady/netscape_index .html.

Matthaei, J. 2001. "Healing Ourselves, Healing Our Economy: Paid Work, Unpaid Work, and the Next Stage of Feminist Economic Transformation." *Review of Radical Political Economics* 33, no. 4: 461–94.

McKay, D. 2002. "Cultivating New Local Futures: Remittance Economies and Land-use Patterns in Ifugao, Philippines." *Journal of Southeast Asian Studies* 34, no. 2: 285–306.

———. 2005. "Scattered Speculations on Surplus: Genealogies of Exchange Labour in Island Southeast Asia." Paper presented in the Department of Human Geography Seminar, RSPAS, ANU, August 15.

Meeker-Lowry, S. 1995. *Invested in the Common Good.* Philadelphia: New Society Publishers.

Mellor, M. 1997. *Feminism and Ecology.* Cambridge, UK: Polity Press.

Mellor, M., J. Hannah, and J. Stirling. 1988. *Worker Cooperatives in Theory and Practice.* Milton Keynes, UK: Open University Press.

Merz, C. 1908. *Report upon the Production and Use of Electric Power.* State of Victoria, Melbourne.

Miller, M. 2002. "Mondragón: Lessons for Our Times." *Social Policy* 32, no. 2: 17–20.

Miller, P. 1994. "Accounting and Objectivity: The Invention of Calculating Selves and Calculable Spaces." In *Rethinking Objectivity: Post-contemporary Interventions,* ed. A. Megill, 239–64. Durham, N.C.: Duke University Press.

Miller, P., and N. Rose. 1990. "Governing Economic Life." *Economy and Society* 19: 1–31.

Mingione, E. 1991. *Fragmented Societies: A Sociology of Economic Life beyond the Market Paradigm.* Oxford, UK: Basil Blackwell.

Mission for Filipino Migrant Workers (HK) Society. 2001. *Migrant Focus Magazine* 1, no. 4.

Mitchell, T. 1995/2002. "Origins and Limits of the Modern Idea of Economy." Unpublished paper, Department of Politics, New York University.

———. 1998. "Fixing the Economy." *Cultural Studies* 12: 82–101.

———. 2002. *Rule of Experts: Egypt, Techno-Politics, Modernity.* Berkeley: University of California Press.

———. 2007. "Culture and Economy." In *Handbook of Cultural Analysis,* ed. T. Bennett and J. Frow. London: Sage Publications.

Monash, J. 1921. "Foreword: Power for Victorian Industries." *The Industrial Australian and Mining Standard,* March 17.

Moreiras, A. 2001. "A Line of Shadow: Metaphysics in Counter-Empire." *Rethinking Marxism* 13, no. 3–4: 216–26.

Morrison, R. 1991. *We Build the Road as We Travel.* Philadelphia: New Society Publishers.

Morton, T. 2000. "Beware the C-word." *Sydney Morning Herald,* November 4, Section 1: 10–11.

Mouffe, C. 2000. *The Democratic Paradox.* London: Verso.

Mumford, L. 1922. *The Story of Utopias.* Revised and reprinted 1959. Gloucester, Mass.: Peter Smith.

Mutersbaugh, T. 2002. "Building Co-ops, Constructing Cooperation: Spatial Strategies and Development Politics in a Mexican Village." *Annals of the Association of American Geographers* 94, no. 4: 756–76.

Nancy, J.-L. 1991a. *The Inoperative Community.* Minneapolis: University of Minnesota Press.

———. 1991b. "Of Being-in-common." In *Community at Loose Ends,* ed. The Miami Theory Collective, 1–12. Minneapolis: University of Minnesota Press.

———. 1992. "La Comparution/The Compearance: From the Existence of 'Communism' to the Community of 'Existence.'" Trans. T. B. Strong. *Political Theory* 20, no. 3: 371–98.

———. 2000. *Being Singular Plural.* Trans. R. D. Richardson and A. E. O'Bryne. Stanford, Calif.: Stanford University Press.

———. 2002. "Nothing But the World." Interview by M. Potte-Bonneville and S. Grelet. Trans. J. Smith. Originally published in French as "Rien que le monde," *Vacarme* 11 (April 2000): 4–12.

Neill, M. 1997. "Toward the New Commons: Working Class Strategies and the Zapatistas." http://www.geocities.com/CapitolHill/3849/commons_paper.

Newman, S. 2000. "Anarchism and the Politics of Ressentiment." *Theory and Event* 4, no. 3. http://muse.jhu.edu/journals/theory_and_event/v004/4.3newman.html.

North, D. C. 1977. "Markets and Other Allocation Systems in History: The Challenge of Karl Polanyi." *Journal of European Economic History* 6: 703–16.

Norton, B. 2001. "Reading Marx for Class." In *Re/Presenting Class: Essays in Postmodern Marxism,* ed. J. K. Gibson-Graham, S. Resnick, and R. Wolff, 23–55. Durham, N.C.: Duke University Press.

Notes from Nowhere. 2003. *We Are Everywhere: The Irresistible Rise of Global Anticapitalism*. London: Verso.

Oakeshott, R. 1973. "Spain's Oasis of Democracy." Supplement to *Observer*, January 21. Reprinted in *Self-Management, Economic Liberation of Man*, ed. J. Vanek, 290–96. Harmondsworth, UK: Penguin.

———. 1978. *The Case for Workers' Co-ops*. London: Routledge and Kegan Paul.

O'Malley P., L. Weir, and C. Shearing. 1997. "Governmentality, Criticism, Politics." *Economy and Society* 26, no. 4: 501–17.

Ormaechea, J. M. 1993. *The Mondragón Cooperative Experience*. Mondragón: Mondragón Corporacion Cooperativa.

Osterweil, M. 2002. "Place and Empire." *Development* 45, no. 2: 113–16.

———. 2004. "Place-based Globalists: Rethinking the *Global* in the Alternative Globalization Movement." Unpublished paper, Department of Anthropology, University of North Carolina, Chapel Hill.

Özselçuk, C. 2003. "Psychoanalysis and the Politics of Research: Treading the Line between Destitution and Reclaiming in Class Transformation." Paper presented at the international conference on "Marxism and the World Stage," University of Massachusetts Amherst.

Pahl, R. 1984. *Divisions of Labour*. Oxford, UK: Basil Blackwell.

Parr, J. 1990. *The Gender of Breadwinners*. Toronto: University of Toronto Press.

———. 1999. *Domestic Goods: The Material, the Moral, and the Economic in the Postwar Years*. Toronto: University of Toronto Press.

Pavlovskaya, M. 2004. "Other Transitions: Multiple Economies of Moscow Households in the 1990s." *Annals of the Association of American Geographers* 94, no. 2: 329–51.

Pearce, J. 1993. *At the Heart of the Community Economy: Community Enterprise in a Changing World*. London: Calouste Gulbenkian Foundation.

Pearce, S. 2000. "Performance Anxiety: The Interaction of Gender and Power in *The Full Monty*." *Australian Feminist Studies* 15, no. 2: 227–36.

Peck, J. 2004. "Geography and Public Policy: Constructions of Neoliberalism." *Progress in Human Geography* 28, no. 3: 392–405.

Peña, D. 1997. *The Terror of the Machine: Technology, Work, Gender, and Ecology on the U.S.-Mexico Border*. Austin: University of Texas Press.

Pickles, J., and A. Smith, eds. 1998. *Theorising Transition: The Political Economy of Post-Communist Transformations*. London: Routledge.

Pierce, L. 2000. *Choosing Simplicity: Real People Finding Peace and Fulfillment in a Complex World*. Carmel, Calif.: Gallagher Press.

Plant, Sadie. 1997. *Zeros + Ones: Digital Women + the New Technoculture*. London: Fourth Estate Ltd.

Polanyi, K. 1944/2001. *The Great Transformation*. Boston, Mass.: Beacon Press.

———. 1968. "The Economy as Instituted Process." In *Primitive, Archaic, and Modern Economies: Essays of Karl Polanyi*, ed. George Dalton, 139–74. Garden City, N.J.: Anchor Books.

Pollin, R., and S. Luce. 1998. *The Living Wage: Building a Fair Economy.* New York: New Press.

Poovey, M. 1998. *A History of the Modern Fact: Problems of Knowledge in the Sciences of Wealth and Society.* Chicago: University of Chicago Press.

Porter, T. 1995. *Trust in Numbers: The Pursuit of Objectivity in Science and Public Life.* Princeton, N.J.: Princeton University Press.

Portes, A., M. Castells, and L. A. Benton, eds. 1989. *The Informal Economy: Studies in Advanced and Less Developing Countries.* Baltimore: The Johns Hopkins University Press.

Potter, B. 1891. *The Cooperative Movement in Great Britain.* London: Swan Sonnenschein.

Power, T. 1996. *Lost Landscapes and Failed Economies: The Search for a Value of Place.* Washington, D.C.: Island Press.

Pratt, A. 1921. "Introduction: Power for Victorian Industries." *Industrial Australian and Mining Standard,* March 17, 5.

Pratt, M. L. 2002. "Why the Virgin of Zapopan Went to Los Angeles: Reflections on Mobility and Globality." Keynote address to the Hemispheric Institute, Lima, Peru, July. http://hemi.ps.tsoa.nyu.edu/eng/seminar/peru/call/mlpratt.shtml.

Pretes, M. 2006. "Renewing the Wealth of Nations." Unpublished PhD thesis, Department of Human Geography, RSPAS, The Australian National University, Canberra.

Primavera, H. 2002. "Wealth, Money, and Power: The Ephemeral 'Argentinean Miracle' of the Exchange Networks." Paper presented at the second panel of the National Journey on Exchange and the Economy of Solidarity organized by the Urban Institute, the National University of General Sarmiento and by the Program of the United Nations for Development, Los Polvorines, Province of Buenos Aires, September.

Putnam, R. D. 2000. *Bowling Alone: The Collapse and Revival of American Community.* London: Simon and Schuster.

Raddon, M-B. 2002. *Community and Money: Men and Women Making Change.* Montreal: Black Rose Books.

Rankin, K. 2001. "Governing Development: Neoliberalism, Microcredit, and Rational Economic Woman." *Economy and Society* 30, no. 1: 18–37.

Read, P. 1996. *Returning to Nothing: The Meaning of Lost Places.* Melbourne: Cambridge University Press.

Rebello, J. 2004. "The Economy and/of Joyful Passions: A Political Economic Ethics of the Virtual." Unpublished paper, Department of Economics, University of Massachusetts Amherst.

Redclift, N., and E. Mingione, eds. 1985. *Beyond Employment: Household, Gender, and Subsistence.* Oxford, UK: Basil Blackwell.

Renooy, P. 1990. *The Informal Economy: Mapping, Measurement, and Social Significance.* Amsterdam: Netherlands Geographical Studies.

Resnick, S., and R. Wolff. 1987. *Knowledge and Class: A Marxian Critique of Political Economy.* Chicago: University of Chicago Press.

———. 2002. *Class Theory and History: Capitalism and Communism in the USSR.* London: Routledge.

Rio, C. 2000. "'This Job Has No End': African American Domestic Workers and Class Becoming." In *Class and Its Others,* ed. J. K. Gibson-Graham, S. Resnick, and R. Wolff, 1–46. Minneapolis: University of Minnesota Press.

Robson, K. 1992. "Accounting Numbers as 'Inscription': Action at a Distance and the Development of Accounting." *Accounting, Organizations and Society* 17: 685–708.

Rose, D. 2002. "Landscapes of Mystery and Desire." Unpublished paper, Centre for Resource and Environmental Studies, The Australian National University, Canberra.

Rose, N. 1996. "Identity, Genealogy, History." In *Questions of Cultural Identity,* ed. S. Hall and P. du Gay, 128–50. London: Sage Publications.

———. 1999. *Powers of Freedom: Reframing Political Thought.* Cambridge: Cambridge University Press.

Rose, N., and P. Miller. 1992. "Political Power beyond the State: Problematics of Government." *British Journal of Sociology* 43: 173–205.

Ross, E. 1970. *A History of the Miners' Federation of Australia.* Sydney: Australasian Coal and Shale Employees Federation.

Ross, R. J. S. 2004. *Slaves to Fashion: Poverty and Abuse in the New Sweatshops.* Ann Arbor: University of Michigan Press.

Ruccio, D. F., and J. Amariglio. 2003. *Postmodern Moments in Modern Economics.* Princeton, N.J.: Princeton University Press.

Ryan, L., and W. Taylor. 1995. "A Critical Review of Problems Associated with the Delineation of 'Regions' for Regional Economic Development Purposes: A Queensland Perspective." *Regional Policy and Practice* 42: 35–47.

Santamaria, B. A. 1945. *The Earth—Our Mother.* Melbourne: Araluen.

Santos, B. de. 2004. "The World Social Forum: Toward a Counter-hegemonic Globalisation (Part I)." In *The World Social Forum: Challenging Empires,* ed. J. Sen, A. Anand, A. Escobar, and P. Waterman, 235–45. New Delhi: Viveka Foundation.

Sauvage, P., ed. 1996. *Reconciling Economy and Society: Towards a Plural Economy.* Paris: OECD.

Schrift, A., ed. 1997. "Introduction: Why Gift?" In *The Logic of the Gift,* 1–22. London: Routledge.

SECV. *See* State Electricity Commission of Victoria.

Sedgwick, E. K. 1990. *Epistemology of the Closet.* Berkeley and Los Angeles: University of California Press.

———. 1993. *Tendencies.* Durham, N.C.: Duke University Press.

———. 1997. "Paranoid Reading and Reparative Reading; or, 'You're So Paranoid, You Probably Think This Introduction Is about You,'" In *Novel Gazing: Queer Readings in Fiction*, 1–37. Durham, N.C.: Duke University Press.

———. 2003. *Touching, Feeling: Affect, Pedagogy, Performativity*. Durham, N.C.: Duke University Press.

Serle, G. 1982. *John Monash: A Biography*. Melbourne: University of Melbourne Press.

Shanin, T. 1990. *Defining Peasants: Essays Concerning Rural Societies*. Oxford, UK: Basil Blackwell.

Sharpe, S. 2002. *A Geography of the Fold*. Unpublished PhD thesis, Department of Human Geography, Macquarie University, North Ryde, NSW, Australia.

Shaw, M., and I. Munro. 2001. "Valley of Despair: A Region Blacked Out by Power Plays." *The Age*, October 23, p. 1.

Sheppard, E. 2005. "Constructing Free Trade: From Manchester Boosterism to Global Management." *Transactions of the Institute of British Geographers* 30: 151–72.

Sheppard, E., and P. Plummer. Forthcoming. "Geography Matters: Agency, Structures, and Dynamics." *Journal of Economic Geography*.

Shuman, M. H. 2000. *Going Local: Creating Self-reliant Communities in a Global Age*. New York: Routledge.

Singer, L. 1991. "Recalling a Community at Loose Ends." In *Community at Loose Ends*, ed. The Miami Theory Collective, 121–30. Minneapolis: University of Minnesota Press.

Smith, C. K. 1973. *Styles and Structures*. New York: Norton.

Smith, N. 1993. "Homeless/Global: Scaling Places." In *Mapping the Futures: Local Cultures, Global Change*, ed. J. Bird, B. Curtis, T. Putnam, G. Robertson, and L. Tickner, 87–119. London: Routledge.

Solnit, R. 2004. *Hope in the Dark: Untold Histories, Wild Possibilities*. New York: Nation Books.

Spinosa, C., F. Flores, and H. L. Dreyfus. 1997. *Disclosing New Worlds: Entrepreneurship, Democratic Action, and the Cultivation of Solidarity*. Cambridge, Mass.: MIT Press.

St. Martin, K. 2004. "Mapping Economic Diversity in the First World: The Case of Fisheries." *Environment and Planning A* 37, no. 6: 959–79.

State Electricity Commission of Victoria (SECV). 1921/1923. *Annual Reports*. Melbourne: Government Printer.

Stengers, I., and I. Prigogine. 1984. *Order Out of Chaos: Man's New Dialogues with Nature*. New York: Bantam.

Stengers, I., and M. Zournazi. 2003. "A 'Cosmo-Politics'—Risk, Hope, Change: A Conversation with Isabelle Stengers." In *Hope: New Philosophies for Change*, ed. M. Zournazi, 244–71. New York: Routledge.

Stodder, J. 2002. "Human Computability and the Institutions of Exchange:

Polanyi's Models." In *Economy and Society,* ed. F. Adaman and P. Devine, 27–63. Montreal: Black Rose Press.

Storper, M. 1997. *The Regional World: Territorial Development in a Global Economy.* New York: Guilford Press.

Suzuki, S. 1970. *Zen Mind, Beginner's Mind,* ed. T. Dixon. New York: Walker/ Weatherhill.

Swyngedouw, E. 1997. "Excluding the Other: The Production of Scale and Scaled Politics." In *Geographies of Economies,* ed. R. Lee and J. Wills, 167–76. London: Routledge.

Thomas, H., and C. Logan. 1982. *Mondragón: An Economic Analysis.* London: George Allen and Unwin.

Thomas Isaac, T. M., and R. W. Franke. 2002. *Local Democracy and Development: The Kerala People's Campaign for Decentralized Planning.* Oxford, UK: Rowman and Littlefield.

Thomas Isaac, T. M., R. W. Franke, and P. Raghavan. 1998. *Democracy at Work in an Indian Industrial Cooperative: The Story of Kerala Dinesh Beedi.* Ithaca, N.Y.: ILR Press and Cornell University Press.

Thomas Isaac, T. M., and P. Heller. 2003. "Democracy and Development: Decentralized Planning in Kerala." In *Deepening Democracy: Institutional Innovations in Participatory Governance,* ed. A. Fund and E. O. Wright, 77–109. London: Verso.

Thrift, N. 1999. "The Place of Complexity." *Theory, Culture and Society* 16, no. 3: 31–69.

———. 2004. "Intensities of Feeling: Towards a Spatial Politics of Affect." *Geografiska Annaler.* Series B: Human Geography 86B, no. 1: 57–78.

Tinker, H. 1965. *Reorientations: Studies on Asia in Transition.* London: Pall Mall Press.

Tippett, G. 1997. "The Valley of the Dole." *Sunday Age,* January 26, p. 5.

Toatu, T. 1993. "The Revenue Equalisation Reserve Fund." In *Atoll Politics: The Republic of Kiribati,* ed. H. Van Trease, 183–90. Christchurch and Suva: Macmillan Brown Centre for Pacific Studies, University of Canterbury, and Institute of Pacific Studies, University of the South Pacific.

Torfing, J. 1999. *New Theories of Discourse: Laclau, Mouffe and Žižek.* Oxford, UK: Blackwell Publishers.

Tucker, R. C., ed. 1972. *The Marx-Engels Reader.* New York: Norton & Company Inc.

Van Den Abbeele, G. 1991. "Introduction." In *Community at Loose Ends,* ed. The Miami Theory Collective, ix–xxvi. Minneapolis: University of Minnesota Press.

Vanek, J. ed. 1975. *Self-Management, Economic Liberation of Man.* Harmondsworth, UK: Penguin Books.

Van Geuns, R., J. Mevissen, and P. Renooy. 1987. "The Spatial and Sectoral Diversity of the Informal Economy." *Tijdschrift voor Economische en Sociale Geografie* 78, no. 5: 389–98.

Van Parijs, P. 2001. *What's Wrong with a Free Lunch?* Boston: Beacon Press.

Varela, F. 1984. "Two Principles of Self-Organization." In *Self-Organization and Management of Social Systems*, ed. H. Ulrich and G. J. B. Probost, 25–32. Berlin: Springer Verlag.

———. 1992. *Ethical Know-how: Action, Wisdom, and Cognition.* Stanford, Calif.: Stanford University Press.

Vaughan, G. 1997. *For-giving: A Feminist Criticism of Exchange.* Austin, Tex.: Plain View Press.

Victoria, State of. 1917. *Report of the Advisory Committee on Brown Coal.* Albert J. Mullett. Melbourne: Government Printer.

Victorian Town and Country Planning Board. 1949. *Future Development of the Latrobe Valley Sub-Region: A Report and Planning Scheme.* Melbourne.

Vlachou, A. 2001. "Nature and Class: A Marxian Value Analysis." In *Re/Presenting Class: Essays in Postmodern Marxism*, ed. J. K. Gibson-Graham, S. Resnick, and R. Wolff, 105–30. Durham, N.C.: Duke University Press.

Wallerstein, I. 2002. "New Revolts against the System." *New Left Review* 18 (November–December): 29–39.

Walters, W. 1999. "Decentring the Economy." *Economy and Society* 28: 312–23.

Waring, M. 1988. *Counting for Nothing: What Men Value and What Women Are Worth.* Auckland and Wellington, New Zealand: Allen and Unwin in association with Port Nicholson Press.

Watts, M. 2003. "Development as Governmentality." *Singapore Journal of Tropical Geography* 24, no. 1: 6–34.

Webb, S., and B. Webb. 1907. *The History of Trade Unionism.* London: Longmans, Green.

———. 1921. *The Consumers' Co-operative Movement.* London: Longmans, Green.

Weekley, K. 2004. "Saving Pennies for the State: A New Role for Filipino Migrant Workers?" *Journal of Contemporary Asia* 34, no. 3: 349–64.

Weiner, H., and R. Oakeshott. 1987. *Worker-Owners: Mondragón Revisited: A New Report on the Group of Cooperatives in the Basque Provinces of Spain.* London: Algo-German Foundation for the Study of Industrial Society.

White, M., and D. Epston. 1990. *Narrative Means to Therapeutic Ends.* New York: W. W. Norton.

Whyte, W. F., and K. K Whyte. 1988/91. *Making Mondragón: The Growth and Dynamics of the Mondragón Cooperative Complex.* Ithaca, N.Y.: ILR, Cornell University.

Wildman, P. 1993. *It's Your Community, It's Your Economy: Understanding the Nuts and Bolts of Your Community Economy.* Nundah, Qld: Prosperity Press.

Williams, C. 2004. *Cash-in-Hand Work: The Underground Sector and the Hidden Economy of Favours.* Basingstoke: Palgrave.

——. 2005. *A Commodified World? Mapping the Limits of Capitalism.* London: Zed Press.

Williams, C., and J. Windebank. 1998. *Informal Employment in the Advanced Economies: Implications for Work and Welfare.* London: Routledge.

Williams, R. 1983. *Keywords: A Vocabulary of Culture and Society.* Rev. ed. Oxford: Oxford University Press.

——. 1989. "The Importance of Community." In *Resources of Hope: Culture, Democracy, Socialism,* ed. R. Gable, 111–19. London: Verso.

Williamson, T., D. Imbroscio, and G. Alperovitz. 2003. *Making a Place for Community: Local Democracy in a Global Era.* London: Routledge.

Wolpe, H., ed. 1980. *The Articulation of Modes of Production.* London: Routledge and Kegan Paul.

Woolcock, M. 1998. "Social Capital and Economic Development: Toward a Theoretical Synthesis and Policy Framework." *Theory and Society* 27: 151–208.

Yang, M. 2000. "Putting Global Capitalism in Its Place: Economic Hybridity, Bataille and Ritual Expenditure." *Current Anthropology* 41, no. 4: 498–99.

Young, I. M. 1990. "The Ideal of Community and the Politics of Difference." In *Feminism/Postmodernism,* ed. L. Nicholson, 300–323. New York: Routledge.

Zaoual, H. 2002. "Can Economic Thinking Be Flexible?" Trans. V. Bawtree. Unpublished paper, Department of Economics, Université du Littoral Côte d'Opale, Dunkerque, France.

Žižek, S. 1990. "Beyond Discourse-Analysis." In *New Reflections on the Revolution of Our Time,* ed. E. Laclau, 249–60. London: Verso.

——. 1998. "The Spectre Is Still Roaming Around: An Introduction" In *The 150th Anniversary Edition of the Communist Manifesto,* K. Marx and F. Engels, 47–52. Arkzin, Zagreb: Bastard Books.

——. 1999. "Whither Oedipus?" In *The Ticklish Subject,* 351–52. London: Verso.

——. 2000. "Holding the Place." In *Contingency, Hegemony, Universality: Contemporary Dialogues on the Left,* ed. J. Butler, E. Laclau, and S. Žižek, 308–29. London: Verso.

——. 2004. "The Ongoing 'Soft Revolution.'" *Critical Inquiry* 30 (Winter): 292–323.

Zournazi, M., ed. 2002. *Hope: New Philosophies for Change.* Annandale, NSW, Australia: Pluto Press.

Previous Publications

Portions of the introduction were originally published as "The Violence of Development: Two Political Imaginaries," *Development* 47, no. 1 (2004): 27–34. Reprinted with permisson of Palgrave Macmillan.

The second half of chapter 1 was originally published as "Class Enchantment," *Theory and Event* 5, no. 3. http://muse.jhu.edu/journals/theory_and_event/v005/5.3gibson-graham.html. Reprinted courtesy of The Johns Hopkins University Press.

A version of chapter 2 was originally published as K. Gibson, "Regional Subjection and Becoming," *Environment and Planning D: Society and Space* 19, no. 6 (2001): 639–67. Reprinted courtesy of Pion Limited, London.

A small portion of chapter 4 originally appeared in J. Cameron and K. Gibson, "Transforming Communities," *Urban Policy and Research* 19, no. 1 (2001): 7–24. Reprinted by permission of Taylor and Francis. www.tandf.co.uk/journals.

A version of chapter 5 was originally published as "Enabling Ethical Economies: Cooperativism and Class." *Critical Sociology* 29, no. 2 (2003): 123–61. Reprinted with permission of Brill Academic Publishers.

Portions of chapter 6 originally appeared in "An Ethics of the Local," *Rethinking Marxism* 15, no. 1 (2003): 49–74. Reprinted by permission of Taylor and Francis. www.tandf.co.uk/journals.

Portions of chapter 6 originally appeared in Community Economies Collective, "Imagining and Enacting Noncapitalist Futures," *Socialist Review* 28, nos. 3 and 4 (2001): 93–153. Reprinted by permission of Taylor and Francis. www.tandf.co .uk/journals.

Portions of chapter 6 originally appeared in "Beyond Global vs. Local: Economic Politics outside the Binary Frame," in *Geographies of Power: Placing Scale,* edited by A. Herod and M. Wright (Oxford: Blackwell Publishers, 2002), 25–60.

Portions of chapter 7 originally appeared in "Surplus Possibilities: Postdevelopment and Community Economies," *Singapore Journal of Tropical Geography* 26, no. 1 (2005): 4–26. Reprinted by permission of Blackwell Publishers.

Index

KATHERINE GIBSON is professor and head of the Department of Human Geography at the Research School of Pacific and Asian Studies, The Australian National University. She has been director of the Centre for Women's Studies at Monash University and directed action research projects in Australia, Papua New Guinea, and the Philippines. JULIE GRAHAM is professor of economic geography and associate department head for geography in the Department of Geosciences, University of Massachusetts Amherst; she is also on the University of Massachusetts faculty in women's studies, labor studies, and regional planning. She has directed action research projects in the Pioneer Valley of Massachusetts. During the past three decades these two authors have collaborated on rethinking economy and economic development, and as J. K. GIBSON-GRAHAM they wrote *The End of Capitalism (As We Knew It): A Feminist Critique of Political Economy* (1996; reprinted by Minnesota in 2006) and were coeditors of two books, *Class and Its Others* (Minnesota, 2000) and *Re/Presenting Class.*